Crises
in U.S.
Foreign
Policy

Michael H. Hunt

YALE UNIVERSITY PRESS *New Haven & London*

Crises
in U.S.
Foreign
Policy

AN

INTERNATIONAL

HISTORY

READER

Designed by Richard Hendel

Set in Minion and Gill types by

Keystone Typesetting Inc., Orwigsburg, Pennsylvania

Printed in the United States of America by

Vail-Ballou Press, Binghamton, New York

Library of Congress Cataloging-in-Publication Data

Hunt, Michael H.

Crises in U.S. foreign policy : an international history reader / Michael H. Hunt.

   p. cm.

Includes bibliographical references and index.

ISBN 0-300-06368-7 (cl : alk. paper). — ISBN 0-300-06597-3 (pb : alk. paper)

1. United States—Foreign relations—20th century—Sources. I. Title.

E744.H885   1996

327.73—dc20   95-22560

               CIP

A catalogue record for this book is available from the British Library.

The paper in this book meets the guidelines for permanence and durability of the Committee on Production Guidelines for Book Longevity of the Council on Library Resources.

10 9 8 7 6 5 4 3 2

Crises in U.S. Foreign Policy

AN INTERNATIONAL HISTORY READER

Designed by Richard Hendel

Set in Minion and Gill types by

Keystone Typesetting Inc., Orwigsburg, Pennsylvania

Printed in the United States of America by

Vail-Ballou Press, Binghamton, New York

Library of Congress Cataloging-in-Publication Data

Hunt, Michael H.

Crises in U.S. foreign policy : an international history reader / Michael H. Hunt.

   p.   cm.

Includes bibliographical references and index.

ISBN 0-300-06368-7 (cl : alk. paper). — ISBN 0-300-06597-3 (pb : alk. paper)

1. United States—Foreign relations—20th century—Sources. I. Title.

E744.H885   1996

327.73—dc20   95-22560

            CIP

A catalogue record for this book is available from the British Library.

The paper in this book meets the guidelines for permanence and durability of the Committee on Production Guidelines for Book Longevity of the Council on Library Resources.

10 9 8 7 6 5 4 3 2

CONTENTS

MAPS

Crises in U.S. Foreign Policy

INTRODUCTION

Foreign policy is about discord and collaboration among nations. That policymakers cope daily with the elements of conflict and cooperation is readily apparent and in the abstract easily grasped. That that coping process works itself out *not* in the confines of one capital or in the minds of one set of policymakers but several is an insight that often receives less attention.

The dangers of a narrow, single-nation focus apply as much to the study of U.S. foreign policy as to that of any other country. From the struggle for independence and national survival in the context of Anglo-French rivalry to the Gulf War fought with the support and within the constraints of an international coalition, the United States has moved on the international stage as one actor among many. The players and plots have changed, but time and again American leaders have had to struggle to understand and deal with their foreign counterparts. While the story of those leaders from George Washington to George Bush is interesting in its own right, our capacity to understand fully the sources and consequences of their foreign policy decisions depends on bringing their foreign counterparts, especially the most hostile of them, into the picture.

These observations lead to four propositions, each fundamental to the purposes of this book and each with an important claim on the attention of students of international relations whatever their orientation or experience.

First, U.S. policy is most fully understood and fairly judged within an international context. While it might be simpler to study crises and other facets of foreign policy chiefly in terms of what Americans have thought and done, that approach is almost bound to miscarry by perpetuating distorted or oversimplified images of the other side. Setting Washington in a global context repays the greater effort it requires. Giving foreign views and calculations parity alongside those of Americans serves, first of all, as a counter to the unilateralist fallacy, the idea that the outcome of a crisis hinges on the actions of one nation. Never so simple, crises are shaped by the divergent perceptions and interacting behavior of all the parties, and any attempt to squeeze a crisis into a narrower, single-nation framework is fundamentally distorting. Giving life to Washington's antagonists serves an additional function—it inoculates us against the tendency to reduce foreign leaders to cartoon figures, whether images of our idealized selves or projections of our own worst fears. Once actors from other nations gain their own voice, foreign policy ceases to be a simple nationalist morality play and becomes a drama that is both complex and morally ambiguous.

This complexity of crisis and the concomitant difficulty of making simple moral judgments once the antagonists' distinct perspectives become equally understood drew me to this project in the first place and remain sources of fascination. Some may worry that this approach carries unsettling hints of moral equivalency and may set in doubt judgments about historical responsibility once controverted but now thought closed. This may be so. But my own commitment is not to a history of blame and censure but to one that opens up and complicates our sense of the past and helps us transcend historical verdicts based solely on a Washington-centered perspective. I am confident that readers, whether old-timers or newcomers, will share with me the pleasure of a past that can engage, unsettle, even provoke.

Second, crises provide an especially useful way of exploring the international dynamic that is at the heart of understanding foreign policy. They have attracted me for much the same reason they have attracted other students of foreign policy and international affairs. Crises are the most serious kind of confrontation between states—those with the potential to precipitate costly armed conflict and the mobilization of state power with widespread and often unanticipated international as well as domestic consequences. Precisely because a crisis is a moment of high risk, it commands the attention of top-level policymakers and thus offers an unusually revealing look into leadership styles under stress and into dominant attitudes toward issues of overarching importance. Crises bring political leaders widely separated by geography and culture into confrontation, with a high potential for costly conflict. The peculiar and fascinating aspect of the phenomenon is the very notion of leaders engaging in this high-stakes game "face to face," figuratively speaking, while in fact literally quite distant in miles, ideology, and psychology.

The third proposition is that primary sources perhaps better than any other kind of historical material can suggest the richness and complexity of the international dynamic. Having before us unmediated the words of figures from other times and other cultures helps us guard against natural impulses toward anachronism and parochialism. Rather than imposing our current attitudes on earlier generations, we must take their categories and concerns seriously. And rather than generalizing from our own culture and personal experience to that of others, we must acknowledge the differences, sometimes profound, that divide us. The use of original evidence can help us in another way—by making those dealing with recent, less accessible crises more sensitive to the documentary and interpretive pitfalls before them. Finally, an emphasis on primary sources provides a reminder of the fundamental importance of language skills for all scholars of international relations. Language is the equivalent of a passport for anyone aspiring to explore interstate tensions in a polyglot world.

Fourth, those who seek to manage crises are inevitably plagued by confusion and misunderstanding. This tragic feature, discussed in some detail in the final chapter, arises in large measure from the very complexity of crises. The policy of any one country is a product of a mix of economic interest, bureaucratic and organizational imperatives, personal attitudes and ambitions, public opinion, and political culture. The international approach adds two more layers of complexity. Not only do we have to account for the intricacies of other countries' policies, but we have to bring them together in an interactive process on which each major participant has a divergent perspective. By making crises complex and dynamic, we highlight the degree to which the world in which policymakers operate is fundamentally unsettled and opaque. Looking out on a complicated and rapidly changing situation, policymakers are forced to make educated guesses, yet their "education" and the information available are seldom adequate to penetrate the confusion that surrounds them.

*   *   *

The documented case studies gathered here had their origins in practical pedagogical needs. I wanted students to have a direct window on policymaking rather than simply see it through the eyes of others in lectures, monographs, and history textbooks. I also wanted that window to open out on other capitals besides Washington. Finally, I wanted students to wrestle with the problems of synthesis and interpretation, and for that they needed some of the same key documents on which historians have based their own, often conflicting accounts. By sharing in weekly discussion sessions their own readings of individual documents, students have learned how divergent appraisals naturally develop into highly individual judgments on the overall meaning of a particular case. Reading and reflecting on primary evidence has thus for me come to occupy a central place in teaching U.S. foreign relations, promoting a more international consciousness while stimulating curiosity and sharpening the skills of critical inquiry.

This book concentrates on seven case studies. In choosing from a long menu of possibilities, I have sought variety. My sample takes the reader across much of the century (from 1914 to 1980), visits different regions, includes a mixed cast of antagonists, and above all draws from cases with fairly well-rounded bodies of documentation. The opening case, treating Woodrow Wilson and World War I, is a classic of the crisis cycle of initial perplexity, high hopes, and ultimate disillusion, and along with the chapter on Pearl Harbor it provides a reminder that crises as a phenomenon are not limited to the Cold War. There is no crisis from the last decade or so because good source materials offering insights on both sides of a conflict, indispensable to a full and interesting account, are still missing for such eligible events as the Gulf War and the intervention in Haiti.

Chapters follow a standard format. Each opens with an introduction that provides background and suggests common-sense ways of understanding the crisis under consideration. In preparing the introductions I sought to put limits on my own interpretive intrusions and above all to avoid placing blame on one side or another. In other words, the introductions are supposed to facilitate readers' access to the documents, so that they can come to their own interpretations. In each case the documents marshaled to illuminate the crisis are mentioned in this introductory treatment, so that readers can set them in topical relation and see them in better context. Each introduction concludes with an invitation to consider key questions in light of the documents to follow. These questions help clear some interpretive space and invite challenges or alternatives to the generalizations embedded in the introductions. Appended to each introduction is a guide to the relevant secondary literature for those wishing to investigate further.

A substantial offering of documents rounds out the chapter. To focus the documentary coverage and keep it manageable, I have made two basic editorial choices. First, I have limited documents on the familiar role of U.S. domestic politics and interest groups except where policymakers themselves refer to them. While I have included those topics in the introductions, I have not been able to accommodate them in the documents without diminishing my central concern with developing the international dimension and the strongly interactive character of crises.

Second, even in documenting the international sphere, I have narrowed the great multiplicity of national voices in each crisis in order to accentuate the counterpoint between the United States and its prime international antagonist. (The only exceptions are the Korean crisis, where the British and Indians appear to highlight differences within the U.S.-led coalition, and the Cuban missile crisis, where I have brought in Fidel Castro as well as Nikita Khrushchev to face off against John Kennedy.) For example, an ideal selection of material on American entry into World War I would include the British alongside the contending Americans and Germans. Similarly, a picture of the Vietnam conflict would leave room for China and Russia.

But this single volume is not meant to serve as a doorstop, and multiplying the international actors in the documents section of each chapter would add only marginally to my argument for the importance of international history. It might even defeat it, by heaping on more detail, more perspectives, and thus even more formidable interpretive challenges than is appropriate for an introductory work. I invite instructors in their lectures to extend my own introductions, and I encourage students in their readings drawn from the suggestions offered here to pursue whatever issues space limits have left inadequately developed in this book.

The documents are laid out in strict chronological order, tracing the sometimes rapid shifts back and forth between Washington and other capitals. These items are accompanied by only a minimum of explanatory material. The sources from which I obtained them are indicated so that those so inclined can compare my excerpts against the original or search for other pertinent documentation and points of view given short shrift in my limited selection.

In editing the documents I have followed the guidelines set forth in *The Chicago Manual of Style* (14th ed., 1993) for ellipsis points. In addition, an omission of one or more paragraphs in full is indicated by a three-dot open ellipsis on a separate line. An omission at the beginning of a document is not marked in any way. Ellipses appearing in the source text are indicated by three closely spaced periods. In some government documents successive paragraphs are often assigned letters or numbers or some combination of both. Where I have judged it might facilitate the reading of that material, I have taken the liberty of ignoring those marks. Readers will encounter two types of brackets in the documents. Square brackets set off my editorial emendations and comments. Angle brackets contain editorial remarks found in the original documents.

Ideally, the documents gathered here would speak for themselves and allow the reader to develop a personal interpretation untainted by my own or others' biases. Alas, that is not possible. The "noble dream" of grasping the past objectively is an illusion that should not ensnare us in sterile debate. In brief, readers should understand that my own interests unavoidably permeate each case. In effect, each of the seven cases is a snapshot taken by one historian today and not the only or final picture. New material is bound to appear that will force revisions, some perhaps fundamental, and disagreement will continue on which pieces of evidence now available are central and which peripheral. The most egregious intrusion of my views is to be found in the introductions, where I have suggested particular ways of thinking about each of the crises as a genuinely international phenomenon. But even the choice of the crises to be included here, and then the selection and editing of relevant documents, reflects my own thinking. I have in turn operated under constraints—the limited availability of documentation, especially on recent crises and above all on the foreign perspective. Six of the seven cases covered here are well documented on the American side. Foreign documentation for three of the cases (World War I, Pearl Harbor, and Korea) is quite good and is at least suggestive for the remaining four.

The book's conclusion seeks to draw out some of the broad implications emerging from these case studies. It argues for the importance *and* the difficulty of understanding crisis in international terms. Following the recent turn of U.S. diplomatic historians toward a more expansive conception of their field, the conclusion reiterates the point that a full and sound understanding of crisis depends on transcending American concerns and sources.

All readers will, I hope, leave this book more sensitive to the dangers of a narrow, parochial approach to the study of U.S. policy, whether in the distant past or in the present. A more global setting—one that allows a prominent place for non-American policymakers and non-American perspectives—is essential not just for understanding the nature of international crisis but for reaching an adequate understanding and evaluation of the U.S. role in world affairs. It is perhaps not too much to hope that education with a more international emphasis can also help us to react with greater sophistication to the crises of our own time.

Wilson and the European War, 1914–1917

REDEFINING THE RULES OF THE GAME

The outbreak of war in Europe in August 1914 created for the United States a crisis that bore hallmarks familiar from the nation's first few decades in world affairs. The assassination of Archduke Ferdinand in Sarajevo triggered a conflict between two alliance systems that divided Europe from the North Sea to the Black Sea. The resulting desperate struggle between the Entente powers (Britain, France, Russia, and Italy after 1915) and the Central powers (Germany, Austria-Hungary, and the Ottoman Empire) resembled the Anglo-French contest that plagued an earlier generation of American policymakers. As in the 1790s and the 1800s, so also now the belligerents launched bloody military campaigns against each other on several fronts and supplemented the military mayhem with economic warfare aimed at civilians no less than at the underpinnings of the other side's military might.

As in the earlier period, the United States sought safety in a policy of neutrality that would keep war at a distance even while protecting trade with the warring nations. But now no less than before, neutrality proved difficult to maintain. Both sides wanted access to American products and capital while denying it to the opposition. The challenge this belligerent pressure posed for American policymakers was the same one confronted a century earlier, but it was compounded now by new technologies that did not easily accommodate to the established rules of neutral rights and obligations.

Adding to the difficulty of maintaining neutrality was the presence of Woodrow Wilson in the White House. His interpretation of the U.S. role as a

Europe during World War I

neutral posed hard choices for Germany that ultimately drove the two countries into a war neither wanted. Moreover, from the outset of the conflict
Wilson's notion of neutrality coexisted with a humanitarian desire to lead
Europe to peace and with a reformer's zeal to refashion a deeply flawed international system along lines consistent with American values. These bold notions were ones that leaders of a weak America a century earlier did not dare
even to entertain. But by 1917 the insistence on general neutrality and isolation
from Europe that had theretofore been basic to U.S. policy had given way to
what had once been undesirable (entanglement in European political affairs)
and even unthinkable (engagement in European war). Wilson's odyssey from
guardian of neutrality to international reformer and the reluctant role the
German government played as foil and precipitant to his reform program
make this crisis one of the most extraordinary of the twentieth century.

*   *   *

The conflict in Europe caught the president by surprise. Sunk in grief over
his first wife's recent death, Wilson called the nation—he especially had in

mind its large population of immigrants—to observe neutrality (Document 1). That neutrality, he reasoned, would carry the United States through what was generally expected to be a short conflict. But the war would not be brief, and so a president with no special preparation in foreign affairs would have to face a complicated three-year crisis. As though anticipating the trial to come, Wilson himself had written on the eve of entering the White House, "It would be the irony of fate if my administration had to deal chiefly with foreign affairs."[1]

Wilson was an introspective, intellectual, and determined man with a well-trained mind and a good knowledge of American politics. Born in Virginia in 1856, he had grown up in a home suffused with religious values. His father was a Presbyterian minister and his mother the daughter of a minister. He attended Princeton, then the University of Virginia law school, and finally Johns Hopkins, where he took a doctorate in government. Seventeen years as a professor established him as an authority on American politics. He then served eight years as the president of Princeton and two as a reform-minded governor of New Jersey. In 1912 he won the Democratic Party nomination for president. When at the age of fifty-seven Wilson gained the White House, his health seemed good. But in fact he suffered from a cerebral vascular disease that had already precipitated one serious stroke in 1896 and another in 1906. The cumulative impact of this chronic, worsening condition on his concentration, equanimity, and judgment is difficult to assess.

The Wilson administration could have responded to the outbreak of World War I in narrow terms, by seeking to preserve the American position as a neutral and the concomitant freedom to trade with the belligerents according to the rules (obligations as well as rights) defined by maritime law. In securing its position as a neutral, Washington had available a strong national tradition of staying aloof from European conflict. The right of neutrals to trade with belligerents had been the bedrock of American policy during the Anglo-French conflict of the 1790s and 1800s, and in 1812 the United States had gone to war against Britain in defense of that right. Neutrality in time of international conflict had remained a central and almost universally accepted principle of American policy through the nineteenth century.

Beginning in the 1890s, the United States joined other powers in an effort to reach formal agreement on rules that would protect neutrals and limit the severity of warfare. The last agreement concluded before the outbreak of war, the 1909 declaration of London, registered a consensus on key aspects of neutrality and belligerency. Signed by Britain, Germany, the United States, and other important maritime countries, the declaration defined the terms under

1. Arthur S. Link, *Wilson the Diplomatist: A Look at His Major Policies* (Baltimore: Johns Hopkins University Press, 1957), 5.

which neutrals would have to observe a naval blockade. It also clarified what goods were contraband (items of an essentially military nature) and hence subject to seizure after the search of a neutral vessel by a belligerent and what goods were "free" and thus not subject to seizure.[2] The U.S. Senate had approved the agreement, while the British and German governments were still seeking legislative approval when war broke out in mid-1914. Immediately thereafter Wilson had called on both Berlin and London to respect its provisions. Berlin agreed, and London refused.

Rather than insulate the United States from the conflict, the recently reenforced system of maritime rights was quickly to embroil the United States in controversy and to force some difficult decisions on the Wilson administration. One source of this turbulence was the temptation felt first by Britain and then by Germany to wage economic warfare. That warfare took as one of its chief objectives the blocking of neutral trade with the other side. Both began testing the limits of American tolerance, though both proceeded cautiously out of fear of alienating a major economic and naval power and precipitating American retaliation. These incursions on neutral rights, tentative as they were, were bound to cause difficulties in any case.

But the situation was made considerably more complex by the introduction of new naval technology. On the British side, the contact mine came into the arsenal. The British navy began to rely heavily on mines to close off the long German coastline and the continental ports that served Germany. This step violated neutral rights because mines could not distinguish neutral from belligerent vessels and thus would destroy both without regard to status. The challenge from the German side was more dramatic. With the main surface fleet bottled up, the German navy began to look to the submarine to challenge Britain's command of the sea and disrupt the flow of goods to the British Isles. But the submarine could abide by the rules formulated for conventional surface warships only at some risk and considerable difficulty. The requirements of "cruiser warfare" stipulated that before sinking any noncombatant vessel a warship had to give warning and provide for the safety of passengers and crew. Thus a submarine would have to come to the surface, where it was visible and vulnerable, and to find some safe place to put those taken from the doomed ship, although the submarine's own cramped quarters offered little option.

While in theory the submarine could play by the rules, British countermeasures raised the costs to prohibitive levels. British merchant vessels began

2. The first part of the declaration deals with blockade and the second with contraband. U.S. Department of State, *Papers Relating to the Foreign Relations of the United States* [hereafter *FRUS*], *1909* (Washington: Government Printing Office, 1914), 318–33.

to fly the flags of neutrals, thus obscuring their identity as belligerents, and even to carry masked guns. When a German submarine surfaced, the British ship could turn on the exposed submarine, destroying it by ramming or gunfire. Faced with such risks, submarine commanders sought other, less dangerous and by necessity less dependable means of identifying enemy vessels and made scant effort to rescue survivors as maritime law required. The chances of mistaken attacks on neutral vessels or loss of neutrals traveling on Entente ships thus increased. In testing the limits of neutral tolerance the British quickly took the initiative. Already in August 1914 British authorities began seizing neutral goods in violation of both the declaration of London and customary rules of maritime law. The Wilson administration responded to these early violations of U.S. neutral rights in September by privately expressing to London a desire for an amicable resolution. In October Washington began quietly protesting violations on a case-by-case basis. This weak American reaction encouraged London to push harder on its economic warfare, chiefly by sowing mines in the North Sea to obstruct trade with neutrals through whom goods might reach Germany. Not until late December did Wilson lodge a general if mildly worded protest. London thought that the note was meant to appease the American public and so continued negotiating individual cases and encroaching on an ever broader range of neutral rights. The British foreign secretary, Sir Edward Grey, was both delighted and surprised by this limited and delayed reaction to seizure of American goods and ships and obstruction of American trade by mines.

London's success provoked Berlin. On 4 February 1915 the German government declared a war zone around Britain and warned that all enemy merchant vessels found there would be subject to submarine attack. Berlin justified this new affront to neutrals on the grounds that the United States and other neutrals had compromised their position by their supine reaction to British inroads. On 16 February the British cabinet agreed on retaliatory measures that in effect blockaded all U.S. trade whether with Germany or European neutrals. London no more than Berlin pretended that it acted in conformity with the established tenets of international law.

These escalating pressures by the two maritime belligerents forced the Wilson administration to reexamine its heretofore weak, ad hoc neutrality policy. The revised policy was the product of a three-way debate. Robert Lansing, the counselor in the State Department and its international law specialist, sought to protect what he understood to be the formal rules of international law. Lansing's boss, Secretary of State William Jennings Bryan, was less concerned with legal technicalities than with maintaining good relations with the powers. The president, who kept the final decision and even the drafting of key diplomatic notes in his own hands, professed a desire to work within the framework of maritime law and to keep out of war. But by degrees he would reject both Lansing's and Bryan's positions and tilt toward the Entente camp.

The new British blockade measures, decided in February and promulgated in March, sparked the first round of discussions, pitting Lansing against Wilson, with Bryan in the role of intermediary. Lansing wanted to stick close to the terms of international law and strenuously hold London "responsible" for any violation of American rights, if for no other reason than to protect precedent and lay the basis for postwar claims. (Lansing seems not to have imagined pressing London to the point that economic or military retaliation would become an issue.) To give way to Britain would, he contended, compromise the tradition of American neutrality, set back efforts to build up an international consensus on maritime law, and harm U.S. commercial interests unfairly impeded by the blockade (Document 5).

Wilson, on the other hand, wanted to accept the British blockade and to trust British officials to enforce trade restrictions in a way that would de facto respect U.S. neutral rights. If the British conduct did not live up to his expectations and did indeed violate American rights, then (he argued) Washington could lodge protests on a case-by-case basis, as it had earlier (Document 6). Wilson had his way. Although he did direct the State Department to object formally to blatant British violations of neutral rights, Wilson made clear to London that his administration would be accommodating and accept future reparations rather than threaten immediate retaliation (Document 7).

Even before reacting to British measures, Wilson had taken a firm stand against submarine warfare. More than a month before the protest to Britain he had announced that he would hold Germany to a "strict accountability" for any submarine attacks on American vessels and for the resulting loss of American life as well as property. In this case Wilson would entertain no policy of delayed settlement or reparations (Document 3).

A German submarine's sinking of the *Lusitania* in May revived the issue and set off a new round of discussions among the trio of U.S. policymakers. The British liner, carrying munitions as well as passengers, had gone down with the loss of 1,198 lives (128 American). In a formal protest that he himself prepared, Wilson advanced the claim that American citizens traveling the high seas on noncombatant belligerent vessels enjoyed protection from attack. Wilson clothed his demand for an immediate halt to the German submarine campaign with the threat of strong but unspecified countermeasures (Document 8).

This time both Bryan and Lansing objected to the emerging tilt in the president's policy. Lansing complained, "We have already been too complacent with Great Britain" (over its violations of neutral rights). Any protest to Germany against the *Lusitania*'s sinking should, he argued, be balanced by a protest to Britain that " 'shows its teeth,' " thus helping to maintain an aura of American "impartiality."[3] Bryan for his part had by early June grown deeply upset. He regarded Wilson's cabinet as pro-Entente and saw the president's own sweeping claims for the right of Americans to travel on belligerent ships and under dangerous conditions as setting the United States on a collision course with Germany.

Wilson was unmoved. On 7 June he conceded to Bryan that he was caught between contradictory popular impulses "to maintain a firm front in respect to what we demand of Germany and yet do nothing that might by any possibility involve us in war."[4] Unable to alter the president's approach and unable to accept the president's strong *Lusitania* protest, a frustrated Bryan resigned so that he could air publicly the concerns that he had been expressing to Wilson privately (Document 10). Wilson promoted an acquiescent Lansing to Bryan's place.

The reading of maritime law that had by mid-1915 come to guide U.S. neutrality policy did indeed set Washington and Berlin at loggerheads. Wilson had embraced the claim that the British and German violations were qualitatively different. Submarines took lives and property, while mines (as he saw it) caused only a loss of property. Critics of Wilson's policy—both in the United States and in Germany—responded that international law contained no such distinction between tolerable and intolerable violations of international law or between violations that harmed people and those which harmed only property. In any case, British mines could be as deadly to neutral lives as any German submarine. Nor did international law allow for selective enforcement, the critics claimed. To submit to transgression of rights was to fail in the responsibilities incumbent on a neutral. Compromising one's protected legal status invited acts of retaliation by the other belligerent power.

Wilson's interpretation of neutral rights was as troubling to Berlin as it had been pleasing to London. The German foreign ministry was perplexed by Wilson's application of strict standards to the German submarine while tolerating the British illegal blockade. The foreign ministry also lamented Washington's ineffectiveness in calling Britain to account for abusing neutral flags and thereby setting genuine neutral vessels under suspicion. Accordingly Berlin ordered its ambassador in Washington to remind the American government that true neutrality required full and equitable, not selective and one-

3. *FRUS: The Lansing Papers, 1914–1920* (2 vols.; Washington: GPO, 1939), 1:296–99.
4. *FRUS: The Lansing Papers,* 1:439.

sided, defense of rights. At the same time it offered to suspend submarine warfare on the condition that the United States cease to bow to British violations of international law (Document 4).

*　*　*

The pro-British course that the president had set can be found, some have contended, in Wilson's unintended misreading of international law. Unversed in its nuances, Wilson may have unthinkingly strayed far from a properly neutral course. It would, however, be too simple to say that Wilson embarked on the road that would lead to war just because he did not understand his obligations and rights as a neutral. Behind his tilt in Britain's favor was a strong personal identification with the British. He admired their political values and institutions, indeed thought them a model that Americans might copy with profit. He cherished British literature, philosophy, and manners. He accepted the notion of an Anglo-American family and regarded the Germans as outsiders whose victory would be a family tragedy.

This sentimental predisposition was already evident shortly after calling the nation to hold to true neutrality. Already by late August 1914 Wilson was privately offering his "condemnation of Germany's part in this war" and predicting the dire consequences to civilization and to U.S. security if Germany won. At the same time, a dispute with Britain, he told the British ambassador in early September, "would be the crowning calamity."[5] In December Wilson offered a reporter a candid appraisal of an embattled Europe consistent with these views (Document 2). This pro-English bias was reenforced most notably by "Colonel" Edward House, a confidante and political backer of the president, whose private diplomacy sought to effect a rapprochement between Washington and London, and by Walter Hines Page, ambassador in London.

The anglophilia that predominated within the Wilson administration was a strong current within elite circles. The editors of the national press, for example, voiced strong support for the British cousins. In fall 1914, even before British propaganda and the controversy over submarine warfare had poisoned views of Germany, 189 editors favored the Entente, only 38 Germany, with 140 not yet clearly committed.[6] This elite bias in favor of Britain came to be shared by much of the public as British propaganda in the United States played on the German occupation army's "rape" of Belgium and the "barbaric" sinking of passenger liners. The public shock and outrage occasioned by loss of life on the *Lusitania* helped consolidate the preponderant view that Britain was the civi-

---

5. Arthur S. Link, ed., *The Papers of Woodrow Wilson* (69 vols.; Princeton: Princeton University Press, 1966–94), 30:462, 472.

6. *Literary Digest* 49 (14 November 1914): 939.

lized combatant in a war of good against evil. The Central powers did find some sympathy, especially among the 15 percent of the population that was Irish-American or German-American. American Jews also strongly favored Germany, either because of cultural ties to that country or out of antipathy to Russia, an Entente power with a starkly antisemitic record.

The general favor shown Britain became a frequent point of comment in the German embassy's reporting home and a general source of irritation, even anger, in Berlin (Document 20). The same themes struck by German officials privately were sounded more forcefully in public—in wartime propaganda. It identified the American cause with the pursuit of profit and with a natural identity of interest with Britain. One such account published in 1916 declared that the Americans, though ostensibly neutral, were "in spirit pure Englishmen" and thus "supply Germany's enemies with all the resources of war." A devotion to money-making even "in the most terrible bloodletting of all time," along with heavy capital investments in Britain, also helped explain the marked American bias.[7]

Where Germans sensed hostility, the British saw in the United States a potential ally ready to be won over. London now reaped the benefits of a long-standing campaign to cultivate the United States as an international partner. As far back as the 1890s, British leaders, recognizing their imperial vulnerability, had purposefully set about resolving serious issues dividing the two countries. Perhaps the most important of these initiatives was the strategic retreat from the U.S. Latin American sphere of influence. Thanks too to the transatlantic cult of Anglo-Saxonism and the growing contact through travel and intermarriage between the elites of the two countries, many Americans looked on Britain with growing favor, while by contrast they saw Germany as a pugnacious expansionist power threatening American interests in Latin America and East Asia, and as an autocracy at odds with American political values. Expansionist dreams that German leaders, military planners, and publicists extended to China, the Philippines, the South Pacific, and even the Western Hemisphere at one time or another from the 1890s down to the eve of war served to fuel this negative American appraisal and inspired naval planning on each side aimed at the other.

Economic interests did (as German observers charged) reenforce pro-British attitudes. Entente war orders began to restore a weak U.S. economy in late 1914, while the blockade of the continent oriented the growing American trade heavily toward the Entente and away from the Central powers. A similar imbalance is reflected in the loans made by American banks. By April 1917, $2.3

7. For an example of that propaganda see Robert Walton, *Over There: European Reactions to Americans in World War I* (Itasca, Ill.: F. E. Peacock, 1971), 72.

		Trade with Belligerents[8] (in millions of dollars)			
	1913	1914	1915	1916	1917
Entente powers	$1207	$1204	$2209	$3642	$3768
Central powers	577	336	62	9	0

billion had gone to the Entente, a mere $27 million to Germany. Like the trade flows, this financial commitment created a vested interest in an Entente victory (though there is little evidence to suggest an influence over Wilson's decisions).

*   *   *

The tilt toward Britain, established early in the war, did not prevent tensions from arising between Washington and London over seizure of American goods and ships. But the submarine issue had by mid-1915 become the more serious and persistent issue, poisoning German-American relations. Responding to Wilson's stiff *Lusitania* protest, German foreign minister Gottlieb von Jagow had expressed regret at the loss of life but insisted that the *Lusitania* was no innocent passenger liner (Document 9). Germany finally stepped away from confrontation in a September 1915 pledge to keep submarines from sinking passenger liners of whatever nationality.

In late 1915 the German high command resurrected the question of unrestricted submarine warfare. Battlefield maps gave cause for deep concern. The western front facing French and British forces had stabilized along a line running through Belgium and northern France, and a struggle of terrible attrition and scant movement to be known as trench warfare had taken hold. On the eastern front German forces had made dramatic advances but still won no decisive victory over Russia. In the opinion of some, a full, vigorous application of the submarine would swiftly—within a matter of months—break the deadlock on the battlefield and bring peace on German terms. By early 1916 the voices arrayed in favor of such a gamble included Grand Admiral Alfred von Tirpitz (then minister of the navy) and General Erich von Falkenhayn (simultaneously minister of war and chief of the general staff) (Document 12). Chancellor Theobald von Bethmann Hollweg resisted, warning that the un-

8. The Entente trade figures cover the United Kingdom, France, and Russia. The Central powers covered here are Germany and Austria-Hungary. American trade with the northern neutrals (Denmark, Holland, Norway, and Sweden) amounted to $224 million in 1913, $257 million in 1914, $398 million in 1915, $256 million in 1916, and $217 million in 1917. U.S. Department of Commerce, Bureau of Foreign and Domestic Commerce, *Statistical Abstracts of the United States, 1920* (Washington: GPO, 1921), 398ff.

leashing of the submarine would have dangerous consequences, not least that of drawing the United States into the conflict on the side of Germany's enemies (Document 13). Virtually from the beginning of the war he had opposed naval pressure for unrestricted submarine warfare. When the navy, despite his objections, had put a submarine blockade in force against the British Isles in February 1915, the sharp U.S. protest had surprised even Bethmann Hollweg and confirmed his opposition.

Austere, tenacious, and stoic, Bethmann Hollweg was an aristocrat who had entered the civil service at age twenty-three and built a record as a reform conservative and a moderate expansionist. Appointed chancellor in 1909, he had proven a devoted servant of a difficult sovereign. The fairly consistent if sometimes grudging support from the kaiser was indispensable to Bethmann Hollweg's success, even to his political survival. Kaiser Wilhelm II, who had come to the throne in 1888, had at least in theory the final word in military as well as foreign policy. In practice he tended to be indecisive. Shallow, insulated, tactless, erratic, given to bluster, his temperament no less than his judgment was the despair of his aides. While Bethmann Hollweg enjoyed wide executive power and direct access to the throne, both the chief of the general staff and the chief of the admiralty staff operated beyond his control, and they too could approach the kaiser directly.

By nature conservative, Bethmann Hollweg feared the unsettling consequences of war. In 1913 he had noted the mounting tensions in Europe with equal measures of worry and prophecy: "It is high time that the great nations quieted down again and pursued peaceful tasks. Otherwise an explosion will occur, which no one desires and which will harm all."[9] When war finally came in the summer of 1914, this patriot turned to the task of defending his country and formulating peace terms that would bring Germany greater security and redeem the mounting sacrifices demanded by the war effort. In the first flush of battle there was talk of the spoils a victorious Germany might gather in: fresh territorial gains to the east and the west, a dependent Belgium and Holland, a dismantled Russian empire, a humbled France, colonial prizes, naval bases, new markets and sources of raw materials, and a large indemnity. Bethmann Hollweg himself at first played with broad goals such as these. But when quick victory eluded Germany, he realized that his government would not impose but rather negotiate peace terms. Many within the political and military elites, however, clung to grandiose goals and were ready to gamble German economic and military power in order to realize them.

9. Quoted in Konrad H. Jarausch, *The Enigmatic Chancellor: Bethmann Hollweg and the Hubris of Imperial Germany* (New Haven: Yale University Press, 1973), 99–100.

Bethmann Hollweg prevailed in the first full-scale debate over unrestricted submarine warfare. Begun in late 1915, the debate ended in March 1916 with the kaiser's call for restraint (Document 14). Submarines were not to go beyond attacking enemy merchant ships around the British Isles, and elsewhere only armed merchant ships were fair game. Enemy passenger ships were off limits.

The torpedoing of the French ferry *Sussex* on 24 March 1916 as it crossed the English Channel set off new controversy with the United States. Although no American lives were lost, Washington lodged a strong protest (Document 15). The subsequent frank exchange between Lansing and the German ambassador made clear that neither side could devise a mutually acceptable way out of the mounting antagonism (Document 16). To avert a collision, Berlin pledged in May 1916 not to let submarines attack without warning and safeguards. But the pledge was explicitly conditioned on the United States' getting Britain to cease its violations of maritime law (Document 17). London's refusal to alter its practices left Berlin in a quandary over how best to employ its submarine weapon. Meanwhile, Wilson's passivity and one-sidedness as a neutral and his seeming naïveté as a statesman determined to play the peacemaker between the warring but precariously stalemated European alliances made German leaders uneasy if not scornful (Document 18).

Through the summer of 1916 Germany's submarine enthusiasts continued to press their case against the doubters with arguments that increasingly won popular support. In August a slight but fatal crack appeared in the chancellor's resistance. After supporting the promotion of the prestigious Paul von Hindenburg as the new chief of general staff (to replace Falkenhayn), Bethmann Hollweg had suggested in the field marshal's presence that the launching of a submarine campaign was ultimately a military decision (Document 19).

That decision was not long in coming. Germany was suffering under the impact of the blockade, and leaders in Berlin were frustrated by the lack of movement on the western front. Popular clamor for using the "decisive" submarine weapon and the Entente's cool response to peace overtures added to the pressure on the chancellor as autumn unfolded. The rising number of submarines in the German arsenal reenforced the confidence of its proponents. Almost one hundred were available, well up from the twenty in operation in early 1915. (Even so, only one third of the submarine fleet could be at sea at any one time.) In addition, the position of Germany's allies, Austria and Turkey, was deteriorating.

In December a confident Admiralty formally presented its case in favor of lifting restrictions on submarine warfare in order to cut vulnerable British supply lines (Document 21). The case persuaded Hindenburg, who was already moving from the ranks of the undecided. In late December he announced to the chancellor that the time had finally come for a decisive military blow (Document 22). Bethmann Hollweg continued to drag his heels, much to the annoyance of the military leaders, but on 9 January, after a high-level conference, the kaiser authorized the campaign scheduled to begin on 1 February 1917 (Document 23).

Outmaneuvered on this critical issue, Bethmann Hollweg dutifully remained in office to save German morale and unity and to serve his sovereign. But his political base was fast eroding under the pressure of political polarization and military intrigue, and the popular Hindenburg and his close military associate Erich Ludendorff had come to dominate the kaiser. In July 1917 Bethmann Hollweg resigned and retired to his family estate, there to die in 1920.

*   *   *

The beginning of the new campaign backed Wilson into a corner. But the submarine challenge alone does not explain his ultimate decision in favor of entering the European conflict. He was also strongly influenced by his search for some goal for U.S. policy that transcended what he regarded as the dry technicalities of maritime law. As Wilson grew increasingly uncomfortable with an American response to war based on narrowly legal grounds, he by degrees broadened American policy concerns. He came to set his sights on new international rules with far-reaching implications for the relations among states and their internal constitution. Ultimately driven toward war by German submarine warfare, Wilson pronounced himself committed to serve humanity through the creation of an enlightened order to replace the selfish and sanguinary one that he had inherited. He would discover, however, that bold recastings of the international system are easier to envision than to implement. His was to fail of support at home no less than abroad.

Hints of the appeal of a policy based on some principle broader and more inspiring than international law had appeared in his earliest response to the war. The attraction seemed even stronger when he spoke in Chicago in January 1916, after more than a year of friction with the belligerents and on the eve of an election campaign in which his neutrality policy was bound to figure as an issue (Document 11). One role that the United States might play, Wilson suggested, was that of peacemaker. Thus shortly before the Chicago speech Wilson sent Colonel House to London, Paris, and Berlin in hopes of promoting a negotiated settlement to the conflict.

The House mission failed to move the combatants toward the peace table, and the colonel came home bearing a bizarre agreement with Sir Edward Grey. This House-Grey memorandum of 22 February 1916 stipulated that Wilson would at a moment acceptable to Britain and France call a conference, which "would secure peace on terms not unfavorable" to them. If Germany refused to attend the conference or once there rejected reasonable terms, then the United States would enter the war on the Entente side.[10] Wilson himself was more concerned with restoring peace than with sending Americans across the sea to fight. He at once watered down the commitment, and the memorandum came to naught. Almost at once the British cabinet, with its scant interest in a compromise, rejected the notion of a Wilson-dominated conference. In the months that followed, growing tensions over maritime rights complicated relations between London and Washington. Wilson was pulled into his reelection campaign—not a time for controversial peace initiatives. Instead Wilson stressed his commitment to keeping out of the European war and to creating after the war a lasting peace founded on a "league of nations," an idea popular among liberal-left groups in the United States, Britain, and Germany.

Wilson's electoral victory over Republican Charles Evans Hughes in November allowed him to return to his search for peace. In December 1916, at the very time Berlin was moving toward a submarine decision, a victorious Wilson sought to promote negotiations by asking the belligerents to state their war aims. Then in January 1917, with his own diplomatic effort stalled, Wilson sought to lay out for himself and the nation a full-blown vision of what he thought the war was about—the creation of a new world order. In a speech to the Senate he presented in embryo the rules that he wanted to govern postwar dealings among nations (Document 25).

The march to war began in February, when the German decision for unrestricted submarine warfare became apparent. Wilson broke diplomatic relations with Berlin and moved under presidential authority to arm American merchant ships traveling through the declared German zone of attack. Conflict on the high seas continued. In addition, Berlin decided to risk the offer of an alliance to Mexico, twice subject to military intervention by Wilson and for several years the field of fruitless German political intrigue (Document 24). The British decoded the offer and passed it on to Washington for release. This stark violation of the Monroe Doctrine fanned the flames of emotion in the United States. When signals reached Berlin in March that the Wilson administration might be seeking some modus vivendi on the maritime issue, the champions of the submarine quickly raised a cry, and the kaiser defiantly ruled out further diplomatic dithering with the Americans. On 18 March 1917 he reacted to news that the Americans were apparently trying to arrange safe passage for their ships en route to Britain: "Now, once and for all, an *end* to negotiations with America. If Wilson wants war, let him make it, and let him

10. Link, *Papers of Woodrow Wilson*, 36:180n (House-Grey memo of 22 February 1916), 262 (Wilson's reaction on 6 March 1916).

then have it."[11] Meanwhile, Wilson displayed considerable resistance to taking that final step, leaving his close confidants troubled by his indecision (Document 26). An Entente in crisis watched anxiously for a resolution. London's treasury was nearly empty, the French army threatened mutiny, and Russia was in the throes of revolution.

In late March Wilson consulted with his cabinet, and it unanimously urged war (Document 27). On 2 April the president appeared before Congress to ask for a war declaration, based in part on what Wilson understood to be a grievous violation of neutral rights and in part on what he hoped American intervention might contribute to a new world of peace and democracy (Document 28). Critics of Wilson's course, such as Senator George W. Norris, a liberal Republican from Nebraska, contended that the United States had indeed not been neutral, had neglected opportunities to force the combatants to respect neutral rights, and would find itself in a war whose costs in both life and treasure might prove high (Document 29). But the critics were in a decided minority, and Congress approved war on 6 April by votes of 82–6 in the Senate and 373–50 in the House.

The war effort on which Wilson and Congress had launched the country would soon be felt in Europe. Defying the boasts of German submarine champions, American troops (eventually to number two million) and a swelling stream of supplies reached the western front. By the summer of 1918 the kaiser was watching his army and navy collapse, and his war-weary subjects were turning rebellious. In November 1918 he went ingloriously into exile in Holland, leaving a politically fractured Germany to save itself.

For a time overwhelmed by the urgent details of military mobilization, Wilson neglected his plans for peace. At last in January 1918 he unveiled to the public his fourteen-point program. The speech that he then delivered had the practical purpose of rallying support for the war effort on the Entente side and stimulating demands for peace in Germany. But it also served formally to lay down the general terms that he expected to guide the postwar settlement and that he had already articulated with force and clarity in his speech to the Senate a year earlier.

Wilson expressed his vision in a set of basic principles: freedom of the seas; free trade, including an open door to formerly closed colonies; disarmament; national self-determination; and, most important of all, respect for a new code of civilized conduct among nations fostered and defended by a League of Nations. The League was at the heart of his plan. "A general association of

11. Carnegie Endowment for International Peace, Division of International Law, comp. and trans., *Official German Documents Relating to the World War* (2 vols.; New York: Oxford University Press, 1923), 2:1335.

nations must be formed under specific covenants for the purpose of affording mutual guarantees of political independence and territorial integrity to great and small states alike."[12]

But above all else Wilson used the occasion once more to voice his personal antipathy to power politics and his dissatisfaction with the narrow concerns of international law. He described World War I as "the culminating and final war for human liberty." In that struggle the American people had to be "ready to devote their lives, their honor, and everything that they possess" in order to set at the foundation of international affairs "the principle of justice to all peoples and nationalities, and their right to live on equal terms of liberty and safety with one another, whether they be strong or weak."[13] This audacious redefinition of the rules of international relations reflected views about the American national mission fermenting in Wilson's mind since the Spanish-American War. The time had come for Americans to put aside their "traditional," limited foreign policy and play a great global role as the promoter of progress.

* * *

International systems are not easily built up—a point that became ever clearer as Wilson's plan for a new world order encountered growing resistance. Already in late 1916 his league idea had drawn conservative fire. In April 1917 some in Congress such as Norris had questioned the premises of Wilson's policy. Britain and France entered their own significant caveats when in October 1918 Germany and Austria-Hungary proposed to Wilson an end to the fighting on the basis of his fourteen points. London and Paris at once took exception to the principle of freedom of the seas and insisted on going beyond his nonpunitive terms by adding reparations to the peace agenda. Still other unsettling demands, mostly territorial, confronted Wilson at the Paris peace conference.

After compromising in Paris to save the League, which was essential to any hope of realizing his new order, the American president returned home to find the domestic opposition almost as intense as the foreign. The Senate, which would have to approve his peace agreements, was divided, with important leaders such as Republican senator Henry Cabot Lodge sharply critical of both Wilson's failure to consult and the terms that he had negotiated. Those terms, the critics contended, did not consistently follow the principle of self-determination and gave too much power to the League of Nations. The League's powers to enforce collective security, for example, infringed on the preroga-

12. President Wilson, address to Congress, 8 January 1918, in Link, *Papers of Woodrow Wilson*, 45:538.

13. Link, *Papers of Woodrow Wilson*, 45:539.

tives of Congress and on U.S. sovereignty. To bring the Senate into line, Wilson turned to the public. His health was now rapidly deteriorating, and in October, while on a cross-country tour, he collapsed from exhaustion (perhaps a stroke), followed on his return to the capital by a serious stroke that paralyzed his left side and shook his mental powers. Still confident that he was right, a bed-ridden Wilson rebuffed compromise. In November the Senate voted down the treaty he had negotiated; a second vote in March 1920 confirmed the rejection. Wilson the man and the politician had suffered near fatal blows.

In retrospect, it is clear that the path Wilson selected—to seek to replace the existing regime of international law—did not succeed. Wilson did have an alternative path open to him that he chose not to follow: he could have held to the established American policy of neutrality. The consensus that the naval powers had reached on the eve of the war had fortified the position of neutrals by clarifying their rights. By holding to a course of genuine neutrality, Wilson could have guaranteed American trade, secured a period of prosperity for the American economy, and altogether avoided the heavy costs of participation in the war. The immediate costs of intervention included the deaths of 130,000 American soldiers and the expenditure of over $30 billion (one-third covered by taxes and the balance by national debt). The long-term monetary costs (including veterans' pensions) were roughly three times higher.

To ensure the belligerents' respect for American neutrality from the outset, Wilson had impressive economic and naval power at his disposal not available to Thomas Jefferson and James Madison when they had confronted European belligerents. Even the threat of depriving one side or the other of access to American resources might quickly have given any offending power serious second thoughts. If the threat and then the actual implementation of economic retaliation had not been enough, Washington had another way to secure respect for its neutrality—by promptly and forcefully threatening to enter the war in defense of its rights against whichever power refused to end its abuses.[14] By late 1916 Germany, rendered desperate by the mounting costs of war, was ready to discount the American role. But an earlier and more even-handed application of American influence might have found Berlin in a more cooperative mood and left London with little choice but to avoid a costly split. Jefferson and Madison had made vigorous but ultimately ineffectual attempts to defend U.S. neutrality. Wilson, backed by the formidable power that had accrued to the nation since the War of 1812, made only feeble attempts to

14. U.S. naval power even in 1914, before Wilson began an intensive program of construction, was sufficient to establish it as a makeweight. The United States then had 25 capital ships (including 10 major battleships called dreadnoughts) compared to Britain's 46 (including 33 dreadnoughts) and Germany's 30 (including 22 dreadnoughts).

maintain a truly neutral stand, and so ironically he ended facing the same stark choice as his predecessors—dishonor or war.

*   *   *

Norris and other critics of intervention raised the critical questions about Wilson's decision to go to war and the attendant attempt to redefine the rules of the international game. To begin with, in what terms do we understand neutrality—as a matter of attitudes, evenhanded treatment of belligerents, formal rules of international law, or the maintenance of amity? And if Wilson strayed from neutrality (however defined), what drew him off course? Was it a distaste for Germany or a preference for Britain? Did considerations of U.S. security, prestige, honor, or economic interest play a larger role? If the Wilson administration had adopted a more evenhanded response to British and German restrictions of U.S. maritime rights, would the combatant powers have softened their economic warfare? Or would at some point growing desperation have forced them to adopt provocative policies, driving Wilson to take sides and ultimately to enter the war anyway? Even if the hardpressed belligerents had not turned on American commerce, would Wilson's own aspirations for a better world, his sentimental attachments to Britain, or his belief in the global danger posed by German ambitions and ruthlessness have gradually pushed him into old-world diplomatic entanglements and old-world battlefields? Finally, how do we evaluate Wilson's postwar plans—as a noble attempt to reform a war-prone world or a high-stakes gamble doomed from the start?

FOR FURTHER READING

The themes of "realism" and "idealism" have dominated studies of Wilson's response to the European conflict. Ernest R. May, *The World War and American Isolation, 1914–1917* (1959), and Daniel M. Smith, *The Great Departure: The United States and World War I* (1965), see Wilson growing ever more sophisticated in his understanding of international politics and ever more "realistic" in his recognition that Germany was a threat to the European balance of power. In a similar vein, Arthur S. Link, the foremost biographer of Wilson, has written approvingly on Wilson's neutrality policy. Link develops his views in detail in the multivolume *Wilson* (1947–   ). His most recent summary treatment can be found in *Woodrow Wilson: Revolution, War, and Peace* (1979). The notions of idealism and realism remain attractive, as can be seen in John Milton Cooper, Jr., *The Warrior and the Priest: Woodrow Wilson and Theodore Roosevelt* (1983), and Lloyd E. Ambrosius, *Wilsonian Statecraft: Theory and Practice of Liberal Internationalism during World War I* (1991).

Some students of Wilson's policy have reacted against the realist-idealist categories of interpretation. N. Gordon Levin, Jr., *Woodrow Wilson and World Politics: America's Response to War and Revolution* (1968), and Arno J. Mayer, *Political Origins of the New Diplomacy, 1917–1918* (1959), highlight economic self-interest and fear of revolutionary upheavals, while John W. Coogan's *The End of Neutrality: The United States, Britain, and Maritime Rights, 1899–1915* (1981), an account that has influenced the treatment here, highlights Wilson's highly consequential deviation from a well-established body of international law. Thomas J. Knock, *To End All Wars: Woodrow Wilson and the Quest for a New World Order* (1992), examines the wartime origins of Wilson's league idea.

Valuable insights into Wilson's personality and point of view can be found in John M. Mulder, *Woodrow Wilson: The Years of Preparation* (1978); Edwin A. Weinstein, *Woodrow Wilson: A Medical and Psychological Biography* (1981); and Niels A. Thorsen, *The Political Thought of Woodrow Wilson, 1875–1910* (1988).

Detailed treatment of German and British policy can be found in the May and Coogan studies (noted above) as well as in Patrick Devlin, *Too Proud to Fight: Woodrow Wilson's Neutrality* (1975), which brings a strong British perspective to Wilson's policy; Konrad H. Jarausch, *The Enigmatic Chancellor: Bethmann Hollweg and the Hubris of Imperial Germany* (1973); Karl E. Birnbaum, *Peace Moves and U-Boat Warfare: A Study of Imperial Germany's Policy towards the United States, April 18, 1916–January 9, 1917* (1958); and Reinhard R. Doerries, *Imperial Challenge: Ambassador Count Bernstorff and German-American Relations, 1908–1917,* trans. Christa D. Shannon (1989). Fritz Fischer, *Germany's Aims in the First World War* (1967), and Gerhard Ritter, *The Sword and the Scepter: The Problem of Militarism in Germany,* trans. Heinz Norden (1969–73), particularly vol. 4, *The Tragedy of Statesmanship—Bethmann Hollweg as War Chancellor (1914–1917)* (1972), offer broad accounts of German wartime policy with sharply differing estimates of war aims. Bradford Perkins, *The Great Rapprochement: England and the United States, 1895–1914* (1968); Holger H. Hervig, *Politics of Frustration: The United States in German Naval Planning, 1889–1941* (1976); and David Stevenson, *The First World War and International Politics* (1988), offer helpful background.

DOCUMENTS

**1   President Woodrow Wilson, address to the nation,
18 August 1914, calling for neutrality following the outbreak
of war in Europe.**[15]

The people of the United States are drawn from many nations, and chiefly from the nations now at war. . . . Some will wish one nation, others another, to succeed in the momentous struggle. It will be easy to excite passion and difficult to allay it. . . . Such divisions among us would be fatal to our peace of mind and might seriously stand in the way of the proper performance of our duty as the one great nation at peace, the one people holding itself ready to play a part of impartial mediation and speak the counsels of peace and accommodation, not as a partisan, but as a friend.

. . . The United States must be neutral in fact as well as in name during these days that are to try men's souls. We must be impartial in thought as well as in action, must put a curb upon our sentiments as well as upon every transaction that might be construed as a preference of one party to the struggle before another.

**2   President Wilson, comments to Herbert Bruce Brougham
of the *New York Times*, 14 December 1914, sizing up the
European conflict.**[16]

The Powers are making the most tremendous display of force in history. . . . [T]he chance of a just and equitable peace, and of the only possible peace that will be lasting, will be happiest if no nation gets the decision by arms; and the danger of an unjust peace, one that will be sure to invite further calamities, will be if some one nation or group of nations succeeds in enforcing its will upon the others.

. . . It seems to me that the Government of Germany must be profoundly changed, and that Austria-Hungary will go to pieces altogether—ought to go to pieces for the welfare of Europe.

. . .

. . . I cannot see now that it would hurt greatly the interests of the United

15. Link, *Papers of Woodrow Wilson*, 30:393–94.
16. Memorandum of a half-hour confidential interview by Brougham, in Link, *Papers of Woodrow Wilson*, 31:458–59.

States if either France or Russia or Great Britain should finally dictate the settlement. England has already extended her empire as far as she wants to—in fact, she has got more than she wants—and she now wishes to be let alone in order that she may bend all her energies to the task of consolidating the ports [parts] of her empire. . . .

3   Secretary of State William Jennings Bryan to U.S. Ambassador to Germany James W. Gerard, 10 February 1915, conveying a protest (drafted by Wilson) against German violation of neutral rights.[17]

If the commanders of German vessels of war . . . should destroy on the high seas an American vessel or the lives of American citizens, it would be difficult for the Government of the United States to view the act in any other light than as an indefensible violation of neutral rights which it would be very hard indeed to reconcile with the friendly relations now so happily subsisting between the two governments.

If such a deplorable situation should arise, . . . the Government of the United States would be constrained to hold the Imperial German Government to a strict accountability for such acts of their naval authorities and to take any steps it might be necessary to take to safeguard American lives and property and to secure to American citizens the full enjoyment of their acknowledged rights on the high seas.

4   German Foreign Minister Gottlieb E. G. von Jagow to U.S. Ambassador Gerard, 16 February 1915, defending German maritime policy.[18]

England has not shrunk from grave violations of international law wherever she could thereby cripple Germany's peaceable trade with neutral countries. . . .

. . . [T]he intention of all these aggressions is to cut off Germany from all supplies and thereby to deliver up to death by famine a peaceful civilian population, a procedure contrary to [the] law of war and every dictate of humanity.

17. Carlton Savage, *Policy of the United States toward Maritime Commerce in War* (2 vols.; Washington: GPO, 1934 and 1936), 2:268.

18. *FRUS, 1915, Supplement: The World War* (Washington: GPO, 1928), 112–15.

The neutrals have not been able to prevent this interception of different kinds of trade with Germany contrary to international law. It is true that the American Government have protested against England's procedure, . . . but in spite of this protest and the protests of the other neutral governments England has not allowed herself to be dissuaded from the course originally adopted. . . .

. . . Germany is to all intents and purposes cut off from oversea supplies with the toleration, tacit or protesting, of the neutrals. . . . On the other hand England with the indulgence of neutral governments is not only being provided with such goods as are not contraband or merely conditional contraband, . . . but also with goods which have been regularly and unquestionably acknowledged to be absolute contraband. . . . [A] trade in arms exists between American manufacturers and Germany's enemies which is estimated at many hundred million marks.

. . .

. . . [T]he secret order of the British Admiralty . . . recommends English merchant vessels to use neutral flags. . . . The English merchant marine has followed this counsel without delay. . . . Moreover, the British Government have armed English merchant vessels and instructed them to resist by force the German submarines. In these circumstances it is very difficult for the German submarines to recognize neutral merchant vessels as such, for even a search will not be possible in the majority of cases, since the attacks to be anticipated in the case of a disguised English ship would expose the commanders conducting a search and the boat itself to the danger of destruction.

. . .

The German Government . . . welcome the fact that the American Government have made representations to the British Government relative to the use of their flag contrary to law and give expression to the expectation that this action will cause England to respect the American flag in future.

In this expectation the commanders of the German submarines have been instructed . . . to abstain from violence to American merchant vessels when they are recognizable as such.

In order to meet in the safest manner all the consequences of mistaking an American for a hostile merchant vessel the German Government recommended that . . . the United States convoy their ships carrying peaceable cargoes and traversing the English seat of maritime war in order to make them recognizable. . . . The German Government are prepared to enter into immediate negotiations with the American Government relative to the manner of convoy. They would, however, be particularly grateful if the American Government would urgently advise their merchant vessels to avoid the English seat of maritime war, at any rate until the flag question is settled.

The German Government resign themselves to the confident hope that the

American Government will recognize the full meaning of the severe struggle which Germany is conducting for her very existence. . . .

5 Robert Lansing (Counselor for the Department of State) to Bryan, memorandum, 24 March 1915, arguing for a firm stand in defense of neutral rights violated by the British blockade.[19]

In formulating a reply to the British note . . . I think that it is important to consider the following:

. . . Unless the reply contains a declaration of the legal rights of the United States based on the principles of international law, with which the press has made the public more or less familiar, the American people will consider the Government either indifferent to or ignorant of its rights. Furthermore, the declaration must be urged with sufficient vigor to remove any impression that the Government is submitting without objection to violations of such rights.

. . . A general statement, I am afraid, which amounts to a practical acceptance of the right asserted by Great Britain to interrupt commerce to Germany passing through neutral ports, regardless of its contraband character, would invite strong criticism and furnish the opponents of the Administration with a plausible argument as to the weakness of our foreign policy.

. . . If the reply of this Government is so worded that it can be construed into an admission that the measures adopted by Great Britain are justified by the conditions and possess, therefore, a degree of legality, it will make the recovery of a claim very difficult. This will also affect public opinion.

. . . The United States in the present war is the guardian of neutrality. For the sake of the future it ought to assert firmly the rights of neutrals. . . .

6 Wilson to Bryan, 24 March 1915, arguing for bowing to the British blockade while holding Britain responsible for violations of U.S. neutral rights.[20]

We are face to face with *something they* [the British] *are going to do,* and they are going to do it no matter what representations we make. We cannot convince them or change them, we can only show them . . . that we mean to hold them to a strict responsibility for every invasion of our rights as neutrals. In short we must make them understand that the discretion which their offi-

---

19. *FRUS: The Lansing Papers,* 1:290.
20. *FRUS: The Lansing Papers,* 1:288–89.

cials are vested with must be exercised in such a way that the extraordinary "blockade" they are instituting will *not* in fact violate our rights as neutral traders on the seas.

. . .

. . . Ought we not to say, in effect: You call this a blockade and mean to maintain it as such; but it is obvious that it is unprecedented in almost every respect, but chiefly in this, that it is a blockade of neutral as well as of belligerent coasts and harbours, which no belligerent can claim as a right. We shall expect therefore that the discretion [left to British government officials] . . . will be exercised to correct what is irregular in this situation and leave the way open to our legitimate trade. If this is not done we shall have to hold you to a strict accountability for every instance of rights violated and injury done; but we interpret [British Foreign Secretary] Sir Edward Grey's note to mean that this is exactly what will be done.

7   Secretary of State Bryan to U.S. Ambassador to Britain Walter Hines Page, 30 March 1915, conveying a protest against British violations of neutral rights.[21]

The note of [the British Foreign Minister] . . . notifies the Government of the United States of the establishment of a blockade which is . . . to include all the coasts and ports of Germany and every port of possible access to enemy territory. But the novel and quite unprecedented feature of that blockade . . . is that it embraces many neutral ports and coasts, bars access to them, and subjects all neutral ships seeking to approach them to the same suspicion that would attach to them were they bound for the ports of the enemies of Great Britain, and to unusual risks and penalties.

It is manifest that such limitations, risks, and liabilities placed upon the ships of a neutral power on the high seas . . . are a distinct invasion of the sovereign rights of the nation whose ships, trade, or commerce are interfered with.

. . .

The possibilities of serious interruption of American trade . . . are so many, and the methods proposed are so unusual and seem liable to constitute so great an impediment and embarrassment to neutral commerce that the Government of the United States . . . apprehends many interferences with its legiti-

21. This protest combined elements of Wilson's and Lansing's positions while omitting any reference to "strict accountability" contained in Wilson's 24 March note to Bryan (above). *FRUS, 1915, Supplement,* 153, 156.

mate trade. . . . It is, therefore, expected that His Majesty's Government . . . will take the steps necessary to avoid them, and, in the event that they should unhappily occur, will be prepared to make full reparation for every act, which under the rules of international law constitutes a violation of neutral rights.

. . .

In conclusion you [Page] will reiterate to His Majesty's Government that this statement of the views of the Government of the United States is made in the most friendly spirit, and in accordance with the uniform candor which has characterized the relations of the two Governments in the past, and which has been in large measure the foundation of the peace and amity existing between the two nations without interruption for a century.[22]

8 Secretary of State Bryan to U.S. Ambassador Gerard, 13 May 1915, conveying a protest (drafted by Wilson) against the sinking of the *Lusitania*.[23]

In view of recent acts of the German authorities in violation of American rights on the high seas which culminated in the torpedoing and sinking of the British steamship *Lusitania* on May 7, 1915, by which over 100 American citizens lost their lives, it is clearly wise and desirable that the Government of the United States and the Imperial German Government should come to a clear and full understanding as to the grave situation which has resulted.

. . .

. . . [The U.S. government is convinced of] the practical impossibility of employing submarines in the destruction of commerce without disregarding those rules of fairness, reason, justice, and humanity, which all modern opinion regards as imperative. It is practically impossible for the officers of a submarine to visit a merchantman at sea and examine her papers and cargo. It is practically impossible for them to make a prize of her; and, if they can not put a prize crew on board of her, they can not sink her without leaving her crew and all on board of her to the mercy of the sea in her small boats. . . .

American citizens act within their indisputable rights in taking their ships and in traveling wherever their legitimate business calls them upon the high seas. . . .

. . .

22. Wilson added this last paragraph at Bryan's suggestion. *FRUS, Lansing Papers*, 1:295–96.

23. *FRUS, 1915, Supplement*, 393, 395–96.

... [The U.S. government] confidently expects ... that the Imperial German Government will disavow the acts of which the Government of the United States complains, ... will make reparation so far as reparation is possible for injuries which are without measure, and ... will take immediate steps to prevent the recurrence of anything so obviously subversive of the principles of warfare. ...

...

The Imperial German Government will not expect the Government of the United States to omit any word or any act necessary to the performance of its sacred duty of maintaining the rights of the United States and its citizens and of safeguarding their free exercise and enjoyment.

9 Foreign Minister Jagow to U.S. Ambassador Gerard, 28 May 1915, defending the submarine sinking of the *Lusitania*.[24]

If neutral vessels have come to grief through the German submarine war during the past few months, by mistake, it is a question of isolated and exceptional cases which are traceable to the misuse of flags by the British Government in connection with carelessness or suspicious actions on the part of captains of the vessels. In all cases where a neutral vessel through no fault of its own has come to grief through the German submarine ..., this Government has expressed its regret at the unfortunate occurrence and promised indemnification where the facts justified it. ...

...

With regard to the loss of life when the British passenger steamer *Lusitania* was sunk, the German Government has already expressed its deep regret to the neutral Governments concerned that nationals of those countries lost their lives on that occasion. ...

The Government of the United States proceeds on the assumption that the *Lusitania* is to be considered as an ordinary unarmed merchant vessel. The Imperial Government begs in this connection to point out that the *Lusitania* was one of the largest and fastest English commerce steamers, constructed with Government funds as auxiliary cruisers, and is expressly included in the navy list published by [the] British Admiralty. It is moreover known to the Imperial Government from reliable information furnished by its officials and neutral passengers that for some time practically all the more valuable English merchant vessels have been provided with guns, ammunition, and other weap-

24. *FRUS, 1915, Supplement,* 419–20.

ons, and reinforced with a crew specially practiced in manning guns. According to reports at hand here, the *Lusitania* when she left New York undoubtedly had guns on board which were mounted under decks and masked.[25]

. . . [T]he British Admiralty by a secret instruction of February of this year advised the British merchant marine not only to seek protection behind neutral flags and markings, but even when so disguised to attack German submarines by ramming them. High rewards have been offered by the British Government as a special incentive for the destruction of the submarines by merchant vessels, and such rewards have already been paid out. In view of these facts, . . . the German commanders are consequently no longer in a position to observe the rules of capture otherwise usual and with which they invariably complied before this. Lastly, the Imperial Government must specially point out that on her last trip the *Lusitania,* as on earlier occasions, had Canadian troops and munitions on board, including no less than 5,400 cases of ammunition destined for the destruction of brave German soldiers. . . . The English steamship company must have been aware of the dangers to which passengers on board the *Lusitania* were exposed under the circumstances. In taking them on board in spite of this the company quite deliberately tried to use the lives of American citizens as protection for the ammunition carried. . . . The company thereby wantonly caused the death of so many passengers. According to the express report of the submarine commander concerned, which is further confirmed by all other reports, there can be no doubt that the rapid sinking of the *Lusitania* was primarily due to the explosion of the cargo of ammunition caused by the torpedo. Otherwise, in all human probability, the passengers of the *Lusitania* would have been saved.

10 Bryan, public statements, 10–11 June 1915, laying out policy concerns that prompted his resignation.[26]

Why should an American citizen be permitted to involve his country in war by traveling upon a belligerent ship, when he knows that the ship will pass through a danger zone? The question is not whether an American citizen has a right, under international law, to travel on a belligerent ship; the question is whether he ought not, out of consideration for his country, if not for his own safety, avoid danger when avoidance is possible.

25. The charge of guns on deck was later proved false. The ship was carrying ammunition, as charged below.

26. *New York Times,* 10 June 1915, p. 2, and 11 June 1915, p. 1.

It is a very one-sided citizenship that compels a government to go to war over a citizen's rights and yet relieve the citizen of all obligations to consider his nation's welfare....

. . .

. . . The most civilized and enlightened—aye, the most Christian—of the nations of Europe are grappling with each other as if in a death struggle. They are sacrificing the best and the bravest of their sons on the battlefield; they are converting their gardens into cemeteries and their homes into houses of mourning; they are taxing the wealth of today and laying a burden of debt on the toil of the future; they have filled the air with thunderbolts more deadly than those of Jove, and they have multiplied the perils of the deep.

Adding fresh fuel to the flame of hate, they have daily devised new horrors, until one side is endeavoring to drown noncombatant men, women, and children at sea, while the other side seeks to starve noncombatant men, women, and children on land. And they are so absorbed in alternate retaliations and in competitive cruelties that they seem, for the time being, blind to the rights of neutrals and deaf to the appeals of humanity. A tree is known by its fruit. The war in Europe is the ripened fruit of the old system.

This is what firmness, supported by force, has done in the Old World[.] [S]hall we invite it to cross the Atlantic? Already the jingoes of our own country have caught the rabies from the dogs of war; shall the opponents of organized slaughter be silent while the disease spreads?

. . .

Some nation must lead the world out the black night of war into the light of that day when "swords shall be beaten into plowshares." Why not make that honor ours? . . .

I I President Wilson, speech in Chicago, 31 January 1916, warning of the danger of war.[27]

[Y]ou have laid upon me the double obligation of maintaining the honor of the United States and of maintaining the peace of the United States. Is it not conceivable that the two might become incompatible? Is it not conceivable that, however great our passion for peace, we would have to subordinate it to our passion for what is right? . . .

Look at the task that is assigned to the United States—to assert the principles of law in a world in which the principles of law have broken down—not the technical principles of law, but the essential principles of right dealing and

27. Link, *Papers of Woodrow Wilson*, 36:66–67, 73.

humanity as between nation and nation. Law is a very complicated term. It includes a great many things that do not engage our affections. But at the basis of the things that we are now dealing with lie the deepest affections of the human heart—the love of life, the love of righteousness, the love of fair dealing, the love of those things that are just and of good report. The things that are rooted in our very spirit are the stuff of the law that I am talking about now.

. . .

. . . America has been cried awake by these voices in the disturbed and reddened night, when fire sweeps sullenly from continent to continent. And it may be that in this red flame of light there will rise again that ideal figure of America holding up her hand of hope and of guidance to the people of the world. . . .

12 Grand Admiral Alfred von Tirpitz (minister of the navy), memorial presented to Chancellor Theobald von Bethmann Hollweg, 8 February 1916, recommending the prompt launching of unrestricted submarine warfare.[28]

The ocean's commerce is the very elixir of life for England, its interruption for any length of time a deadly danger, its permanent interruption absolutely fatal within a short time. Every attack upon England's transoceanic communication is therefore a blow in the direction of the termination of the war. The more the losses take place with merciless regularity at the very gates of the island kingdom, the more powerful will be the material and moral effect on the English people. In spite of its former resources, England will not be able to make a successful defense against the attacks of submarines directed against its transoceanic commerce, provided they are well planned. That is precisely why a timely U-boat[29] war is the most dangerous and, if vigorously carried on, the form of warfare which will unconditionally decide the war to England's disadvantage.

. . .

. . . [A]ccording to my view and the opinion of the Chief of the Admiralty Staff, if we were to adopt at once the unrestricted use of the U-boat weapon, England . . . would have to give in by the fall of this year.

. . .

28. *Official German Documents,* 2:1122, 1125–26. This recommendation was promptly and formally endorsed by the chief of the general staff, General Erich von Falkenhayn. Ibid., 2:1129–30.

29. U-boat is shorthand for underwater boat or submarine.

From the very beginning, the attitude of the United States toward us has not been a friendly one. The close racial feeling which bound the greater part of the population to England, together with the combinations of English and American economic forces which have constantly resulted in more and more intimate relations in this direction, necessarily resulted in the antagonism referred to. . . . America is directly interested in the fate of England's economic existence, and, as a logical consequence, in England's intention to crush Germany. . . . It follows that the United States, whether they desire to be so or not, are directly interested in our defeat, and have become a direct enemy of Germany.

13 Chancellor Bethmann Hollweg's memorial, presented to Kaiser Wilhelm II, 29 February 1916, opposing unrestricted submarine warfare.[30]

The break with America [brought about by unrestricted submarine warfare] will have the following practical consequences:

. . . All of its financial resources will be put at the disposal of the Entente, and England will gladly include in the bargain the results of its financial dependence on the United States . . . if she can only succeed in cementing together the entire Anglo-Saxon world in one military brotherhood, united for the purpose of our destruction. Even if money alone can not determine the outcome of the war, the financial aid proffered by the United States will constitute a very material increase of our opponents' resources.

. . .

The provisioning of [German-occupied Belgium and northern France] by means of American foodstuffs will cease. . . .

. . . [P]articipation by the United States in this war would necessarily bring about the supplying of our opponents with further war material. . . . Moreover, no one who is acquainted with American conditions will entertain any doubt that the American sporting spirit, based upon its English prototype, would result in bringing over to our opponents volunteer contingents which one can surely venture to estimate at a few hundred thousands.

. . .

So the question comes down to this, whether our position is so desperate that we are bound to play a win-all lose-all game in which our existence as a world Power and our whole future as a nation would be at stake, whereas the chances of winning, that is, the prospect of crushing England by next fall, are uncertain. This question is to be answered unqualifiedly in the negative.

30. *Official German Documents*, 2:1134–36, 1138.

... It is certainly reasonable to argue that our military successes in the west, the failure of the great and long-heralded enemy offensives in the spring, the increasing financial straits of the Entente, and the absence of all prospects of starving us out in the current year, will so increase the general recognition of the fact in England that the prolongation of the war is a bad business, even from the standpoint of British interests, as to make England desist from attempting to carry on the war to the point of our exhaustion. We are cutting ourselves off from the benefits of all these possibilities if, through the adoption of unrestricted U-boat warfare, we drive the United States, and with the United States still other neutral Powers, into making war upon us. ... Therefore there devolves upon us the task of carrying on the U-boat war in such a way as to make it possible to avoid the break with the United States. In this case, we shall be able to list as pure profit all the injuries which we inflict upon England. That these injuries are not inconsiderable is evidenced by the results of the restricted U-boat war carried on since the summer of 1915. The increased number of U-boats which are now at our disposal would increase results many times over.

...

... In the meantime, it is essential that *Lusitania* cases, even if an armed liner is involved, be not repeated. A new *Lusitania* case would, under any and all conditions, bring about a break with the United States. A strict order that liners are not to be sunk, even if they are armed, is therefore absolutely essential to an understanding with the United States. Such an order would not have a definitely detrimental effect upon the practical results of the U-boat war.

...

... [D]angerous complications would arise with the United States if, in the destruction of merchant ships, our submarines were ... to confuse unarmed ships with armed ships, passenger steamers with freight steamers, neutral ships with enemy ships, and in this way injure American interests. Isolated cases occurring from time to time could undoubtedly be settled by means of apology and indemnities; on the other hand, the occurrence of numerous cases ... would certainly lead to a break. ...

14 Chancellor Bethmann Hollweg, personal letter to Foreign Minister Jagow, 5 March 1916, recounting his winning of the kaiser's support at an imperial conference.[31]

On the evening of the 2d instant, I handed over my memorial to His Majesty. ... On the 3d, after breakfast, His Majesty told me that he fully agreed

31. The conference was held at the general headquarters in Charleville, France, near the

with the stand taken in the memorial. That we had far too few U-boats to overcome Great Britain, and that he would not permit the "folly" of provoking America into a war. . . .

. . .

. . . On [the 5th], after church, His Majesty visited me in my garden. . . . He stated . . . that if we were to challenge England to come out and fight us on the seas, in the face of a break with the United States, every Englishman would give up his last shirt before he would capitulate; that he was still banking on the commercial instinct of the British to finally make it clear to them that they have nothing to gain by continuing the war.

15 Secretary of State Lansing to U.S. Ambassador Gerard, 18 April 1916, note for the German government protesting the sinking of the *Sussex*.[32]

The *Sussex* had never been armed; was a vessel known to be habitually used only for the conveyance of passengers across the English Channel; and was not following the route taken by troopships or supply ships. About 80 of her passengers, non-combatants of all ages and sexes, including citizens of the United States, were killed or injured.

. . .

The Government of the United States has been very patient. At every stage of this distressing experience of tragedy after tragedy it has sought to be governed by the most thoughtful consideration of the extraordinary circumstances of an unprecedented war and to be guided by sentiments of very genuine friendship for the people and Government of Germany. . . .

. . .

If it is still the purpose of the Imperial Government to prosecute relentless and indiscriminate warfare against vessels of commerce by the use of submarines without regard to what the Government of the United States must consider the sacred and indisputable rules of international law and the universally recognized dictates of humanity, the Government of the United States is at last forced to the conclusion that there is but one course it can pursue. Unless the Imperial Government should now immediately declare and effect an abandonment of its present methods of submarine warfare against pas-

western front. *Official German Documents*, 2:1139–40, 1142. For another firsthand account, see Walter Görlitz, *The Kaiser and His Court: The Diaries, Notebooks and Letters of Admiral Georg Alexander von Müller, Chief of the Naval Cabinet, 1914–1918*, trans. Mervyn Savill (New York: Harcourt, Brace, and World, 1964), 140–43.

32. *FRUS, 1916, Supplement: The World War* (Washington: GPO, 1929), 232, 234.

senger and freight-carrying vessels, the Government of the United States can have no choice but to sever diplomatic relations with the German Empire altogether. . . .

16 Secretary of State Lansing and German Ambassador Count Johann Heinrich von Bernstorff, meeting on 20 April 1916, discussing the submarine as a weapon of war following the sinking of the *Sussex*.[33]

L.— . . . I do not know how your Government can modify submarine warfare and make it effective and at the same time obey the law and the dictates of humanity.

B.—Humanity. Of course war is never humane.

L.—"Humanity" is a relative expression when used with "war" but the whole tendency in the growth of international law in regard to warfare in the past 125 years has been to relieve non-combatants of needless suffering.

B.—Of course I think it would be an ideal state of affairs, but our enemies violate all the rules and you insist on their being applied to Germany.

L.—One deals with life; the other with property.

B.—Yes.

L.—The German method seems reckless to me. It is as if a man who has a very dim vision should go out on the street with a revolver in search of an enemy and should see the outline of a figure and should immediately fire on him and injure him seriously and then go up and apologize and say he made a mistake. I do not think that would excuse him. That seems to be the course pursued by your submarine commanders—they fire first and inquire afterwards.

. . .

B.— . . . [A] declaration to my Government to absolutely abandon submarine warfare . . . would mean the overthrow of the Chancellor.

L.—Probably you would get a more radical man. I realize that.

. . .

L.— . . . The only possible course is an abandonment of submarine warfare, whether limited or not would depend on the terms. I would want to see an abandonment first and then possibly a discussion could follow as to how submarine warfare can be conducted within the rules of international law and entire safety of non-combatants. . . .

B.—Then I am to understand that you do not recognize the law of retaliation?

---

33. Memo of conversation by Lansing, in Savage, *Policy of the United States*, 2:481–83.

L.—We do not recognize retaliation when it affects the rights of neutrals.

B.—The British retaliate by stopping all commerce to Germany.

L.—It is a very different thing. The right to life is an inherent right, which man has from birth; the right of property is a purely legal right.

B.—Only in this case, England's methods affect the lives of non-combatants of Germany.

17 Foreign Minister Jagow to U.S. Ambassador Gerard, 4 May 1916, settling the *Sussex* case on condition that Britain end violations of neutral rights.[34]

[I]nstructions have been issued to the German war-craft to observe the general principles of international law covering the question of visit, search, and destruction of merchant ships, and not to sink merchant ships, even inside the restricted war zone, without warning, unless they take to flight or offer resistance, and to observe the care necessary for the preservation of human lives.

. . .

The German Government . . . entertains no doubt that the Government of the United States from now on will most earnestly demand and insist that the Government of Great Britain will immediately undertake a full observance of those principles of international law which were generally recognized as such before the war. . . . If the steps taken by the Government of the United States should not lead to the desired result of bringing about an observance of the laws of humanity by all the belligerent nations, the German Government would then be brought face to face with a new situation concerning which it would be forced to reserve for itself complete freedom of action. . . .

18 Foreign Minister Jagow to Ambassador in the United States Count Bernstorff, 7 June 1916, offering guidelines for handling the Wilson administration.[35]

[O]ur concession in the submarine question with regard to the United States is regarded as impracticable in many broad and influential circles in Germany. Should President Wilson continue his inactive course with regard to England, it is greatly to be feared that even that portion of German public

34. *Official German Documents,* 2:972–73.
35. *Official German Documents,* 2:977–78.

opinion which has up to this time supported the attitude of the Government, will join those who are opposed to the Government's policies, and that the entire public opinion of Germany will insistently demand the resumption of submarine warfare in its earlier forms. The Imperial Government would then be still less in a position to forestall this demand for any length of time because of the fact that all the military authorities regard and recommend, as they did before, unrestricted U-boat warfare as the only really effective war measure which could bring about the complete defeat of England. . . . As regards Mr. Wilson's purpose to bring about a peace by mediation, . . . the fact is that we entertain but little hope for the result of the exercise of good office by one whose instincts are all in favor of the English point of view, and who, in addition to this, is so naive a statesman as President Wilson. . . . [I]f the progress of the war were to continue favorable for us, a peace founded on the absolute *status quo ante* would be unacceptable to us. As the President interprets his rôle, to wit, that of a Lord Protector designated to uphold everything which, in his opinion, constitutes right and justice, there is reason to fear that our refusal to conclude peace on these terms might induce him to go over openly into the camp of our enemies. . . . [I]t will be the duty of your Excellency to prevent President Wilson from approaching us with a positive proposal to mediate. . . .

19 High-level German conference, 31 August 1916, discussing unrestricted submarine warfare.[36]

[CHIEF OF THE ADMIRALTY STAFF ADMIRAL HENNING VON HOLTZENDORFF:] [I]t is within our power to break England's determination to carry on the war to the end of the year; . . . if we renounce the use of the U-boat weapon we may have reason to believe that this means *finis Germaniae*.

. . .

[FOREIGN MINISTER JAGOW:] Even assuming that England would become exhausted as the result of the U-boat war, the question still remains whether she will conclude peace on that account. We have seen that France, which has long since been bled white, is upheld by her hope based on the other Allies. In this way, England, too, will exert the most desperate efforts and will keep herself on her feet by the hope which she will entertain concerning the remaining Allies. Whether under these conditions the newly-joined Allies will make peace is very questionable.

36. This conference was held at the general headquarters at Pless near the eastern front. *Official German Documents*, 2:1155–59, 1161–62.

...

[MINISTER OF THE TREASURY DR. KARL HELFFERICH:] [T]he British supplies in the way of breadstuffs and the product of the new crop assure a capacity for maintenance for the period of from four to five months without any further importations. Moreover, we can not bank upon an immediate stoppage of the British ocean commerce, since only 5 per cent of the arriving ships are destroyed monthly. . . . If in the period of from four to six months, 4 million of the tonnage of the British merchant fleet are destroyed, England will still have at her disposal 8 million tons, which will make it readily possible for her to meet her own needs. Therefore, such a result of the U-boat war would hardly be sufficient to force her to capitulation. It is true that commercial activities will be rendered most difficult and that the price of foodstuffs will rise. But we ourselves have had occasion to see to what extent the endurance of a people will hold out, and that even meager provisions go very far under competent management. The assumption is erroneous that the British organization and the determination to hold out would fail in England. . . .

. . . The assumption that the hostile attitude of the United States can not reach a higher pitch so far as we are concerned, is erroneous. Up to the present time, the Allies have received from the United States in the way of loans $1,250,000,000. In the case of war, America will stand ready with all of its reserves available for the cause of the Allies, which will then become the cause of the United States. America will desire to win the war as quickly as possible and will summon all its energies for putting this wish into execution. Acting in cooperation with England, the very strongest kind of pressure can be exerted upon the neutral Powers to join the Entente. . . . I see nothing but catastrophe following the application of the U-boat weapon at this time. . . .

. . .

[CHANCELLOR BETHMANN HOLLWEG:] I take the stand that the decision of the U-boat question must depend very greatly on the estimate of the military situation made by the Supreme High Command. According to the view of Field Marshal v. Hindenburg, with whom I have had a preliminary conference, no decision, either *pro* or *con,* can be reached as long as the military situation . . . is not clear. . . .

. . . It is certain that a complete blockade from and to England can not be carried out, because U-boats can undertake nothing in the night time. We can lay down no iron ring around England, and, moreover, our blockade can be broken by the accompaniment of transports by war-ships. . . .

. . .

[CHIEF OF THE GENERAL STAFF FIELD MARSHAL PAUL VON HINDENBURG:] We would shout with joy if we could begin the U-boat war immediately, but it is a very serious question. . . . It is impossible to render a decision at this time. I will inform you of the time when this can be done.

20 Counselor of the German Embassy in Washington, K. A. Haniel von Haimhausen, personal letter to the chancellor's representative at the German General Headquarters, Col. Karl Georg von Treutler, 10 November 1916, analyzing the American political scene.[37]

[T]he feeling, above all in high society and in the press, is, as you know, almost exclusively "pro-Ally." In view of the close connection with England, from the standpoint of history, blood, speech, society, finance, culture, etc.— and, in many of these relations, also with France—this should cause no particular surprise. And in addition to this there are Belgium, the *Lusitania,* and the fact that here we are considered responsible for the war, in spite of all proofs to the contrary. Notwithstanding his commercial instincts, the American is *very* sentimental—often hysterically so—and in the case referred to commercial instinct and sentiment point in the same direction. However inconceivable and disgusting this attitude may appear to us, we shall have to reckon with it. . . .

. . . Very many American politicians gifted with insight agree upon the point that if the U-boat question could once be allowed to rest in peace for a moderate length of time—not only from the point of view of actual performance by the avoidance of "mistakes," but also from that of public discussion, —the [U.S.] Government would be forced to take steps against England. For the present the Allies and their friends make use of the U-boat danger as a shield and a diversion. . . .

There is one point on which we must be absolutely clear. A withdrawal from, or even a material limitation of, the exercise of the so-called concession which we made to the United States this spring in connection with the U-boat war, means war with the United States. . . . No government and no party would venture, without committing political suicide, to give in to Germany on this question, which is one involving the lives of American citizens, after America has so definitely announced what it considers its international rights. . . .

. . .

. . . [War with Germany] would immediately be carried on by setting in full motion America's endless resources in man-power, money, war industries,

37. *Official German Documents,* 2:1183–86.

ships, etc. Nor are we to expect any effective opposition to be supplied by the German-American element here. They would not be able, nor would they attempt, to bear the brunt of such a national tempest. The days of the *Lusitania* proved this to be the fact.

21 Chief of the Admiralty Staff Admiral Henning von Holtzendorff to Chief of the General Staff General Field Marshal Paul von Hindenburg, 22 December 1916, laying out the argument for all-out submarine warfare.[38]

It is necessary that the war be fought out to a definite decision before August, 1917, unless it is to result in the exhaustion of all the belligerents, and hence in a termination which will be fatal for us. Our enemies Italy and France have received such a staggering blow, economically speaking, that it is only by the energy and force of England that they are still kept on their feet. If we can succeed in breaking the backbone of England's resistance, the war will immediately be terminated in our favor. But the backbone of England consists in the cargo space used for bringing to England those imports necessary for the maintenance of life, which assure her credit in foreign countries.

. . .

. . . [A]s things stand at present, England will be forced to sue for peace within five months as the result of launching an unrestricted U-boat war. But this is true only in case ruthless U-boat warfare is carried on; it would not follow as the result of the limited U-boat war on commerce which is being carried on at this time, even if all armed vessels were to be considered as open to attack.

. . .

. . . [W]ar with the United States is so serious a question that all steps should be taken to avoid it. But in my opinion also the fear of such a break should not overawe us at the crucial moment to the extent of causing us to renounce the use of the weapon which promises us victory.

. . . [The effect of the United States' coming into war] could at best be practically negligible with regard to shipping space. . . . We may attribute an equal paucity of results in the case of American troops which, on account of absence of cargo space, would not be able to be brought over in any considerable numbers; and to American money, which can never take the place of transportation and shipping space. The only question to be considered is the attitude which America would assume towards the question of concluding

38. *Official German Documents*, 2:1214–16, 1218–19.

peace—the peace for which England would be forced to sue. We can not suppose that the United States would then determine to carry on the war against us single-handed, as it has no means at its disposal for taking definite steps against us, whereas its commerce would be damaged by our U-boats. On the other hand, it is to be expected that the United States would support the conclusion of such a peace, in order to resume normal commercial relations at the earliest possible moment.

. . .

. . . If we fail to make use of this opportunity, which so far as can be foreseen, is our last, I can see no alternative than that of mutual exhaustion, without its being possible for us to terminate the war in such a way as to guarantee our future as a world Power.

In order to obtain the necessary results in time, the unrestricted U-boat war must commence by February 1 at the latest. . . .

22 Chief of the General Staff Hindenburg, telegram to Chancellor Bethmann Hollweg, 23 December 1916, throwing support behind unrestricted submarine warfare.[39]

On the occasion of the conference . . . at the end of August, your Excellency made the decision on the question of launching of an unrestricted U-boat war depend upon my statement of opinion that from the military standpoint the time had come. This moment will be the end of January. . . . [W]e should not allow our opponents any considerable time in which to complete undisturbed their preparations for the decisive battle on land.

23 Chief of the General Staff Hindenburg and Chancellor Bethmann Hollweg, exchange of views at a high-level political-military conference, 9 January 1917, reaching consensus on a new submarine policy (endorsed by Kaiser Wilhelm II).[40]

[BETHMANN HOLLWEG:] If His Majesty commands that a ruthless U-boat war

39. *Official German Documents*, 2:1201–2. For Hindenburg's follow-up telegrams of 26 December 1916 and 8 January 1916 reiterating his determination, see ibid., 2:1204–5.

40. This conference was held at midday at the general headquarters at Pless. *Official German Documents*, 2:1320–21. (Apparently the transcription is a paraphrase, since certain phrases are in quotation marks.) After a pro forma imperial conference in the evening of 9 January 1917 Kaiser Wilhelm II ordered the Admiralty to launch unrestricted submarine war "with the greatest vigor on the 1st of February" and to "immediately take all the necessary

shall be launched, [I] will endeavor to succeed in keeping America "out of it." . . .

. . .

The U-boat war is the "last card." A very serious decision. "But if the military authorities consider the U-boat war essential, I am not in a position to contradict them."

. . .

. . . America's assistance, in case she enters the war, will consist in the delivery of food supplies to England, financial support, delivery of airplanes and the dispatching of corps of volunteers.

[HINDENBURG:] We can take care of that. The opportunity for the U-boat war is such that it can perhaps never become as favorable again; we can carry it on and we must carry it on.

[BETHMANN HOLLWEG:] Of course, if success beckons, we must follow.

[HINDENBURG:] We would reproach ourselves later if we let the opportunity pass by.

24 German Foreign Minister Arthur Zimmermann to German Ambassador Bernstorff, telegram, 16 January 1917, proposing a German alliance with Mexico against the United States.[41]

For your Excellency's exclusively personal information and transmission to the Imperial Minister at Mexico by safe hands:

. . .

It is our purpose on the 1st of February to commence the unrestricted U-boat war. The attempt will be made to keep America neutral in spite of it all.

In case we should not be successful in this, we propose Mexico an alliance upon the following terms: Joint conduct of war. Joint conclusion of peace. Ample financial support and an agreement on our part that Mexico shall gain back by conquest the territory lost by her at a prior period in Texas, New Mexico, and Arizona. Arrangement as to details is entrusted to your Excellency. Your Excellency will make the above known to the President [of Mexico] in strict confidence at the moment that war breaks out with the United States, and you will add the suggestion that Japan be requested to take part at once and that he simultaneously mediate between ourselves and Japan.

---

steps" to prevent the Entente and neutral powers from gaining advance knowledge of the coming campaign. Ibid., 1210. The meeting on this occasion is described in Görlitz, *The Kaiser and His Court*, 230.

41. *Official German Documents*, 2:1337.

25 President Wilson, address to the Senate, 22 January 1917, delineating the framework for a lasting and just peace.[42]

In every discussion of the peace that must end this war it is taken for granted that that peace must be followed by some definite concert of power which will make it virtually impossible that any such catastrophe should ever overwhelm us again. Every lover of mankind, every sane and thoughtful man must take that for granted.

. . .

It is inconceivable that the people of the United States should play no part in that great enterprise. To take part in such a service will be the opportunity for which they have sought to prepare themselves . . . ever since the days when they set up a new nation in the high and honourable hope that it might . . . show mankind the way to liberty. . . . But they owe it to themselves and to the other nations of the world to state the conditions under which they will feel free to render it.

. . .

. . . It will be absolutely necessary that a force be created as a guarantor of the permanency of the settlement so much greater than the force of any nation now engaged or any alliance hitherto formed or projected that no nation, no probable combination of nations could face or withstand it. If the peace presently to be made is to endure, it must be a peace made secure by the organized major force of mankind.

. . .

The equality of nations upon which peace must be founded if it is to last must be an equality of rights; the guarantees exchanged must neither recognize nor imply a difference between big nations and small, between those that are powerful and those that are weak. Right must be based upon the common strength, not upon the individual strength, of the nations upon whose concert peace will depend. . . . Mankind is looking now for freedom of life, not for equipoises of power.

. . . No peace can last, or ought to last, which does not recognize and accept the principle that governments derive all their just powers from the consent of the governed, and that no right anywhere exists to hand peoples about from sovereignty to sovereignty as if they were property. . . .

. . .

So far as practicable, moreover, every great people now struggling towards a

42. At the time of this speech Germany had not yet made public its submarine decision. Link, *Papers of Woodrow Wilson*, 40:534–39.

full development of its resources and of its powers should be assured a direct outlet to the great highways of the sea. . . .

And the paths of the sea must alike in law and in fact be free. The freedom of the seas is the *sine qua non* of peace, equality, and cooperation. . . .

. . . There can be no sense of safety and equality among the nations if great preponderating armaments are henceforth to continue here and there to be built up and maintained. The statesmen of the world must plan for peace and nations must adjust and accommodate their policy to it as they have planned for war and made ready for pitiless contest and rivalry. . . .

. . .

I am proposing, as it were, that the nations should with one accord adopt the doctrine of President Monroe as the doctrine of the world: that no nation should seek to extend its polity over any other nation or people, but that every people should be left free to determine its own polity, its own way of development, unhindered, unthreatened, unafraid, the little along with the great and powerful.

I am proposing that all nations henceforth avoid entangling alliances which would draw them into competitions of power, catch them in a net of intrigue and selfish rivalry, and disturb their own affairs with influences intruded from without. There is no entangling alliance in a concert of power. When all unite to act in the same sense and with the same purpose all act in the common interest and are free to live their own lives under a common protection.

I am proposing government by the consent of the governed; that freedom of the seas which in international conference after conference representatives of the United States have urged with the eloquence of those who are the convinced disciples of liberty; and that moderation of armaments which makes of armies and navies a power for order merely, not an instrument of aggression or of selfish violence.

These are American principles, American policies. We could stand for no others. And they are also the principles and policies of forward looking men and women everywhere, of every modern nation, of every enlightened community. They are the principles of mankind and must prevail.

26 Colonel Edward House, diary entry on a White House visit, 1 February 1917, describing Wilson's reaction to the German declaration of unrestricted submarine warfare.[43]

The President was sad and depressed and I did not succeed at any time

43. Link, *Papers of Woodrow Wilson*, 41:87.

during the day in lifting him into a better frame of mind. He was deeply disappointed at the sudden and unwarranted action of the German Government. . . .

. . .

The question we discussed longest was wh[e]ther it was better to give Bernstorff his passports immediately or wait until the Germans committed some overt act. When Lansing came this discussion was renewed and we all agreed that it was best to give him his passports at once, because by taking that course, there was a possibility of bringing the Germans to their senses. . . .

The President was insistent that he would not allow it to lead to war if it could possibly be avoided. He reiterated his belief that it would be a crime for this Government to involve itself in the war to such an extent as to make it impossible to save Europe afterward. He spoke of Germany as "a madman that should be curbed." I asked if he thought it fair to the Allies to ask them to do the curbing without doing our share. He noticeably winced at this, but still held to his determination not to become involved if it were humanly possible to do otherwise.

27 President Wilson, meeting with his cabinet, 20 March 1917 (2:30–5 p.m.), canvasing opinion on policy toward Germany.[44]

[T]he President said that he desired advice from the Cabinet on our relations with Germany and the course which should be pursued. He began with a review of his actions up to the present time . . . [including notably a break in diplomatic relations with Germany and the arming of American ships traveling into the German submarine zone].

He went on to say that he did not see from a practical point of view what else could be done to safeguard American vessels more than had already been done unless we declared war or declared that a state of war existed, which was the same thing; and that the power to do this lay with Congress.

. . .

After the President had finished [Secretary of the Treasury William G. McAdoo said] . . . that we might just as well face the issue and come out squarely in opposition to Germany, whose Government represented every evil in history; that, if we did not do so at once, the American people would compel action and we would be in the position of being pushed forward instead of

44. Lansing, memorandum of the meeting, in Link, *Papers of Woodrow Wilson*, 41:437–44.

leading, which would be humiliating and unwise. He further said that he believed that we could best aid the Allies against Germany by standing back of their credit, by underwriting their loans, and that they were sorely in need of such aid. He felt, however, that we could do little else, and doubted whether we could furnish men.

. . .

[Secretary of Agriculture David F.] Houston, who followed, said that he agreed with McAdoo that it would create a most unfortunate, if not disastrous, impression on the American public as well as in Europe if we waited any longer to take a firm stand now that Germany had shown her hand. . . .

[Secretary of Commerce William C.] Redfield . . . was for declaring war and doing everything possible to aid in bringing the Kaiser to his knees. . . .

[Secretary of War Newton D.] Baker . . . said that he considered the state of affairs called for drastic action with as little delay as possible. . . . He said that the recent German outrages showed that the Germans did not intend to modify in the least degree their policy of inhumanity and lawlessness, and that such acts could mean only one thing, and that was war.

. . .

. . . I [Lansing] said that the revolution in Russia, which appeared to be successful, had removed the one objection to affirming that the European War was a war between Democracy and Absolutism; that the only hope of a permanent peace between all nations depended upon the establishment of democratic institutions throughout the world; that no League of Peace would be of value if a powerful autocracy was a member, and that no League of Peace would be necessary if all nations were democratic; and that in going into the war at this time we could do more to advance the cause of Democracy than if we failed to show sympathy with the democratic powers in their struggle against the autocratic government of Germany.

. . .

I . . . urged the propriety of taking advantage of the aroused sentiment of the people since it would have a tremendous influence in keeping Congress in line. . . . I must have spoken with vehemence because the President asked me to lower my voice so that no one in the corridor could hear.

The President said that he did not see how he could speak of a war for Democracy or of Russia's revolution in addressing Congress. I replied . . . that he could do so indirectly by attacking the character of the autocratic government of Germany as manifested by its deeds of inhumanity, by its broken promises, and by its plots and conspiracies against this country.

To this the President only answered, "Possibly."

. . . I felt strongly that to go to war solely because American ships had been sunk and Americans killed would cause debate, and that the sounder basis was the duty of this and every other democratic nation to suppress an autocratic government like the German because of its atrocious character and because it was a menace to the national safety of this country and of all other countries with liberal systems of government. Such an arraignment would appeal to every liberty-loving man the world over. . . .

When I had finished, Secretary [of Labor William B.] Wilson . . . said: "Mr. President, I think we must recognize the fact that Germany has made war upon this country and, therefore, I am for calling Congress together as soon as possible. . . . [W]e should enter the war with the determination to employ all our resources to put an end to Prussian rule over Germany which menaces human liberty and peace all over the world. I do not believe we should employ half-measures or do it half-heartedly."

. . .

. . . [Secretary of the Navy Josephus Daniels] spoke in a voice which was low and trembled with emotion. His eyes were suffused with tears. He said that he saw no other course than to enter the war. . . .

. . .

When at last every Cabinet officer had spoken and all had expressed the opinion that war was inevitable and that Congress ought to be called in extraordinary session as soon as possible, the President in his cool, unemotional way said: "Well, gentlemen, I think that there is no doubt as to what your advice is. I thank you."

The President, during the discussion or at the close, gave no sign what course he would adopt. . . .

28 President Wilson, address to Congress, 2 April 1917, asking for a declaration of war.[45]

International law had its origin in the attempt to set up some law which would be respected and observed upon the seas, where no nation had right of dominion and where lay the free highways of the world. By painful stage after stage has that law been built up, with meagre enough results . . . but always with a clear view, at least, of what the heart and conscience of mankind demanded. This minimum of right the German Government has swept aside. . . . I am not now thinking of the loss of property involved, immense and

45. Link, *Papers of Woodrow Wilson*, 41:520–21, 523–27.

serious as that is, but only of the wanton and wholesale destruction of the lives of non-combatants, men, women, and children, engaged in pursuits which have always, even in the darkest periods of modern history, been deemed innocent and legitimate. Property can be paid for; the lives of peaceful and innocent people cannot be. The present German submarine warfare against commerce is a warfare against mankind.

. . .

. . . [A]rmed neutrality, it now appears, is impracticable. Because submarines are in effect outlaws when used as the German submarines have been used against merchant shipping, it is impossible to defend ships against their attacks. . . . Armed neutrality . . . is likely only to produce what it was meant to prevent; it is practically certain to draw us into the war without either the rights or the effectiveness of belligerents. There is one choice we cannot make, we are incapable of making: we will not choose the path of submission and suffer the most sacred rights of our Nation and our people to be ignored or violated. The wrongs against which we now array ourselves are no common wrongs; they cut to the very roots of human life.

With a profound sense of the solemn and even tragical character of the step I am taking and of the grave responsibilities which it involves, but in unhesitating obedience to what I deem my constitutional duty, I advise that the Congress declare the recent course of the Imperial German Government to be in fact nothing less than war against the government and people of the United States; that it formally accept the status of belligerent which has thus been thrust upon it; and that it take immediate steps not only to put the country in a more thorough state of defense but also to exert all its power and employ all its resources to bring the Government of the German Empire to terms and end the war.

. . .

. . . Our object . . . is to vindicate the principles of peace and justice in the life of the world as against selfish and autocratic power and to set up amongst the really free and self-governed peoples of the world such a concert of purpose and of action as will henceforth ensure the observance of those principles. . . .

We have no quarrel with the German people. We have no feeling towards them but one of sympathy and friendship. It was not upon their impulse that their government acted in entering this war. It was not with their previous knowledge or approval. It was a war determined upon as wars used to be determined upon in the old, unhappy days when peoples were nowhere consulted by their rulers and wars were provoked and waged in the interest of dynasties or of little groups of ambitious men who were accustomed to use their fellow men as pawns and tools. . . . Cunningly contrived plans of deception or aggression, carried, it may be, from generation to generation, can be worked out and kept from the light only within the privacy of courts or behind the carefully guarded confidences of a narrow and privileged class. They are happily impossible where public opinion commands and insists upon full information concerning all the nation's affairs.

A steadfast concert for peace can never be maintained except by a partnership of democratic nations. No autocratic government could be trusted to keep faith within it or observe its covenants. . . . Only free peoples can hold their purpose and their honor steady to a common end and prefer the interests of mankind to any narrow interest of their own.

Does not every American feel that assurance has been added to our hope for the future peace of the world by the wonderful and heartening things that have been happening within the last few weeks in Russia? Russia was known by those who knew it best to have been always in fact democratic at heart. . . . The autocracy that crowned the summit of her political structure, long as it had stood and terrible as was the reality of its power, was not in fact Russian in origin, character, or purpose; and now it has been shaken off and the great, generous Russian people have been added in all their naïve majesty and might to the forces that are fighting for freedom in the world, for justice, and for peace. Here is a fit partner for a League of Honour.

. . .

. . . The world must be made safe for democracy. Its peace must be planted upon the tested foundations of political liberty. We have no selfish ends to serve. We desire no conquest, no dominion. We seek no indemnities for ourselves, no material compensation for the sacrifices we shall freely make. We are but one of the champions of the rights of mankind. We shall be satisfied when those rights have been made as secure as the faith and the freedom of nations can make them.

. . .

. . . It is a fearful thing to lead this great peaceful people into war, into the most terrible and disastrous of all wars, civilization itself seeming to be in the balance. But the right is more precious than peace, and we shall fight for the things which we have always carried nearest our hearts,—for democracy, for the right of those who submit to authority to have a voice in their own governments, for the rights and liberties of small nations, for a universal dominion of right by such a concert of free peoples as shall bring peace and safety to all nations and make the world itself at last free. . . . America is privileged to spend her blood and her might for the principles that gave her birth and happiness and the peace which she has treasured. God helping her, she can do no other.

29 Senator George W. Norris (Republican, Nebraska), speech in the Senate, 4 April 1917, opposing U.S. involvement in the European conflict.[46]

No close student of recent history will deny that both Great Britain and Germany have, on numerous occasions since the beginning of the war, flagrantly violated in the most serious manner the rights of neutral vessels and neutral nations under existing international law as recognized up to the beginning of this war by the civilized world.

. . .

. . . Under international law no belligerent Government has the right to place submerged mines in the high seas. Neither has it any right to take human life without notice by the use of submarines. . . . In carrying out these two policies, both Great Britain and Germany have sunk American ships and destroyed American lives without provocation and without notice. There have been more ships sunk and more American lives lost from the action of submarines than from English mines in the North Sea; for the simple reason that we finally acquiesced in the British war zone and kept our ships out of it, while in the German war zone we have refused to recognize its legality and have not kept either our ships or our citizens out of its area. . . .

. . .

. . . What was our duty as a Government and what were our rights when we were confronted with these extraordinary orders declaring these military zones? First, we could have defied both of them and could have gone to war against both of these nations for this violation of international law and interference with our neutral rights. Second, we had the technical right to defy one and to acquiesce in the other. Third, we could, while denouncing them both as illegal, have acquiesced in them both and thus remained neutral with both sides, although not agreeing with either as to the righteousness of their respective orders. We could have said to American shipowners that, while these orders are both contrary to international law and are both unjust, we do not believe that the provocation is sufficient to cause us to go to war for the defense of our rights as a neutral nation, and, therefore, American ships and American citizens will go into these zones at their own peril and risk. Fourth, we might have declared an embargo against the shipping from American ports of any merchandise to either one of these Governments that persisted in maintaining its military zone. We might have refused to permit the sailing of any ship from any American port to either of these military zones. In my judgment, if we had

46. U.S. Senate, *Congressional Record,* 65th Cong., 1st Sess. (Washington: GPO, 1917), 212–14.

pursued this course, the zones would have been of short duration. England would have been compelled to take her mines out of the North Sea in order to get any supplies from our country. When her mines were taken out of the North Sea[,] then the German ports upon the North Sea would have been accessible to American shipping and Germany would have been compelled to cease her submarine warfare in order to get any supplies from our Nation into German North Sea ports.

. . . We have loaned many hundreds of millions of dollars to the allies in this controversy. While such action was legal and countenanced by international law, there is no doubt in my mind but the enormous amount of money loaned to the allies in this country has been instrumental in bringing about a public sentiment in favor of our country taking a course that would make every bond worth a hundred cents on the dollar and making the payment of every debt certain and sure. Through this instrumentality and also through the instrumentality of others who have not only made millions out of the war in the manufacture of munitions, etc., and who would expect to make millions more if our country can be drawn into the catastrophe, a large number of the great newspapers and news agencies of the country have been controlled and enlisted in the greatest propaganda that the world has ever known, to manufacture sentiment in favor of war. It is now demanded that the American citizens shall be used as insurance policies to guarantee the safe delivery of munitions of war to belligerent nations. The enormous profits of munition manufacturers, stockbrokers, and bond dealers must be still further increased by our entrance into the war. . . .

. . .

. . . We are going into war upon the command of gold. We are going to run the risk of sacrificing millions of our countrymen's lives in order that other countrymen may coin their lifeblood into money. And even if we do not cross the Atlantic and go into the trenches, we are going to pile up a debt that the toiling masses that shall come many generations after us will have to pay. . . .

. . .

The troubles of Europe ought to be settled by Europe, and wherever our sympathies may lie, disagreeing as we do, we ought to remain absolutely neutral and permit them to settle their questions without our interference. We are now the greatest neutral nation. Upon the passage of this [war] resolution we will have joined Europe in the great catastrophe and taken America into entanglements that will not end with this war, but will live and bring their evil influences upon many generations yet unborn.

The Road to Pearl Harbor, 1931–1941

THE DANGERS OF DRIVING IN THE FAST LANE

On the morning of 7 December 1941 a Japanese naval task force launched a surprise attack on Pearl Harbor. In what President Franklin D. Roosevelt described in an address to the nation as "a day that will live in infamy," the attack killed twenty-four hundred Americans, destroyed or immobilized seven battleships (the backbone of the Pacific fleet), and crippled the air force on Hawaii.

The sense of outrage expressed by Roosevelt in reaction to the sneak attack persisted after the war. In war crimes trials held in Tokyo the victors indicted Japan's leaders for having violated treaties, flouted the principle of liberty, and committed war crimes and crimes against humanity. Dominated by a "criminal, militaristic clique," so the charges read, Japanese policymakers had launched an "aggressive war" with the goal of securing in cooperation with Germany and Italy the "domination of the whole world."[1] In the United States those who had had a hand in prewar policy toward Japan repeated the indictment. In 1949 one former official described Japan's leaders as "a reckless, determined and ruthless military group [which] succeeded in imposing its will upon an irresolute nation." Another, writing with privileged access to the diplomatic record, charged that Japan, in league with Hitler's Germany and Mussolini's Italy, had "bent its efforts toward bringing the world under their

---

1. Quoted in Richard H. Minear, *Victor's Justice: The Tokyo War Crimes Trial* (Princeton: Princeton University Press, 1971), 24–25.

combined control." Even today the feelings of injured innocence and images of Japanese aggression and treachery still live in the American imagination and strongly color our understanding of the road to Pearl Harbor.[2]

That road was arguably more tortuous and far longer than the conventional wisdom suggests. Its beginnings can be found in the simultaneous rise of two Pacific powers, each with a distinctive set of concerns that combined to create an increasingly tangled, troubled relationship. It might be useful to think of the United States and Japan by the 1930s as two drivers competing for the same lane at ever higher speeds and with ever greater determination to shut the other out. As the rivalry sharpened, the difficulties of maintaining control and the reluctance to back out of the competition grew ever greater. There may be more than enough blame to go around for the pileup that finally took place.

*   *   *

The roots of confrontation go back to the turn of the century. By the time of Japan's victory over Russia in 1905, the tensions between the two emergent Pacific powers had become marked. American policymakers were beginning in broad terms to see relations with Japan through the prism of two issues— immigration and the open door in China—but split on how to handle them.

On one side were accommodationists, who gave high priority to reaching an understanding with Japan. They were uneasy with the emergence of the open-door doctrine, which made the United States a claimant to the China market and defender of China's administrative and territorial integrity and thus thrust the United States directly into the sphere of an increasingly power- ful Japan. Better to acknowledge Japan's leading role in northeast Asia and China and in return secure Japan's cooperation in resolving the nettlesome immigration problem, accommodationists argued. Policymakers in Washing- ton could not wish away the hostility directed at Japanese immigrants, par- ticularly on the West Coast. The only sensible solution likely to avoid mount- ing popular ill-will between the two countries was to seek Tokyo's cooperation in limiting the flow of immigrants and thus in dampening the nativist move- ment so offensive to Japanese.

President Theodore Roosevelt was the foremost American advocate of ac- commodation. In 1905 he arranged for prompt recognition of Japan's newly won control over Korea, gaining in return Tokyo's recognition of American control over the Philippines. In 1908 Roosevelt arranged another bargain that

2. Quotes from Joseph W. Ballantine, "Mukden to Pearl Harbor: The Foreign Policies of Japan," *Foreign Affairs* 27 (July 1949): 651; and Herbert Feis, "War Came at Pearl Harbor: Suspicions Considered," *Yale Review*, n.s., 45 (March 1956): 389. For a survey of public views in the United States as well as Japan on the fiftieth anniversary of the bombing, see *New York Times*, 8 December 1991, pp. 1, 24, 26.

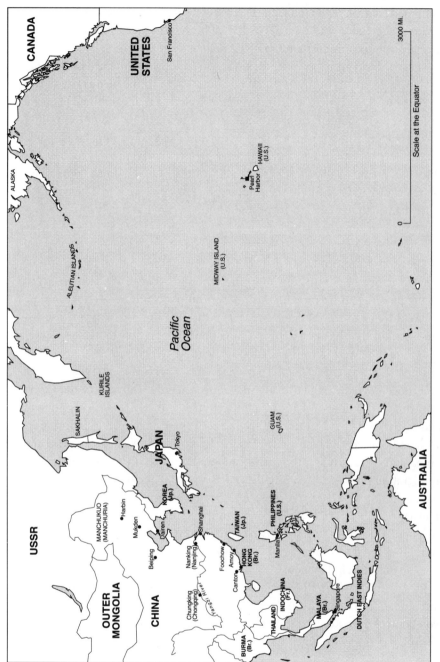

East and Southeast Asia before Pearl Harbor

quieted an acrimonious dispute over Manchuria (China's northeastern provinces), while also concluding a "gentlemen's agreement" that committed Tokyo to restricting immigration on its own in place of formal U.S. exclusion legislation humiliating to Japan. After leaving the White House Roosevelt pressed his successor, William Howard Taft, to continue these policies (Document 1). New accommodationists appeared in the Wilson administration in the person of Edward House and Robert Lansing. Lansing entered into the most notable trade of the Wilson years when in 1917 he secured from Ambassador Ishii Kikujiro an acknowledgement of the open door in China in exchange for an American recognition of Japan's "special interests" there. Both sides secretly pledged to respect the status quo in the Pacific.

The alternative approach, championed by confrontationists, rejected linkage between U.S. immigration policy and the open door in China. They refused to see immigration as anything but a domestic issue in which Japanese sensibilities had no proper part. In their view Japan would simply have to accept whatever restrictions Congress imposed. For this group, the core policy defining relations with Japan was the open door. It offered a basis for contesting Japanese pretensions to regional hegemony, for promoting American economic and cultural influence in China, and even for defending China's political integrity. The fate of the open door became for confrontationists a symbol of the long-term prospects for American standing in East Asia and thus well worth the price of tensions with Japan. President Taft and his secretary of state, Philander C. Knox, were the first U.S. leaders to stake out this position (Document 2). Woodrow Wilson was also attracted to the defense of China, especially in 1915, when Japan placed a long list of demands before China that would have formally established the latter's subordination to the former. For a time the world war and Lansing's advice diverted Wilson from a hard line. Tensions revived at the Paris peace conference, where Japan fought to hold on to Chinese territory seized during the war and failed to extract a formal admission of racial equality from the European and American leaders.

The Republican policymakers that dominated the scene through the 1920s returned to a policy of accommodation. Charles Evans Hughes, the secretary of state in the Harding administration, called the Washington conference of 1921–1922 with an eye to creating a new understanding among the Pacific powers. The conference produced a set of linked agreements that defined that understanding. A five-power naval agreement contained a transpacific naval race. It set the ratio of capital naval vessels of the United States, Britain, and Japan at 5:5:3 and froze construction of western Pacific island defenses, a provision that offset somewhat Japan's lower capital ship figure. A nine-power agreement registered for the first time formal international acceptance of the open-door principle in China, while committing the powers to coordinate their response to the nationalist fervor sweeping that country. Finally, a four-power agreement guaranteed the status quo in the Pacific. As a final contribution to a new era of amity, Japan agreed to surrender disputed Chinese territory, to remove troops sent into the far eastern part of Russia during World War I, and to relinquish an alliance with Britain that faced growing criticism in the United States as well as in British Commonwealth countries.

The Washington conference bargain stood as the high-water mark of Japan's own attempt to devise a cooperative approach. That search for harmonious relations had its inception in the late nineteenth-century effort to end a self-imposed isolation and to come to terms with the Western-defined system of international relations. As the Japanese proponents of cooperation understood it, that system sanctioned the free movement of peoples and goods. The Japanese people could thus be sure of an opportunity for trade and immigration and hence increasing national prosperity. Moreover, in keeping with prevailing practices of that system, Japan could expect to win from the other powers acceptance of its regional security claims. Finally, Japanese accommodationists assumed that their country as the most advanced in Asia would come to stand on an equal footing alongside other civilized countries in a culturally diverse world. Yamagata Aritomo, an oligarch who helped create a modern army and played a prominent role in government affairs down to his death in 1922, articulated this set of beliefs that in fact dominated policy into the 1920s. He contended that Japan could find a peaceful place in the Pacific even though the task would involve some delicate handling of China and the Anglo-Americans (Document 3).

But some leaders in Tokyo looked across the Pacific and found reason to doubt the possibility of good relations with Washington. These doubts had begun to appear already between the 1890s and 1910s as American policy and attitudes seemed to challenge the very principles on which Japan had come to base its policy of accommodation. The dramatic U.S. territorial leap across the Pacific in 1898—into Guam, Hawaii, and the Philippines—blocked Japanese immigration and raised a potential security threat, especially as the United States became an increasingly formidable naval power. In addition, the attacks, both political and physical, on Japanese within the United States seemed to reveal racial arrogance and stirred popular resentment and patriotic protest.

Through the 1920s Japanese advocates of a more confrontational course gained strength as the hopes inspired by the Washington conference faded. Even accommodationists who thought of themselves as liberal and Western-oriented grew skeptical of the prospects for acceptance of Japan as a great power and the Japanese as a civilized people (Document 4). In 1922 the United States raised its tariff, a blow for protectionism that augured ill for the 40 percent of Japan's export trade then absorbed by the United States. In 1924 the

U.S. Congress singled out Japanese for an immigration ban. Japan's ambassador protested against this measure "stigmatizing them as unworthy and undesirable in the eyes of the American people."[3] Secretary of State Hughes stressed his regret at the measure. But Congress stood firm, and President Calvin Coolidge bowed to domestic pressure. Then between 1929 and 1931 the global depression cut exports in half, producing social and economic unrest in Japan and setting off a worldwide assault on the principle of free trade. Faced with economic hard times, the U.S. Congress in 1930 again raised the tariff.

A China aroused against foreign domination remained a bone of contention. Tokyo sought a solution to the China problem through coordination with Washington and London, an approach associated with the name of Shidehara Kijuro, who served as foreign minister for much of the time between 1924 and 1931. The Anglo-Saxon powers, however, proved cool to joint action, and so Tokyo finally acted alone to defend its extensive interests, above all in Manchuria. In 1928 Japanese forces assassinated Zhang Zuolin, the Manchurian warlord, and clashed with Chinese forces in Shandong. Criticism by outraged Americans soon followed, confirming the failure of the Washington conference powers to arrive at a common stand on China.

By the late 1920s right-wing groups were calling for a dramatic reorientation of Japan's policy at home and abroad. They wanted to renovate Japanese culture by promoting spiritual solidarity and the virtues of imperial rule and to assert a pan-Asian policy in which Japan would serve as the guide and protector of vulnerable and disordered neighbors (foremost China). Only a Japan purified of Western materialism, individualism, liberalism, and Marxism would be a fit leader for this new Asia (Document 5). When in 1930 Prime Minister Hamaguchi Osachi accepted continued naval restrictions in the interest of good relations with the United States and Britain, critics charged that he had left Japan vulnerable to attack by the Anglo-American powers. Against this backdrop of political discontent, Hamaguchi himself was shot by an assassin.

The Manchurian crisis of 1931–1932 strengthened the hand of confrontationists in both countries and marked the clear beginning of the road to Pearl Harbor. In September 1931 Japanese army units in Manchuria launched a military offensive. They acted to turn back a rising tide of Chinese nationalist sentiment that threatened long-nurtured Japanese interests in that resource-rich, thinly populated region, a prized part of the informal Japanese empire but also a bulwark to Japan's adjoining Korean colony. Civilians and military leaders in Tokyo harbored a variety of doubts about this insubordinate initiative, not least that excessive force would alienate the other powers. But they

3. U.S. Department of State, *Foreign Relations of the United States* [hereafter *FRUS*], *1924* (2 vols.; Washington: Government Printing Office, 1939), 2:373.

went along as a matter of national prestige, out of a shared vision of Japan's dominance in East Asia and from fear of militant elements in the armed forces.

Now, as on other occasions, Emperor Hirohito favored the course of accommodation. He sought to limit the military's initiative and thereby avoid a clash with the United States and Britain. He exercised his restraining influence through the questions, concerns, and doubts that he or his advisers could pose in meetings with government and military leaders. But he was restrained by precedents against blatant imperial intervention, by his own preference for a constitutional monarchy that reigned but did not rule, and by cautious advisers, the most influential of whom was the elder statesman Saionji Kimmochi. As a sovereign widely regarded as divine, the emperor was safest standing above the political fray. Even the little that he dared do to promote accommodation raised the ire of militants within the military.

The seizure of Manchuria convinced American confrontationists that Japan had become a direct, disturbing threat to the United States. Better than anyone else Henry L. Stimson, Herbert Hoover's secretary of state, articulated that position. Initially he had thought that he could restrain the "reactionary," "aggressive" military by prodding pro-Western, civilian "moderates" in Tokyo to take a stand. When Tokyo failed to call its army back into line with what he regarded as the accepted norms of civilized behavior, Stimson hardened his stand. He argued that the United States as an advanced nation had an obligation to rally the international community in defense of basic standards of decency and law. President Hoover, however, ruled out any retaliation that carried a risk of war. He thought that the economic crisis at home deserved top priority and that the public would not support a more forceful policy toward Japan (Document 6).

Stimson could thus only issue paper declarations and hint at stronger action. In early January 1932 he announced what would come to be known as the Stimson doctrine: the United States would not recognize the fruits of Japanese conquests in China. The next month, after Japanese forces extended their military campaign to Shanghai, Stimson made a veiled warning that the exercise of "arbitrary force" might well provoke the United States into beginning a naval buildup in the Pacific, thus in effect overthrowing the Washington conference restrictions.[4] In both cases Stimson took his stand on the principle of the open door (accepted by Japan in the 1922 nine-power treaty) and on the 1928 Kellogg-Briand treaty, which committed Japan, the United States, and

4. The nonrecognition note of 7 January 1932 and Stimson's broader warning of 23 February 1932 (contained in a letter to Senator William Borah, the chair of the Foreign Relations Committee) are in *FRUS: Japan, 1931–1941* (2 vols.; Washington: GPO, 1943), 1:76, 83–87.

other signatories to renounce warfare as a tool of national policy (except in self-defense!). These agreements were, he contended, the very foundation of any just, orderly international system. A failure to defend the enlightened legal principles embodied in those agreements would unleash the floodwaters of chaos and barbarism.

Verbal condemnation continued into the Roosevelt years. It did not prevent Japan from consolidating its hold on Manchuria in the form of a puppet state (Manchukuo). And fears of a possible U.S. military challenge strengthened those advocating a naval buildup and the creation of a security state with control of national resources and popular support essential to assuring regional dominance. Japanese intellectuals, the military, and patriotic groups saw their country isolated and threatened by Anglo-American strategic as well as cultural domination in East Asia. Governments that sought to buck the tide of this sentiment became the target of attempted military coups in 1932 and 1936.

Policy reflected this emergent consensus behind greater strategic and economic autonomy that was critical to withstanding outside attack. In 1933 Japan quit the League of Nations over the Manchurian issue and between 1934 and 1936 began to move to a war footing. Identifying the combined American and British fleets as a major threat to Japanese security, Tokyo broke free of the naval restrictions first laid down in 1921–1922 and began building up the navy in anticipation of war. Seeking allies, Japan concluded a pact with Germany in 1936 directed against the Soviet Union.

The next step in strengthening Japan's position had already in the early 1930s become a matter of debate. Some, most notably the navy, wanted to concentrate on preparing for war with the United States in the Pacific. One faction within the army saw the Soviet Union with its strong military and dangerous revolutionary ideology as the major threat to Japan and thus wanted to focus military preparation to the north. But others in the army wanted to subjugate unruly Chinese nationalists, supposedly inspired by Soviet bolshevism and clearly hostile to Japanese influence. The Japanese army raised the stakes on this third front when in July 1937 it went into action against the Nationalist regime led by Chiang Kai-shek, provoking a Chinese declaration of war. Chinese resistance proved unexpectedly stubborn. The Nationalist government fought a rear-guard resistance, abandoning the coast and the capital (Nanjing) and retreating to Chongqing, deep in the interior.

Prince Konoe Fumimaro led Japan along most of the remaining stretch of road winding to Pearl Harbor. Born in 1891 of an aristocratic family, he had been raised in a tradition of service to the throne. A first-class education had awakened in him an interest in Western radical philosophers, while travel abroad and attendance at the Paris peace conference carried him toward a critical view of the Anglo-American powers that would stay with him. They wanted, so Konoe believed, to freeze the global status quo to the disadvantage of the have-nots, including notably such rising powers as Japan and Germany, and to perpetuate to their own considerable advantage an international system of economic imperialism. His political career, launched in 1921, quickly carried him to the patriotic right and to prominence by the early 1930s. A sterling pedigree, intelligence, and casual style made him a popular figure.

In June 1937, just on the eve of intensified conflict in China, the forty-five-year-old Konoe became prime minister. He held that position until January 1939, returned to power in late July 1940, and remained in office until October 1941. His leadership would sustain Japan's expansionist trajectory. Despite his own practical doubts about the wisdom of a military offensive against the Chinese Nationalists in mid-1937, Konoe bowed to the initiative of forces in the field. Army proponents of pacification promised a short mopping-up campaign but instead delivered a long Sino-Japanese war of attrition that would ultimately merge with the broader global conflict. The next year Konoe personally proclaimed a "new order," a union of Manchukuo, Japan, and China under Japanese leadership. Konoe's foreign minister sought to reassure deeply agitated Americans that this initiative would not only promote stability in East Asia and guarantee Japan's security but also leave the United States a residue of economic opportunity (Documents 9 and 10). The notion of a "new order," which had taken shape in the wake of the Manchurian incident, would assume grander dimensions as Japan extended its territorial reach, becoming the Greater East Asia Co-Prosperity Sphere.

* * *

These Japanese measures accelerated the race toward Pearl Harbor. The American public quickly registered its resentment. Already in October 1937, in the first months of the Sino-Japanese war, a poll revealed that only 1 percent of those surveyed sympathized with Japan, while 59 percent took China's side. By May 1939 support for Japan was still minuscule (2 percent), and those expressing sympathy for China had climbed to 74 percent.[5] This pronounced public bias reflected a long-term fascination with China as a market (even though by any economic measure Japan was more important) and as a stage for playing out the national mission in the Pacific (even though Japan stood closer by, with its own nationalist script in hand). The public saw a victimized China in desperate need of help from its traditional friend, the United States. Japanese, on the other hand, increasingly figured as violent, subhuman brutes bent on

5. George H. Gallup, *The Gallup Poll: Public Opinion, 1935–1971* (3 vols.; New York: Random House, 1972), 1:72–73, 159–60.

smashing civilized values. The unprovoked attack by Japanese aircraft on the U.S. gunboat *Panay* on the Yangzi River in December 1937 and the Japanese army's savage occupation of China's capital, Nanjing, that same month, with horrendous and gratuitous loss of civilian life, helped freeze this image of a country gone badly wrong.

By degrees the Roosevelt administration translated this mounting animus against Japan into a policy that moved beyond verbal censure. The president and his aides sought with growing resolve to bring Japan into line—to end the invasion of China and check expansion into Southeast Asia. They sought to work their will through the gradual application of economic, diplomatic, and naval sanctions meant not to provoke war but to drive home to Japanese "moderates" the costs of expansion and force them to bring the "militarists" under control.

Roosevelt played a crucial role in putting some teeth into earlier expressions of disapproval—but only after overcoming deep personal doubts about the wisdom of overseas commitments. As an assistant secretary of the navy during World War I, Roosevelt had gloried in the exercise of American power. He professed himself a disciple of intervention in Mexico, of the doctrine of a major blue-water navy, and of Wilson's own dream of better ordering the world. Running as the Democratic Party's vice-presidential nominee in 1920, he stayed true to his Wilsonian faith by arguing for membership in the League of Nations. His defeat in that election and the growing national reaction against American intervention in World War I made Roosevelt more sensitive to the war's tragic waste of life and the dangers of entanglement in foreign crises.

After his presidential election in 1932 Roosevelt met with Stimson and endorsed the policy of nonrecognition. But while FDR agreed that Japan had violated international morality and international law, he still concluded that domestic economic crisis and public antipathy to even a hint of another foreign war dictated a nonconfrontational approach to Japan (Document 7). He was further restrained by the passage of neutrality laws in 1935, which were meant to prevent a repeat of Wilson's entanglement of the country in war.

By 1937 the rise of twin international threats—Japan in East Asia and Germany in Europe—began to reawaken the Wilsonian in FDR. In his "quarantine speech" of October 1937, he strongly condemned outlaw states, a transparent reference to Japan as well as Germany and Italy, and warned of the peril they posed. But even this major effort to alert the public to the revival of aggression was replete with contradictions—between the dire developments he saw abroad and his pious desire to promote peace (Document 8). The caution that continued to mark Roosevelt's public stance into 1939 was notably evident in his reaction to the outbreak of war in Europe (Document 11). After putting his reelection campaign behind him in fall 1940, Roosevelt moved with vigor to win public support for aid to those on the frontlines facing the aggressors. Germany and Japan threatened not just their neighbors but the United States as well, he now contended. His public comments were by late 1940 and early 1941 closely aligned with his private views, as revealed by his exchange with the American ambassador in Japan (Documents 15–17).

In the course of 1941 Roosevelt put together the coalition that would ultimately win World War II. In August he met with Prime Minister Winston Churchill off the coast of Newfoundland in a dramatic demonstration of the emergent Anglo-American alliance. Despite strong public opposition to steps that might entangle the United States in another round of European warfare, Roosevelt rebutted these "isolationist" fears and made the case for aid to Britain as critical to that country's survival and American security. Roosevelt had already taken a strong stand in the Atlantic to assure supplies got to Britain, and by the fall he was locked in an undeclared naval war with Germany. He also brought Stalin into the fold following Hitler's attack on the Soviet Union in June. China too was part of the coalition—but compared to Britain or Russia it occupied a distinctly secondary place.

While FDR concentrated on building this international coalition, Secretary of State Cordell Hull attended to day-to-day management of Japan. A Tennessee lawyer and prominent Democrat, Hull had provided Roosevelt key southern support in the 1932 election and had received as his reward the State Department. Like Roosevelt, Hull was a Wilsonian in his general foreign policy outlook. He was also a staunch free trader. The open door in China was as sacrosanct as Japan's autarkic policy was repugnant. He thus agreed in principle with Stimson's earlier indictment of the Japanese challenge to international order, civilized behavior, and the open door (Document 14).

But in practice Hull was cautious in his handling of Japan, prompting other cabinet members with bolder views to grumble and sometimes intrude with their own more forceful schemes. Secretary of the Treasury and Roosevelt intimate Henry Morgenthau, as well as Secretary of the Interior Harold Ickes, stood from the first at the head of those supporting resistance to Japan. In June 1940 their voices were strengthened when Roosevelt appointed the Republicans Henry L. Stimson and Frank Knox to head the War and Navy Departments respectively. Stimson still clung to his view that the Japanese were bluffing, that international pressure would force them to behave, and that silence and half-measures only served to encourage their aggression.

The president and his chief advisers steadily stepped up pressure on Japan. In December 1938 the administration granted a loan to Chiang's Nationalist government for the purchase of arms and supplies, and more loans followed to encourage China's resistance. By that same year Roosevelt was well launched on a naval building program aimed as much at securing the Pacific as the Atlantic. Roosevelt had begun favoring the navy as soon as he had entered office, restoring funds and making plans for a long-range buildup of the fleet. Appropriations continued steadily upward so that by 1937 they had doubled. In January 1938 he asked Congress for another round of building, and in May he got it.

By 1940 Roosevelt was flexing his military muscle in ways that Tokyo could not miss. In May, following the fall of France, Roosevelt decided to leave the Pacific fleet at Pearl Harbor rather than base it on the West Coast. He wanted it to serve as a visible, forceful reminder to Tokyo of the steel and powder behind U.S. policy. In late July, in the wake of mounting Japanese pressure on French and Dutch holdings in Southeast Asia, FDR signed a bill to create a two-ocean force through a 70 percent expansion of the navy. Total U.S. arms production had already outstripped Japan's (though the output had to be shared with anti-German allies). In such a critical category as aircraft output the United States had almost a threefold advantage over Japan, and the gap would steadily widen in the American favor.

Finally, the administration began to apply economic pressure. This turned out to be the most potent American weapon, and it supplied, contrary to Washington's intention, the single strongest push toward war. In July 1939 Washington announced that it would terminate the commercial treaty with Japan, setting the basis for an embargo that would deprive Japan of its third largest market. In July 1940 Washington followed through on the threat by imposing a limited embargo on scrap iron, steel, and high-octane aviation fuel after Japanese forces moved into the northern part of French Indochina. Then in September the Roosevelt administration made the scrap-metal embargo total. In July 1941 came what was probably the most consequential step. Provoked by further Japanese penetration into Indochina, Washington froze Japanese assets in the United States, in effect preventing the purchase of U.S. oil (amounting to four-fifths of Japan's oil supply). The U.S. government was able to cut off the remaining fraction from the East Indies by securing the cooperation of Dutch and British authorities.

Even at this point in 1941 the Roosevelt administration did not want war. American military leaders preferred some kind of modus vivendi with Japan that would allow them to concentrate limited resources on the more dangerous foe, Germany. They gave priority to securing the Atlantic supply bridge to embattled Britain and to getting material assistance to the USSR. Only considerably later, after they had had time to push forward military preparations and expand production, would they be ready for a war on a second front with Japan (Document 29). But getting in the way of a modus vivendi for the Roosevelt administration were the long-standing commitments to safeguarding international law and the open door. To this were added the newer concerns with protecting the Southeast Asian colonies of Britain, France, and the Netherlands, allies in the struggle against Hitler. Finally, a compromise with Japan would betray the Chinese resistance, perhaps even undermine it, while also shaking Soviet confidence in its newfound capitalist partners. Both Churchill and Chiang argued forcefully to Roosevelt their opposition to any American accommodation with Tokyo.

A public opinion still sharply skewed against Japan helped sustain a policy of pressure. By late October 1941, 64 percent of Americans surveyed were ready to oppose Japan even at the risk of war, and only 25 percent were not ready to run that risk. (Queries about the European conflict posed in early November revealed a more cautious attitude: 63 percent opposed a declaration of war against Germany, while only 26 percent supported such a measure.)[6]

∗   ∗   ∗

Confronted by a hostile United States, Tokyo watched the international scene for opportunities to strengthen its strategic position. Nineteen thirty-nine proved a bad year: the Chinese continued their resistance; Soviet forces got the best of Japanese troops in a clash on the borders of Manchukuo; and the Germans concluded a pact in August with Japan's Soviet foe. But the fall of France to Germany in June 1940 opened the way for Japan's occupation of northern French Indochina, legitimized by agreement in September with the French collaborationist regime in Vichy. Not only were Indochina's resources virtually in hand but now those of British Malaya and the Dutch East Indies were in easy reach. While carrying Japan toward greater economic self-sufficiency, this southward advance was also to help cut outside support to the Chinese Nationalists.

The future looked bright—so reasoned the government of Konoe (just returned to power in July 1940). Britain, now under siege, was expected to capitulate, leaving Germany triumphant in Europe and the United States isolated. Japan could more comfortably contemplate a move south against the exposed European colonies if it had German backing that would in turn give pause to the Americans. In the decision to move closer to Germany, Konoe was guided by his strong-willed foreign minister, Matsuoka Yosuke. In September Tokyo concluded the Tripartite Pact with Berlin and Rome and at the same time confidently formalized its claims to a pan-Asian co-prosperity sphere (Documents 12 and 13).

Once more a Japanese government had taken the initiative despite the doubts of the emperor. He dreaded the prospect of war with the Anglo-

6. Gallup, *Gallup Poll*, 1:306–7.

American powers and now openly expressed his fear that Japan lacked the resources to survive such a collision while bogged down in China. Indeed, in September 1940, just after the decision to ally with Germany and Italy, he pressed Konoe, "I have often heard that in the map problems of the Naval Staff College, Japan is always the loser in a Japanese-American war. Can you reassure me about that?" He added, "I am very concerned over this situation. What would happen in the event that Japan should become a defeated nation?"[7]

The optimistic assessment of the Konoe government prevailed and carried over into 1941. In April it reached a neutrality agreement with the Soviet Union, thus safeguarding one of Japan's flanks. Then in June Germany launched its surprise attack on the USSR. Hitler's forces tying down both the British and the Soviets created an irresistible strategic opportunity. Japan's leaders met in conference early in July to consider how to exploit it (Document 19). At the end of the month imperial forces pushed into southern Indochina.

In parallel with these developments in 1941 Japan conducted a diplomatic offensive in Washington to secure a peaceful settlement. Like Roosevelt, Konoe wanted to avoid war, though (also like Roosevelt) without compromising principles or position in Asia. In February a high-level emissary, Admiral Nomura Kichisaburo, arrived to conduct secret talks with Hull. Nomura had limited diplomatic experience; his chief recommendation was that he had known Roosevelt when serving as naval attaché in Washington during World War I. In mid-April, after some preliminary exchanges, Hull presented four simple, abstract principles drawn from earlier U.S. policy to serve as the basis for their talks: respect for territorial integrity and sovereignty of all states; noninterference in the internal affairs of other countries; support for equality, including equality of commercial opportunity; and adjustment of the status quo only by peaceful means.

By July the talks, begun with high hopes, had for Tokyo become an irritant, in large measure because Hull's fixed principles left little room for maneuver (Documents 18 and 20). Belatedly responding to the unexpectedly vehement American opposition to the Tripartite Pact, Konoe sought to sweeten the atmosphere. He eased Matsuoka, the author of that pact, out of the government. Konoe also assured Washington that the bonds between Tokyo and Berlin were not so tight as to prevent an accommodation with the United States. But other issues still stood in the way: Japan's invasion of China and occupation of northern Indochina, U.S. economic pressure on Japan and aid to China, deep mutual resentments, and the naval race on which both sides were engaged. Verbal formulas, no matter how artfully contrived, were no

7. Quoted in Stephen S. Large, *Emperor Hirohito and Showa Japan: A Political Biography* (London: Routledge, 1992), 100.

match for this formidable array of problems. Even so, the line of communications remained open until early December, with Japanese and American diplomats gamely engaging in semantic contortions in an effort to find a formula that could bridge their differences and forestall war.

For Konoe's government, the freeze on assets at the end of July cast a pall over the diplomacy and set off intense and anguished discussions. The alternatives seemed now reduced to confrontation with a more powerful United States or capitulation to American demands and sinking to the ranks of second-class powers. With the oil reserves steadily dwindling, the navy pressed for some action before the loss of the strategic reserve immobilized the fleet. At best that reserve would last for two years, and war would exhaust it in eighteen months. Japanese leaders now traced out the strategic logic that led inescapably to Pearl Harbor. The East Indies was the only major nearby source. Seizure of that Dutch colony would guarantee just enough oil to meet Japanese requirements. Taking the Dutch and other adjacent colonies, however, Japanese strategists assumed, would precipitate armed American retaliation. Thus it was necessary to neutralize American power in the Pacific at the same time that Japan's forces moved deeper into Southeast Asia.

In a frenzy of activity Tokyo began to prepare the task force to attack Pearl Harbor and the Philippines while still seeking through diplomacy some last-minute solution to the quest for oil that now drove Japanese strategy (Documents 21 and 23). Prime Minister Konoe even went so far as to press in August for a face-to-face meeting with Roosevelt to negotiate a general agreement that would head off the looming showdown. But Roosevelt regarded such a summit meeting as the reward for a resolution of U.S.-Japan disagreements, not the means to that end. With no acceptable grounds for compromise evident, he had Hull parry the proposal (Documents 22 and 24).

Time had run out for Konoe. The Americans had given him the cold shoulder, and in any case Konoe's army minister, Tojo Hideki, firmly resisted any compromise on the China question; the sacrifices of the military and the honor of the nation forbad retreat. War preparations were in full gear. And although the navy had private doubts about challenging the United States, Konoe could not get its leaders to call for a basic policy reappraisal that might give more time for diplomacy. On 16 October he resigned, to be replaced by Tojo.

The new government continued the intense discussions of the strike against the United States. Though himself a hard-liner, Tojo bowed to pressure from the emperor's advisers to search one last time for a way to avoid war. He had the new foreign minister, Togo Shigenori, make one last diplomatic effort (Documents 25–28). But Togo failed to draw Hull into even a temporary bargain that would avert military action. Hull insisted that any deal depended on Japan's respecting the four principles laid down at the outset of his talks with Nomura and withdrawing all its forces from both China and Indochina.[8] And both Hull and Roosevelt emphasized their visceral aversion to coming to terms with a Japan tied to Germany (Documents 30 and 31).

Tojo's government could only embrace war, presenting that decision formally to the emperor on 1 December (Document 32). On 7 December, as the Japanese embassy in Washington struggled to decode a message breaking off the stalled talks, a Japanese naval task force launched its aircraft. Nomura walked into Hull's office even as American warships settled to the bottom of Pearl Harbor (Document 33).

American pressure had produced the war that that very pressure had been intended to preclude or at least delay. By holding to its determination to bring Japan into line, the Roosevelt administration lost its minimum strategic requirement, the time to mobilize for war on two fronts. Now Roosevelt asked Congress for a declaration of war against Japan, and he called the public to rally and crush the nation guilty of shocking treachery (Document 34). When Hitler responded with his own declaration of war against the United States, the circle of global conflict was closed.

The last lap of the Japanese-American contest for preeminence in East Asia was marked by a failure of intelligence almost as striking as the failure of the policy of pressure. American intelligence had broken the Japanese code (through the operation known as MAGIC) and made clear to FDR in late November that an attack was coming. Some historians have thus concluded that the president invited the attack as a back-door entry into war with Germany, a war to which the public would not otherwise agree. But a close examination reveals that American intelligence, overwhelmed by raw information and confused by "static," could not determine with precision where Japan would aim its blow. Even so, the American military might have better weathered the attack if not for a breakdown in communications that left forces in Hawaii at a lower level of readiness than the military command in Washington had called for. The unwanted war thus began with losses more serious than they need have been—and with considerably greater success than Japanese naval planners had anticipated. Roosevelt was stunned, and Tokyo was exultant. Japan's gamble had paid off handsomely—so at least it seemed for the moment.

*   *   *

The long and complicated road Japan and the United States followed to Pearl Harbor is littered with difficult but intriguing interpretive questions.

8. Hull's outline of terms for an agreement, handed to Nomura, 26 November 1941, in *FRUS: Japan, 1931–1941*, 2:768–70.

What issues finally triggered the test of arms between Japanese and Americans? When did the two sides reach a point of no return in their souring relationship—or did grounds for accommodation continue to exist into late 1941? Does the responsibility for the collision lie with Japanese policymakers? Were they, as some Americans charged, guilty of serious moral failings? Did Tokyo fundamentally and disastrously overestimate its own strength? Or should Henry L. Stimson, Franklin D. Roosevelt, and Cordell Hull also be called before the dock of history? Were those American leaders guilty in their own fashion—of a muddled policy, caught halfway between a determination not to let Japanese aggression pass in silence and an aversion to taking up arms? Or are they more fundamentally at fault for a racist reluctance to accept the Japanese as equals and concede to Japan its own sphere of influence? Did either side discard reasonable alternatives to war? Might a more forceful U.S. policy have checked Japan's expansion—or would such a policy have heightened tension and led to an early war when the United States would have been even less prepared to fight than in late 1941? Can judgments on ultimate responsibility and alternative courses be fruitfully drawn at all?

Pearl Harbor and the ensuing war in the Pacific marked a watershed in U.S.-Japan relations. Ironically, it took a major conflict to break the cycle of suspicion and fear building in Japanese-American relations since the turn of the century. Prewar leaders most closely associated with a course of confrontation were swept away. Konoe, for example, took poison rather than submit to the humiliation of trial by the victors, and Tojo was executed after botching a suicide attempt. A Japan cleansed by defeat and subjected to a reformist, New Deal–style occupation would emerge as a major Cold War ally of the United States and in time as an economic powerhouse flourishing under the American security umbrella. Was war the only way to break the cycle of confrontation and finally reach an accommodation?

FOR FURTHER READING

Until the late 1960s writing on the origins of the Japanese-American conflict was preoccupied with apportioning blame, directed either at Japanese leaders or Franklin Roosevelt. James B. Crowley, *Japan's Quest for Autonomy: National Security and Foreign Policy, 1930–1938* (1966), and his essay, "A New Deal for Japan and Asia: One Road to Pearl Harbor," in Crowley, ed., *Modern East Asia: Essays in Interpretation* (1970), were path-breaking works that began to introduce a more international, less judgmental perspective.

Other equally international accounts soon followed, including notably Christopher Thorne, *The Limits of Foreign Policy: The West, the League and the Far Eastern Crisis of 1931–1933* (1972); Dorothy Borg and Shumpei Okamoto, eds., *Pearl Harbor as History: Japanese-American Relations, 1931–1941* (1973); Stephen E. Pelz, *Race to Pearl Harbor: The Failure of the Second London Naval Conference and the Onset of World War II* (1974); Charles Neu, *The Troubled Encounter: The United States and Japan* (1975); Akira Iriye, *Power and Culture: The Japanese-American War, 1941–1945* (1981); Iriye, *The Origins of the Second World War in Asia and the Pacific* (1987); and John W. Dower, *War without Mercy: Race and Power in the Pacific War* (1986). Gordon W. Prange's popular *At Dawn We Slept: The Untold Story of Pearl Harbor* (1981) recounts in detail the climactic events of 1941, with an emphasis on both the American and Japanese militaries.

Particularly helpful in amplifying the Japanese side of the story are Yoshitake Oka, *Konoe Fumimaro: A Political Biography,* trans. Shumpei Okamoto and Patricia Murray (1983); William Miles Fletcher III, *The Search for a New Order: Intellectuals and Fascism in Prewar Japan* (1982); James W. Morley, ed., "Japan's Road to the Pacific War" (1976–94), a five-volume series containing translations of important accounts by Japanese scholars; and Saburo Ienaga, *The Pacific War, 1931–1945: A Critical Perspective on Japan's Role in World War II,* trans. Frank Baldwin (1978). Ienaga, which first appeared in Japan in 1968, deserves singling out as a lively, broadly cast study with a strong point of view.

Important treatment of U.S. policy can be found in Robert Dallek, *Franklin D. Roosevelt and American Foreign Policy, 1932–1945* (1979); Waldo Heinrichs, *Threshold of War: Franklin D. Roosevelt and American Entry into World War II* (1988); Irvine H. Anderson, Jr., *The Standard-Vacuum Oil Company and United States East Asian Policy, 1933–1941* (1975); Jonathan G. Utley, *Going to War with Japan, 1937–1941* (1985), best read for its insights on Cordell Hull; and Roberta Wohlstetter, *Pearl Harbor: Warning and Decision* (1962), a study of the American intelligence failure that rebuts the charge that Roosevelt sought to draw Japan into war. J. Garry Clifford offers a helpful review of the recent literature in "Both Ends of the Telescope: New Perspectives on FDR and American Entry into World War II," *Diplomatic History* 13 (Spring 1989).

Anyone interested in digging into collections of primary sources can turn to Ralph E. Shaffer, ed., *Toward Pearl Harbor: The Diplomatic Interchange between Japan and the United States, 1899–1941* (1991); Joyce C. Lebra, ed., *Japan's Greater East Asia Co-Prosperity Sphere in World War II: Selected Readings and Documents* (1975); and Nobutaka Ike, trans. and ed., *Japan's Decision for War: Records of the 1941 Policy Conferences* (1967).

DOCUMENTS

1   Theodore Roosevelt to President William Howard Taft, 22 December 1910, criticizing his administration's policy of challenging Japan in Manchuria.[9]

Our vital interest is to keep the Japanese out of our country, and at the same time to preserve the good will of Japan. The vital interest of the Japanese, on the other hand, is in Manchuria and Korea. It is therefore peculiarly our interest not to take any steps as regards Manchuria which will give the Japanese cause to feel, with or without reason, that we are hostile to them, or a menace—in however slight a degree—to their interests. Alliance with China, in view of China's absolute military helplessness, means of course not an additional strength to us, but an additional obligation which we assume; . . . and as regards Manchuria, if the Japanese choose to follow a course of conduct to which we are averse, we cannot stop it unless we are prepared to go to war, and a successful war about Manchuria would require a fleet as good as that of England, plus an army as good as that of Germany. . . .

. . . [W]hereas our interests in Manchuria are really unimportant, and not such that the American people would be content to run the slightest risk of collision about them, our interest in keeping the Japanese out of our own country is vital. . . .

2   Secretary of State Philander C. Knox, reply to Theodore Roosevelt (prepared for Taft but never sent), 7 January 1911, insisting on both defense of rights in China and rejection of Japanese immigrants.[10]

[A]lthough I am aware that some Japanese statesmen have recently attempted to connect [the Manchurian and immigration questions], . . . I am unable to see any essential connection between them.

We have an expressed treaty right to control the immigration of Japanese

9. Elting E. Morison et al., eds., *The Letters of Theodore Roosevelt* (8 vols.; Cambridge: Harvard University Press, 1951–54), 7:189–90.

10. William Howard Taft Papers, presidential series 7, file 26, Manuscript Division, Library of Congress, Washington.

laborers to our territory and we have likewise a treaty right to equal opportunity in Manchuria. . . .

. . .

. . . [Y]our letter seems to imply that there is no alternative between silently renouncing our historic policy [of the open door] in China whenever it may cross the interest of another power and being prepared to go to war in defense of that policy. Whether the American people would ever go to war or not in defense of our interests in China I am not prepared to say. It might depend upon the nature of the provocation. But in any case it certainly is not for us to prejudice our case at the start by admitting to the world that we would *not*, under any circumstances, go to war. . . .

. . . [I]n any event I think it would be much better for us to stand consistently by our principles even though we fail in getting them generally adopted.

3   Prince Yamagata Aritomo to Prime Minister Okuma Shigenobu, August 1914, urging solidarity with China and accommodation with the United States.[11]

There are people in our country who rely excessively on the military prowess of our empire and who believe that against China the application of force alone will suffice to gain our objectives. But the problems of life are not so simple as to permit of their solution by the use of force alone. The principal aim of our plan today should be to improve Sino-Japanese relations and to instill in China a sense of abiding trust in us....

The recent international situation points to an increasing intensity in racial rivalry from year to year. . . . When the present great conflict in Europe is over and when the political and economic order [is] restored, the various countries will again focus their attention on the Far East and the benefits and rights they might derive from this region. When that day comes, the rivalry between the white and the non-white races will become violent, and who can say that the white races will not unite with one another to oppose the colored peoples?

Now among the colored peoples of the Orient, Japan and China are the only two countries that have the semblance of an independent state. . . . Thus, if the colored races of the Orient hope to compete with the so-called culturally advanced white races and maintain friendly relations with them while retain-

11. Ryusaku Tsunoda et al., eds. and trans., *Sources of Japanese Tradition* (2 vols.; New York: Columbia University Press, 1964), 2:207–8. The omission in the first paragraph appears in the source text.

ing their own cultural identity and independence, China and Japan, which are culturally and racially alike, must become friendly and promote each other's interests. . . .

. . . America is rich, and of late she is giving great attention to the commerce, industry, and trade of China. Moreover, the great European war has not deterred her in the least. . . . And the government of China, suspicious of the true motives of our empire, and as a means of restraining our activities in China, has been turning to America. If we fail to dissipate China's suspicion of us, she will rapidly turn against us and instead turn more and more to America. America herself will take advantage of such a situation and will increasingly extend her influence over China.

. . . [I]t is advisable, for the realization of our China policy, not to aggravate America's feelings toward us nor needlessly to arouse her suspicions over our actions. . . .

4 K. K. Kawakami, "A Japanese Liberal's View," November 1921, voicing frustration over the international restrictions placed on Japan.[12]

[T]he Caucasian race, having completed the occupation of Europe and the Americas, has conquered and secured control of the whole of Australasia, almost all Africa, the greater part of Asia, as well as the adjacent islands. And the Caucasian peoples who control so vast a territory number only 623,000,000. . . .

. . .

. . . [T]he Caucasian nations are always on the alert to exclude outside enterprises, and especially those of non-Caucasian peoples, from the territories they control. Even where they profess to follow the principles of free trade, they set up a barrier against non-Caucasian immigration. Moreover, by reason of their priority and their accumulated wealth, they have so firmly intrenched themselves that outsiders, most of all non-Caucasian outsiders, find little chance to launch new enterprises in competition with them.

. . .

. . .[I]t is not only the question of land shortage and overpopulation that weigh[s] heavily upon Japan. Equally depressing is the fact that she has not within her own confines adequate mineral resources essential to modern industry. She depends almost entirely upon foreign countries for iron ores. Of

12. *The Nation* 113 (9 November 1921): 530–31. Kiyoshi Karl Kawakami (1875–1949), a journalist and longtime resident of the United States, was a frequent commentator on Pacific affairs during the interwar period, usually along lines favorable to Japan.

coal she has little that can be used in the steel industry. But the most serious handicap is the lack of petroleum, a material which is becoming more and more important in transportation and in manufacturing industries. If you watch the chessboard of European and American diplomacy, you cannot fail to see how each nation is trying to outwit the other in gaining control of oil resources in different parts of the world.

And here is Japan, struggling to solve, partly at least, her population problems by becoming an industrial and trading nation, and yet harassed by the lack of three essential materials of industry—oil, iron, and coal. If she steps an inch out of her narrow precincts and tries to obtain, say in Siberia or China, the privilege of working such mineral resources, down comes the sword of Damocles in the shape of protest, official or otherwise, from the Western nations.

5 Amur Society, statement of 1930, calling for national strength and discipline essential for realizing Japan's imperial mission.[13]

Japan's status among the empires of the world has risen until today she ranks as one of the three great powers, and from this eminence she can support other Asiatic nations. . . .

However, in viewing recent international affairs it would seem that the foundation established by the great Meiji emperor [reigned 1867–1912] is undergoing rapid deterioration. The disposition of the gains of the war with Germany was left to foreign powers, and the government, disregarding the needs of national defense, submitted [at the Washington conference] to unfair demands to limit our naval power. Moreover, the failure of our China policy made the Chinese more and more contemptuous of us, so much so that they have been brought to demand the surrender of our essential defense lines in Manchuria and Mongolia. Furthermore, in countries like the United States and Australia our immigrants have been deprived of rights which were acquired only after long years of struggle, and we now face a highhanded anti-Japanese expulsion movement which knows no bounds. Men of purpose and of humanity who are at all concerned for their country cannot fail to be upset by the situation.

When we turn our attention to domestic affairs, we feel more than deep

---

13. The ultranationalist Amur (or Black Dragon) Society was organized in 1901 by former samurai who wished to promote Japan's influence in East Asia. It began to focus in the 1920s on the strains developing within Japanese society. Tsunoda et al., *Sources of the Japanese Tradition*, 2:256–58.

concern. There is a great slackening of discipline and order. Men's hearts are become corrupt. Look about you! Are not the various government measures and establishments a conglomeration of all sorts of evils and abuses? The laws are confusing, and evil grows apace. The people are overwhelmed by heavy taxes, the confusion in the business world complicates the livelihood of the people, the growth of dangerous thought threatens social order, and our national polity, which has endured for three thousand years, is in danger. This is a critical time for our national destiny; was there ever a more crucial day? . . .

. . .

. . . [W]e are resolved to reform the moral corruption of the people, restore social discipline, and ease the insecurity of the people's livelihood by relieving the crises in the financial world, restore national confidence, and increase the national strength, in order to carry out the imperial mission to awaken the countries of Asia. . . .

6   Secretary of State Henry L. Stimson, diary entries, October 1931–January 1932, describing his and President Herbert Hoover's divergent reactions to the Japanese occupation of Manchuria.

—Account of cabinet meeting, 9 October 1931:[14]

[Hoover's] main proposition in this conference was not to allow under any circumstances anybody to deposit that baby [Manchuria] on our lap; and second, not to get ourselves into a humiliating position, in case Japan refused to do anything to what he called our scraps of paper or paper treaties. . . . The question of the "scraps of paper" is a pretty crucial one. We have nothing but "scraps of paper." This fight has come on in the worst part of the world for peace treaties. The peace treaties of Modern Europe made out by the Western nations of the world no more fit the three great races of Russia, Japan, and China, who are meeting in Manchuria, than, as I put it to the Cabinet, a stovepipe hat would fit an African savage. Nevertheless they are parties to these treaties and the whole world looks on to see whether the treaties are good for anything or not, and if we lie down and treat them like scraps of paper nothing will happen, and in the future the peace movement will receive a blow that it will not recover from for a long time. As I pointed out to the President in Cabinet, if Japan runs amok, Congress will never let him cut a single dollar off on navies.

14. Henry L. Stimson diaries, vol. 18, pp. 111–12 (microfilm ed. reel 3), Stimson Papers, Manuscripts and Archives, Yale University Library, New Haven, Conn.

—Reflections after a private meeting with Hoover, 7 November 1931:[15]

It looks now as if the military element in Japan might get control of the situation and oust the Government at any time. So the President and I discussed . . . what we would do under such circumstances. Any such thing as an embargo or an attempt to put on economic pressure he ruled out on the ground that it was as [*sic*] step which would be provocative and lead to war. His idea was that we might withdraw our Ambassador, and, if we did so, he would give out a statement at the same time putting war out of the question, an announcement that we would not under any event go to war and that that was contrary to our present policy and to all the treaties and contrary to the views of the world. Of course, the argument on the other side of this is manifest, it would remove from Japan any fear of any further economic blockade. . . .

I concur with him as to the danger of a blockade leading to war. It is almost a belligerent step. . . .

—Reflections after a private meeting with Hoover, 27 November 1931:[16]

In the first place, probably an embargo, if joined in by all the world against Japan, would be a very brief event. She would have to surrender very quickly. It would, therefore, not be a strain upon the rest of the governments. In the next place, it would seem now that the militaristic elements in Japan could learn only through suffering and not by the sanctions of public opinion, which we in America are committed to and deem enough for ourselves. In the third place, it would be a tremendous loss to the higher motives and higher policies if Japan really gets away with this, if the army teaches itself, Japan, and the rest of the world that the higher efforts towards peace by the rest of the world can be successfully defied in the way in which Japan is now defying them. The poor old President is in a bad plight. As he says, he has been making speeches against sanctions of force all this time and he cannot reverse himself. . . .

—Account of cabinet meeting, 26 January 1932:[17]

[T]he President stated his view forcibly and emphatically. . . . [H]e felt that the mere size of China, 350,000,000 [people] as he expressed it, always had succeeded and would succeed in throwing off the efforts of other nations like Japan to penetrate it and dominate it. He believes now that in time China would throw Japan out of Manchuria and that she would throw her out of the Yangtze Valley. He had no doubt, however, that Japan was going ahead now. . . . He pointed out strongly the folly of getting into a war with Japan on this

15. Stimson diaries, vol. 19, pp. 18–19 (microfilm ed. reel 4).
16. Stimson diaries, vol. 19, p. 103 (microfilm ed. reel 4).
17. Stimson diaries, vol. 20, pp. 100–111 (microfilm ed. reel 4).

subject; that such a war could not be localized or kept within bounds, and that it would mean the landing of forces in the Far East which we had no reason or sense in doing. He said he would fight for Continental United States as far as anybody, but he would not fight for Asia. . . . He said that he thought [Stimson's 7 January nonrecognition] note would take rank with the greatest papers of this country, and that that was the safe course for us to follow now rather than by getting into a war in China.

. . . I told him then that the only difference I could see between his point and mine was that in respect to the reliance which I felt we could put upon America's strength both economically and military. I quoted Roosevelt's saying, "Speak softly but carry a big stick." I told him that I thought that this represented a great truth; that we were responsible for our words. I was against putting any threat into words. I thought we had a right to rely upon the unconscious elements of our great size and military strength; that I knew Japan was afraid of that, and I was willing to let her be afraid of that without telling her that we were not going to use it against her. The difference which I have just mentioned is really the great difference and difficulty which I have with the President's policy. He has not got the slightest element of even the faintest kind of bluff. He is too likely to let the other fellow know the element against ourselves which the other fellow might not guess. I am a thorough believer in the policy of not drawing until you are ready to shoot, but when you have a case where the chances are a thousand to one that you will not be drawn into a fight, I am willing to let our size and strength speak for itself and not to disclaim publicly our willingness to fight if it becomes essential. . . .

7   Secretary of State Cordell Hull, meeting with Japanese Ambassador Saito Hiroshi, 16 May 1934, discussing Japanese claims to regional preeminence.[18]

[The Japanese ambassador stated that] his Government did feel that it had a special interest in preserving peace and order in China. He then repeated the same formula that his government had been putting out for some weeks about the superior duty or function of his government to preserve peace and of its special interest in the peace situation in—to quote his words—"Eastern Asia". . . . [Hull responded] that my hope and prayer was that all the civilized nations of the world, including Japan, should work together and in a perfectly friendly and understanding way so as to promote to the fullest extent the

18. Saito was a professional diplomat appointed to Washingtion in December 1933. Hull memorandum of the meeting, 19 May 1934, in *FRUS: Japan 1931–1941*, 1:234–36.

welfare of their respective peoples and at the same time meet their duties to civilization and to the more backward populations of the world; and that my Government would always be ready and desirous of meeting his Government fully half-way in pursuing these latter objectives.

I then remarked that . . . just now there was considerable inquiry everywhere as to just why his government singled out the clause or formula about Japan's claiming superior and special interests in the peace situation in "Eastern Asia" and her superior rights or duties in connection with the preservation of peace there; and that many were wondering whether this phrase or formula had ulterior or ultimate implications partaking of the nature of an overlordship of the Orient or definite purpose to secure preferential trade rights as rapidly as possible in the Orient or "Eastern Asia"—to use the Japanese expression. The Ambassador commenced protesting that this was not the meaning contemplated or intended. . . .

. . . [Hull said] that this was peculiarly a time when our civilized countries should be especially vigilant to observe and to preserve both legal and moral obligations. . . .

8   President Franklin D. Roosevelt, speech in Chicago, 5 October 1937, calling for an international "quarantine" in the face of Japan's invasion of China and German remilitarization.[19]

[T]he hopes of mankind for a continuing era of international peace were raised to great heights when [in 1928] more than sixty nations solemnly pledged themselves not to resort to arms in furtherance of their national aims and policies. The high aspirations expressed in the Briand-Kellogg Peace Pact and the hopes for peace thus raised have of late given way to a haunting fear of calamity. The present reign of terror and international lawlessness began a few years ago.

It began through unjustified interference in the internal affairs of other nations or the invasion of alien territory in violation of treaties; and has now reached a stage where the very foundations of civilization are seriously threatened. . . .

. . .

There is a solidarity and interdependence about the modern world, both technically and morally, which makes it impossible for any nation completely to isolate itself from economic and political upheavals in the rest of the world,

19. Samuel I. Rosenman, ed., *The Public Papers and Addresses of Franklin D. Roosevelt, 1937* (New York: Macmillan, 1941), 407, 409–11.

especially when such upheavals appear to be spreading and not declining. There can be no stability or peace either within nations or between nations except under laws and moral standards adhered to by all. International anarchy destroys every foundation for peace. . . .

. . .

. . . The peace, the freedom and the security of ninety percent of the population of the world is being jeopardized by the remaining ten percent who are threatening a breakdown of all international order and law. Surely the ninety percent who want to live in peace under law and in accordance with moral standards that have received almost universal acceptance through the centuries, can and must find some way to make their will prevail.

. . .

When an epidemic of physical disease starts to spread, the community approves and joins in a quarantine of the patients in order to protect the health of the community against the spread of the disease.

. . .

War is a contagion, whether it be declared or undeclared. It can engulf states and peoples remote from the original scene of hostilities. We are determined to keep out of war, yet we cannot insure ourselves against the disastrous effects of war and the dangers of involvement. . . .

. . .

America hates war. America hopes for peace. Therefore, America actively engages in the search for peace.

9   Prime Minister Konoe Fumimaro, 3 November 1938, formally staking Japan's claim to a "New Order in East Asia."[20]

What Japan seeks is the establishment of a new order which will insure the permanent stability of East Asia. In this lies the ultimate purpose of our present military campaign [in China].

This new order has for its foundation a tripartite relationship of mutual aid and co-ordination between Japan, Manchoukuo and China in political, economic, cultural and other fields. Its object is to secure international justice, to perfect the joint defence against Communism, and to create a new culture and realize a close economic cohesion throughout East Asia. This indeed is the way to contribute toward the stabilization of East Asia and the progress of the world.

What Japan desires of China is that that country will share in the task of

20. *FRUS: Japan, 1931–1941*, 1:478.

bringing about this new order in East Asia. She confidently expects that the people of China will fully comprehend her true intentions and that they will respond to the call of Japan for their co-operation. Even the participation of [China's Nationalist] Government would not be rejected. . . .

Japan is confident that other Powers will on their part correctly appreciate her aims and policy and adapt their attitude to the new conditions prevailing in East Asia. . . .

10 Foreign Minister Arita Hichiro, comments to a U.S. embassy official, 19 November 1938, justifying Japan's claims to a "New Order."[21]

Japan, like other nations, was maintaining military and naval forces adequate for national defense needs. However, there was another method by which pressure could be exerted on Japan, and that was by withholding from her foreign markets and raw materials necessary for her existence. Her army and navy would be useless against pressure applied in that form. It had, there-fore, become necessary for Japan to place herself in a position to resist that method of applying pressure, and she was now in process of putting herself in that position by acquiring certain access to necessary raw materials.

. . . He could say definitely that Japan has no intention whatever of assim-ilating politically any part of China or of "Manchukuo," and he saw no incon-sistency between that statement and the settled policy of economically linking together the three countries in order to provide for their common security. Such an arrangement would not necessarily be exclusive of American and other foreign enterprise and capital. What the Japanese Government has in mind is that the new bloc, while providing Japan a market and a source for raw materials, will offer other countries an opportunity for trade and for invest-ments. . . .

. . . When he came into office, he decided that it would be mischievous as well as useless to attempt to reconcile the principle of the open door, as understood in the United States and elsewhere abroad, with the new situation which Japan was endeavoring to bring about. . . .

. . .

He realized that there were extended historical and even sentimental asso-ciations in the United States with regard to that [open-door] principle. . . . [H]e was confident that by quiet discussion between the two governments and

21. The official who recorded Arita's remarks was Eugene H. Dooman, counsellor of the U.S. embassy. *FRUS: Japan, 1931–1941*, 1:802–5.

by refraining from engaging in disputes through exchanges of official notes which are later made public, substantial progress could be made toward an eventual satisfactory solution of the present difficulty.

I I President Roosevelt, national radio address from the White House, 3 September 1939, reacting to the outbreak of war in Europe set off by the German invasion of Poland.[22]

For four long years a succession of actual wars and constant crises have shaken the entire world and have threatened in each case to bring on the gigantic conflict which is today unhappily a fact.

. . .

You must master at the outset a simple but unalterable fact in modern foreign relations between nations. When peace has been broken anywhere, the peace of all countries everywhere is in danger.

. . .

This Nation will remain a neutral nation, but I cannot ask that every American remain neutral in thought as well. Even a neutral has a right to take account of facts. Even a neutral cannot be asked to close his mind or his conscience.

I have said not once, but many times, that I have seen war and that I hate war. I say that again and again.

I 2 Japanese Imperial Conference, 19 September 1940, discussing an alliance with Germany and Italy (the Tripartite Pact) and the likely American reaction.[23]

[PRESIDENT OF THE PRIVY COUNCIL HARA YOSHIMICHI:] [T]his Pact is a treaty of alliance with the United States as its target. Germany and Italy hope to prevent American entry into the European war by making this Pact public.

22. Samuel I. Rosenman, ed., *The Public Papers and Addresses of Franklin D. Roosevelt, 1939* (New York: Macmillan, 1941), 460–63.

23. Nobutaka Ike, ed. and trans., *Japan's Decision for War: Records of the 1941 Policy Conferences* (Stanford, Calif.: Stanford University Press, 1967), 9–10, 12. Imperial conferences were formal gatherings before the emperor intended to ratify policy around which a consensus had developed. It was opened by the prime minister followed by others with prepared statements. The president of the Privy Council (a group of advisers to the emperor) would then raise questions nominally to inform the emperor and lay the basis for the handing down of an imperial sanction for the conference decisions.

Recently the United States has been acting as a watchdog in Eastern Asia in place of Great Britain. She has applied pressure to Japan, but she has probably been restraining herself in order to prevent Japan from joining Germany and Italy. But when Japan's position becomes clear with the announcement of this Pact, she will greatly increase her pressure on us, she will greatly step up her aid to Chiang [Kai-shek], and she will obstruct Japan's war effort. I assume that the United States, which has not declared war on Germany and Italy, will put economic pressure on Japan without declaring war on us. She will probably ban the export of oil and iron, and will refuse to purchase goods from us. She will attempt to weaken us over the long term so that we will not be able to endure war. The Director of the Planning Board has said that all available steps will be taken to obtain iron and oil, but the results are uncertain. Also the Foreign Minister's statement shows that we cannot obtain iron and oil right away, and that in any case the amount will be restricted. You cannot carry on a war without oil. The capital in Netherlands East Indies oil is British and American, and the Dutch Government has fled to England; so I think it will be impossible to obtain oil from the Netherlands East Indies by peaceful means. I would like to hear the Government's views on this.

. . .

[FOREIGN MINISTER MATSUOKA YOSUKE:] If Japan would abandon all, or at least half, of China, it might be possible for the time being to shake hands with the United States; but [American] pressure on Japan will certainly not come to an end in the future. The Presidential election that is coming up very shortly is especially dangerous. Roosevelt, who has high ambitions, will stop at nothing to achieve them if he believes that he is in danger. He might well undertake a war against Japan, or enter the war in Europe. Both of the Presidential candidates can build up their popularity by condemning Japan. Minor military clashes between Japan and the United States in China could easily lead to war. At present, American sentiment against Japan has become stronger, and this cannot be remedied by a few conciliatory gestures. Only a firm stand on our part will prevent a war. Of course, we should firmly suppress any useless anti-British and anti-American activities. . . .

. . .

HARA: The United States is a self-confident nation. Accordingly, I wonder if our taking a firm stand might not have a result quite contrary to the one we expect.

MATSUOKA: I see your point; but Japan is not Spain. We are a great power with a strong navy in Far Eastern waters. To be sure, the United States may adopt a stern attitude for a while; but I think that she will dispassionately take her interests into consideration and arrive at a reasonable attitude. As to whether she will stiffen her attitude and bring about a critical situation, or will levelheadedly reconsider, I would say that the odds are fifty-fifty.

13 Pact uniting Germany, Italy, and Japan, concluded in Berlin, 27 September 1940.[24]

The Governments of Japan, Germany and Italy, considering it as the condition precedent of any lasting peace that all nations of the world be given each its own proper place, have decided to stand by and co-operate with one another in regard to their efforts in Greater East Asia and the regions of Europe respectively wherein it is their prime purpose to establish and maintain a new order of things calculated to promote mutual prosperity and welfare of the peoples concerned. . . .

ARTICLE 1
Japan recognizes and respects the leadership of Germany and Italy in the establishment of a new order in Europe.

ARTICLE 2
Germany and Italy recognize and respect the leadership of Japan in the establishment of a new order in Greater East Asia.

ARTICLE 3
Japan, Germany and Italy agree to cooperate in their efforts on the aforesaid lines. They further undertake to assist one another with all political, economic and military means when one of the three Contracting Parties is attacked by a power at present not involved in the European War or in the Sino-Japanese Conflict.

14 Secretary of State Hull and Ambassador to the United States Kensuke Horinouchi, meeting of 8 October 1940, exchanging views on the scrap-iron and steel embargo imposed by the Roosevelt administration.[25]

I said that it was really amazing for the Government of Japan, which has been violating in the most aggravating manner valuable American rights and

24. *FRUS: Japan, 1931–1941*, 2:165.
25. Hull memorandum of conversation, in *FRUS: Japan, 1931–1941*, 2:226–27.

interests throughout most of China . . . to question the fullest privilege of this Government . . . to impose the proposed scrap iron and steel embargo, and that to go still further and call it an unfriendly act was still more amazing in the light of the conduct of the Japanese Government in disregarding all law, treaty obligations and other rights and privileges and the safety of Americans while it proceeded at the same time to seize territory by force to an ever-increasing extent. . . .

The Ambassador again said that he very much regretted the serious differences between our two countries. . . . He added that any Japanese or any American must know that strife between the two countries would be extremely tragic for both alike. . . . I went on to say that we have stood for law and order and treaty observance and justice along with genuine friendliness between our two countries; that it was clear now, however, that those who are dominating the external policies of Japan are, as we here have believed for some years, bent on the conquest by force of all worthwhile territory in the Pacific Ocean area. . . .

The Ambassador undertook to repeat the old line of talk about how fair Japan proposed to be with respect to all rights and privileges of foreign nations within its conquered territory. . . .

. . . I made it clear that it is the view of this Government that two nations, one in Europe and one in Asia, are undertaking to subjugate both of their respective areas of the world, and to place them on an international order and on a social basis resembling that of 750 years ago. In the face of this world movement, extending itself from day to day, peaceful and interested nations are to be held up to denunciation and threats if they dare to engage in any lawful acts or utterances in opposition to such wide movements of world conquest.

15 Ambassador Joseph C. Grew in Tokyo to President Roosevelt, letter of 14 December 1940, appraising the prospects for a policy of pressure against Japan.[26]

Only insuperable obstacles will now prevent the Japanese from digging in permanently in China and from pushing the southward advance, with economic control as a preliminary to political domination in the areas marked down. Economic obstacles, such as may arise from American embargoes, will seriously handicap Japan in the long run, but meanwhile they tend to push the Japanese onward in a forlorn hope of making themselves economically self-sufficient.

26. *FRUS, 1940*, vol. 4 (Washington: GPO, 1955), 469–71.

History has shown that the pendulum in Japan is always swinging between extremist and moderate policies, but as things stand today we believe that the pendulum is more likely to swing still further toward extremes than to reverse its direction. . . .

. . .

A progressively firm policy on our part will entail inevitable risks—especially risks of sudden uncalculated strokes [by Japan] . . . which might enflame the American people—but in my opinion those risks are less in degree than the far greater future dangers which we would face if we were to follow a policy of *laisser-faire*.

. . . The principal point at issue, as I see it, is not whether we must call a halt to the Japanese program, but when.

It is important constantly to bear in mind the fact that if we take measures "short of war" with no real intention to carry those measures to their final conclusion if necessary, such lack of intention will be all too obvious to the Japanese who will proceed undeterred, and even with greater incentive, on their way. Only if they become certain that we mean to fight if called upon to do so will our preliminary measures stand some chance of proving effective and of removing the necessity for war. . . .

If by such action we can bring about the eventual discrediting of Japan's present leaders, a regeneration of thought may ultimately take shape in this country, permitting the resumption of normal relations with us and leading to a readjustment of the whole Pacific problem.

16 President Roosevelt, national radio address from the White House, 29 December 1940, calling for the United States to become an "arsenal of democracy."[27]

[O]n September 27, 1940 . . . three powerful nations, two in Europe and one in Asia, joined themselves together in the threat that if the United States of America interfered with or blocked the expansion program of these three nations—a program aimed at world control—they would unite in ultimate action against the United States.

. . .

Some of our people like to believe that wars in Europe and in Asia are of no concern to us. But it is a matter of most vital concern to us that European and

27. Samuel I. Rosenman, ed., *The Public Papers and Addresses of Franklin D. Roosevelt, 1940* (New York: Macmillan, 1941), 634–35, 639–41, 643.

Asiatic war-makers should not gain control of the oceans which lead to this hemisphere.

. . .

If Great Britain goes down, the Axis powers will control the continents of Europe, Asia, Africa, Australasia, and the high seas—and they will be in a position to bring enormous military and naval resources against this hemisphere. It is no exaggeration to say that all of us, in the Americas, would be living at the point of a gun. . . .

. . .

The history of recent years proves that shootings and chains and concentration camps are not simply the transient tools but the very altars of modern dictatorships. They may talk of a "new order" in the world, but what they have in mind is only a revival of the oldest and the worst tyranny. In that there is no liberty, no religion, no hope.

. . .

Our national policy is not directed toward war. Its sole purpose is to keep war away from our country and our people.

Democracy's fight against world conquest is being greatly aided, and must be more greatly aided, by the rearmament of the United States and by sending every ounce and every ton of munitions and supplies that we can possibly spare to help the defenders who are in the front lines. . . .

. . .

We must be the great arsenal of democracy. For us this is an emergency as serious as war itself. We must apply ourselves to our task with the same resolution, the same sense of urgency, the same spirit of patriotism and sacrifice as we would show were we at war.

17   President Roosevelt to Ambassador Grew, letter of 21 January 1941, putting policy toward Japan in the context of a global struggle.[28]

[T]he fundamental proposition is that we must recognize that the hostilities in Europe, in Africa, and in Asia are all parts of a single world conflict. We must, consequently, recognize that our interests are menaced both in Europe and in the Far East. We are engaged in the task of defending our way of life and our vital national interests wherever they are seriously endangered.

28. Drafted by Alger Hiss working under Stanley K. Hornbeck, the State Department's senior specialist on East Asia. *FRUS,* 1941, vol. 4 (Washington: GPO, 1956), 6–8.

Our strategy of self-defense must be a global strategy which takes account of every front and takes advantage of every opportunity to contribute to our total security.

You [ask] . . . whether our getting into war with Japan would so handicap our help to Britain in Europe as to make the difference to Britain between victory and defeat. In this connection it seems to me that we must consider whether, if Japan should gain possession of the region of the Netherlands East Indies and the Malay Peninsula, the chances of England's winning in her struggle with Germany would not be decreased thereby. . . . The British need assistance along the lines of our generally established policies at many points, assistance which in the case of the Far East is certainly well within the realm of "possibility" so far as the capacity of the United States is concerned. Their defense strategy must in the nature of things be global. Our strategy of giving them assistance toward ensuring our own security must envisage both sending of supplies to England and helping to prevent a closing of channels of communication to and from various parts of the world, so that other important sources of supply will not be denied to the British and be added to the assets of the other side.

. . .

. . . [T]he problems which we face are so vast and so interrelated that any attempt even to state them compels one to think in terms of five continents and seven seas. . . .

18 Secretary of State Hull, comments to Ambassador Nomura Kichisaburo, 21 June 1941, indicting Japan's alignment with Germany.[29]

At a time when Nazi Germany had invaded some fifteen or twenty countries the Japanese Minister for Foreign Affairs was declaring in effect that measures of resistance by countries not already actually invaded would call for action by Japan under the Tripartite Pact. This would be like saying that if a tiger should break loose in the countryside and if a villager living a mile or so away from where the tiger is committing depredations and killing neighbors should go out and attack the tiger in order to protect his own family[,] the action of the villager would constitute aggression.

. . .

It seemed to us that the Japanese Government would decide either to as-

29. Memorandum prepared by Joseph W. Ballantine, in *FRUS: Japan, 1931–1941,* 2:483–84.

sume control of those elements in the Japanese body politic which supported Nazi Germany and its policies of aggression or to allow those elements to take over entire charge of Japan's policies. If the Japanese Government decided before it was too late that Hitler was dangerous to Japan and if then Japan decided to come forward with a program which offered a basis for cooperation along peaceful courses, we should be glad to consider such a program.

19 Japanese Imperial Conference, summary of decisions reached at the 2 July 1941 meeting, contemplating war with the United States and Britain.[30]

I. POLICY

1. The Imperial Government is determined to follow a policy which will result in the establishment of the Greater East Asia Co-Prosperity Sphere and world peace, no matter what international developments take place.

2. The Imperial Government will continue its efforts to effect a settlement of the China Incident and seek to establish a solid basis for the security and preservation of the nation. This will involve an advance into the Southern Regions [Southeast Asia] and, depending on future developments, a settlement of the Soviet Question as well.

3. The Imperial Government will carry out the above program no matter what obstacles may be encountered.

II. SUMMARY

1. Steps will be taken to bring pressure on the Chiang Regime from the Southern approaches in order to bring about its surrender. . . .

2. In order to guarantee national security and preservation, the Imperial Government will continue all necessary diplomatic negotiations with reference to the southern regions and also carry out various other plans as may be necessary. In case the diplomatic negotiations break down, preparations for a war with England and America will also be carried forward. . . .

   In carrying out the plans outlined in the foregoing article, we will not be deterred by the possibility of being involved in a war with England and America.

3. Our attitude with reference to the German-Soviet War will be based on

30. U.S. Congress, *Hearings before the Joint Committee on the Investigation of the Pearl Harbor Attack*, 79th Cong., 1st and 2nd Sess. (39 parts; Washington: GPO, 1946), pt. 20, pp. 4018–19.

the spirit of the Tri-Partite Pact. However, we will not enter the conflict for some time but will steadily proceed with military preparations against the Soviet [Union] and decide our final attitude independently. At the same time, we will continue carefully correlated activities in the diplomatic field.

In case the German-Soviet War should develop to our advantage, we will make use of our military strength, settle the Soviet question and guarantee the safety of our northern borders.

. . .

4. In carrying out the preceding article all plans, especially the use of armed forces, will be carried out in such a way as to place no serious obstacle in the path of our basic military preparations for a war with England and America.

5. In case all diplomatic means fail to prevent the entrance of America into the European War, we will proceed in harmony with our obligations under the Tri-Partite Pact. However, with reference to the time and method of employing our armed forces we will take independent action.

6. We will immediately turn our attention to placing the nation on a war basis and will take special measures to strengthen the defenses of the nation.

20 Japanese Liaison Conferences, 10 and 12 July 1941, discussing Hull's 21 June comments to Japan's ambassador.[31]

—Conference of 10 July:[32]

[ADVISER TO THE FOREIGN MINISTER SAITO YOSHIE:] The present world, divided into those who are for the maintenance of the status quo and those who are for its destruction, the democracies and the totalitarian states, is in the midst of a war. Hull's reply is for the status quo and for democracy. It is obvious that America sent it after consultation with Britain and China. Thus I think the countries that are for the status quo are getting together to put pressure on Japan. . . .

. . .

Hull's "Oral Statement"[33] contains especially outrageous language. . . . His

31. Liaison conferences were informal meetings at which the government and the military high command could seek agreement.

32. Ike, *Japan's Decision*, 94, 96–97.

33. A written statement given by Hull to the Japanese ambassador at their meeting on 21

attitude is one of contempt for Japan. I have been in the foreign service for a long time. This language is not the kind one would use toward a country of equal standing: it expresses an attitude one would take toward a protectorate or a possession. These words are inexcusable.

—Conference of 12 July:[34]

[FOREIGN MINISTER MATSUOKA:] [W]hen I read the "Oral Statement," I really felt that we should reject it immediately. It is indeed absurd. . . . [T]he United States regards Japan as either her protectorate or her dependency. . . . It is characteristic of Americans to be high-handed toward the weak. The "Statement" considers Japan a weak, dependent country. . . . I propose here and now that we reject the "Statement," and that we discontinue negotiations with the United States.

. . .

ARMY CHIEF OF STAFF SUGIYAMA [GEN]: I myself agree with the Foreign Minister's views. However, we among the military believe it is appropriate on this occasion to leave room for negotiation. It is not [yet] suitable to tell the United States that we might cut off diplomatic relations, since in the near future we plan to move troops into French Indochina, and since in the North [in Manchuria, located adjacent to the Soviet Union] we are directly faced with the grave necessity of strengthening the Kwantung Army [Japan's army in Manchuria].

MATSUOKA: I believe that the American attitude will not change, no matter what attitude Japan takes. It is the nature of the American people to take advantage of you if you show weakness. Therefore, I believe it is better to take a strong position on this occasion.

. . .

. . . [G]iven the situation, the American President is trying to lead his country into the war. There is, however, one thread of hope, which is that the American people might not follow him. The President has even managed somehow to get things that appear rather difficult to get. He finally managed to get elected three times. Roosevelt is a real demagogue. We probably cannot prevent American entry into the war in the end. . . . Japanese-American accord has been my cherished wish ever since I was young. I think there is no hope, but let us try until the very end. . . .

WAR MINISTER TOJO [HIDEKI]: Even if there is no hope, I would like to persist

---

June. It reiterated Hull's direct statement (document 18) to the ambassador but in more formal and restrained terms. *FRUS: Japan, 1931–1941*, 2:485–86.

34. Ike, *Japan's Decision*, 99–102.

to the very end. I know it is difficult; but it will be intolerable if we cannot establish the Greater East Asia Co-prosperity Sphere and settle the China Incident. Because of the Tripartite Pact, can't we at least prevent the formal participation of the United States in the war? Of course, since the "Oral Statement" affects the dignity of our national polity,[35] I believe we cannot help but reject it, in line with the Foreign Minister's judgment. However, if we sincerely convey to the Americans what we, as Japanese, believe to be right, won't they be inwardly moved?

   . . .

NAVY MINISTER OIKAWA [KOSHIRO]: According to Navy reports, it appears that Secretary of State Hull and others are not prepared to provoke a Pacific war. Since Japan does not wish to engage in a Pacific war, isn't there room for negotiation?

MATSUOKA: Is there room? What will they accept?

OIKAWA: Well, something minor.

MATSUOKA: If we say we will not use force in the South, they will probably listen. Is there anything else they would accept?

OIKAWA: Won't they accept the security of the Pacific? The Open Door Policy in China?

MATSUOKA: . . . They sent this kind of letter because they believe that we give in easily. . . .

21   Tokyo to the Japanese embassy in Washington, cable of 31 July 1941, explaining pressures prompting the move into French Indochina.[36]

Commercial and economic relations between Japan and third countries, led by England and the United States, are gradually becoming so horribly strained that we cannot endure it much longer. Consequently, our Empire, to save its very life, must take measures to secure the raw materials of the South Seas. Our Empire must immediately take steps to break asunder this ever-strengthening chain of encirclement which is being woven under the guidance and with the participation of England and the United States, acting like a cunning dragon seemingly asleep. That is why we decided to obtain military bases in French Indo-China and to have our troops occupy that territory.

35. The Japanese phrase used here was *kokutai*, meaning roughly "national structure," with the emperor at the core.

36. This despatch was decoded and made available to U.S. policymakers. *Pearl Harbor Attack: Hearings*, pt. 12, p. 9.

22 President Roosevelt, oral statement to Ambassador Nomura, 17 August 1941, warning against any further expansion by Japan.[37]

Notwithstanding [American efforts to negotiate a settlement in the Pacific], the Government of Japan has continued its military activities and its disposals of armed forces at various points in the Far East and has occupied Indochina with its military, air and naval forces.

. . .

Such being the case, this Government now finds it necessary to say to the Government of Japan that if the Japanese Government takes any further steps in pursuance of a policy or program of military domination by force or threat of force of neighboring countries, the Government of the United States will be compelled to take immediately any and all steps which it may deem necessary toward safeguarding the legitimate rights and interests of the United States and American nationals and toward insuring the safety and security of the United States.

23 Japanese Imperial Conference, 6 September 1941, resolving to prepare for war while continuing to negotiate.

—Agenda:[38]

In view of the increasingly critical situation, especially the aggressive plans being carried out by America, England, Holland and other countries, the situation in Soviet Russia and the Empire's latent potentialities, the Japanese Government will proceed as follows in carrying out its plans for the southern territories [as presented in the July 2 conference].

1. Determined not to be deterred by the possibility of being involved in a war with America (and England and Holland) in order to secure our national existence, we will proceed with war preparations so that they [will] be completed approximately toward the end of October.

2. At the same time, we will endeavor by every possible diplomatic means to have our demands agreed to by America and England. . . .

3. If by the early part of October there is no reasonable hope of having our demands agreed to in the diplomatic negotiations mentioned above, we will immediately make up our minds to get ready for war against America (and England and Holland).

37. *FRUS: Japan, 1931–1941,* 2:556–57.
38. *Pearl Harbor Attack: Hearings,* pt. 20, pp. 4022–23.

. . .

I. Japan's Minimum Demands in her Negotiations with America (and England).

1. America and England shall not intervene in or obstruct a settlement by Japan of the China incident.

. . .

2. Japan is prepared to withdraw her troops from French Indo–China as threat to the defense of the Empire.

. . .

3. America and England will cooperate with Japan in her attempt to obtain needed raw materials.

. . .

II. Maximum Concessions by Japan.

. . .

1. Japan will not use French Indo-China as a base for operations against any neighboring countries with the exception of China.

. . .

2. Japan is prepared to withdraw her troops from French Indo-China as soon as a just peace is established in the Far East.

3. Japan is prepared to guarantee the neutrality of the Philippine Islands.

—Discussion:[39]

[NAVY CHIEF OF STAFF NAGANO OSAMI:] A number of vital military supplies, including oil, are dwindling day by day. This will cause a gradual weakening of our national defense, and lead to a situation in which, if we maintain the status quo, the capacity of our Empire to act will be reduced in the days to come. Meanwhile, the defenses of American, British, and other foreign military facilities and vital points in the Far East, and the military preparedness of these countries, particularly of the United States, are being strengthened with great speed. By the latter half of next year America's military preparedness will have made great progress, and it will be difficult to cope with her. Therefore, it must be said that it would be very dangerous for our Empire to remain idle and let the days go by.

Accordingly, if our minimum demands, which are necessary for the self-preservation and self-defense of our Empire, cannot be attained through diplomacy, and ultimately we cannot avoid war, we must first make all preparations, take advantage of our opportunities, undertake aggressive military operations with determination and a dauntless attitude, and find a way out of our difficulties.

39. Ike, *Japan's Decision,* 139–40, 148, 151.

. . . We can anticipate that America will attempt to prolong the war, utilizing her impregnable position, her superior industrial power, and her abundant resources.

Our Empire does not have the means to take the offensive, overcome the enemy, and make them give up their will to fight. Moreover, we are short of resources at home, so we would very much like to avert a prolonged war. However, if we get into a prolonged war, the most important means of assuring that we will be able to bear this burden will be to seize the enemy's important military areas and sources of materials quickly at the beginning of the war, making our operational position tenable and at the same time obtaining vital materials from the areas now under hostile influence. If this first stage in our operations is carried out successfully, our Empire will have secured strategic areas in the Southwest Pacific, established an impregnable position, and laid the basis for a prolonged war, even if American military preparedness should proceed as scheduled. What happens thereafter will depend to a great extent on overall national power . . . and on developments in the world situation.

. . .

[DIRECTOR OF THE PLANNING BOARD SUZUKI TEIICHI:] . . . [A]s a result of the present overall economic blockade imposed by Great Britain and the United States, our Empire's national power is declining day by day.

Our liquid fuel stockpile, which is the most important, will reach bottom by June or July of next year, even if we impose strict wartime control on the civilian demand.

Accordingly, I believe it is vitally important for the survival of our Empire that we make up our minds to establish and stabilize a firm economic base. . . . I believe that if important areas in the South were to fall into our hands without fail in a period of three or four months, we could obtain such items as oil, bauxite, nickel, crude rubber, and tin in about six months, and we would be able to make full use of them after two years or so.

. . .

[PRESIDENT OF THE PRIVY COUNCIL HARA:] . . . [A]t the present time some people are opposed to the adjustment of relations between Japan and the United States. They might be patriots, but I feel a great anxiety when I see that some people are opposed to what the Government is doing. It is indeed deplorable that some people will resort to direct action [attacks on government officials and offices thought to favor a conciliatory policy] when our nation has its very destiny at stake. . . .

. . .

[EMPEROR HIROHITO, closing the conference by reading a poem composed by his grandfather, the Meiji emperor:] "All the seas in every quarter are as brothers to one another. Why, then, do the winds and waves of strife rage so turbulently throughout the world?"[40]

24 Secretary of State Hull to Ambassador Nomura, oral statement of 2 October 1941, fending off a Japanese proposal for a summit meeting between Roosevelt and Konoe to seek a last-minute settlement.[41]

[T]his Government has endeavored to make clear that what it envisages is a comprehensive program calling for the application uniformly to the entire Pacific area of liberal and progressive principles. From what the Japanese Government has so far indicated in regard to its purposes this Government derives the impression that the Japanese Government has in mind a program which would be circumscribed by the imposition of qualifications and exceptions to the actual application of those principles.

If this impression is correct, can the Japanese Government feel that a meeting between the responsible heads of government under such circumstances would be likely to contribute to the advancement of the high purposes which we have mutually had in mind?

. . . [I]t is the President's earnest hope that discussion of the fundamental questions may be so developed that such a meeting can be held. It is also the President's hope that the Japanese Government shares the conviction of this Government that, if the Governments of Japan and of the United States are resolved to give those principles practical and comprehensive application, the two Governments can work out a fundamental rehabilitation of the relations between the United States and Japan and contribute to the bringing about of a lasting peace with justice, equity and order in the whole Pacific area.

25 Tokyo to the Japanese embassy in Washington, cable of 21 October 1941, stressing the limited time left to break the diplomatic deadlock.[42]

The new cabinet [under Tojo] differs in no way from the former one in its sincere desire to adjust Japanese–United States relations on a fair basis. Our

40. This surprise intervention by the usually silent emperor was meant to stress the importance of diplomacy.

41. Tokyo had put the summit proposal before the Roosevelt administration in early August. *FRUS: Japan, 1931–1941*, 2:660–61.

42. This despatch was decoded and made available to U.S. policymakers. *Pearl Harbor Attack: Hearings*, pt. 12, p. 81.

country has said practically all she can say in the way of expressing of opinions and setting forth our stands. We feel that we have now reached a point where no further positive action can be taken by us except to urge the United States to reconsider her views.

We urge, therefore, that, choosing an opportune moment, . . . [you] let it be known to the United States by indirection that our country is not in a position to spend much more time discussing this matter. . . .

26 Japanese Liaison Conference, 1 November 1941, discussing military options in a tense seventeen-hour session.[43]

FINANCE MINISTER KAYA [OKINORI]: If we go along, as at present, without war, and three years hence the American fleet comes to attack us, will the Navy have a chance of winning or won't it? ⟨He asked this several times.⟩

NAVY CHIEF OF STAFF NAGANO [OSAMI]: Nobody knows.

KAYA: Will the American fleet come to attack us, or won't it?

NAGANO: I don't know. I think the chances are 50–50.

KAYA: I don't think they will come. If they should come, can we win the war on the seas? ⟨He could not very well ask the Supreme Command whether we would lose.⟩

NAGANO: We might avoid war now, but go to war three years later; or we might go to war now and plan for what the situation will be three years hence. I think it would be easier to engage in a war now. The reason is that now we have the necessary foundation for it.

KAYA: If there were chances of victory in the third year of the war, it would be all right to go to war; but according to Nagano's explanation, this is not certain. Moreover, I would judge that the chances of the United States making war on us are slight, so my conclusion must be that it would not be a good idea to declare war now.

FOREIGN MINISTER TOGO [SHIGENORI]: I, too, cannot believe that the American fleet would come and attack us. I don't believe there is any need to go to war now.

NAGANO: There is a saying, "Don't rely on what won't come." The future is uncertain; we can't take anything for granted. In three years enemy defenses in the South will be strong, and the number of enemy warships will also increase.

KAYA: Well, then, when can we go to war and win?

43. Ike, *Japan's Decision*, 201–4.

NAGANO: Now! The time for war will not come later! ⟨He said this with great emphasis.⟩

. . .

NAVY VICE CHIEF OF STAFF ITO [SEIICHI] ⟨he suddenly says at this point⟩: As far as the Navy is concerned, you can negotiate until November 20.

TSUKADA [KO; Army Vice Chief of Staff]: As for the Army, negotiations will be all right until November 13, but no later.

TOGO: You say there must be a deadline for diplomacy. As Foreign Minister, I cannot engage in diplomacy unless there is a prospect that it will be successful. I cannot accept deadlines or conditions if they make it unlikely that diplomacy will succeed. You must obviously give up the idea of going to war. ⟨Thus Togo from time to time speaks of no war and the maintenance of the status quo.⟩

. . .

TOGO: November 13 is outrageous. The Navy says November 20.

TSUKADA: Preparations for military operations are tantamount to military operations. Airplanes, surface vessels, and submarines are going to collide, I tell you. Thus the time for ending diplomatic negotiations must be the day prior to the time when preparations for military operations will be so intense as to be tantamount to military operations. That day is November 13.

NAGANO: Small collisions are incidents, and not war.

[PRIME MINISTER] Tojo and Togo: We are going to undertake both diplomacy and military operations simultaneously; so you must give your word that if diplomacy is successful we will give up going to war.

TSUKADA: That's impossible. It will be all right until November 13; but after that you will throw the Supreme Command into confusion.

SUGIYAMA [Gen; Army Chief of Staff] and Nagano: This will endanger the Supreme Command.

NAVY MINISTER SHIMADA [SHIGETARO] ⟨to Navy Vice Chief Ito⟩: It will be all right to negotiate until two days before the outbreak of war, won't it?

TSUKADA: Please keep quiet. What you've just said won't do. What deadline does the Foreign Minister want?

Thus the deadline for diplomatic negotiations became the subject of heated debate. A twenty-minute recess was called. . . . [T]he Army Chief of Staff decided that "it would be all right to carry on negotiations until November 30." Meanwhile, the Navy Chief of Staff also . . . discussed the matter. The meeting was reconvened.

TOJO: Can't we make it December 1? Can't you allow diplomatic negotiations to go on even for one day more?

TSUKADA: Absolutely not. We absolutely can't go beyond November 30. Absolutely not.

SHIMADA: Mr. Tsukada, until what time on the 30th? It will be all right until midnight, won't it?

TSUKADA: It will be all right until midnight.

27 Tokyo to the Japanese embassy in Washington, cable of 4 November 1941, voicing urgency and frustration as time runs out on negotiations.[44]

Conditions both within and without our Empire are so tense that no longer is procrastination possible, yet in our sincerity to maintain pacific relationships between the Empire of Japan and the United States of America, we have decided, as a result of these deliberations, to gamble once more on the continuance of the parleys, but this is our last effort. . . .

When the Japanese-American meetings began, who would have ever dreamt that they would drag out so long? Hoping that we could fast come to some understanding, we have already gone far out of our way and yielded and yielded. The United States does not appreciate this, but through thick and thin sticks to the self-same propositions she made to start with. Those of our people and of our officials who suspect the sincerity of the Americans are far from few. Bearing all kinds of humiliating things, our Government has repeatedly stated its sincerity and gone far, yes, too far, in giving in to them. There is just one reason why we do this—to maintain peace in the Pacific. . . . This time we are showing the limit of our friendship; this time we are making our last possible bargain, and I hope that we can thus settle all our troubles with the United States peaceably.

28 Japanese Imperial Conference, 5 November 1941, formally reaffirming the decision to prepare for war while negotiating.[45]

[PRIME MINISTER TOJO:] The Government and the Army and Navy sections of Imperial Headquarters have held eight Liaison Conferences. . . . As a result of this, we have come to the conclusion that we must now decide to go to war, set the time for military action at the beginning of December, concentrate all of our efforts on completing preparations for war, and at the same time try to break the impasse by means of diplomacy. . . .

44. This despatch was decoded and made available to U.S. policymakers. *Pearl Harbor Attack: Hearings*, pt. 12, pp. 92–93.

45. Ike, *Japan's Decision*, 211–13, 220, 229–30, 236–38.

. . .

[FOREIGN MINISTER TOGO:] The successful conclusion of the China Incident and the establishment of the Greater East Asia Co-prosperity Sphere would assure the existence of our Empire and lay the foundations for stability in East Asia. To achieve these objectives, our Empire must be prepared to sweep away any and all obstacles.

. . .

Since the outbreak of the China Incident, both the British and American Governments have obstructed our advance on the continent. On the one hand, they have aided Chiang; on the other hand, they have checked our activities in China or have stepped up their economic measures against us. Needless to say, Great Britain, which has acquired more interests than anyone else in East Asia, took all kinds of measures to obstruct us from the beginning. The United States, cooperating with her, abrogated the Japanese-American Trade Agreement, limited or banned imports and exports, and took other measures to increase her pressure on Japan. Particularly since our Empire concluded the Tripartite Pact, the United States has taken steps to encircle Japan by persuading Great Britain and the Netherlands to join her and by cooperating with the Chiang regime. Since the start of the German-Soviet war [June 1941], she has taken unfriendly action against us by supplying oil and other war materials to the Soviet Union through the Far East, despite warnings from our Government. As soon as our Empire sent troops into French Indochina . . . America's actions became increasingly undisguised. Not only did she cut off economic relations between Japan and the United States, with Central and South America going along with her, under the guise of freezing our assets; but also, in cooperation with Great Britain, China, and the Netherlands, she threatened the existence of our Empire and tried harder to prevent us from carrying out our national policies. Accordingly, our Empire, which is the stabilizing force in East Asia, was compelled to try to overcome the impasse by showing firmness and determination.

President Roosevelt has stressed, as his national policy, the rejection of "Hitlerism"—that is, policies based on force—and he has continued to aid Great Britain, which is almost tantamount to entering the war, by utilizing the economically superior position of the United States. At the same time . . . he has adopted a policy of firm pressure on Japan. In the middle of April of this year unofficial talks were begun, seeking a general improvement in relations between Japan and the United States. . . . The American Government, however, maintained an extremely firm attitude . . . and refused to make any concessions. . . . Moreover, she has taken many measures to tighten the encirclement of Japan—strengthening of military facilities in the South; encouragement to Chiang through economic assistance, supplying arms, and sending military missions; meetings with military leaders in Singapore and Manila; and holding frequent military and economic conferences in Batavia,[46] Hong Kong, etc. There has been nothing to demonstrate her sincerity. Hence we cannot help but regretfully conclude that there is no prospect of the negotiations coming to a successful conclusion quickly if things continue as they have in the past.

. . .

[PRESIDENT OF THE PLANNING BOARD SUZUKI:] In brief, it is by no means an easy task to carry on a war against Great Britain, the United States, and the Netherlands—a war that will be a protracted one—while still fighting in China, and at the same time maintain and augment the national strength needed to prosecute a war over a long period of time. . . .

. . .

[PRIME MINISTER TOJO:] We sent a large force of one million men [to China], and it has cost us well over 100,000 dead and wounded, [the grief of] their bereaved families, hardship for four years, and a national expenditure of several tens of billions of yen. We must by all means get satisfactory results from this. If we should withdraw troops stationed in China under the Japanese-Chinese treaty, China would become worse than she was before the Incident. She would even attempt to rule Manchuria, Korea, and Formosa [Taiwan]. We can expect an expansion of our country only by stationing troops. This the United States does not welcome. However, the stationing of troops that Japan insists upon is not at all unreasonable.

Concerning the Japanese-American conference of heads of state, we do not agree with each other. The United States insists that the meeting be held after the major questions have been agreed upon; whereas Japan proposes to settle the major questions at the talks.

. . .

[HARA:] . . . According to the briefing given today, the present American attitude is not just the same as the previous one, but is even more unreasonable. Therefore, I regret very much that the negotiations have little prospect of success.

It is impossible, from the standpoint of our domestic political situation and of our self-preservation, to accept all of the American demands. We must hold fast to our position. As I understand it, the Japanese-Chinese problem is the important point in the negotiations, and there is suspicion that the United States is acting as spokesman for the [Nationalist] Chungking regime. . . .

On the other hand, we cannot let the present situation continue. If we

46. The capital of the Dutch East Indies, now known as Djakarta.

miss the present opportunity to go to war, we will have to submit to American dictation. Therefore, I recognize that it is inevitable that we must decide to start a war against the United States. I will put my trust in what I have been told: namely, that things will go well in the early part of the war; and that although we will experience increasing difficulties as the war progresses, there is some prospect of success.

. . . I do not believe that the present situation would have developed out of just the China Incident. We have come to where we are because of the war between Germany and Great Britain. What we should always keep in mind here is what would happen to relations between Germany and Great Britain and Germany and the United States, all of them being countries whose population belongs to the white race, if Japan should enter the war. Hitler has said that the Japanese are a second-class race, and Germany has not declared war against the United States. Japan will take positive action against the United States. In that event, will the American people adopt the same attitude toward us psychologically that they do toward the Germans? Their indignation against the Japanese will be stronger than their hatred of Hitler. . . . [W]e must be prepared for the possibility that hatred of the yellow race might shift the hatred now being directed against Germany to Japan. . . .

. . . [W]e must . . . exercise constant care to avoid being surrounded by the entire Aryan race—which would leave Japan isolated—and take steps now to strengthen relations with Germany and Italy. . . . [D]on't let hatred of Japan become stronger than hatred of Hitler, so that everybody will in name and in fact gang up on Japan. . . .

TOJO: . . . There is still some hope for success. The reason the United States agreed to negotiate with us is that they have some weaknesses: (1) they are not prepared for operations in two oceans; (2) they have not completed strengthening their domestic structure; (3) they are short of materials for national defense (they have only enough for one year); and so on.

. . . The United States has from the beginning believed that Japan would give up because of economic pressure; but if they recognize that Japan is determined, then that is the time we should resort to diplomatic measures. . . .

If we enter into a protracted war, there will be difficulties. . . . But how can we let the United States continue to do as she pleases, even though there is some uneasiness? Two years from now we will have no petroleum for military use. Ships will stop moving. When I think about the strengthening of American defenses in the Southwest Pacific, the expansion of the American fleet, the unfinished China Incident, and so on, I see no end to difficulties. We can talk about austerity and suffering, but can our people endure such a life for a long time? The situation is not the same as it was during the Sino-Japanese War [1894–1895]. I fear that we would become a third-class nation after two or three years if we just sat tight. . . .

29 Chief of Naval Operations Admiral Harold Stark and Army Chief of Staff General George Marshall, joint memorandum to President Roosevelt, 5 November 1941, calling for postponing conflict in the Pacific.[47]

At the present time the United States Fleet in the Pacific is inferior to the Japanese Fleet, and cannot undertake an unlimited strategic offensive in the Western Pacific. In order to be able to do so, it would have to be strengthened by withdrawing practically all naval vessels from the Atlantic except those assigned to local defense forces. An unlimited offensive by the Pacific Fleet would require tremendous merchant tonnage, which could only be withdrawn from services now considered essential. The result of withdrawals from the Atlantic of naval and merchant strength might well cause the United Kingdom to lose the Battle of the Atlantic in the near future.

The current plans for war against Japan in the Far East are to conduct defensive war, in cooperation with the British and Dutch, for the defense of the Philippines and the British and Dutch Indies. . . .

. . .

The Chief of Naval Operations and the Chief of Staff are in accord in the following conclusions:

(a) The basic military policies and strategy agreed to in the United States–British Staff conversations remain sound. The primary objective of the two nations is the defeat of Germany. If Japan be defeated and Germany remain undefeated, decision will still not have been reached. In any case, an unlimited offensive war should not be undertaken against Japan, since such a war would greatly weaken the combined effort in the Atlantic against Germany, the most dangerous enemy.

(b) War between the United States and Japan should be avoided while building up the defensive forces in the Far East, until such time as Japan attacks or directly threatens territories whose security to the United States is of very great importance. . . .

. . .

47. *Pearl Harbor Attack: Hearings,* pt. 14, pp. 1061–62.

(c) If war with Japan cannot be avoided, it should follow the strategic lines of existing war plans; i.e., military operations should be primarily defensive, with the object of holding territory, and weakening Japan's economic position.

30 Ambassador Nomura to Secretary of State Hull, 20 November 1941, proposing final terms for a peaceful settlement.[48]

1. Both the Governments of Japan and the United States undertake not to make any armed advancement into any of the regions in the South-eastern Asia and the Southern Pacific area excepting the part of French Indo-China where the Japanese troops are stationed at present.

2. The Japanese Government undertakes to withdraw its troops now stationed in French Indo-China upon either the restoration of peace between Japan and China or the establishment of an equitable peace in the Pacific area.

In the meantime the Government of Japan declares that it is prepared to remove its troops now stationed in the southern part of French Indo-China to the northern part of the said territory upon the conclusion of the present arrangement. . . .

3. The Governments of Japan and the United States shall cooperate with a view to securing the acquisition of those goods and commodities which the two countries need in Netherlands East Indies.

4. The Governments of Japan and the United States mutually undertake to restore their commercial relations to those prevailing prior to the freezing of the assets.

The Government of the United States shall supply Japan a required quantity of oil.

5. The Government of the United States undertakes to refrain from such measures and actions as will be prejudicial to the endeavors for the restoration of general peace between Japan and China.

31 President Roosevelt and Secretary of State Hull, comments to Ambassadors Nomura and Kurusu Saburo, 27 November 1941, blaming Japanese hard-liners for the failure of negotiations.[49]

The President proceeded to express the grateful appreciation of himself

48. *FRUS: Japan, 1931–1941*, 2:755–56.

49. Kurusu Saburo came to Washington in mid-November to assist Nomura in the final effort to avoid war. Hull memorandum, in *FRUS: Japan, 1931–1941*, 2:770–72.

and of this Government to the peace element in Japan which has worked hard in support of the movement to establish a peaceful settlement in the Pacific area. . . . The President added that in the United States most people want a peaceful solution of all matters in the Pacific area. He said that he does not give up yet although the situation is serious. . . . The President then made [the point] . . . that Japan's own best interests will not be served by following Hitlerism and courses of aggression. . . . If, however, Japan should unfortunately decide to follow Hitlerism and courses of aggression, we are convinced beyond any shadow of doubt that Japan will be the ultimate loser.

. . .

The President further referred to the matter of encirclement that Japan has been alleging. He pointed out that the Philippines were being encircled by Japan so far as that is concerned.

I [Hull] made it clear that . . . everyone knows that the Japanese slogans of co-prosperity, new order in East Asia and a controlling influence in certain areas, are all terms to express in a camouflaged manner the policy of force and conquest by Japan and the domination by military agencies of the political, economic, social and moral affairs of each of the populations conquered; and that so long as they move in that direction and continue to increase their cultural relations, military and otherwise with Hitler through such instruments as the Anti-Comintern Pact and the Tripartite Pact . . . , there could not be any real progress made on a peaceful course.

32 Japanese Imperial Conference, 1 December 1941, registering the failure of diplomacy and giving the green light for the attack on Pearl Harbor.[50]

[FOREIGN MINISTER TOGO:] America's policy toward Japan has consistently been to thwart the establishment of a New Order in East Asia, which is our immutable policy. We must recognize that if we were to accept their present proposal [for ending the conflict with China as the precondition for a Japanese-American settlement], the international position of our Empire would be reduced to a status lower than it was prior to the Manchurian Incident, and our very survival would inevitably be threatened.

First, China under Chiang's control would increasingly come to rely on Britain and the United States. . . . We would be forced to retreat completely from the mainland, and as a result our position in Manchuria would neces-

50. Ike, *Japan's Decision*, 270–73, 281–83.

sarily be weakened. Any hope of settling the China Incident would be swept away, root and branch.

Second, Britain and the United States would gain control over these regions. The prestige of our Empire would fall to the ground, and our role as stabilizer would be destroyed. Our great undertaking, the establishment of a New Order in East Asia, would be nipped in the bud.

Third, the Tripartite Pact would be reduced to a dead letter, and the reputation of our Empire abroad would decline.

...

[TOJO HIDEKI, concurrently Prime Minister, War Minister, and Minister for Home Affairs:] The so-called nationalistic organizations [in Japan] have advocated a strong foreign policy; and once diplomatic negotiations end in failure, they will very likely demand that we move southward at once. Even the owners of small and medium-sized enterprises, whose livelihood has been much affected by the recent strengthening of economic controls—to say nothing of the laboring and peasant classes—are clearly aware of the position in which our country finds itself, and their spirits are high. It appears that they tend to want the Government to take an unambiguous position in executing a strong policy. There are, however, some within our large nation who would like to avoid war as much as possible at this time; but even these people have made up their minds that as long as the United States refuses to acknowledge our legitimate position, does not remove the economic blockade, and refuses to abandon her policy of oppressing Japan, our moving southward is inevitable; and if this action leads to a clash between Japan and the United States, this also cannot be helped.

...

[PRESIDENT OF THE PRIVY COUNCIL HARA:] In negotiating with the United States, our Empire hoped to maintain peace by making one concession after another. But to our surprise, the American position from beginning to end was to say what Chiang Kai-shek wanted her to say, and to emphasize those ideals that she had stated in the past. The United States is being utterly conceited, obstinate, and disrespectful. It is regrettable indeed. We simply cannot tolerate such an attitude.

If we were to give in, we would give up in one stroke not only our gains in the Sino-Japanese and Russo-Japanese wars [of 1894–1895 and 1904–1905], but also the benefits of the Manchurian Incident. This we cannot do. We are loath to compel our people to suffer even greater hardships, on top of what they have endured during the four years since the China Incident. But it is clear that the existence of our country is being threatened, that the great achievements of the Emperor Meiji would all come to nought, and that there is nothing else we can do. Therefore, I believe that if negotiations with the United States are hopeless, then the commencement of war, in accordance with the decision of the previous Imperial Conference, is inevitable.

. . .

[TOJO:] I would now like to make one final comment. At the moment our Empire stands at the threshold of glory or oblivion. We tremble with fear in the presence of His Majesty. We subjects are keenly aware of the great responsibility we must assume from this point on. Once His Majesty reaches a decision to commence hostilities, we will all strive to repay our obligations to him, bring the Government and the military ever closer together, resolve that the nation united will go on to victory, make an all-out effort to achieve our war aims, and set His Majesty's mind at ease.

I now adjourn the meeting.

⟨During today's Conference, His Majesty nodded in agreement with the statements being made, and displayed no signs of uneasiness. He seemed to be in an excellent mood, and we were filled with awe.⟩

33 Ambassador Nomura, meeting with Secretary of State Hull, 7 December 1941, announcing an end to talks.

—The U.S. State Department account:[51]

The Japanese Ambassador asked for an appointment to see the Secretary at 1:00 p.m., but later telephoned and asked that the appointment be postponed to 1:45 as the Ambassador was not quite ready. The Ambassador and Mr. Kurusu [Saburo] arrived at the Department at 2:05 p. m. and were received by the Secretary at 2:20 [one hour after the beginning of the attack on Pearl Harbor].

The Japanese Ambassador stated that he had been instructed to deliver at 1:00 p.m. the document [which follows] which he handed the Secretary, but that he was sorry that he had been delayed owing to the need of more time to decode the message. . . .

. . .

. . . The Secretary as soon as he had finished reading the document turned to the Japanese Ambassador and said,

". . . In all my fifty years of public service I have never seen a document that was more crowded with infamous falsehoods and distortions—infamous falsehoods and distortions on a scale so huge that I never imagined until today that any Government on this planet was capable of uttering them."

51. Memorandum prepared by Joseph W. Ballantine, in *FRUS: Japan, 1931–1941,*2:786–87.

The Ambassador and Mr. Kurusu then took their leave without making any comment.

—The formal Japanese statement handed to Hull:[52]

The American Government, obsessed with its own views and opinions, may be said to be scheming for the extension of the war. While it seeks, on the one hand, to secure its rear by stabilizing the Pacific Area, it is engaged, on the other hand, in aiding Great Britain and preparing to attack, in the name of self-defense, Germany and Italy, two Powers that are striving to establish a new order in Europe. Such a policy is totally at variance with the many principles upon which the American Government proposes to found the stability of the Pacific Area through peaceful means.

Whereas the American Government, under the principles it rigidly upholds, objects to settle international issues through military pressure, it is exercising in conjunction with Great Britain and other nations pressure by economic power. Recourse to such pressure as a means of dealing with international relations should be condemned as it is at times more inhumane than military pressure.

. . . [T]he American Government desires to maintain and strengthen, in coalition with Great Britain and other Powers, its dominant position it has hitherto occupied not only in China but in other areas of East Asia. It is a fact of history that the countries of East Asia for the past hundred years or more have been compelled to observe the *status quo* under the Anglo-American policy of imperialistic exploitation and to sacrifice themselves to the prosperity of the two nations. The Japanese Government cannot tolerate the perpetuation of such a situation since it directly runs counter to Japan's fundamental policy to enable all nations to enjoy each its proper place in the world.

34 President Roosevelt, national radio address from the White House, 9 December 1941, condemning the attack on Pearl Harbor.[53]

The sudden criminal attacks perpetrated by the Japanese in the Pacific provide the climax of a decade of international immorality.

Powerful and resourceful gangsters have banded together to make war upon the whole human race. Their challenge has now been flung at the United States

---

52. *FRUS: Japan, 1931–1941*, 2:791.

53. Samuel I. Rosenman, ed., *The Public Papers and Addresses of Franklin D. Roosevelt, 1941* (New York: Harper and Brothers, 1950), 522–23, 526, 528.

of America. The Japanese have treacherously violated the long-standing peace between us. Many American soldiers and sailors have been killed by enemy action. American ships have been sunk; American airplanes have been destroyed.

The Congress and the people of the United States have accepted that challenge.

Together with other free peoples, we are now fighting to maintain our right to live among our world neighbors in freedom and in common decency, without fear of assault.

. . .

The course that Japan has followed for the past ten years in Asia has paralleled the course of Hitler and Mussolini in Europe and in Africa. Today, it has become far more than a parallel. It is actual collaboration so well calculated that all the continents of the world, and all the oceans, are now considered by the Axis strategists as one gigantic battlefield.

. . .

. . . We must be set to face a long war against crafty and powerful bandits. The attack at Pearl Harbor can be repeated at any one of many points, points in both oceans and along both our coast lines and against all the rest of the hemisphere.

It will not only be a long war, it will be a hard war. That is the basis on which we now lay all our plans. That is the yardstick by which we measure what we shall need and demand; money, materials, doubled and quadrupled production—ever-increasing. The production must be not only for our own Army and Navy and Air Forces. It must reinforce the other armies and navies and air forces fighting the Nazis and the war lords of Japan throughout the Americas and throughout the world.

. . .

. . . [T]he United States can accept no result save victory, final and complete. Not only must the shame of Japanese treachery be wiped out, but the sources of international brutality, wherever they exist, must be absolutely and finally broken.

3

The Origins of the Cold War, 1943–1952

THE ANATOMY OF A LONG CRISIS

The Cold War is a crisis unusual in its long, slow, complex, and uneven unfolding. Yet it was to have powerful ramifications among, as well as within, states around the world. By early 1945 strains over the postwar settlement began to intrude into the Soviet-American alliance. As tension between the two sides mounted through the late 1940s, Harry Truman and Joseph Stalin each sought to mobilize political and military resources at home and to enlist allies on a global scale. But direct U.S.-Soviet conflict did not result. Indeed, the chances for such a conflict diminished as Truman's and Stalin's successors grew sensitive to the costs and dangers of the rivalry and as they began the search for a modicum of restraint and stability in superpower relations. The effort to escape the Cold War would prove as long, slow, complex, and uneven as the process of interaction that had created it in the first place.

*   *   *

The alliance that carried the United States and the Soviet Union (along with Britain and China) to victory over the Axis powers was built above all on military necessity, not shared political or cultural values. The U.S. government had greeted the birth of the Bolshevik regime in 1917 with ideological hostility and even joined the intervention in the ensuing Russian civil war. Washington did not recognize Moscow until 1933 (the last power to do so), and even then relations between governments headed by Stalin and Franklin Roosevelt developed under the whip of global economic crisis and Japanese and German

Europe at the End of World War II

expansion. While FDR moved steadily toward an anti-Axis stand, Stalin shifted in 1939 to appeasement of Hitler. The surprise German attack on the USSR in June 1941 suddenly brought the Soviet and American leaders together against their new common enemy. Another surprise, the Pearl Harbor attack in December, made them formal allies.

The early stages of that alliance cast the USSR in the dependent role. Overrun by German forces, Stalin desperately needed supplies and the prompt opening of a second front in Europe that would draw away German divisions. Roosevelt was forthcoming with substantial aid, but repeated delays in opening military operations in Europe left Stalin fuming. In November 1942 American and British troops did go into action in North Africa, moving in mid-1943 into Italy; however, the overdue cross-channel invasion did not take place until June 1944.

By then Stalin's forces were on the offensive in Europe, and it was Roosevelt who needed Soviet military help in what was expected to be the last bloody phase of the war against Japan. In early February 1945, at the Yalta conference, Stalin agreed to enter the Pacific War within three months after the end of the

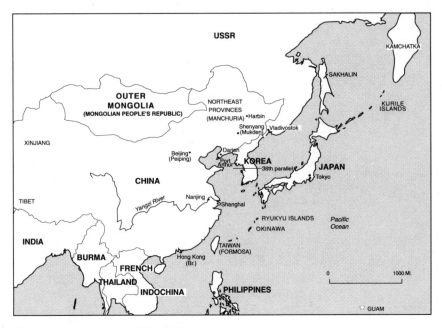

East Asia at the End of World War II

European war, asking in return the Kurile Islands, the southern half of Sakhalin, and a sphere of influence in China's northeast provinces (Manchuria). In early May Germany surrendered, and three months later Stalin made good on his promise to join the fight against Japan. Exposed to conventional and atomic bombing and now opposed by an overwhelming coalition, Japan surrendered. The alliance had triumphed.

Well before that moment of triumph Roosevelt and Stalin had tried to glimpse the shape of the postwar world. What they each saw gave them hope that wartime cooperation might continue long after the guns fell silent.

Roosevelt's views had undergone a striking evolution. He had entered the conflict in the name of the Wilsonian principles laid out in the Atlantic Charter that he had issued with British prime minister Winston Churchill in August 1941. It called for no spoils for the victors; freedom of the seas; self-determination and support for democracy; restoration of conquered states; international economic cooperation, free trade, and equal access to resources; and "the abandonment of the use of force" in favor of a "permanent system of general security."[1] Publicly, at least, FDR held to these principles, reiterating them during the war and moving toward the creation of a new league of nations.

1. U.S. Department of State, *Foreign Relations of the United States* [hereafter *FRUS*], *1941*, vol. 1 (Washington: Government Printing Office, 1958), 367–69.

Privately, however, FDR began to rethink his goal for the immediate postwar period. He foresaw a time of transition and compromise during which the allies had to maintain their working relationship. Simple universal principles should not get in the way of reconciling their divergent but not necessarily contradictory interests. In concrete terms this meant accepting Moscow's ambitions along the Soviet periphery as well as the continued existence of the British empire. Already in fall 1941 FDR had considered the formation of a postwar Anglo-American police force. By 1942 his plan envisioned the inclusion of the Soviet Union and China as well. He told Soviet foreign minister Vyacheslav Molotov in May that he wanted the four to create "a peace which would last 25 years, at least the lifetime of the present generation."[2] A year later he confirmed his commitment to a four-power condominium in the postwar period that would control Japan and Germany, preside over the United Nations as a forum for the international community, and generally maintain the peace (Document 1).

Stalin's attitudes toward the capitalist powers that had become his allies appear to have undergone an equally striking adjustment. His introversion and the limited documentation leave those attitudes less than crystal clear. Born Joseph Vissarionovich Dzugashvili in Georgia in 1879, he had attended seminary before embracing another religion, that of the struggling Bolshevik Party. He took as his new party name Stalin ("man of steel"), an identity that belied his personality but suggests the kind of control that he fixed on the Soviet party and state by the late 1920s.

Stalin had good reason to doubt his wartime bedfellows. He had witnessed their armed intervention against the new Bolshevik regime. He had seen Britain and the United States refuse to cooperate against an aggressive Hitler in the late 1930s, leaving Russia isolated and vulnerable. He had watched them, even as allies, work together to take the Italian surrender, casting the Soviet Union in the role of spectator. And he had suffered through repeated Anglo-American military delays until after the USSR had turned the tide of war against the Germans and victory was in sight. He had then complained to his allies that their delays in opening a second front—first promised for 1942, then 1943, then 1944—"leaves the Soviet Army . . . to do the fighting alone, almost single-handed, against an enemy that is still very strong and formidable."[3]

Stalin, however, defied this legacy of suspicion by searching for a way to avoid a postwar confrontation. In November 1943 he pronounced his alliance

2. *FRUS, 1942*, vol. 3 (Washington: GPO, 1961), 568–69.

3. Ministry of Foreign Affairs of the U.S.S.R., ed., *Correspondence between the Chairman of the Council of Ministers of the U.S.S.R. and the Presidents of the U.S.A. and the Prime Ministers of Great Britain during the Great Patriotic War of 1941–1945* (2 vols.; Moscow: Foreign Languages Publishing House, 1957), 2:70.

with the two major capitalist powers in good shape despite "different ideologies and social systems."[4] At the same time he associated himself with the broad Anglo-American war aims first articulated in the Atlantic Charter. A speech delivered a year later went even farther in espousing hopes for cooperation in the postwar period (Document 2).

Stalin's postwar position appears to have rested on his calculation that the Soviet-American relationship could prove mutually advantageous. In Stalin's view, FDR represented the progressive side of American capitalism, intent on promoting the reforms needed to stabilize the domestic system and stave off economic crisis. Part of that effort would be directed toward securing markets for excess production and investing surplus capital. Stalin could help Roosevelt hold economic crisis at bay and at the same time speed Soviet reconstruction by opening the USSR to American goods and capital. Such a course would not only help avert the renewal of capitalist rivalry and conflict but also gain time for the USSR to rebuild. Cooperation would also assure international acceptance of the Red Army's recovery of territory lost to Japan in 1905 and during World War I and give legitimacy to Russia's newly won dominance in eastern Europe, especially in the states that had sided with Germany during the war (Bulgaria, Hungary, and Romania) and above all in Poland.

In February 1945 Stalin joined Roosevelt and Churchill at the Yalta conference. There they sought to look beyond allied victory (already in sight) to the terms of the postwar settlement. The future of Poland at once became the most sensitive issue.

By the time of that meeting Polish-Soviet relations were tangled. Stalin had himself participated in the most recent phase of the three-century-old rivalry between Poland and Russia. He had served with the Bolshevik forces pushing the Polish invaders back toward Warsaw in 1920. He had cooperated with Hitler in the partition of Poland in 1939. And he had killed thousands of captured officers and others from the Polish elite the next year at Katyn. During the latter stages of World War II Stalin had insisted on a territorial adjustment by which Poland would give up land in the east for German land in the west. Moving the Polish-Soviet border westward was anathema to Polish nationalists even though Poland gained German eastern territory by way of compensation.

Stalin thought he saw in Stanislaus Mikolajczyk, a prominent Polish moderate associated with a government in exile in London, a possible leader for a coalition government who would not only accept the territorial change but

4. Stalin speech, 6 November 1943, in Joseph Stalin, *The Great Patriotic War of the Soviet Union* (New York: International Publishers, 1945), 67.

also try to work with the USSR. But Mikolajczyk's more conservative colleagues in the Polish government in London were in no mood for a deal with Stalin. In its own bid for power the London government ordered its 300,000-man underground army to take German-occupied Warsaw before the Red Army could arrive. Instead, the German Army crushed the rising. Through the drama Stalin did nothing to assist the Polish force.

By the eve of the Yalta conference Stalin had come to rely on the Polish Communist Party even though both Stalin and his "puppets" were wary of each other. He had executed the party leadership in 1937, and the reorganized Polish party was still, Stalin recognized, weak and divided—a poor instrument for administering Poland—and might need propping up by the USSR. The Polish party for its part knew that it needed the Red Army to gain and maintain power. But its dependency carried with it the risk of alienating Polish nationalists, stirring up the fires of anti-Russian feeling, and diminishing its own legitimacy within Poland.

At Yalta Stalin had to defend his unilateral decision to work through the Communist-controlled provisional government based in Lublin. He justified his action on the grounds of immediate wartime necessity and long-term Soviet security interests. Roosevelt conceded the legitimacy of Stalin's concerns while pressing for an allied agreement on self-determination and the creation of a broad-based Polish government. Churchill was even more emphatic in defense of an independent Poland (Documents 3 and 4). The conference closed with a declaration on liberated Europe pledging respect for democratic forms and providing a diplomatic mechanism for constituting a generally acceptable Polish government. It made no reference to Soviet security interests (Document 5).

*   *   *

The final phase of the war inevitably proved politically as well as militarily turbulent. The collapse and surrender of German forces in May and then of Japanese forces in August confronted allied leaders with a rapidly changing military situation and then peace a year or more earlier than generally expected. Postwar issues left unresolved or even unforeseen at earlier wartime conferences now required resolution, with little time for consultation and compromise.

In April 1945, with the German Third Reich in ruins and Japan under constant aerial bombardment, FDR died at his vacation retreat at Warm Springs, Georgia. His death not only added greatly to the difficulty of coordinating allied policy but also defined a watershed in U.S.-Soviet relations. Roosevelt's policy had been highly personal. An extraordinarily private man, he had not shared his thinking with most of his aides, nor had he articulated his postwar vision to the public in any but formal Wilsonian terms. Thus his postwar plans for cooperation virtually died with him.

The man who moved into the White House and who would bear responsibility for the last phase of the war and for the peace-making was familiar neither with Roosevelt's approach, nor with his wartime strategy and commitments, nor even with international affairs more generally. Harry S. Truman had grown up in Independence, Missouri. He was successful in local politics, and after ten generally undistinguished years in the Senate he had been selected in 1944 as a bland replacement on the Democratic ticket for the more liberal and controversial vice president, Henry Wallace. Roosevelt's death at a crucial juncture in the war thrust a sixty-one-year-old Truman into a genuinely difficult situation. Not only had he to act in the shadow of the great man and beloved leader. But having seen FDR only eight times in his last year, Truman had to take up the burden with perhaps less insight into Roosevelt's thinking than anyone else in the upper levels of the administration. Truman confessed to feeling overwhelmed and inadequate to the task.

With little preparation and no time for real education, a president in need of guidance fell back on his own general views. Woodrow Wilson, in whose war Truman had fought, was one source of inspiration. Truman's reading of history was another. It led him to think of international affairs in terms of a contest between civilization and barbarism waged by a succession of major powers. As he saw it, the United States had tried once under Wilson to become a force for good in world affairs but had retreated—with disastrous results. Roosevelt's leadership had brought the country a second chance, and it was Truman's responsibility to see that the country made good on it.

Truman also depended on advisers inherited from the Roosevelt administration. They were divided, however, forcing him to chose from contradictory advice, beginning with the issue of Poland. On the one side was a coalition of political conservatives and anti-Soviet diplomats previously ignored by FDR. They urged taking a firm line toward the USSR. Specifically, they argued that Poland was a test case of Soviet intentions toward the postwar world and of the American commitment to self-determination. This group included W. Averell Harriman (ambassador to the USSR), George F. Kennan (Harriman's lieutenant in the Moscow embassy), Joseph Grew (number-two man in the State Department and for a time acting secretary of state), Charles Bohlen (the State Department's Soviet expert), James Forrestal (secretary of the navy and later Truman's secretary of defense), and Senator Arthur Vandenberg (Michigan Republican and exponent of a bipartisan foreign policy).

On the other side was a diverse group that had worked closely with Roosevelt through the war. They questioned the wisdom of a hard-line policy on

Poland. They argued that a diplomacy of compromise was essential to the final phase of the war against Japan and could sustain good overall relations with Stalin into the postwar period. This group included the prominent New Dealers Harry Hopkins (FDR's close assistant), Harold Ickes (secretary of the interior), Joseph Davies (former ambassador to the Soviet Union), Henry Wallace (who had moved to head the Department of Commerce after surrendering the vice presidency), and Henry Morgenthau (secretary of the treasury), and two architects of the war effort, General George C. Marshall (army chief of staff) and Henry L. Stimson (secretary of war).

From the start the new president tilted to the side of the hard-liners. They offered clear-cut advice that was consistent with his general outlook as well as his desire to show himself, despite his inexperience, a tough, decisive policymaker. A new tone became strikingly evident when Truman held his first high-level discussions on Soviet policy in late April (Documents 6 and 7). While the hard-liners stayed on as his chief policy advisers, the former FDR intimates began to leave, some quietly because of age or illness but others in anger over the increasingly belligerent tone of policy.

Truman's get-tough attitude did not translate at once into a clear shift in policy. He needed Soviet support in bringing the Pacific War to a close, and the public wanted peace and demobilization, not a renewal of international conflict. Through the spring Truman's divided impulse was reflected in a variety of ways. During a White House visit he confronted Molotov over Soviet misconduct in Poland, and the Truman administration brusquely terminated lend-lease aid to the USSR. In private Truman professed to be militantly committed to peace. He felt that the United States was the power best suited to achieve it even if it took force (Document 8). The new president then sent Harry Hopkins to Moscow in May for an exchange of views with Stalin. The talks went over familiar ground rather than creating a fresh understanding.

Two months later, at the Potsdam conference of the Big Three—the United States, Great Britain, and the Soviet Union—Truman used both cajolery and hard bargaining to try to bring Stalin into line (Document 10). Policy continued unsettled into the fall, while Truman focused on domestic issues and left foreign policy to his new secretary of state, James F. Byrnes. Appointed just before the Potsdam conference, Byrnes brought confidence but not experience to his job. After thirty years representing South Carolina in Congress, he had directed wartime mobilization and in his only foreign policy foray had attended the Yalta conference (but not the critical horse-trading sessions). While Byrnes did not adopt Roosevelt's approach, neither did he assume a settled anti-Soviet stance. Guided chiefly by Truman and Byrnes, U.S. policy had recognized the Soviet-backed Polish government in early July and then at Potsdam had insisted on changes in the Bulgarian and Romanian governments as the price of recognition. With the war over in August, Washington resolved to contain the Soviet Union in China and to keep the Soviets out of any meaningful role in the occupation of Japan. Meanwhile, the U.S. armed forces demobilized and at the same time acquired a global system of bases.

The handling of the atomic bomb, already looming large in U.S. policy, was a straw revealing the direction of the political wind in Washington. The product of a crash program initiated by Roosevelt, the bomb proved itself on 16 July while Truman was at Potsdam wrestling over the shape of the postwar world. When the president received the news of the successful test on 21 July, he appeared "tremendously pepped up." He told Stimson that "it gave him an entirely new feeling of confidence."[5] Casually, three days later, Truman passed on the news to Stalin, who feigned indifference.

While virtual unanimity of opinion existed on dropping the remaining two bombs in the American arsenal on Japan, views on the place of the new weapon in postwar policy were less clear. In September, with the war over, Stimson tried to formulate a fresh approach that would bring this new weapon of mass destruction under international control before it poisoned relations with the Soviet Union (Document 11). Truman, however, took the alternative, and ultimately preponderant, view: that the United States should not risk its nuclear monopoly and that a growing arsenal of atomic bombs would help keep the peace and win any war. Reflecting Truman's preferences, U.S. policy through the late 1940s downplayed arms control and instead gave increasing attention to the development and deployment of nuclear weapons, culminating in the decision in 1950 to produce a "super" bomb many times more powerful than the type first tested in 1945.[6]

In early 1946 hard-line attitudes on the American side grew firmer, and any lingering official doubts about the need for confrontation disappeared. Truman's impatience both with Moscow and with Byrnes's inconclusive, freelance effort to reach some compromise played a part (Document 12). So too did a speech by Stalin in February 1946, which was widely interpreted in Washington as a declaration of hostility (Document 13). And confirming fears of Soviet intentions was the voice of experts such as George Kennan, whose "long telegram" from the Moscow embassy was avidly read in American government circles (Document 14). Moreover, Soviet behavior itself gave support to the growing consensus on the Soviet threat. Soviet troops continued their

5. Henry L. Stimson diaries, vol. 52, p. 31 (microfilm ed., reel 9), Stimson Papers, Manuscripts and Archives, Yale University Library, New Haven, Conn.

6. The first atomic weapons were based on a fission process, while the later thermonuclear or hydrogen bombs gained their greater power from fusion.

occupation of China's northeast. In Iran, the Soviet Union left occupation forces in place after the war, supported a separatist movement in the northwest (Azerbaijan), and pressed Tehran for an oil concession. When civil war began in Greece in May, the Soviet Union appeared to be the sponsor of the leftist insurgency. Next door in Turkey, Moscow applied pressure for access rights from the Black Sea to the Mediterranean through the Dardanelles.

Alarm bells began to ring in Washington, and Truman began to play a more active role in shaping policy. A string of protests and warnings were soon on their way to Moscow. Outraged by this apparent pattern of Soviet expansion, Truman roundly condemned fellow Americans who did not share his feelings and privately vented his anger at Stalin as well as American labor leaders who were making his life difficult (Documents 15 and 17). In July the president poured out his frustration to White House aide Clark Clifford and gave instructions to prepare a report developing his critical views. The resulting analysis, prepared after consultation with the national-security bureaucracy, reached Truman in late September. Its hard-line stance toward the Soviet Union articulated views that Truman either had already espoused or was strongly inclined toward (Document 18).

The ascendant attitude in Washington at last found expression in a general policy of containment. It was announced by Truman in March 1947 along with a request to Congress for support for embattled Greece and Turkey. The president took the occasion to articulate the fundamental principle behind the containment policy: the United States would support any free people threatened by communist aggression or subversion (Document 20). In June George Marshall, Byrnes's successor as secretary of state, proposed a program of economic aid to ensure stability in the vital western European sector of the containment line. And the next month, in a widely read essay, Kennan (disguised as "X") put before the public the strategic and moral implications of the Truman administration's new course (Document 22).

The drift toward a new war, with the old one still a fresh memory, stirred up controversy. Some prominent political figures questioned the administration's reading of Soviet policy and offered their own, less alarming interpretation. Henry Wallace, Truman's secretary of commerce, moved along those lines in a speech at New York's Madison Square Garden in September 1946, just as the chill began to penetrate Soviet-American relations (Document 16). Truman then fired him. The journalist Walter Lippmann had already in late 1945 asked, in a perceptive review of postwar developments, if Washington and London had been wise to challenge a Soviet sphere of interest in eastern Europe secured by the Red Army. In fall 1947—after global containment had taken form— Lippmann warned that such a sweeping policy would in practice prove inflexible and costly and might divert the United States into strategically peripheral areas.[7]

* * *

Stalin had his own worries through these first postwar years. He could take satisfaction from the gains won by the Red Army on both his western and eastern frontiers. But those gains had come at a cost. Stalin presided over a blasted land. The USSR had lost some ten million soldiers on the battlefield or in prison camps. (American deaths came to only 3 percent of that number.) Total Soviet deaths including civilians were as high as twenty-seven million. Major population centers were in ruins, famine threatened survivors, and resistance to the return of Soviet rule erupted in partisan warfare that continued to the end of the decade.

Moreover, Stalin confronted former allies who were increasingly open in their resentment of his wartime gains, suspicious of his postwar intentions, and determined to yield him no more ground. Despite the exchange of views at Yalta, Poland had remained a key point of contention. In early April 1945 Stalin offered his understanding of the formula for creating a Polish government. "[T]he three of us regarded the Polish Provisional Government [the Lublin group] as the government now functioning in Poland and subject to reconstruction as the government that should be the core of a new Government of National Unity." But, he complained, the British and American ambassadors in Moscow, who were supposed to be working with Foreign Minister Molotov on drawing other political groups into that government, sought instead "its abolition and the establishment of an entirely new government."[8]

The ill omens on the prospects for cooperation continued. Immediately after victory in Europe and despite the Soviet commitment to join in the war against Japan, the Truman administration made its abrupt and awkwardly executed decision to cut off lend-lease and persisted in an approach to the postwar eastern European settlement that made little allowance for Soviet interests. Truman surrounded the American atomic bomb project with secrecy, and at Potsdam he informed Stalin of the first successful test in only the most terse and casual terms. Stalin had already in 1942 given his blessings to the Soviet Union's own nuclear project and provided it with the fruits of Soviet

7. Lippmann, "A Year of Peacemaking," *Atlantic Monthly* 178 (December 1946): 35–40; Lippmann, *The Cold War* (originally published in 1947; reprint New York: Harper and Row, 1972), esp. 7, 14–15, 18–19, 24, 26, 35–36, 50–52. *The Cold War* draws together a series of articles Lippmann published in the *New York Herald Tribune* critically evaluating the position of "X" (George Kennan).

8. Stalin to Roosevelt, 7 April 1945, in Ministry of Foreign Affairs of the U.S.S.R., *Correspondence*, 1:314.

atomic espionage. But he accorded it prime priority, putting Lavrenti Beria in charge, only after the Potsdam conference and the destruction of Hiroshima demonstrated that the bomb could serve as a weapon of political pressure. Then, despite the Soviet Union's intervention in the Pacific War, Stalin found himself effectively excluded from a real role in the postwar occupation of Japan. By early 1946 Washington was beginning to challenge Soviet positions in northeast China and Iran.

Stalin's reaction to these developments seems to have been restrained. He maintained a rough working relationship with the Truman administration, and in his meetings with Hopkins in May and Truman in July 1945 he sought an understanding that would ratify Soviet wartime gains and win acceptance of Soviet standing as a power in the postwar world. Though irritated by U.S. policy, he couched his comments to both Hopkins and Truman in the language of realpolitik and accommodation (Documents 9 and 10).

In fall 1945 Stalin took almost three months off to recuperate from the strains of war leadership. When he returned from his Black Sea vacation in December, he held to a moderate line of policy. In his election speech of February 1946 (the one that elicited such concern in Washington) Stalin focused on the tasks of rebuilding at home and gave short shrift to international affairs. He still referred to the United States and Britain as "freedom-loving" states (Document 13). The next month the Soviet leader decried the agitation of "warmongers," singling out Churchill with his belief (as Stalin put it) that "only English-speaking nations are superior nations, who are called upon to decide the destinies of the entire world." In September Stalin offered public assurances that he felt cooperation was still possible between countries with different ideologies.[9] To calm Washington's ire he also staged a series of retreats, pulling his forces out of China's northeast, Iran, and several points in Scandinavia as well as abandoning his claim to a trusteeship over the former Italian colony of Tripolitania (now part of Libya).

Stalin's stance is notable because he eschewed the allusions to "capitalist encirclement" and the need for military readiness that others in the Kremlin had begun to invoke. In this stance he reflected his long-held belief that a war among the imperialists was a far more likely prospect than an attack on the USSR by an imperialist coalition. Guided by this belief, Stalin's cautious policy sought to avoid provocations that might create a hostile coalition and to give time for rivalry among the capitalists to ripen into a war that would bury capitalism.

But the Soviet leadership was not in agreement on this point. Molotov, Stalin's long-time associate and foreign minister since 1939, preferred to put

9. Stalin's comments of 13 March and 24 September 1946, in *J. V. Stalin on Post-War International Relations* (London: Soviet News, 1947), 3, 11–13.

the emphasis on intersystemic war (imperialist versus socialist) while not publicly challenging Stalin's emphasis on the likelihood of conflict among the leading capitalist powers. Known as "iron ass" for his astonishing work ethic, Molotov was as insular as Stalin but more anti-Western and more inclined to see in U.S. policy considerable danger to Soviet security. Just days before Stalin's election speech Molotov discussed the prospects for a new world war "encouraged by insatiable imperialists." In May he deplored the American effort "to establish naval and airbases in all parts of the globe," behind which he saw "advocates of a new imperialist domination of the world."[10] In September the Soviet ambassador in Washington offered support for Molotov's views (indeed he may have been inspired by them). The ambassador's alarmist treatment of American policy seemed to strike directly at the assumptions built into Stalin's analysis earlier in the year (Document 19).

Through the first half of 1947 Stalin remained hopeful of avoiding estrangement. When Truman laid down his doctrine, drawing an ideological line across the world, Stalin responded with a cool reaffirmation of the possibilities of cooperation (Document 21). Stalin frowned on the leftist resistance in Greece, and he called on Yugoslavia, Albania, and Bulgaria to terminate their support. Moreover, he did not immediately reject the Marshall Plan. He went so far as to send a delegation led by Molotov to Paris to explore the intentions behind the plan.

Almost at once Stalin reversed himself in what was to prove a watershed decision for Soviet policy. He had finally concluded that the United States was trying to use its economic power to tighten its grip on western Europe and to dislodge the USSR from its advanced position in eastern Europe. Soviet intelligence in London had sent word of Anglo-American consultations over how best to direct the Marshall Plan against Soviet interests, while Molotov reported from his preliminary soundings in Paris that Britain and France were "now in dire straits," so that only submission to U.S. interference would enable them "to overcome their economic difficulties."[11] Stalin decided to withdraw his delegation and closed the door to participation by the eastern Europeans.

10. Molotov speech of 6 February 1946 and statement published in Moscow on 27 May 1946, in V. M. Molotov, *Problems of Foreign Policy: Speeches and Statements, April 1945–November 1948* (Moscow: Foreign Languages Publishing House, 1949), 34, 39. For evidence of Molotov's divergent analysis of international affairs, see *Molotov Remembers: Inside Kremlin Politics—Conversations with Felix Chuev*, ed. and trans. Albert Resis (Chicago: Ivan R. Dee, 1993), 205–6, 306–7.

11. Quoted in Mikhail M. Narinsky, "The Soviet Union and the Marshall Plan" (Washington: Working Paper no. 9, the Cold War International History Project, Woodrow Wilson International Center for Scholars, March 1994), 47.

Thereafter Stalin took a tougher line. In September he pulled the most important European Communist parties more tightly under his control through a new coordinating body, the Communist Information Bureau (Cominform). Addresses delivered at the time by Politburo members Andrei Zhdanov and Molotov defined the new policy with its emphasis on the American drive to world domination. The United States was seeking a solution to its economic problems through domination of the industrially advanced areas of western Europe along with Japan, penetration of the colonial world, and creation of a cordon sanitaire around the USSR. These leaders concomitantly played down national rivalry and the threat of war within the capitalist world that might pit the United States against Britain. In a world sharply divided into two ideological camps—one socialist and the other capitalist—such divisions among capitalists, they reasoned, paled by comparison (Documents 23 and 24).

By 1948 Stalin had good reason for alarm. The United States had an atomic monopoly (though not the capacity, he realized, to wage a sustained nuclear assault), an unrivaled strategic bombing capability, and a mastery of the high seas. American might was even then being augmented by the resources of the two former enemies, Germany and Japan. Stalin for his part commanded a military force of 2.9 million men, down from 11.4 million at the end of World War II and of debatable combat effectiveness. Washington's estimates at the time of 4.5–4.7 million men made the Soviets seem a more formidable threat to western Europe than in fact they were. Any invasion force would have at once encountered 800,000 western European troops. Seen in broader terms, the 1.8 million Americans and the one million British still under arms were a match to the Soviets in numbers alone, although scattered around the globe. Already in 1947 Stalin had halted demobilization, and in 1949 and 1950 he would launch a major military buildup.

A Communist coup in February 1948 against a Czech government seeking to follow a middle way and the imposition of one-party states elsewhere in eastern Europe registered the measurable hardening of Soviet policy. And these developments would be followed in 1949 by the first of the purge trials meant to guarantee the complete reliability of these neighboring regimes. Stalin's determination to clamp down encountered resistance in Josip Tito's Yugoslavia, and in June 1948 the Cominform expelled the Yugoslavs. That same month Stalin brought his initiatives to a climax when he placed a blockade on Berlin. He wanted to disrupt the Anglo-American-French effort to unite their zones of occupation. When an American airlift nullified the blockade, he abandoned crude pressure in May 1949 in favor of diplomacy. As the United States moved toward the creation of a European military alliance (the North Atlantic Treaty Organization, or NATO) and toward West German membership, the Soviet leader countered with his own proposal for a united but demilitarized Germany. Washington was not interested.

*   *   *

With doctrinal lines of conflict laid down and tensions mounting in Europe, the Cold War gained impetus. Both sides offered increasingly strident, militarized, and global definitions of the contest that had now begun. Washington was driven in that direction by a series of new alarums, which Truman met with the advice of Secretary of State Marshall (succeeded in 1949 by Dean Acheson) and Secretary of Defense James Forrestal. To the 1948 coup in Czechoslovakia and the Berlin blockade were added in 1949 the news of the first Soviet nuclear test and the Communist victory in China over U.S.-backed Nationalist forces. In 1950 American policymakers were shaken by the conclusion of a Sino-Soviet alliance and then the invasion of South Korea.

These developments fed Truman's own sense of self-righteousness and belligerence (Document 25). They also stimulated efforts within the foreign-affairs bureaucracy to reconsider overall U.S. policy. The formal drafting process initiated in the summer of 1948 yielded its first major statement, a National Security Council[12] report (NSC-20/4) of November 1948. Truman made its conclusions the basis for U.S. policy toward the USSR (Document 26). In April 1950 the National Security Council put forward a fresh appraisal (NSC-68). It offered a stark, even cataclysmic picture of ideological struggle in the offing and concluded with proposals for a major increase in the defense budget (Document 28). Truman immediately approved the general outlines of NSC-68 but asked for more information on the costs of the programs recommended in its conclusion. Whatever doubts Truman harbored on the costs of waging the Cold War vanished with the outbreak of fighting in Korea; in late September he fully embraced NSC-68 and authorized a tripling of defense spending.

At the end of the decade the public firmly lined up behind Truman after some wavering about what to expect from the Soviet Union. Asked during the last months of the war in Europe whether Russia could be trusted to cooperate in the postwar period, a majority (55 percent) of the public had said "yes," with 31 percent responding "no." A year later, with the war over and the first public tests with the USSR underway, a survey found the numbers reversed (35 percent "yes" and 52 percent "no"). By December 1946 the public had gone through yet another shift, now splitting evenly (43 percent "yes" and 40 percent "no") over

12. The National Security Council had been created in 1947 to help the president formulate and coordinate overall foreign and strategic policy by bringing together his chief advisers, assuring him their considered views, and enabling him to be certain his decisions were properly implemented.

whether the Soviets would cooperate with the United States. Finally, two years later, in January 1949, the public had settled into a decidedly Cold War mood: only 16 percent thought Russia wanted peace and 72 percent firmly embraced the contrary view espoused by Truman and his advisers.[13]

On the Soviet side the Cold War began to take ever clearer shape between 1949 and Stalin's death in March 1953. The creation of NATO in 1949 and above all the integration of West Germany into that military alliance realized Stalin's worst fears. He now faced an anti-Soviet militarist revival and a capitalist line of encirclement stretching from Turkey to Norway. As the situation in Europe grew grimmer, Stalin looked elsewhere for revolutionary allies, especially among national-liberation movements, to counter the global U.S. containment policy. Like the United States, the USSR began to enlist "third-world" allies, including the victorious Communists in China, the Viet Minh at war with France in Vietnam, and Kim Il Sung in North Korea.

Even so, Stalin remained sanguine that he could avoid war. He stressed to a Chinese delegation in mid-1949 the powerful role that demands for international peace could play in winning time for the USSR to rebuild its economy and strengthen its defenses (Document 27). In February 1952, with barely a year of life left, Stalin returned to his long-held belief in the overriding importance of the contradictions developing within the capitalist camp. He discounted the dangers of a war breaking out between the socialist world that he led and the American-dominated camp, and he still put his bets on rivalry and ultimately conflict between the United States and its associates, especially Britain and France. Just as past conflicts among the capitalists (the two world wars) had weakened them and advanced the socialist cause (first sparking the Bolshevik revolution and then paving the way for the creation of the socialist bloc), so too future wars would pit capitalist against capitalist and eventually plunge them into their final convulsion (Document 29).

As superpower competition gained headway, it began to feed fears on both sides. Those fears eventually prompted increased diplomatic dialogue and the renewal of summit meetings in 1955 after a decade of estrangement. Those fears meant the Cold War would remain cold. Already in 1952 a Harry Truman near the end of his presidency commented soberly on the ghastly destruction that a third world war would visit on civilians no less than combatants (Document 30). Dwight Eisenhower's own early appraisal of U.S. policy, NSC-162/2 of October 1953, focused even more broadly on the dangers and costs of the Cold War. It expressed a fiscal conservatism at odds with the Truman administra-

13. The missing percentages are the "undecided." George H. Gallup, *The Gallup Poll: Public Opinion, 1935–1971* (3 vols.; New York: Random House, 1972), 1:492 (survey of 22–27 February 1945), 565 (28 February–5 March 1946), 617 (13–18 December 1946), and 2:788 (7–12 January 1949).

tion's ultimate view that the economy could sustain a large defense budget over the long haul, and Eisenhower proceeded to rein in military spending. Moreover, NSC-162/2 reflected a growing recognition of the emerging nuclear balance of terror. By the mid-1950s Eisenhower was acknowledging that nuclear war with the Soviet Union would yield no clear winner. He left office with yet a third Cold War danger on his mind. His "farewell address" of January 1961 warned that an emerging military-industrial complex threatened democratic institutions.[14]

The Soviet side was also engaged in second thoughts following Stalin's death in March 1953. In February 1956, at the Twentieth Congress of the Communist Party of the Soviet Union, Nikita Khrushchev sounded cooperative international themes even as he attacked Stalin's domestic political legacy. He argued that a new global war was not inevitable, implying that neither war within the capitalist system nor war between the capitalists and socialists was on the horizon. The two sides could enjoy friendly relations even as they engaged in a competition to determine which system would yield its people the greatest benefits. Indeed, he contended that the United States and the USSR had to coexist, even cooperate, under a nuclear threat which, Khrushchev hinted, had altered the nature of international relations. Moscow no less than Washington was now ready to concede that nuclear war would have no winners.[15]

*　*　*

Historical accounts of the origins of the Cold War are legion, and the debates over it extend all the way back to the late 1940s and continue down to the present. Two basic questions have dogged those trying to make sense of the beginnings of this superpower conflict.

First, when did the Cold War begin? Some analysts trace the origins back to the antagonisms spawned at once by the Bolshevik revolution, and others point to a date as late as 1950 and the outbreak of the Korean War. Much of the disagreement here turns on which indices offer the best measure of the growing distance between the two countries. For example, should we pay more

14. National Security Council document 162/2, 29 October 1953 (approved by Eisenhower as a statement of policy, 30 October 1953), in *FRUS, 1952–1954*, vol. 2 (Washington: GPO, 1983), esp. 576, 578–79, 586, 588–89; Eisenhower diary entry, 23 January 1956, summarizing likely effects of nuclear war, in *The Eisenhower Diaries*, ed. Robert H. Ferrell (New York: Norton, 1981), 311–12; Eisenhower's "farewell address" of 17 January 1961, in *Public Papers of the Presidents* [hereafter *PPP*]: *Dwight D. Eisenhower, 1960–61* (Washington: GPO, 1961), 1035–40.

15. Nikita S. Khrushchev, *Report of the Central Committee, CPSU to the XXth Congress of the Communist Party of the Soviet Union* (New York: New Century Publishers, 1956), esp. 17–18, 28–30, 33–34.

attention to ideological hostility, political antagonism, or military buildups? Similarly, should we give more weight to private comments and calculations than to public statements?

Second, which of the major powers was responsible for starting the Cold War? Some lay primary blame on Stalin, and others assign guilt to American leaders (while differing over whether Roosevelt shares culpability with Truman). The generic argument over responsibility follows similar lines regardless of whether blame is placed on Washington or Moscow. Essentially levelheaded policymakers, so the argument goes, sought to protect the vital interests of their country without giving in to the ideologues within their own ranks. But leaders in the other capital, increasingly driven by an aggressive outlook and by hegemonic aspirations, repeatedly violated those interests, thus strengthening the ideologues and eventually provoking justified counteractions. Mounting tensions were in turn exacerbated by systemic pressures generated by World War II—the bipolar distribution of military power, the instabilities resulting from widespread wartime destruction and the crushing of Axis power, and the mounting pressures for decolonization.

Harry Truman's policy was marked by indecision in 1945, but thereafter he seemed to see his course, in broad terms at least, fairly clearly. Joseph Stalin, by contrast, seems to have had greater difficulty deciding how best to deal with his former allies, alternately provoking and placating them at least until mid-1947. He promoted his political clients in most of the states occupied by the Red Army, demanded a colonial trusteeship, put pressure on Turkey, left his troops in Iran and China's northeast beyond their appointed time, and looted parts of Germany and China. On the other hand, he accepted the declaration on liberated Europe, discouraged the Greek resistance (even at the cost of strains with its Yugoslav sponsors), kept his distance from the Chinese Communists, acquiesced to American control in occupied Japan, relinquished a chance to impose governments in Austria and Finland, allowed free elections in Hungary and Czechoslovakia, kept the large French and Italian Communist parties within a parliamentary framework, and withdrew his troops from their forward position in Czechoslovakia, Austria, Scandinavia, and ultimately Iran and China. Precisely how (or even if) Stalin saw this patchwork as a coherent policy and where he thought he was headed are questions for readers to consider. Now is not too soon; even fuller documentation may not provide the basis for a definitive answer.

Placing this crisis in a firmly international context does not make interpretation any easier. Indeed, it may render the dynamics of the crisis even more complex and thus even harder to understand. Can a convincing case for a particular ignition point be made, and can the issue of responsibility be fruitfully addressed? Or was Soviet-American interaction a seamless web—

making compelling judgments about the beginning point for the Cold War and about responsibility for it impossible to draw? Whatever the conclusions that may emerge, these documents will certainly make clear why students of the Cold War have found their interpretive enterprise both fascinating and frustrating.

FOR FURTHER READING

Much of the literature on the origins of the Cold War has been shaped by a search for blame. Notable among the general studies that make the best case for U.S. policy by stressing either its "realism" or its "prudence" are John Lewis Gaddis, *The United States and the Origins of the Cold War, 1941–1947* (1972), and Melvyn P. Leffler, *A Preponderance of Power: National Security, the Truman Administration, and the Cold War* (1992). More critical readings of U.S. policy can be found in Gabriel Kolko, *The Politics of War: Allied Diplomacy and the World Crisis of 1943–1945* (1968); Joyce Kolko and Gabriel Kolko, *The Limits of Power: The World and United States Foreign Policy, 1945–1954* (1972); Daniel Yergin, *Shattered Peace: The Origins of the Cold War and the National Security State* (1977); and Lloyd Gardner, *Architects of Illusion: Men and Ideas in American Foreign Policy, 1941–1949* (1970). Jerald A. Combs, *American Diplomatic History: Two Centuries of Changing Interpretations* (1983), chaps. 14–15, 19, and Peter Novick, *That Noble Dream: The "Objectivity Question" and the American Historical Profession* (1988), pp. 445–57, provide reviews of the controversy generated by these two contending viewpoints.

Special studies of U.S. policy deserving of note include Robert Dallek, *Franklin D. Roosevelt and American Foreign Policy, 1932–1945* (1979); William E. Pemberton, *Harry S. Truman: Fair Dealer and Cold Warrior* (1989); Robert L. Messer, *The End of an Alliance: James F. Byrnes, Roosevelt, Truman, and the Origins of the Cold War* (1982); Les K. Adler and Thomas G. Paterson, "Red Fascism: The Merger of Nazi Germany and Soviet Russia in the American Image of Totalitarianism, 1930s-1950s," *American Historical Review* 75 (April 1970); Paterson, *Soviet-American Confrontation: Postwar Reconstruction and the Origin of the Cold War* (1973); Martin Sherwin, *A World Destroyed: The Atomic Bomb and the Grand Alliance* (1975); Walter LaFeber, "American Policy-makers, Public Opinion, and the Outbreak of the Cold War, 1945–50," in *The Origins of the Cold War in Asia,* ed. Yonosuke Nagai and Akira Iriye (1977); Bruce R. Kuniholm, *The Origins of the Cold War in the Near East: Great Power Conflict and Diplomacy in Iran, Turkey, and Greece* (1980); and Michael J. Hogan, *The Marshall Plan: America, Britain, and the Reconstruction of Western Europe, 1947–1952* (1987).

Perhaps the most useful insights on Soviet policy can be found in Albert Resis, *Stalin, the Politburo, and the Onset of the Cold War, 1945–1946* (pamphlet,

1988), and Vladislav Zubok and Constantine Pleshakov, "The Soviet Union," in *The Origins of the Cold War in Europe: International Perspectives*, ed. David Reynolds (1994), both treatments that I have relied on heavily above. But see also the fresh findings in David Holloway, *Stalin and the Bomb: The Soviet Union and Atomic Energy, 1939–1956* (1994), and in Karel Krátký on Czech-Soviet relations and Leonid Gibianski on the Soviet-Yugoslav split, both in *The Soviet Union in Eastern Europe, 1945–89*, ed. Odd Arne Westad et al. (1994). Older, still noteworthy accounts include William Taubman, *Stalin's American Policy: From Entente to Detente to Cold War* (1982); Vojtech Mastny, *Russia's Road to the Cold War: Diplomacy, Warfare and the Politics of Communism, 1941–1945* (1979); Mastny, "Stalin and the Militarization of the Cold War," *International Security* 9 (Winter 1984/85); and Matthew A. Evangelista, "Stalin's Postwar Army Reappraised," *International Security* 7 (Winter 1982/83).

DOCUMENTS

**1   President Franklin D. Roosevelt to George W. Norris,
      letter, 21 September 1943, describing the basis for great-power
      relations in the postwar period.[16]**

[W]e should have a trial or transition period after the fighting stops—we might call it even a period of trial and error.

Peoples all over the world are shell shocked—and they will require a period of recuperation before final terms are laid down in regard to boundaries, transfers of population, free intercourse, the lowering of economic barriers, planning for mutual reconstruction, etc. It has long been my thought that the world cannot successfully take up all these things if fear of war hangs over the world.

Therefore, I have been visualizing a superimposed—or if you like it, super-assumed—obligation by Russia, China, Britain and ourselves that we will act as sheriffs for the maintenance of order during the transition period. Such a period might last two or even three or four years. And, in the meantime, through the holding of many special conferences the broad ideals which you and I have in mind might be cleared up.

**2   Premier Joseph Stalin, speech of 6 November 1944, describing
      the basis for great-power relations in the postwar period.[17]**

[T]he alliance between the U.S.S.R., Great Britain, and the United States is founded not on casual, short-lived considerations but on vital and lasting interests. There need be no doubt that having stood the strain of over three years of war and being sealed with the blood of nations risen in defense of their liberty and honor, the fighting alliance of the democratic powers will all the more certainly stand the strain of the concluding phase of the war.

. . .

. . . But winning the war is not in itself synonymous with insuring for the nations lasting peace and guaranteed security in the future. The thing is not

16. Norris was a liberal Republican from Nebraska who retired from the Senate the year of this letter after forty years of service. Elliott Roosevelt, ed., *F.D.R.: His Personal Letters* (4 vols.; New York: Duell, Sloan and Pearce, 1947–50), 4:1446–47.

17. Stalin, *The Great Patriotic War*, 139–42.

only to win the war but also to render new aggression and new war impossible, if not forever then at least for a long time to come.

After her defeat Germany will of course be disarmed both in the economic and the military-political sense. It would however be naïve to think that she will not attempt to restore her might and launch new aggression. . . .

. . .

Well, what means are there to preclude fresh aggression on Germany's part . . . ?

There is only one means to this end, in addition to the complete disarmament of the aggressive nations: that is, to establish a special organization made up of representatives of the peace-loving nations to uphold peace and safeguard security; to put the necessary minimum of armed forces required for the averting of aggression at the disposal of the directing body of this organization, and to obligate this organization to employ these armed forces without delay if it becomes necessary to avert or stop aggression and punish the culprits.

. . .

Can we expect the actions of this world organization to be sufficiently effective? They will be effective if the great powers which have borne the brunt of the war against Hitler['s] Germany continue to act in a spirit of unanimity and accord. They will not be effective if this essential condition is violated.

3   President Roosevelt, Premier Stalin, and Prime Minister Winston Churchill, meeting at the Yalta conference, 6 February 1945, sparring over the future of Poland.[18]

[Roosevelt said that] he wished to see the creation of a representative government which could have the support of all the great powers and which could be composed of representatives of the principal parties of Poland . . . [and] that Poland should maintain the most friendly and co-operative relations with the Soviet Union.

. . .

[Stalin said that] . . . for the Russians [the Polish situation] was a question . . . of honor because Russia had many past grievances against Poland and desired to see them eliminated. It was [also] a question of strategic security not only because Poland was a bordering country but because throughout history

18. Meeting minutes by Charles E. Bohlen (assistant to the secretary of state), in *FRUS: The Conferences at Malta and Yalta, 1945* (Washington: GPO, 1955), 667, 669–71.

Poland had been the corridor for attack on Russia. . . . Since it was impossible by the force of Russian armies alone to close from the outside this corridor, it could be done only by Poland's own forces. It was very important, therefore, to have Poland independent, strong and democratic. . . .

. . .

[Regarding the make-up of the Polish government Stalin said]: As a military man I demand from a country liberated by the Red Army that there be no civil war in the rear. The men in the Red Army are indifferent to the type of government as long as it will maintain order and they will not be shot in the back. The [Moscow-backed] Warsaw, or Lublin, government has not badly fulfilled this task. There are, however, agents of the London government [of Polish conservatives in exile] who claim to be agents of the underground forces of resistance. I must say that no good and much evil comes from these forces. . . .

. . . [Churchill expressed doubts] that the Lublin government represents more than one third of the people and would be maintained in power if the people were free to express their opinion. . . . [T]he British Government could not agree to recognizing the Lublin government of Poland.

4   President Roosevelt to Premier Stalin, letter written at Yalta, 6 February 1945, seeking common ground on Poland.[19]

I am greatly disturbed that the three great powers do not have a meeting of minds about the political setup in Poland. It seems to me that it puts all of us in a bad light throughout the world to have you recognizing one government while we and the British are recognizing another in London. I am sure this state of affairs should not continue and that if it does it can only lead our people to think there is a breach between us, which is not the case. I am determined that there shall be no breach between ourselves and the Soviet Union. Surely there is a way to reconcile our differences.

I was very much impressed with . . . your determination that your rear must be safeguarded as your army moves into Berlin. You cannot, and we must not, tolerate any temporary government which will give your armed forces any trouble of this sort. . . .

. . .

It goes without saying that any interim government which could be formed as a result of our conference with the Poles here would be pledged to the holding of free elections in Poland at the earliest possible date. I know this is

19. *FRUS: The Conferences at Malta and Yalta*, 727–28.

completely consistent with your desire to see a new free and democratic Poland emerge from the welter of this war.

5 U.S.-Soviet-British declaration at Yalta, 12 February 1945, providing a blueprint for postwar regimes.[20]

[On a liberated Europe:] The establishment of order in Europe and the rebuilding of national economic life must be achieved by processes which will enable the liberated peoples to destroy the last vestiges of Nazism and Fascism and to creat[e] democratic institutions of their own choice. . . .

To foster the conditions in which the liberated peoples may exercise these rights, the three governments will jointly assist the people in any European liberated state or former Axis satellite state in Europe . . . to form interim governmental authorities broadly representative of all democratic elements in the population and pledged to the earliest possible establishment through free elections of governments responsive to the will of the people; and . . . to facilitate where necessary the holding of such elections.

. . .

[On Poland:] We reaffirm our common desire to see established a strong, free, independent and democratic Poland. . . .

6 President Harry S. Truman, meeting with Ambassador to the Soviet Union W. Averell Harriman, 20 April 1945, discussing the basis for future policy toward the Soviet Union.[21]

[Harriman] said that he thought the Soviet Union had two policies which they thought they could successfully pursue at the same time—one, the policy of cooperation with the United States and Great Britain, and the other, the extension of Soviet control over neighboring states through unilateral action. He said that he thought our generosity and desire to cooperate was being misinterpreted in Moscow by certain elements around Stalin as an indication that the Soviet Government could do anything that it wished without having any trouble with the United States. He said that he thought the Soviet

20. Signed 11 February 1945 and released to the press on 12 February. *FRUS: The Conferences at Malta and Yalta,* 972–73.

21. Also in attendance: Secretary of State Edward R. Stettinius and Under Secretary of State Joseph Grew. Memorandum of conversation by Bohlen, in *FRUS, 1945,* vol. 5 (Washington: GPO, 1967), 231–34.

Government did not wish to break with the United States since they needed our help in order to reduce the burden of reconstruction and that he felt we had nothing to lose by standing firm on issues that were of real importance to us. . . . The President [said] that he intended to be firm with the Russians and make no concessions from American principles or traditions for the fact of winning their favor. He said he felt that only on a give and take basis could any relations be established.

Ambassador Harriman said that in effect what we were faced with was a "barbarian invasion of Europe," that Soviet control over any foreign country did not mean merely influence on their foreign relations but the extension of the Soviet system with secret police, extinction of freedom of speech, etc., and that we had to decide what should be our attitude in the face of these unpleasant facts. He added that he was not pessimistic and felt that we could arrive at a workable basis with the Russians but that this would require a reconsideration of our policy and the abandonment of the illusion that for the immediate future the Soviet Government was going to act in accordance with the principles which the rest of the world held to in international affairs. He said that obviously certain concessions in the give and take of negotiation would have to be made. The President said that he thoroughly understood this and said that we could not, of course, expect to get 100 percent of what we wanted but that on important matters he felt that we should be able to get 85 percent.

. . .

In concluding the interview the President stated that he fully realized that he was not up on all details of foreign affairs and would rely on the Secretary of State and his Ambassadors to help him in this matter but that he did intend to be firm in his dealings with the Soviet Government. . . .

7   President Truman, meeting with his chief foreign policy advisers, 23 April 1945, discussing alternative approaches to the Soviet Union.[22]

THE PRESIDENT said that he had told Mr. [Vyacheslav] Molotov [visiting Soviet foreign minister] last night that he intended fully to carry out all the agreements reached by President Roosevelt at the Crimea [Yalta]. He added that he felt our agreements with the Soviet Union so far had been a one way street and that could not continue; it was now or never. He intended to go on with the plans for San Francisco [the meeting to organize the United Nations]

22. Memorandum of conversation by Bohlen, in *FRUS, 1945*, 5:253–55.

and if the Russians did not wish to join us they could go to hell. The President then asked in rotation the officials present for their view.

... [Secretary of War Henry L. Stimson] said in the big military matters the Soviet Government had kept their word and that the military authorities of the United States had come to count on it. In fact he said that they had often been better than their promise. He said it was important to find out what motives they had in mind in regard to these border countries and that their ideas of independence and democracy in areas that they regarded as vital to the Soviet Union are different from ours. .... In this case he said that without fully understanding how seriously the Russians took this Polish question we might be heading into very dangerous water. He remarked that 25 years ago virtually all of Poland had been Russian.

[Secretary of Navy James V. Forrestal] said that he felt that this difficulty over Poland could not be treated as an isolated incident, that there had been many evidences of the Soviet desire to dominate adjacent countries and to disregard the wishes of her allies. He said he had felt that for some time the Russians had considered that we would not object if they took over all of Eastern Europe into their power. He said it was his profound conviction that if the Russians were to be rigid in their attitude we had better have a show down with them now than later.

AMBASSADOR HARRIMAN . . . remarked that the real issue was whether we were to be a party to a program of Soviet domination of Poland. He said obviously we were faced with a possibility of a real break with the Russians but he felt that if properly handled it might be avoided....

MR. STIMSON observed that he would like to know how far the Russian reaction to a strong position on Poland would go. He said he thought that the Russians perhaps were being more realistic than we were in regard to their own security.

ADMIRAL [William] LEAHY [Chief of Staff to the President] said that he had left Yalta with the impression that the Soviet Government had no intention of permitting a free government to operate in Poland.... In his opinion the Yalta agreement was susceptible to two interpretations. He added that he felt that it was a serious matter to break with the Russians but that we should tell them that we stood for a free and independent Poland.

THE SECRETARY OF STATE [Edward R. Stettinius] . . . said he felt that [the Yalta decision on Poland] was susceptible of only one interpretation.

... [Army Chief of Staff General George C. Marshall] said from the military point of view the situation in Europe was secure but that they hoped for Soviet participation in the war against Japan at a time when it would be useful to us. The Russians had it within their power to delay their entry into the Far Eastern war until we had done all the dirty work. He said the difficulties with the Russians . . . usually straightened out. He was inclined to agree with Mr. Stimson that possibility of a break with Russia was very serious.

MR. STIMSON observed that he agreed with General Marshall and that he felt that the Russians would not yield on the Polish question. He said we must understand that outside the United States with the exception of Great Britain there was no country that understood free elections; that the party in power always ran the election. . . .

. . . The President [said that the] issue was the execution of agreements entered into between this Government and the Soviet Union. He said he intended to tell Mr. Molotov that we expected Russia to carry out the Yalta decision. . . .

. . .

The President [added] that he was satisfied that from a military point of view there was no reason why we should fail to stand up to our understanding of the Crimean [Yalta] agreements. . . .

8 President Truman, diary entry, 22 May 1945, musing on postwar great-power relations.[23]

To have a reasonably lasting peace the three great powers must be able to trust each other and they must themselves honestly want it. They must also have the confidence of the *smaller* nations. Russia hasn't the confidence of the small nations, nor has Britain. We have. I want peace and I'm willing to fight for it. It is my opinion we'll get it.

9 Premier Stalin, comments to special U.S. emissary Harry Hopkins in Moscow, 27 May 1945, on growing tensions with the United States.[24]

[Stalin said that it was the Soviet government's] impression that the American attitude towards the Soviet Union had perceptibly cooled once it

23. Robert H. Ferrell, ed., *Off the Record: The Private Papers of Harry S. Truman* (New York: Harper and Row, 1980), 35. Original source: President's Secretary's Files, Box 333, 1945, Papers of Harry S. Truman, Truman Library, Independence, Mo.

24. Also in attendance: Harriman and Soviet interpreter V. N. Pavlov. Memorandum by Bohlen, in *FRUS: The Conference of Berlin (The Potsdam Conference), 1945* (2 vols.; Washington: GPO, 1960), 1:32–33, 39–40.

became obvious that Germany was defeated, and that it was as though the Americans were saying that the Russians were no longer needed. He said he would give [some] examples:

. . .

. . . [A]t Yalta it had been agreed that the existing [Polish] government was to be reconstructed and that anyone with common sense could see that this meant that the present government was to form the basis of the new. He said no other understanding of the Yalta Agreement was possible. Despite the fact that they were simple people the Russians should not be regarded as fools. . . .

. . . [T]he manner in which [Lend Lease] had been [terminated] had been unfortunate and even brutal. . . . If the refusal to continue Lend Lease was designed as pressure on the Russians in order to soften them up then it was a fundamental mistake. . . . [R]eprisals in any form would bring about the exact opposite effect.

. . .

. . . [Stalin said that] any talk of an intention to Sovietize Poland was stupid. He said even the Polish leaders, some of whom were communists, were against the Soviet system since the Polish people did not desire collective farms or other aspects of the Soviet system. In this the Polish leaders were right since the Soviet system was not exportable—it must develop from within on the basis of a set of conditions which were not present in Poland. He said all the Soviet Union wanted was that Poland should not be in a position to open the gates to Germany and in order to prevent this Poland must be strong and demo-cratic. . . . [H]e fully recognized the right of the United States as a world power to participate in the Polish question and that the Soviet interest in Poland does not in any way exclude those of England and the United States. . . . He said the Soviet Government had recognized the Warsaw Government and concluded a treaty with it [on 21 April 1945] at a time when their Allies did not recognize this government. These were admittedly unilateral acts which would have been much better left undone but the fact was they had not met with any under-standing on the part of their Allies. The need for these actions had arisen out of the presence of Soviet troops in Poland and it would have been impossible to have waited until such time as the Allies had come to an agreement on Poland. The logic of the war against Germany demanded that the Soviet rear be as-sured and the Lublin Committee had been of great assistance to the Red Army at all times. . . .

MARSHAL STALIN said that he felt that we should examine the composition of the future Government of National Unity. He said there were eighteen or twenty ministries in the present Polish Government and that four or five of these portfolios could be given representatives of other Polish groups taken from the list submitted by Great Britain and the United States. . . .

10 President Truman's views expressed at the Potsdam conference, July 1945.

—Diary entries, 17 and 18 July, describing meetings with Stalin:[25]

Just spent a couple of hours with Stalin. . . . He'll be in the Jap War on August 15th. Finis Japs when that comes about. . . . I can deal with Stalin. He is honest—but smart as hell.

. . .

. . . Stalin's luncheon was a most satisfactory meeting. I invited him to come to the U.S. . . . He said he wanted to cooperate with U.S. in peace as we had cooperated in War but it would be harder. Said he was grossly misunderstood in U.S. and I was misunderstood in Russia. I told him that we each could help to remedy that situation in our home countries. . . .

—Comments to Stalin and Churchill, 21 July, on the future of Poland:[26]

THE PRESIDENT pointed out that the United States is very much interested in the Polish elections. There are six million Poles in the United States. A free election in Poland reported to the United States by a free press would make it much easier to deal with these Polish people. . . .

—Comments to Stalin and Churchill, 23 July, on the future of the Balkans:[27]

THE PRESIDENT said [responding to Stalin's demand for a Soviet voice in control of the Turkish straits] that . . . [h]e had come to the conclusion after a long study of history that all the wars of the last two hundred years had originated in the area from the Black Sea to the Baltic and from the eastern frontier of France to the western frontier of Russia. In the last two instances the peace of the whole world had been overturned; by Austria in the case of the previous war, and by Germany in the case of this war. He thought it should be the business of this Conference and of the coming peace conference to see that this did not happen again. . . .

THE PRESIDENT then continued that . . . our ambition was to have a Europe that was sound economically and which could support itself. He wanted a Europe that would make Russia, England, France and all other countries in it happy and with which the United States can trade and be happy as well as prosperous. . . .

25. "Ross" folder, Box 322, President's Secretary's Files, Papers of Harry S. Truman. Alternative copy: Eduard Mark, "'Today Has Been A Historical One': Harry S Truman's Diary of the Potsdam Conference," *Diplomatic History* 4 (Summer 1980): 322–23.

26. State Department minutes, in *FRUS: Conference of Berlin*, 2:206.

27. Minutes by Harriman, in *FRUS: Conference of Berlin*, 2:303–4.

—Exchange with Stalin and Churchill, 24 July, on the status of Italy and the eastern European states:[28]

TRUMAN: The first question before us is the statement on the admission of Italy, neutrals, and other satellites to the United Nations.

. . .

STALIN: To ease the situation of all satellite countries, all of them should be mentioned on an equal basis. The artificial distinction drawn [by the United States and Britain between Italy and the other satellites] prompts us to believe that satellites other than Italy are put in a leprous category. Such a distinction tends to discredit the Soviet armies. Italy was the first to surrender, but she did more harm than any other satellite state. . . .

Is the Italian government really more democratic than the governments of Hungary, Rumania, Bulgaria and Finland? Is it more responsible? No elections have been held in Italy. It is not clear to me that the benevolent attitude towards Italy has been shown to the other satellites. Italy's position has been eased by the renewal of diplomatic relations. Now a second step [a peace treaty] is proposed. Yes, let us take the second step towards Italy. But let us also take the first step towards the other satellites. That would be just. You can renew diplomatic relations with the other satellites and then you can make a peace treaty with Italy first.

CHURCHILL: We are in general agreement with the United States. . . . We have been unable to get information, or to have free access to the satellite states. As soon as we have proper access to them, and proper governments are set up, we will recognize them—not sooner. . . .

. . .

STALIN: No one of these governments can prevent access to information to the Allied governments. There were restrictions on the Soviet government's representatives in Italy.

TRUMAN: We are asking reorganization of these governments along democratic lines.

STALIN: The other satellites have democratic governments closer to the people than does Italy.

TRUMAN: I have made clear we will not recognize these governments until they are reorganized.

—Diary entry, 25 July, reacting to the successful atomic bomb test:[29]

[W]e think we have found the way to cause a disintegration of the atom. An experiment in the New Mexico desert was startling—to put it mildly. . . .

28. Notes by Benjamin V. Cohen, in *FRUS: Conference of Berlin,* 2:370–71.

29. "Ross" folder, Box 322. Alternative copy: Mark, " 'Today Has Been A Historical One,' " 323–24.

The explosion was visible for more than 200 miles and audible for 40 miles and more.[30]

This weapon is to be used against Japan between now and August 10th. I have told the Sec. of War, Mr. Stimson, to use it so that military objectives and soldiers and sailors are the target and not women and children. Even if the Japs are savages, ruthless, merciless and fanatic, we as the leader of the world for the common welfare cannot drop this terrible bomb on the old Capitol [*sic*; Kyoto] or the new [Tokyo].

. . . [W]e will issue a warning statement asking the Japs to surrender and save lives. I'm sure they will not do that, but we will have given them the chance. It is certainly a good thing for the world that Hitler[']s crowd or Stalin's did not discover this atomic bomb. It seems to be the most terrible thing ever discovered, but it can be made the most useful.

—Diary entry, 26 July, on the nature of the regime in Moscow:[31]

[T]he Russian variety [of communism] . . . isn't communism at all but just police government pure and simple. A few top hands just take clubs, pistols and concentration camps and rule the people on the lower levels.

The Communist Party in Moscow is no different in its methods and actions toward the common man than were the Czar and the Russian Nobleman (so called: they were anything but noble.) Nazis and Facists [*sic*] were worse. It seems that Sweden, Norway, Denmark and perhaps Switzerland have the only real people[']s governments on the Continent of Europe. But the rest are a bad lot from the standpoint of the people who do not believe in tyrany [*sic*].

11 Secretary of War Henry L. Stimson to President Truman, 11 September 1945, proposing talks with the Russians to avoid a nuclear arms race.[32]

[W]hen in Potsdam I talked with you about the question whether we could be safe in sharing the atomic bomb with Russia while she was still a

30. Truman's entry here draws on the information in a report (received in Potsdam on 21 July) from the overall head of the atomic bomb project, General Leslie R. Groves, describing the first successful test at Alamogordo, New Mexico.

31. "Ross" folder, Box 322. Alternative copy: Mark, " 'Today Has Been A Historical One,' " 324–25.

32. Stimson's communication consisted of a cover letter and a memorandum laying out in general terms his proposal. He personally presented both to Truman and then discussed his proposal. *FRUS, 1945*, vol. 2 (Washington: GPO, 1971), 41–43.

police state and before she put into effect provisions assuring personal rights of liberty to the individual citizen.

I still recognize the difficulty and am still convinced . . . of the ultimate importance of a change in Russian attitude toward individual liberty but I have come to the conclusion that it would not be possible to use our possession of the atomic bomb as a direct lever to produce the change. I have become convinced that any demand by us for an internal change in Russia as a condition of sharing in the atomic weapon would be so resented that it would make the objective we have in view less probable.

. . .

[Proposal:]

. . . I consider the problem of our satisfactory relations with Russia as not merely connected with but as virtually dominated by the problem of the atomic bomb. . . . These relations may be perhaps irretrievably embittered by the way in which we approach the solution of the bomb with Russia. For if we fail to approach them now and merely continue to negotiate with them, having this weapon rather ostentatiously on our hip, their suspicions and their distrust of our purposes and motives will increase. . . .

The chief lesson I have learned in a long life is that the only way you can make a man trustworthy is to trust him; and the surest way to make him untrustworthy is to distrust him and show your distrust.

If the atomic bomb were merely another though more devastating military weapon to be assimilated into our pattern of international relations, it would be one thing. . . . But I think the bomb instead constitutes merely a first step in a new control by man over the forces of nature too revolutionary and dangerous to fit into the old concepts. . . .

. . .

My idea of an approach to the Soviets would be a direct proposal after discussion with the British that we would be prepared in effect to enter an arrangement with the Russians, the general purpose of which would be to control and limit the use of the atomic bomb as an instrument of war and so far as possible to direct and encourage the development of atomic power for peaceful and humanitarian purposes. Such an approach might more specifically lead to the proposal that we would stop work on the further improvement in, or manufacture of, the bomb as a military weapon, provided the Russians and the British would agree to do likewise. It might also provide that we would be willing to impound what bombs we now have in the United States provided the Russians and the British would agree with us that in no event will they or we use a bomb as an instrument of war unless all three Governments agree to that use. We might also consider including in the arrangement a covenant with the U.K. [United Kingdom] and the Soviets providing for the exchange of benefits of future developments whereby atomic energy may be applied on a mutually satisfactory basis for commercial or humanitarian purposes.

12 President Truman to Secretary of State James F. Byrnes, letter (unsent) of 5 January 1946, arguing for a firm line against Soviet expansion around the world.[33]

I think we ought to protest with all the vigor of which we are capable [against] the Russian program in Iran. There is no justification for it. It is a parallel to the program of Russia in Latvia, Estonia and Lithuania. It is also in line with the high handed and arbitrary manner in which Russia acted in Poland.

. . .

Iran was our ally in the war. Iran was Russia's ally in the war. . . . Yet now Russia stirs up rebellion and keeps troops on the soil of her friend and ally, Iran.

There isn't a doubt in my mind that Russia intends an invasion of Turkey and the seizure of the Black Sea Straits to the Mediterranean. Unless Russia is faced with an iron fist and strong language another war is in the making. Only one language do they understand—"How many divisions have you?"

I do not think we should play compromise any longer. We should refuse to recognize Rumania and Bulgaria until they comply with our requirements; we should let our position on Iran be known in no uncertain terms and . . . we should maintain complete control of Japan and the Pacific. We should rehabilitate China and create a strong central government there. We should do the same for Korea.

Then we should insist on the return of our ships from Russia and force a settlement of the Lend-Lease Debt of Russia.

I'm tired babying the Soviets.

13 Premier Stalin, radio address, 9 February 1946, offering a broad review of World War II and current concerns.[34]

[The Second World War] was the inevitable result of the development of world economic and political forces on the basis of modern monopoly capital-

---

33. Ferrell, *Off the Record*, 79–80. Original source: President's Secretary's Files, Box 333, 1946, Papers of Harry S. Truman.

34. Stalin delivered the speech in the Bolshoi Theater in Moscow after his nomination as

ism. Marxists have declared more than once that the capitalist system of world economy harbors elements of general crises and armed conflicts and that, hence, the development of world capitalism in our time proceeds not in the form of smooth and even progress but through crises and military catastrophes.

The fact is, that the unevenness of development of the capitalist countries usually leads in time to violent disturbance of equilibrium in the world system of capitalism, that group of capitalist countries which considers itself worse provided than others with raw materials and markets usually making attempts to alter the situation and repartition the "spheres of influence" in its favor by armed force. The result is a splitting of the capitalist world into two hostile camps and war between them.

. . .

That does not mean of course that the Second World War is a copy of the first. . . .

. . . [U]nlike the First World War, the Second World War against the Axis states from the very outset assumed the character of an anti-fascist war, a war of liberation, one the aim of which was also the restoration of democratic liberties. The entry of the Soviet Union into the war against the Axis states could only enhance, and indeed did enhance, the anti-fascist and liberation character of the Second World War.

It was on this basis that the anti-fascist coalition of the Soviet Union, the United States of America, Great Britain, and other freedom-loving states came into being. . . .

And so, what are the results of the war?

. . .

Our victory means, first of all, that our Soviet social order . . . has successfully passed the ordeal in the fire of war and has proved its unquestionable vitality.

. . .

Second, our victory means . . . that our multinational Soviet State has stood all the trials of war and has proved its vitality.

. . .

Third, our victory means . . . that the Red Army bore up heroically under all the trials of war, utterly routed the armies of our enemies and came out of the war as a victor.

. . .

---

a deputy to the Supreme Soviet. U.S. House of Representatives, Committee on Foreign Affairs, *The Strategy and Tactics of World Communism,* Supplement I, *One Hundred Years of Communism, 1848–1948* (Washington: GPO, 1948; House document #619), 168–71, 176–77.

Now a few words about the Communist Party's plans of work for the immediate future. As is known these plans are set forth in the new Five-Year Plan which is shortly to be endorsed. The principal aims of the new Five-Year Plan are to rehabilitate the ravaged areas of the country, to restore the prewar level in industry and agriculture, and then to surpass this level in more or less substantial measure. . . .

. . .

As regards the plans for a longer period ahead, the Party means to organize a new mighty upsurge in the national economy, which would allow us to increase our industrial production, for example, three times over as compared with the prewar period. . . . Only under such conditions can we consider that our homeland will be guaranteed against all possible accidents.[35] (*Stormy applause.*) That will take three more Five-Year Plans, I should think, if not more. But it can be done and we must do it. (*Stormy applause.*)

14 U.S. Chargé in the Soviet Union George F. Kennan to the State Department, "long telegram" of 22 February 1946, analyzing Soviet policy.[36]

At bottom of Kremlin's neurotic view of world affairs is traditional and instinctive Russian sense of insecurity. . . . [Russian rulers] have always feared foreign penetration, feared direct contact between Western world and their own, feared what would happen if Russians learned truth about world without or if foreigners learned truth about world within. And they have learned to seek security only in patient but deadly struggle for total destruction of rival power, never in compacts and compromises with it.

. . . After establishment of Bolshevist regime, Marxist dogma . . . became a perfect vehicle for sense of insecurity with which Bolsheviks, even more than previous Russian rulers, were afflicted. In this dogma, with its basic altruism of purpose, they found justification for their instinctive fear of outside world, for the dictatorship without which they did not know how to rule, for cruelties they did not dare not to inflict, for sacrifices they felt bound to demand. In the name of Marxism they sacrificed every single ethical value in their methods and tactics. Today they cannot dispense with it. It is fig leaf of their moral and intellectual respectability. Without it they would stand before history, at best, as only the last of that long succession of cruel and wasteful Russian rulers who have relentlessly forced country on to ever new heights of military power in

35. This phrase was also translated at the time as "our country will be insured against any eventuality." *Vital Speeches of the Day* 12 (1 March 1946): 303.

36. *FRUS, 1946*, vol. 6 (Washington: GPO, 1969): 699–700, 706–7.

order to guarantee external security of their internally weak regimes. . . . [Their dogma depicts the] outside world as evil, hostile and menacing, but as bearing within itself germs of creeping disease and destined to be wracked with growing internal convulsions until it is given final *coup de grace* by rising power of socialism and yields to new and better world. This thesis provides justification for that increase of military and police power of Russian state, for that isolation of Russian population from outside world, and for that fluid and constant pressure to extend limits of Russian police power which are together the natural and instinctive urges of Russian rulers. Basically this is only the steady advance of uneasy Russian nationalism. . . . But in new guise of international Marxism, with its honeyed promises to a desperate and war torn outside world, it is more dangerous and insidious than ever before.

. . .

. . . [W]e have here a political force committed fanatically to the belief that with US there can be no permanent *modus vivendi,* that it is desirable and necessary that the internal harmony of our society be disrupted, our traditional way of life be destroyed, the international authority of our state be broken, if Soviet power is to be secure. This political force has complete power of disposition over energies of one of world's greatest peoples and resources of world's richest national territory, and is borne along by deep and powerful currents of Russian nationalism. In addition, it has an elaborate and far flung apparatus for exertion of its influence in other countries, an apparatus of amazing flexibility and versatility, managed by people whose experience and skill in underground methods are presumably without parallel in history. Finally, it is seemingly inaccessible to considerations of reality in its basic reactions. . . . Problem of how to cope with this force . . . [is] undoubtedly greatest task our diplomacy has ever faced and probably greatest it will ever have to face. . . .

15 President Truman, note to himself [June 1946], expressing frustration over obstacles to his policies at home and abroad.[37]

Call in [leaders of the major unions at the forefront of labor unrest]. Tell them that patience is exhausted. Declare an emergency—call out the troops. Start industry and put anyone to work who wants to work. If any leader interferes, courtmartial him. [The head of the United Mine Workers John L.]

37. Monte M. Poen, ed., *Strictly Personal and Confidential: The Letters Harry Truman Never Mailed* (Boston: Little, Brown, 1982), 31. The ellipsis represents an omission in the published text. Original source: "Personal Memos, 1946," Box 333, President's Secretary's Files.

Lewis ought to have been shot in 1942, but Franklin [Roosevelt] didn't have the guts to do it.... Adjourn Congress and run the country.

Get plenty of Atomic Bombs on hand—drop one on Stalin, put the United Nations to work and eventually set up a free world.

16 Secretary of Commerce Henry A. Wallace, speech in New York, 12 September 1946, defining the basis for cooperative U.S.-Soviet relations.[38]

To achieve lasting peace, we must study in detail just how the Russian character was formed—by invasions of Tartars, Mongols, Germans, Poles, Swedes, and French; by the czarist rule based on ignorance, fear, and force; by the intervention of the British, French, and Americans in Russian affairs from 1919 to 1921; by the geography of the huge Russian land mass situated strategically between Europe and Asia; and by the vitality derived from the rich Russian soil and the strenuous Russian climate. Add to all this the tremendous emotional power which Marxism and Leninism gives to the Russian leaders—and then we can realize that we are reckoning with a force which cannot be handled successfully by a "Get tough with Russia" policy. . . .

. . .

. . . [W]e should recognize that we have no more business in the *political* affairs of eastern Europe than Russia has in the *political* affairs of Latin America, western Europe, and the United States. We may not like what Russia does in eastern Europe. . . .

But whether we like it or not the Russians will try to socialize their sphere of influence just as we try to democratize our sphere of influence. This applies also to Germany and Japan. We are striving to democratize Japan and our area of control in Germany, while Russia strives to socialize eastern Germany.

. . .

Russia must be convinced that we are not planning for war against her and we must be certain that Russia is not carrying on territorial expansion or world domination through native communists faithfully following every twist and turn in the Moscow party line. But in this competition, we must insist on an open door for trade throughout the world. There will always be an ideological conflict—but that is no reason why diplomats cannot work out a basis for both systems to live safely in the world side by side.

38. John Morton Blum, ed., *The Price of Vision: The Diary of Henry A. Wallace* (Boston: Houghton Mifflin, 1973), 664–68. Identical copy in *Vital Speeches of the Day* 12 (1 October 1946): 738–41.

. . .

In the United States . . . the people can be organized for peace—even though a large segment of our press is propagandizing our people for war in the hope of scaring Russia. And we who look on this war-with-Russia talk as criminal foolishness must carry our message direct to the people—even though we may be called communists because we dare to speak out.

17 President Truman, memo of 19 September 1946, registering deep disagreement with Henry Wallace.[39]

Mr. Wallace spent two and one half hours talking to me yesterday. I am not sure he is as fundamentally sound intellectually as I had thought. . . .

He is a pacifist one hundred percent. He wants us to disband our armed forces, give Russia our atomic secrets and trust a bunch of adventurers in the Kremlin Politburo. I do not understand a "dreamer" like that. . . . The Reds, phonies and the "parlor pinks" seem to be banded together and are becoming a national danger.

I am afraid that they are a sabotage front for Uncle Joe Stalin. They can see no wrong in Russia's four and one half million armed forces, in Russia's loot of Poland, Austria, Hungary, Rumania, Manchuria. They can see no wrong in Russia's living off the occupied countries to support the military occupation.

18 Special Counsel to the President Clark M. Clifford to President Truman, top-secret report of 24 September 1946 on "American Relations with the Soviet Union."[40]

As long as the Soviet Government maintains its present foreign policy, based upon the theory of an ultimate struggle between Communism and Capitalism, the United States must assume that the U.S.S.R. might fight at any time for the twofold purpose of expanding the territory under communist control and weakening its potential capitalist opponents. The Soviet Union was able to flow into the political vacuum of the Balkans, Eastern Europe, the Near East,

39. Truman memorandum quoted in extenso in Margaret Truman, *Harry S. Truman* (New York: William Morrow, 1973), 317–18.

40. George Elsey, Clifford's junior in the White House staff, helped in drafting this report. Thomas H. Etzold and John Lewis Gaddis, eds., *Containment: Documents on American Policy and Strategy, 1945–1950* (New York: Columbia University Press, 1978), 65–68, 70–71. Original source: Book Collection, Harry S. Truman Library.

Manchuria and Korea because no other nation was both willing and able to prevent it. Soviet leaders were encouraged by easy success and they are now preparing to take over new areas in the same way. The Soviet Union, as Stalin euphemistically phrased it, is preparing "for any eventuality."[41]

. . .

The language of military power is the only language which disciples of power politics understand. The United States must use that language in order that Soviet leaders will realize that our government is determined to uphold the interests of its citizens and the rights of small nations. Compromise and concessions are considered, by the Soviets, to be evidences of weakness and they are encouraged by our "retreats" to make new and greater demands.

. . .

. . . [I]n order to maintain our strength at a level which will be effective in restraining the Soviet Union, the United States must be prepared to wage atomic and biological warfare. A highly mechanized army, which can be moved either by sea or by air, capable of seizing and holding strategic areas, must be supported by powerful naval and air forces. . . .

. . .

The United States, with a military potential composed primarily of highly effective technical weapons, should entertain no proposal for disarmament or limitation of armament as long as the possibility of Soviet aggression exists. . . .

. . .

In addition to maintaining our own strength, the United States should support and assist all democratic countries which are in any way menaced or endangered by the U.S.S.R. Providing military support in case of attack is a last resort; a more effective barrier to communism is strong economic support. Trade agreements, loans and technical missions strengthen our ties with friendly nations and are effective demonstrations that capitalism is at least the equal of communism. . . .

. . .

There are some trouble-spots which will require diligent and considered effort on the part of the United States if Soviet penetration and eventual domination is to be prevented. In the Far East, for example, this country should continue to strive for a unified and economically stable China, a reconstructed and democratic Japan, and a unified and independent Korea. We must ensure Philippine prosperity and we should assist in the peaceful solution, along noncommunistic lines, of the political problems of Southeast Asia and India.

41. Clifford refers here to Stalin's 9 February 1946 speech (Document 13).

. . .

Only a well-informed public will support the stern policies which Soviet activities make imperative and which the United States Government must adopt. The American people should be fully informed about the difficulties in getting along with the Soviet Union, and the record of Soviet evasion, misrepresentation, aggression and militarism should be made public.

. . .

Even though Soviet leaders profess to believe that the conflict between Capitalism and Communism is irreconcilable and must eventually be resolved by the triumph of the latter, it is our hope that they will change their minds and work out with us a fair and equitable settlement when they realize that we are too strong to be beaten and too determined to be frightened.

19 Soviet ambassador to the United States Nikolai Novikov to Foreign Minister Vyacheslav M. Molotov, 27 September 1946, analyzing U.S. policy.[42]

The foreign policy of the United States, which reflects the imperialist tendencies of American monopolistic capital, is characterized in the postwar period by a striving <u>for world supremacy</u>.[43] This is the real meaning of the many statements by President Truman and other representatives of American ruling circles: that the United States has the right to lead the world. . . .

. . .

[1.] Europe has come out of the war with a completely dislocated economy. . . . All of the countries of Europe and Asia are experiencing a colossal need for consumer goods, industrial and transportation equipment, etc. Such a situation provides American monopolistic capital with <u>prospects for enormous shipments of goods and the importation of capital</u> into these countries—a circumstance that would permit it to infiltrate their national economies.

Such a development would mean a serious strengthening of the economic

42. While Novikov was in Paris working with Molotov, his boss pressed for an analysis of U.S. policy. Novikov objected that he had neither time nor documentation. Molotov insisted. Handed the report at the end of the month, the foreign minister went over it carefully. Albert Resis review, *Russian History* 20 (1993): 403–5. Underlining here indicates sections Molotov marked for attention. This telegram comes from the Soviet Foreign Ministry archives. It was supplied by Vladimir Shustov and translated by John Glad. Kenneth M. Jensen, ed., *Origins of the Cold War: The Novikov, Kennan, and Roberts 'Long Telegrams' of 1946* (Washington: United States Institute of Peace Research, 1991), 3–8, 10–16.

43. Molotov marginal query: "A difference from [the] prewar [period]?"

position of the United States in the whole world and would be a stage on the road to world domination by the United States.

. . .

[Meanwhile] despite all of the economic difficulties of the postwar period connected with the enormous losses inflicted by the war and the German fascist occupation, the Soviet Union continues to remain economically independent of the outside world and is rebuilding its national economy with its own forces.

At the same time the USSR's international position is currently stronger than it was in the prewar period. Thanks to the historical victories of Soviet weapons, the Soviet armed forces are located on the territory of Germany and other formerly hostile countries, thus guaranteeing that these countries will not be used again for an attack on the USSR. In formerly hostile countries, such as Bulgaria, Finland, Hungary, and Romania, democratic reconstruction has established regimes that have undertaken to strengthen and maintain friendly relations with the Soviet Union. In the Slavic countries that were liberated by the Red Army or with its assistance—Poland, Czechoslovakia, and Yugoslavia—democratic regimes have also been established that maintain relations with the Soviet Union on the basis of agreements on friendship and mutual assistance.

. . .

Such a situation in Eastern and Southeastern Europe cannot help but be regarded by the American imperialists as an obstacle in the path of the expansionist policy of the United States.

[2.] The foreign policy of the United States is not determined at present by the circles in the Democratic party that (as was the case during Roosevelt's lifetime) strive to strengthen the cooperation of the three great powers that constituted the basis of the anti-Hitler coalition during the war. The ascendance to power of President Truman, a politically unstable person but with certain conservative tendencies, and the subsequent appointment of [James] Byrnes as Secretary of State meant a strengthening of the influence on U.S. foreign policy of the most reactionary circles of the Democratic party. The constantly increasing reactionary nature of the foreign policy course of the United States . . . laid the groundwork for close cooperation in this field between the far right wing of the Democratic party and the Republican party. This cooperation of the two parties . . . took shape in both houses of Congress in the form of an unofficial bloc of reactionary Southern Democrats and the old guard of the Republicans headed by [Senator Arthur] Vandenberg and [Senator Robert] Taft. . . .

. . .

3. Obvious indications of the U.S. effort to establish world dominance are also to be found in the increase in military potential in peacetime and in the establishment of a large number of naval and air bases both in the United States and beyond its borders.

In the summer of 1946, for the first time in the history of the country, Congress passed a law on the establishment of a peacetime army, not on a volunteer basis but on the basis of universal military service. The size of the army, which is supposed to amount to about one million persons as of July 1, 1947, was also increased significantly. . . . At the present time, the American navy occupies first place in the world, leaving England's navy far behind, to say nothing of those of other countries.

Expenditures on the army and navy have risen colossally, amounting to 13 billion dollars according to the budget for 1946–47 (about 40 percent of the total budget of 36 billion dollars). This is more than ten times greater than corresponding expenditures in the budget for 1938, which did not amount to even one billion dollars.

. . .

The establishment of American bases on islands that are often 10,000 to 12,000 kilometers from the territory of the United States and are on the other side of the Atlantic and Pacific oceans clearly indicates the offensive nature of the strategic concepts of the commands of the U.S. army and navy. . . .

. . .

[4.] One of the stages in the achievement of dominance over the world by the United States is its understanding with England concerning the partial division of the world on the basis of mutual concessions. . . . [Those two countries have agreed to include] Japan and China in the sphere of influence of the United States in the Far East, while the United States, for its part, has agreed not to hinder England either in resolving the Indian [demands for independence] or in strengthening its influence in Siam [Thailand] and Indonesia.

. . .

[5.] In recent years American capital has penetrated very intensively into the economy of the Near Eastern countries, in particular into the oil industry. . . .

In expanding in the Near East, American capital has English capital as its greatest and most stubborn competitor. The fierce competition between them is the chief factor preventing England and the United States from reaching an understanding on the division of spheres of influence in the Near East. . . .

. . .

The irregular nature of relations between England and the United States in the Near East is manifested in part also in the great activity of the American naval fleet in the eastern part of the Mediterranean Sea. Such activity cannot help but be in conflict with the basic interests of the British Empire. These actions on the part of the U.S. fleet undoubtedly are also linked with American oil and other economic interests in the Near East.

. . . The strengthening of U.S. positions in the Near East and the establishment of conditions for basing the American navy at one or more points on the Mediterranean Sea . . . signify the emergence of a new threat to the security of the southern regions of the Soviet Union.

[6.] Relations between the United States and England are determined by two basic circumstances. On the one hand, the United States regards England as its greatest potential competitor; on the other hand, England constitutes a possible ally for the United States. Division of certain regions of the globe into spheres of influence of the United States and England would create the opportunity, if not for preventing competition between them, which is impossible, then at least of reducing it. At the same time, such a division facilitates the achievement of economic and political cooperation between them.

England needs American credits for reorganizing its economy, which was disrupted by the war. To obtain such credits England is compelled to make significant concessions. . . .

. . . At recent international conferences the United States and England have closely coordinated their policies, especially in cases when they had to oppose the policy of the Soviet Union. . . .

The ruling circles of the United States obviously have a sympathetic attitude toward the idea of a military alliance with England, but at the present time the matter has not yet culminated in an official alliance. . . .

. . .

The current relations between England and the United States, despite the temporary attainment of agreements on very important questions, are plagued with great internal contradictions and cannot be lasting.

. . .

[7.] The "hard-line" policy with regard to the USSR[:] . . . [T]he United States no longer follows a policy of strengthening cooperation among the Big Three (or Four) but rather has striven to undermine the unity of these countries. The objective has been to impose the will of other countries on the Soviet Union. . . . [The United States has given its blessings to efforts] to undermine or completely abolish the principle of the veto in the Security Council of the United Nations. This would give the United States opportunities to form among the Great Powers narrow groupings and blocs directed primarily against the Soviet Union, and . . . would transform the United Nations into an Anglo-Saxon domain in which the United States would play the leading role.

The present policy of the American government with regard to the USSR is also directed at limiting or dislodging the influence of the Soviet Union from neighboring countries. In implementing this policy in former enemy or Allied countries adjacent to the USSR, the United States attempts . . . to support reactionary forces with the purpose of creating obstacles to the process of democratization of these countries. In so doing, it also attempts to secure positions for the penetration of American capital into their economies. Such a policy is intended to weaken and overthrow the democratic governments in power there, which are friendly toward the USSR, and replace them in the future with new governments that would obediently carry out a policy dictated from the United States. . . .

. . .

. . . [T]he United States is considering the possibility of terminating the Allied occupation of German territory before the main tasks of the occupation—the demilitarization and democratization of Germany—have been implemented. This would create the prerequisites for the revival of an imperialist Germany, which the United States plans to use in a future war on its side. One cannot help seeing that such a policy has a clearly outlined anti-Soviet edge and constitutes a serious danger to the cause of peace.

The numerous and extremely hostile statements by American government, political, and military figures with regard to the Soviet Union and its foreign policy . . . are echoed in an even more unrestrained tone by the overwhelming majority of the American press organs. Talk about a "third war," meaning a war against the Soviet Union, and even a direct call for this war—with the threat of using the atomic bomb—such is the content of the statements on relations with the Soviet Union by reactionaries at public meetings and in the press. . . .

The basic goal of this anti-Soviet campaign of American "public opinion" is to exert political pressure on the Soviet Union and compel it to make concessions. Another, no less important goal of the campaign is the attempt to create an atmosphere of war psychosis among the masses, who are weary of war, thus making it easier for the U.S. government to carry out measures for the maintenance of high military potential. . . .

20 President Truman, address to Congress, 12 March 1947, linking defense of freedom worldwide to a program of aid for Greece and Turkey.[44]

At the present moment in world history nearly every nation must choose between alternative ways of life. The choice is too often not a free one.

44. *PPP: Harry S. Truman, 1947* (Washington: GPO, 1963), 178–80.

One way of life is based upon the will of the majority, and is distinguished by free institutions, representative government, free elections, guarantees of individual liberty, freedom of speech and religion, and freedom from political oppression.

The second way of life is based upon the will of a minority forcibly imposed upon the majority. It relies upon terror and oppression, a controlled press and radio, fixed elections, and the suppression of personal freedoms.

I believe that it must be the policy of the United States to support free peoples who are resisting attempted subjugation by armed minorities or by outside pressures.

I believe that we must assist free peoples to work out their own destinies in their own way.

I believe that our help should be primarily through economic and financial aid which is essential to economic stability and orderly political processes.

. . .

Should we fail to aid Greece and Turkey in this fateful hour, the effect will be far reaching to the West as well as to the East.

We must take immediate and resolute action.

I therefore ask the Congress to provide authority for assistance to Greece and Turkey [in the form of a $400 million grant, the despatch of civilian and military advisers, and the training of Greek and Turkish personnel].

. . .

The seeds of totalitarian regimes are nurtured by misery and want. They spread and grow in the evil soil of poverty and strife. They reach their full growth when the hope of a people for a better life has died.

We must keep that hope alive.

The free peoples of the world look to us for support in maintaining their freedoms.

If we falter in our leadership, we may endanger the peace of the world—and we shall surely endanger the welfare of this Nation.

21 Premier Stalin, meeting with Harold Stassen, 9 April 1947, affirming the possibility of peaceful coexistence.[45]

[STASSEN:] [W]e have two economic systems that are very different. . . . I would be interested to know if you think these two economic systems can exist together in the same modern world in harmony with each other?

45. Stassen was a Republican politician and perennial presidential candidate. The inter-

STALIN: Of course they can. The difference between them is not important so far as co-operation is concerned. The systems in Germany and the United States are the same but war broke out between them. The U.S. and U.S.S.R. systems are different but we didn't wage war against each other and the U.S.S.R. does not propose to. If during the war they could co-operate, why can't they today in peace . . . ? Of course, if there is no desire to co-operate, even with the same economic system they may fall out as was the case with Germany.

STASSEN: . . . [T]here have been many statements about not being able to co-operate. Some of these were made by the Generalissimo [Stalin] himself before the war. . . .

   . . .

STALIN: There was not a single Party congress or plenary session of the Central Committee of the Communist Party at which I said or could have said that co-operation between the two systems was impossible. I did say that there existed capitalist encirclement and danger of attack on the U.S.S.R. . . .

   . . .

STASSEN: . . . It seems to me we have been successful in America in preventing the monopoly of capitalism and the imperialistic trend, and that the workers have made greater progress through use of the strength of their vote and their freedom than Karl Marx or Frederick Engels thought they could make. . . .

STALIN: Let us not mutually criticize our systems. Everyone has the right to follow the system he wants to maintain. Which one is better will be said by history. We should respect the systems chosen by the people, and whether the system is good or bad is the business of the American people. . . .

   . . . Some people call the Soviet system totalitarian. Our people call the American system monopoly capitalism. If we start calling each other names with the words monopolist and totalitarian, it will lead to no co-operation.

We must start from the historical fact that there are two systems approved by the people. Only on that basis is co-operation possible. If we distract each other with criticism, that is propaganda.

. . . I am not a propagandist but a business-like man. We should not be sectarian. When the people wish to change the systems they will do so. When we met with Roosevelt to discuss the questions of war, we did not call each other names. We established co-operation and succeeded in defeating the enemy.

---

view appeared in the *New York Times* on 4 May 1947. Joseph Stalin, *For Peaceful Coexistence: Postwar Interviews,* ed. Alexander Trachtenberg (New York: International Publishers, 1951), 32–35.

22 George Kennan (writing under the pseudonym "X"), "The Sources of Soviet Conduct," July 1947, advocating a policy of containment.[46]

[T]he Soviet pressure against the free institutions of the western world is something that can be contained by the adroit and vigilant application of counter-force at a series of constantly shifting geographical and political points, corresponding to the shifts and manoeuvres of Soviet policy. . . .

. . .

. . . [T]he possibilities for American policy are by no means limited to holding the line and hoping for the best. It is entirely possible for the United States to influence by its actions the internal developments, both within Russia and throughout the international Communist movement, by which Russian policy is largely determined. This is not only a question of the modest measures of informational activity which this government can conduct in the Soviet Union and elsewhere, although that, too, is important. It is rather a question of the degree to which the United States can create among the peoples of the world generally the impression of a country which knows what it wants, which is coping successfully with the problems of its internal life and with the responsibilities of a World Power, and which has a spiritual vitality capable of holding its own among the major ideological currents of the time. To the extent that such an impression can be created and maintained, the aims of Russian Communism must appear sterile and quixotic, the hopes and enthusiasm of Moscow's supporters must wane, and added strain must be imposed on the Kremlin's foreign policies. . . .

. . .

It would be an exaggeration to say that American behavior unassisted and alone could exercise a power of life and death over the Communist movement and bring about the early fall of Soviet power in Russia. But the United States has it in its power to increase enormously the strains under which Soviet policy must operate, to force upon the Kremlin a far greater degree of moderation and circumspection than it has had to observe in recent years, and in this way to promote tendencies which must eventually find their outlet in either the break-up or the gradual mellowing of Soviet power. . . .

. . .

. . . [T]he thoughtful observer of Russian-American relations will find no cause for complaint in the Kremlin's challenge to American society. He will rather experience a certain gratitude to a Providence which, by providing the American people with this implacable challenge, has made their entire security

46. *Foreign Affairs* 25 (July 1947): 576, 581–82.

as a nation dependent on their pulling themselves together and accepting the responsibilities of moral and political leadership that history plainly intended them to bear.

23 Andrei Zhdanov (member of the Soviet Politburo), speech at the founding of the Cominform in Poland, late September 1947, calling for coordinated Communist resistance to the American threat.[47]

A new alignment of political forces has arisen. The more the war recedes into the past, the more distinct become two major trends in post-war international policy, corresponding to the division of the political forces operating on the international arena into two major camps[:] the imperialist and anti-democratic camp, on the one hand, and the anti-imperialist and democratic camp, on the other. The principal driving force of the imperialist camp is the U.S.A. Allied with it are Great Britain and France. . . . The imperialist camp is also supported by colony-owning countries, such as Belgium and Holland, by countries with reactionary anti-democratic regimes, such as Turkey and Greece, and by countries politically and economically dependent on the United States, such as the Near-Eastern and South-American countries and China.

The cardinal purpose of the imperialist camp is to strengthen imperialism, to hatch a new imperialist war, to combat Socialism and democracy, and to support reactionary and anti-democratic pro-fascist regimes and movements everywhere.

. . .

The anti-fascist forces comprise the second camp. This camp is based on the U.S.S.R. and the new democracies [of central and eastern Europe]. It also includes countries that have broken with imperialism and have firmly set foot on the path of democratic development, such as Rumania, Hungary and Finland. Indonesia and Viet Nam are associated with it; it has the sympathy of India, Egypt and Syria. The anti-imperialist camp is backed by the labour and democratic movement and by the fraternal Communist parties in all countries, by the fighters for national liberation in the colonies and dependencies,

47. The Cominform organizing meeting was held 22–27 September in Szklarska Poreba in southwestern Poland with the Communist parties of the Soviet Union, Poland, Hungary, Czechoslovakia, Romania, Bulgaria, Yugoslavia, Italy, and France in attendance. U.S. House of Representatives, Committee on Foreign Affairs, *The Strategy and Tactics of World Communism*, Supplement I, *One Hundred Years of Communism, 1848–1948*, 216–17, 223–24, 229. Alternative source: A. Zhdanov, *The International Situation* (Moscow: Foreign Languages Publishing House, 1947), 17–18, 34, 45–46.

by all progressive and democratic forces in every country. The purpose of this camp is to resist the threat of new wars and imperialist expansion, to strengthen democracy and to extirpate the vestiges of fascism.

. . .

. . . [T]he expansionist ambitions of the United States find concrete expression in the Truman doctrine and the Marshall Plan. . . .

The main features of the Truman doctrine as applied to Europe are as follows:

1. Creation of American bases in the Eastern Mediterranean with the purpose of establishing American supremacy in that area.

2. Demonstrative support of the reactionary regimes in Greece and Turkey as bastions of American imperialism against the new democracies in the Balkans. . . .

3. Unintermitting pressure on the countries of the new democracy, as expressed in false accusations of totalitarianism and expansionist ambitions, in attacks on the foundations of the new democratic regime[s], in constant interference in their domestic affairs, in support of all anti-national, anti-democratic elements within these countries, and in the demonstrative breaking off of economic relations with these countries with the idea of creating economic difficulties, retarding their economic development, preventing their industrialization, and so on.

The Truman doctrine, which provides for the rendering of American assistance to all reactionary regimes which actively oppose the democratic peoples, bears a frankly aggressive character. . . . Progressive public elements in the USA and other countries vigorously protested against the provocative and frankly imperialistic character of Truman's announcement.

The unfavorable reception which the Truman doctrine was met with accounts for the necessity of the appearance of the Marshall Plan which is a more carefully veiled attempt to carry through the same expansionist policy.

The vague and deliberately guarded formulations of the Marshall Plan amount in essence to a scheme to create a bloc of states bound by obligations to the United States, and to grant American credits to European countries as a recompense for their renunciation of economic, and then of political, independence. Moreover, the cornerstone of the Marshall Plan is the restoration of the industrial areas of Western Germany controlled by the American monopolies.

It is the design of the Marshall Plan . . . to render aid in the first place, not to the impoverished victor countries, America's allies in the fight against Germany, but to the German capitalists, with the idea of bringing under American sway the major sources of coal and iron needed by Europe and by Germany, and of making the countries which are in need of coal and iron dependent on the restored economic might of Germany.

. . .

. . . The need for mutual consultation and voluntary coordination of action between individual [European Communist] parties has become particular[l]y urgent at the present juncture. . . .

. . . [T]here has devolved upon the Communists the special historical task of leading the resistance to the American plan for the enthrallment of Europe, and of boldly denouncing all coadjutors of American imperialism in their own countries. . . . The Communists must be the leaders in enlisting all anti-fascist and freedom-loving elements in the struggle against the new American expansionist plans for the enslavement of Europe.

24 Foreign Minister Molotov, speech, 6 November 1947, analyzing American imperialism.[48]

[A] lot of advertisement is being given to various American projects connected now with the "Truman doctrine," now with the "Marshall plan." Reading about all these American plans of "aid to Europe," "aid to China," and so forth, one might think that America's domestic problems have already been solved long ago, and that all that remains is for her to order the affairs of other countries by prescribing for them her own policy and governments of such composition as she finds desirable. Actually, this is not so. If the domestic affairs of the U.S.A. were not causing its ruling circles great uneasiness, especially in connection with the approaching economic crisis, there would not be such an abundance of economic projects for United States expansion. . . .

. . . [The United States] is constantly setting up new naval and air bases in all parts of the globe, and is even adapting whole countries for such purposes, especially those lying near to the territory of the Soviet Union. Who nowadays does not complain of the pressure of American imperialism in this respect! . . .

As we know, a sort of new religion has become widespread among expansionist circles in the U.S.A.: having no faith in their own internal forces, they put their faith in the secret of the atomic bomb . . . which, it is generally known, is not a means of defence but a weapon of attack. . . .

48. Speech delivered to a meeting of the Moscow Soviet in celebration of the thirtieth anniversary of the Bolshevik revolution. Molotov, *Problems of Foreign Policy,* 487–88, 493. Variant translation: U.S. House of Representatives, Committee on Foreign Affairs, *The Strategy and Tactics of World Communism,* Supplement I, *One Hundred Years of Communism, 1848–1948,* 231–32, 235.

. . .

. . . [A] sober view of the matter will show that nowadays to indulge in new imperialist gambles is to play a dangerous game with the destiny of capital-ism. . . . [I]f the anti-imperialist and democratic camp unites its forces and avails itself of all its opportunities, it will compel the imperialists to be more sensible and restrained. (*Applause*) It is to be presumed that capitalism has no interest in expediting its own downfall. (*Laughter. Applause.*)

25 President Truman, national radio broadcast from the University of California, Berkeley, 12 June 1948, blaming the USSR for postwar international frictions.[49]

We fought through World War II with only one purpose: to destroy the tyrants who tried to impose their rule on the world and enslave the people. . . .

. . .

Why then, after such great exertions and huge expenditures, do we live today in a twilight period, between war so dearly won and a peace that still eludes our grasp?

The answer is not hard to find.

It lies largely in the attitude of one nation—the Soviet Union.

Long before the war the United States established normal diplomatic and commercial relations with the Soviet Union. In doing so we demonstrated our belief that it was possible to get along with a nation whose economic and political system differs sharply from ours.

. . .

. . . The Soviet Government has rejected the invitation to participate, freely and on equal terms, in a great cooperative program for reconstruction of Europe [the Marshall plan]. It has constantly maneuvered for delay and for propaganda effect in every international conference. It has used the veto exces-sively and unreasonably in the Security Council of the United Nations. . . . It has used indirect aggression against a number of nations in Eastern Europe and extreme pressure against others in the Middle East. It has intervened in the internal affairs of many other countries by means of Communist parties di-rected from Moscow.

The refusal of the Soviet Union to work with its wartime allies for world recovery and world peace is the most bitter disappointment of our time.

49. *PPP: Harry S. Truman, 1948* (Washington: GPO, 1964), 337–40. Truman struck the themes of this speech in a draft prepared earlier (in mid-April). Ferrell, *Off the Record,* 131–33.

. . .

What is needed is a will for peace. What is needed is the abandonment of the absurd idea that the capitalistic nations will collapse and that the instability in international affairs will hasten their collapse, leaving the world free for communism. It is possible for different economic systems to live side by side in peace, one with the other, provided one of these systems is not determined to destroy the other by force.

. . .

We have sought to help free nations protect themselves against aggression. We know that peace through weakness has proved to be a dangerous illusion. We are determined, therefore, to keep strong for the sake of peace.[50]

. . .

The only expansion we are interested in is the expansion of human freedom and the wider enjoyment of the good things of the earth in all countries.

26 National Security Council report 20/4, 23 November 1948, "U.S. Objectives with Respect to the ussr to Counter Soviet Threats to U.S. Security."[51]

The will and ability of the leaders of the USSR to pursue policies which threaten the security of the United States constitute the greatest single danger to the U.S. within the foreseeable future.

Communist ideology and Soviet behavior clearly demonstrate that the ultimate objective of the leaders of the USSR is the domination of the world. Soviet leaders hold that the Soviet communist party is the militant vanguard of the world proletariat in its rise to political power, and that the USSR, base of the world communist movement, will not be safe until the non-communist nations have been so reduced in strength and numbers that communist influence is dominant throughout the world. The immediate goal of top priority since the recent war has been the political conquest of western Europe. The resistance of the United States is recognized by the USSR as a major obstacle to the attainment of these goals.

. . .

50. Here Truman's April draft spoke more bluntly: "Our friends the Russkies understand only one language—how many divisions have you—actual or potential." Ferrell, *Off the Record*, 133.

51. Truman approved the conclusions of the report on 24 November 1948. The report was based on a draft by the State Department's Policy Planning Staff headed by George Kennan. *FRUS, 1948*, vol. 1, pt. 2 (Washington: GPO, 1976), 663, 668–69.

[Peacetime aims of U.S. policy:]

a. To encourage and promote the gradual retraction of undue Russian power and influence from the present perimeter areas around traditional Russian boundaries and the emergence of the satellite countries as entities independent of the USSR.

b. To encourage the development among the Russian peoples of attitudes which may help to modify current Soviet behavior and permit a revival of the national life of groups evidencing the ability and determination to achieve and maintain national independence.

c. To eradicate the myth by which people remote from Soviet military influence are held in a position of subservience to Moscow and to cause the world at large to see and understand the true nature of the USSR and the Soviet-directed world communist party, and to adopt a logical and realistic attitude toward them.

d. To create situations which will compel the Soviet Government to recognize the practical undesirability of acting on the basis of its present concepts and the necessity of behaving in accordance with precepts of international conduct, as set forth in the purposes and principles of the UN charter.

. . .

In the event of war with the USSR . . . [w]ar aims supplemental to our peace-time aims should include:

a. Eliminating Soviet Russian domination in areas outside the borders of any Russian state allowed to exist after the war.

b. Destroying the structure of relationships by which the leaders of the [Soviet] Communist Party have been able to exert moral and disciplinary authority over individual citizens, or groups of citizens, in countries not under communist control.

c. Assuring that any regime or regimes which may exist on traditional Russian territory in the aftermath of war:

(1) Do not have sufficient military power to wage aggressive war.

(2) Impose nothing resembling the present iron curtain over contacts with the outside world.

27 Premier Stalin, comments to a Chinese Communist delegation, 11 July 1949, predicting favorable prospects for peace.[52]

The people of every country have just emerged from the disasters of war. Having still not recovered from catastrophe, they are not likely to endorse

52. Shi Zhe, a translator accompanying the Chinese delegation, recorded this response to questions posed by the delegation head, Liu Shaoqi, about the prospects for a third world

war. So long as the people of every country do not want to fight, war cannot arise. We can make use of this opportunity to restore and develop economic construction. How long this period will be—fifteen years or perhaps twenty years—is very difficult to forecast. We must make full use of this time in order to expand our national economies and strengthen ourselves. If we really become quite strong, then war may not arise.

. . .

We should mobilize the people to oppose war and support peace. Provided that the people are not misled and do oppose war, war maniacs will find it difficult to get their way. . . .

. . .

It is important to take advantage of the interval between wars to vigorously develop and strengthen economic construction, expand production, and build national defense. The more formidable our strength, the smaller the possibility of war. The reason is that it is the weak and the poor who invariably get bullied by others.

The people's strength has always been of decisive significance. The people in today's world are getting stronger—nothing like their weakness in the past. It is important to treasure and cherish the people's strength!

In sum, we don't fear war, we oppose war, and will do everything possible to prevent war.

28 National Security Council report 68, 7 April 1950, "United States Objectives and Programs for National Security."[53]

[T]his Republic and its citizens in the ascendancy of their strength stand in their deepest peril.

The issues that face us are momentous, involving the fulfillment or destruction not only of this Republic but of civilization itself. . . .

. . .

The Kremlin regards the United States as the only major threat to the achievement of its fundamental design. There is a basic conflict between the

---

war, the international situation, and the international communist movement. My translation from Shi Zhe with Li Haiwen, *Zai lishi juren shenbian: Shi Zhe huiyilu* (Alongside the giants of history: Shi Zhe's memoir) (Beijing: Zhongyang wenxian, 1991), 406–7. For an alternative translation by Chen Jian, see *Chinese Historians* 6 (Spring 1993): 78–79.

53. The report was drafted by Paul Nitze, head of the State Department's Policy Planning Staff. Truman gave his conditional approval on 12 April 1950. *FRUS, 1950*, vol. 1 (Washington: GPO, 1977), 238–41, 265–67, 285.

idea of freedom under a government of laws, and the idea of slavery under the grim oligarchy of the Kremlin. . . . The idea of freedom, moreover, is peculiarly and intolerably subversive of the idea of slavery. . . .

. . .

The assault on free institutions is world-wide now, and in the context of the present polarization of power a defeat of free institutions anywhere is a defeat everywhere. . . .

Thus unwillingly our free society finds itself mortally challenged by the Soviet system. No other value system is so wholly irreconcilable with ours, so implacable in its purpose to destroy ours, so capable of turning to its own uses the most dangerous and divisive trends in our own society, no other so skill-fully and powerfully evokes the elements of irrationality in human nature everywhere, and no other has the support of a great and growing center of military power.

. . .

. . . [T]here are risks in making ourselves strong. A large measure of sacrifice and discipline will be demanded of the American people. They will be asked to give up some of the benefits which they have come to associate with their freedoms. . . .

. . .

It is estimated that, within the next four years, the U.S.S.R. will attain the [atomic] capability of seriously damaging vital centers of the United States, provided it strikes a surprise blow and provided further that the blow is opposed by no more effective opposition than we now have programmed. Such a blow could so seriously damage the United States as to greatly reduce its superiority in economic potential.

. . .

A further increase in the number and power of our atomic weapons is necessary in order to assure the effectiveness of any U.S. retaliatory blow. . . . Greatly increased general air, ground and sea strength, and increased air de-fense and civilian defense programs would also be necessary to provide reason-able assurance that the free world could survive an initial surprise atomic attack of the weight which it is estimated the U.S.S.R. will be capable of delivering by 1954 and still permit the free world to go on to the eventual attainment of its objectives. Furthermore, such a build-up of strength could safeguard and increase our retaliatory power, and thus might put off for some time the date when the Soviet Union could calculate that a surprise blow would be advantageous. This would provide additional time for the effects of our policies to produce a modification of the Soviet system.

. . .

A program for rapidly building up strength and improving political and economic conditions will place heavy demands on our courage and intelligence; it will be costly; it will be dangerous. But half-measures will be more costly and more dangerous, for they will be inadequate to prevent and may actually invite war. Budgetary considerations will need to be subordinated to the stark fact that our very independence as a nation may be at stake.

29 Premier Stalin, remarks on economic issues, I February 1952, insisting on the inevitability of crisis in the capitalist system and the possibility of the Soviet Union's avoiding war.[54]

[As a result of World War II] Germany and Japan were put out of action as competitors of the three major capitalist countries: the U.S.A., Great Britain and France. But at the same time China and European people's democracies broke away from the capitalist system and, together with the Soviet Union, formed a united and powerful socialist camp confronting the camp of capitalism. The economic consequences of the existence of two opposite camps was that the single all-embracing world market disintegrated, so that now we have two parallel world markets also confronting one another.

. . .

. . . [I]t follows from this that the sphere of exploitation of the world's resources by the major capitalist countries (U.S.A., Britain, France) will not expand, but contract; that their opportunities for sale in the world market will deteriorate, and that their industries will be operating more and more below capacity. . . .

. . . They are trying to offset these difficulties with the "Marshall Plan," the war in Korea, frantic rearmament, and industrial militarization. But that is very much like a drowning man clutching at a straw.

. . .

Some comrades hold that, owing to the development of new international conditions since the Second World War, wars between capitalist countries have ceased to be inevitable. They consider that the contradictions between the socialist camp and the capitalist camp are more acute than the contradictions among the capitalist countries; that the U.S.A. has brought the other capitalist

54. Stalin is here intervening to settle a theoretical debate on political economy stirred up in November 1951 by Eugen Varga. Varga, who had just after the war argued unsuccessfully against the notion of imminent capitalist crisis, once more and no less futilely challenged Stalinist orthodoxy—this time by questioning the idea of splits emerging within the capitalist camp. "Remarks on Economic Questions Connected with the November Discussion," in Joseph Stalin, *Economic Problems of Socialism in the U.S.S.R.* (New York: International Publishers, 1952), 26–30.

countries sufficiently under its sway to be able to prevent them going to war among themselves and weakening one another; that the foremost capitalist minds have been sufficiently taught by the two world wars and the severe damage they caused to the whole capitalist world, not to venture to involve the capitalist countries in war with one another again—and that, because of all this, wars between capitalist countries are no longer inevitable.

These comrades are mistaken. . . .

Outwardly, everything would seem to be "going well": the U.S.A. has put Western Europe, Japan and other capitalist countries on rations; Germany (Western), Britain, France, Italy and Japan have fallen into the clutches of the U.S.A. and are meekly obeying its commands. But it would be mistaken to think . . . that these countries will tolerate the domination and oppression of the United States endlessly, that they will not endeavor to tear loose from American bondage and take the path of independent development.

. . . Would it not be truer to say that capitalist Britain, and, after her, capitalist France, will be compelled in the end to break from the embrace of the U.S.A. and enter into conflict with it in order to secure an independent position and, of course, high profits?

. . .

It is said that the contradictions between capitalism and socialism are stronger than the contradictions among the capitalist countries. Theoretically, of course, that is true. . . . Yet the Second World War began not as a war with the U.S.S.R., but as a war between capitalist countries. Why? Firstly, because war with the U.S.S.R., as a socialist land, is more dangerous to capitalism than war between capitalist countries; for whereas war between capitalist countries puts in question only the supremacy of certain capitalist countries over others, war with the U.S.S.R. must certainly put in question the existence of capitalism itself. Secondly, because the capitalists, although they clamor, for "propaganda" purposes, about the aggressiveness of the Soviet Union, do not themselves believe that it is aggressive, because they are aware of the Soviet Union's peaceful policy and know that it will not itself attack capitalist countries.

. . .

Consequently, the struggle of the capitalist countries for markets and their desire to crush their competitors proved in practice to be stronger than the contradictions between the capitalist camp and the socialist camp.

. . .

. . . [I]t follows from this that the inevitability of wars between the capitalist countries remains in force.

. . .

To eliminate the inevitability of war, it is necessary to abolish imperialism.

30 President Truman, farewell remarks, 21 November 1952, stressing the burdens of Cold War leadership and the dangers of nuclear war.[55]

We are at the top, and the leader of the free world—something that we did not anticipate, something that we did not want, but something that has been forced on us. It is a responsibility which we should have assumed in 1920. We did not assume it then. We have to assume it now, because it has again been thrust on us. It is our duty, under Heaven, to continue that leadership in the manner that will prevent a third world war—which would mean the end of civilization. The weapons of destruction have become so powerful and so terrible that we can't even think of another all-out war. It would then bring into the war not only the fighting men . . . but the whole civilian population of every country involved would be more thoroughly exposed to death and de-struction than would the men at the front.

. . .

. . . [T]he Presidential Office is the most powerful Office that has ever existed in the history of this great world of ours. Genghis Khan, Augustus Caesar, great Napoleon Bonaparte, or Louis Fourteenth—or any other of the great leaders and executives of the world—can't even compare with what the President of the United States himself is responsible for, when he makes a decision. . . .

55. Remarks delivered before a CIA orientation course, in *The CIA under Harry Truman*, ed. Michael Warner (Washington: History Staff of the CIA Center for the Study of Intelligence, 1994), 472. Alternative copy: *PPP: Harry S. Truman, 1952–53* (Washington: GPO, 1966), 1061.

4

The Sino-American Collision in Korea, 1948–1951

RIDING THE ROLLER COASTER

On 25 June 1950 North Korean forces invaded the south, and before the year was out both the United States and China had intervened in the peninsular conflict to protect their respective Korean allies. Washington and then Beijing set off on a dramatic roller-coaster ride. Alarmed by developments on the peninsula, first one, then the other reluctantly climbed on board. Once underway, each in turn experienced exhilaration over the prospect of an unexpected victory. But when that victory eluded their grasp, Chinese and Americans found themselves plunged into intensified conflict. Shaken by the careening ride, leaders in each country looked for ways to stabilize and then end a conflict that neither had wanted in the first place. A year after the fighting started, Beijing and Washington were ready, however grudgingly, to help each other step off.

*   *   *

The war in the Pacific thrust Korea into the consciousness of American policymakers for the first time since Japan had asserted control in 1905. But the sudden end of the war found Washington resolved on nothing beyond the ultimate goal of Korean independence. With Soviet forces marching down the

I am grateful to *Political Science Quarterly* for permission to draw on my article "Beijing and the Korean Crisis, June 1950–June 1951," *Political Science Quarterly* 107 (Fall 1992): 453–78, in preparing the introduction to this chapter.

peninsula in August 1945, the Truman administration rushed American troops to the south. That decision guaranteed a U.S. voice in that country's future while immediately thrusting on the army occupation duties below the thirty-eighth parallel, a line that was supposed to separate the two foreign forces only temporarily.

By 1947 the intensifying Cold War and the failure of talks aimed at Korean unification under United Nations (UN) auspices forced Washington to decide what to do with its zone of occupation. Military planners contended that Korea was strategically peripheral. They lacked the troops to garrison South Korea permanently and in any case expected that any fighting in Korea or another locale would quickly result in a global war against the Soviet Union. That war would, they assumed, unfold much as World War II had—with first priority given to Europe and Korea's rescue coming only at the end. For the moment, however, Washington was not ready to surrender some fifteen million Koreans in the south to communism or set in doubt its international credibility. Indeed, a formal statement of policy, crafted in April 1948, committed the Truman administration to strengthening containment in South Korea even while getting American troops out (Document 2).

In keeping with this policy the U.S. military government closed down in August 1948, and by mid-1949 the last American combat units had gone. At the same time Washington sought to build up a government around Syngman Rhee as an offset to Kim Il Sung's Soviet-backed regime in the north. Boasting a strong anti-Japanese record and an American education (including a Princeton Ph.D. earned under Woodrow Wilson), Rhee had returned to Korea in October 1945 to become the chief adviser to the American occupation commander and then leader of the government put together in 1948 to replace the Americans. But by the spring of 1950 the new regime was running into serious difficulties. The economy was faltering; Rhee himself suffered repudiation at the polls; and repression had driven the left into armed resistance. Moreover, Rhee's American advisers grumbled not only about his political ineptness and stubbornness but also about his wild talk about marching north to unify the country. The Truman administration wanted stability, not crisis, on the peninsula.

For a revolutionary Chinese regime, Korea was for the moment an even more peripheral concern and a crisis even less welcome. In October 1949, following a decisive victory over Chiang Kai-shek's Nationalists, the Chinese Communist Party (CCP) had formally proclaimed the People's Republic of China (PRC). In the months immediately following, the socialist-bloc states, joined by some Asian neutrals (such as Burma, India, and Indonesia) as well as the British, Swiss, Dutch, and Scandinavians, offered diplomatic recognition. The United States held notably aloof, and the doors to the United Nations closed shut, thus challenging the international standing of the new Chinese state.

Domestically the CCP had already by late 1949 begun to deal with a daunting array of problems. Above all, the economy needed repair. Industrial production after a decade of conflict had fallen to roughly half of its prewar peak, and agricultural output was down by a quarter. Land reform in newly liberated areas, the suppression of armed resistance, and demobilization of an army of four million were other pressing tasks.

The CCP had an immediate agenda for securing China's border regions. But Korea, despite its intimate cultural and strategic links to China, especially the provinces of the northeast, did not figure prominently on that agenda. At the top was the reconquest of Tibet, preparations for taking Taiwan, and the conclusion of an alliance with the USSR. Following the formal establishment of the PRC, Beijing did quickly exchange diplomatic recognition with Pyongyang. By then Beijing had already begun to repatriate Koreans who had fought in the Chinese civil war, and by June 1950 some fifty thousand to seventy thousand had crossed the Yalu River into Korea to strengthen Kim's army.

Though the United States and the PRC had sought to limit their involvement in Korea, both were vulnerable to a rapid policy shift. The pivot for U.S. policy was a strong anticommunism. It was reflected in the thinking of Dean Acheson, the patrician northeasterner appointed secretary of state in 1949. Trained as a lawyer, Acheson would serve in effect as Truman's counsel, a trusted adviser in private and a loyal, vigorous advocate in public. Acheson immediately took up the primary burden of defending a failed China policy and working out the details of a new one.

His task was complicated by substantial public hostility to the Chinese Communists and opposition to contacts with them. Polling done between June 1949 and May 1950 consistently indicated that respondents who claimed to follow events in China opposed diplomatic recognition by a two-to-one margin. A May 1949 survey on trade ties was almost as negative, with 46 percent ready to discontinue trade and 34 percent inclined to continue it.[1] Even more outspoken was a collection of pro-Nationalist congressmen who joined other vocal public figures in warning against any diplomatic overture to Beijing. The Truman administration, they charged, had not done enough to save China from communism. Recognition now would in their view be tantamount to a shameful betrayal of an old ally in favor of a reprehensible Soviet puppet.

To still the public debate over who had "lost China," Acheson offered in July

1. George H. Gallup, *The Gallup Poll: Public Opinion, 1935–1971* (3 vols.; New York: Random House, 1972), 2:831, 868, 915.

1949 his own analysis, blaming the Nationalists for the debacle (Document 7). In January 1950 he took a tougher line that emphatically equated the Chinese revolution with a Russian takeover. He also revealed what the military planners had long before decided—that Korea fell beyond the U.S. defense perimeter in the Pacific (Document 11). The conclusion of a Sino-Soviet treaty in February 1950 seemed to confirm the subservient role of the CCP, an unnatural position that would eventually (Acheson believed) lead China along the path of Tito's Yugoslavia and out from under Soviet domination. Waiting for a Sino-Soviet split was for Acheson an attractive low-cost, low-risk strategy that would leave Europe where it belonged—at the center of American policy.

But Acheson's China policy did not go far enough fast enough for many in the grip of more restless anticommunism, including the president himself. While Acheson wanted to contain China and wait, Truman instinctively leaned toward a more aggressive course of isolating and punishing the PRC. In April 1948, with CCP victory a growing possibility, Truman denounced the Communists and rejected diplomatic contacts (Document 1). Again, at a cabinet meeting on 19 January 1949, Truman concluded a discussion of the political transition in China by announcing, "We can't be in a position of making any deal with a Communist regime."[2] In mid-1949 the Truman administration set off on a course of economic pressure against the mainland (despite the unhappiness of the British government and American firms interested in China), and in October Truman himself voiced support not for recognition of the PRC but for a naval blockade applied by the Nationalists.

At the same time Truman refused to make a definitive break with the Nationalists on Taiwan, which looked more and more attractive as a base of operations against the mainland. In a carefully prepared public statement in early January 1950 he emphasized that his administration had no intention of getting drawn into China's internal conflict; however, his denial in that same statement of any intention of establishing a U.S. military presence on Taiwan was intentionally qualified by the phrase "at this time."[3] A major, high-level survey of Asian policy, concluded in December 1949, mixed Truman's hardline views on the China question with Acheson's hopes for a Sino-Soviet split and the military leaders' resistance to becoming overextended in Asia (Document 9).

The Truman administration's China policy fed the hostility and suspicion of Mao Zedong (Mao Tse-tung), the dominant figure within the CCP. No knee-

2. Notes on cabinet meeting, 19 January 1949, Matthew J. Connelly Papers, Harry S. Truman Library, Independence, Mo.

3. *Public Papers of the Presidents: Harry S. Truman* [hereafter *PPP: HST*], *1950* (Washington: Government Printing Office, 1965), 11.

jerk anti-imperialist, he had for a time sought to develop ties to Washington, most energetically in 1944–1945. Even as late as the spring of 1949, with his triumphant forces crossing the Yangzi River to take control of the Nationalist capital of Nanjing, Mao was not averse to any links to Washington that would help isolate the Nationalists, neutralize the threat of an American-sponsored intervention, and secure access to technology and trade. And so he sanctioned an invitation to the American ambassador to travel from Nanjing to Beijing for a quiet exchange of views (Document 5). But Mao believed that Washington was more interested in challenging than accommodating the Chinese revolution. Already in CCP meetings in January and March 1949 he had expressed concerns about the possibility of a coordinated U.S.-Nationalist invasion that would in turn enlist resistance forces still operating within China, including a million or more remnant Nationalist troops, covert missions dispatched from Taiwan, bandits numbering as high as one million, and others opposed to the new regime (Documents 3 and 4).

At these meetings and repeatedly on other occasions through the year Mao balanced his fears and hopes in a formula that made diplomatic relations by any power conditional on treating China as an equal, respecting Chinese sovereignty, and breaking relations with the defeated Nationalists. Washington's demands for a privileged position for its diplomats and other residents in China while continuing to recognize the Nationalists touched a raw nerve among leaders long resentful of foreign arrogance and interference. When Acheson's defense of the administration's China policy in July identified middle-of-the-roaders as China's best hope, he had put his finger on another raw nerve—Mao's long-standing concerns with integrating into the revolutionary fold important segments of the urban population (in particular groups identified by the CCP as the petty and national bourgeoisie and the intellectuals). In August Mao publicly lashed back (Document 8).

While relations with the United States festered, Mao cultivated the USSR. His relationship with Joseph Stalin had earlier been cautious and sometimes strained. In the year before the outbreak of the Korean War Mao sought to close the gap and calm Moscow's concerns that the CCP was allowing too wide a circle of nonparty people a political role in the new regime. He himself offered public assurances to Moscow in June 1949 that China stood with the community of people's democracies while seeking to destroy the illusion within China that his regime might follow some kind of neutralist path (Document 6). Liu Shaoqi, the second-ranking Party leader, then left for Moscow to open high-level talks aimed at securing help in China's reconstruction and a strategic commitment to deter intervention. Mao (now chair of the recently created PRC as well as the CCP Central Committee) followed in December. After two months of arduous negotiations Mao and Zhou Enlai (premier and foreign minister of the PRC) were able to get a security treaty stipulating that China and the USSR would "immediately render military and other assistance with all the means at its disposal" to the other if attacked by Japan or one of its allies.[4] They also got limited economic aid. The price was concessions to the USSR in China's northeast and in Outer Mongolia (Document 10).

Parallel to the Moscow-Beijing talks, Kim Il Sung and Stalin discussed war. In early 1950 Kim put forward plans for an invasion that would unify Korea. The Korean leader guaranteed success: the United States had openly placed Korea outside its defense perimeter, and Rhee's position in the south was demonstrably weak. Stalin, who had already in late 1948 pulled the last of the Soviet troops from North Korea and in the winter of 1949–50 sent Kim offensive weapons, gave his approval, expecting that the war would be a strictly Korean affair with the Americans sitting on the sidelines. Even so, he asked Kim in an April meeting in Moscow to get Mao's approval. At a meeting the next month in Beijing Mao gave Kim a less than enthusiastic endorsement. Like Stalin, Mao approved on the assumption that the United States would not defend South Korea and that Kim would win the promised quick victory.

*   *   *

Americans, Chinese, Koreans, and Soviets had each contributed to assembling the machinery for the Korean crisis; Kim's invasion on 25 June set it in motion. Truman initially flew back to Washington from Independence to meet with his advisers at Blair House, the president's residence while the White House underwent major renovations. The assembled U.S. policymakers would quickly decide to climb aboard the roller coaster.

The president, Acheson, and other participants in those discussions interpreted the invasion as a bald Soviet challenge that required a strong response. However, fearing that this local probe was but a prelude to global war, Washington immediately sought to stem the attack by limited use of air and naval power (Document 12). On the twenty-seventh Truman publicly proclaimed his support for embattled South Korea. By then he had armed himself with a UN resolution calling for action in South Korea "to repel the armed attack and to restore international peace and security in the region."[5] At the same time Truman linked the defense of Korea to the China question by announcing that

4. Grant Rhode and Reid Whitlock, *Treaties of the People's Republic of China, 1949–1978* (Boulder, Colo.: Westview, 1980), 15b.

5. U.S. Department of State, *Foreign Relations of the United States* [hereafter *FRUS*], *1950*, vol. 7 (Washington: GPO, 1976), 211. The UN Security Council had been able to act on this resolution on 27 June because the Soviet representative, Jacob Malik, was boycotting the sessions in protest over exclusion of the PRC. On 7 July the council created a unified military command under U.S. leadership.

he was sending the Seventh Fleet to "neutralize" the Taiwan Strait and block any Communist invasion attempt. Finally, he announced measures to strengthen anticommunists in the Philippines and Indochina (Document 13).

At last, on the twenty-ninth, with intelligence reports giving no support to the view that Korea was merely a feint before the Kremlin struck elsewhere, Truman authorized the use of American troops in the resistance, and the Joint Chiefs of Staff issued guidelines for General Douglas MacArthur, the commander of American forces in the Pacific as well as the willful and semi-independent proconsul in Japan. Those guidelines reflected Washington's resolve not to become locked in a wider conflict with Soviet forces (Document 15). Though in fact Truman had made a commitment to fighting an Asian land war, he denied at a press conference that day that the country was at war. Pressed by reporters, he explained that the United States was engaged in a "police action" against a "bunch of bandits" from North Korea.[6]

Once committed to the war, the Truman administration proceeded to reverse itself in a reprise of the opportunism governing the Kim-Stalin calculations that had triggered the conflict in the first place. For a time during the summer the fate of MacArthur's forces, hemmed in around Pusan on the tip of the peninsula, seemed in doubt. While some lower-level officials called for making unification the goal of the war, the Central Intelligence Agency (CIA) argued for caution (Document 17). Calls for caution were even stronger from the closely allied British and the prominent Asian neutral, India (Document 16). Acheson used his skills as an advocate to keep at least the British in line through the summer and into the fall (Documents 21 and 28).

Success at stabilizing the Pusan defenses and at building up MacArthur's command paved the way for a policy shift. On 11 September Truman approved a formal recommendation from his high-level advisers to cross the thirty-eighth parallel and thus attempt the first "roll-back" of communist control of the Cold War. Then four days later the landing at Inchon, a port midway up the west coast, turned the tide of battle. This risky operation caught North Korean forces off guard and sent them retreating in disarray back north of the thirty-eighth parallel. On 27 September the Joint Chiefs, having secured the president's explicit approval, gave MacArthur permission to continue north while again emphasizing the importance of avoiding a broader conflict. On 9 October the Joint Chiefs gave MacArthur latitude to use his own judgment in case he encountered Chinese units (Documents 18 and 22).

Success now seemed guaranteed. On 1 October MacArthur called on North Korean forces, now on the run, to submit to unconditional surrender. On 7

6. *PPP: HST, 1950,* 504.

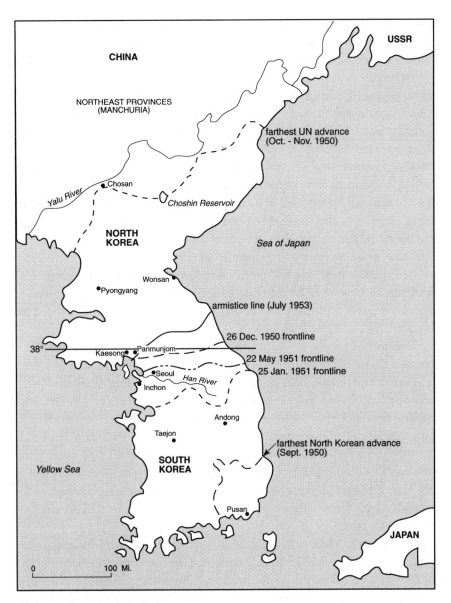

The Korean War, 1950–1953

October the UN endorsed the American decision to unify Korea by force of arms, and U.S. forces crossed the thirty-eighth parallel the next day. On 15 October Truman flew to Wake Island for a meeting with the triumphant commander, perhaps in part to secure for the Democrats some of the credit for the Korean victory before the upcoming November congressional election.

MacArthur, a self-proclaimed expert on "oriental psychology," assured Truman that the Chinese would not intervene and that American troops would be on their way home by Christmas (Document 25).

Washington was equally confident of quick victory despite a stream of warnings coming out of Beijing and evidence of Chinese troop movements. Private signals sent through India were in Washington's estimate tainted by neutralist bias, while China's own public statements seemed sheer propaganda, not to be taken seriously. American officials reassured themselves that China would not jump into a war that was for all practical purposes over. The CIA, shifting its position, now supported the mood of optimism (Document 23). The CIA and MacArthur held to a sanguine reading of the situation even into late October and early November, as the evidence of a Chinese military intervention steadily mounted (Documents 27 and 29). The Truman administration's chief response from mid-September to mid-November was repeatedly to ask UN neutrals to advise Beijing to calm down and accept a fait accompli. Finally, on 16 November Truman himself appeared at a press conference with a formal statement explaining that efforts to unify Korea were not intended to threaten China and would go forward (Document 30).

China moved only a step or two behind the United States toward boarding the roller coaster. Beijing's first response to American intervention in late June had been notably cautious, as much concerned with indicting American "neutralization" of Taiwan as intervention in Korea (Documents 14). At virtually the same time, however, the leadership of the CCP began preparing in secret for the possibility of military trouble in the north. On 30 June Zhou ordered Chinese military observers to North Korea, and he hastened diplomatic personnel to Pyongyang to effect the long-delayed opening of an embassy. On 7 July Mao endorsed a proposal by the CCP's Military Affairs Committee to assemble a large force in the northeast to defend the border and if necessary to cross over to fight.

By early August more than a quarter of a million troops had advanced to the Yalu River. By then Mao was urging haste on Gao Gang, whose responsibility for Party and military affairs in the northeast also put him in charge of logistical support for any operations in Korea. As MacArthur prepared his Inchon landing, Mao revealed his own resolve in off-the-record remarks on 5 September before the Council of the Central People's Government. He acknowledged the specter of an American atomic attack but claimed that he would not be intimidated.[7] On 17 September, in the immediate aftermath of Inchon, the

7. Consistent with Mao's position, Beijing publicly dismissed the nuclear threat either to a lightly industrialized and heavily agricultural China or to land warfare in Korea. Even so,

Military Affairs Committee dispatched an advance team to Korea to lay the groundwork for intervention. By then American incursions along the coast had become regular and worrisome events. The mounting Korean crisis had also come to eclipse Taiwan in importance, and so on 11 August the Military Affairs Committee decided to delay any decision on an invasion of the island until 1952.

By the end of September the rapid collapse of Kim's army forced the CCP toward a definitive decision on intervention. Stalin's insistence on keeping a low profile in Korea even in the midst of an impending disaster left little choice but to push the Chinese forward. Stalin raised with Mao the possibility of Kim setting up a government in exile. Meanwhile he had his personal representative in Pyongyang urge Kim to look to China for rescue while authorizing emergency delivery of military supplies. On 1 October, with South Korean forces crossing the thirty-eighth parallel, both Kim and Stalin requested China's help. Efforts to warn Washington of the risks of a military collision, thus far ineffectual in checking the UN advance, now went through their last phase. On 30 September Zhou publicly aired Beijing's concerns (Document 19). But words, it was becoming clear, carried scant weight in Washington.

On 1 October Mao and his colleagues broke away early from the public celebration of the PRC's first anniversary to hold the first of a series of high-level meetings within the CCP headquarters compound at Zhongnanhai in Beijing. Mao favored immediate and resolute action, but he encountered doubts. (Precisely who among the leadership voiced doubts is still not definitively documented, although Lin Biao's name appears most frequently.) Chinese troops were not ready for combat and once in Korea would operate in a rapidly deteriorating battlefield situation against a strong foe. Intervention would place fresh burdens on a war-weary population and might provoke a direct, damaging attack on China. The new Chinese state needed time to consolidate its control. Finally, Soviet assistance was uncertain. Why not delay or limit assistance to Korea?

During the first round of decision-making, between 2 and 8 October, Mao got his way. On 2 October he extracted from his colleagues—Liu Shaoqi, Zhou Enlai, Gao Gang, army commander-in-chief Zhu De, and acting army chief of staff Nie Rongzhen—an agreement that Chinese forces would march on 15 October. They also agreed on Peng Dehuai as the commander of the Chinese forces. Mao then cabled Stalin with this news and indicated his need for Soviet military support (Document 20). Meetings in Zhongnanhai continued until

---

the government ordered bomb shelters prepared in cities, some industrial plants removed from vulnerable urban sites, and civil defense education begun.

finally, on 8 October, Mao gave the formal orders for Chinese forces to prepare to move across the Yalu River and do battle with U.S troops then crossing the thirty-eighth parallel. At the same time he sent Zhou to meet with Stalin and informed Kim of the forthcoming support. North Korea and China at once established a military liaison.[8]

On 10 October a second round of consultations in Zhongnanhai began, set off by Zhou Enlai's unsettling report of his interview with Stalin at Sochi on the Black Sea. Stalin had revealed that he would not for the moment provide air cover in Korea. The Soviet air force, he explained, needed more time for preparation before being engaged even in the defense of Chinese airspace.[9] On 11–12 October Mao not only suspended his intervention order but also recalled Peng and Gao to Beijing. A Political Bureau meeting on 13 October and Mao's subsequent discussions with Peng on military operations produced a consensus in favor of proceeding cautiously with intervention and avoiding a forceful challenge to the United States. Mao now cabled Zhou, still in Moscow, the terms on which China was acting and made clear that the intervening force would consist not of the six divisions that Stalin had urged earlier in the crisis but of fifteen divisions together with supporting units for a total of 260,000 troops (Document 24). Finally, on 15 October, with Kim calling for haste in the dispatch of support, Mao issued an order for intervention no later than 17 October (soon pushed back to the eighteenth).

Even now, Beijing hesitated. Peng's subordinates had concluded that their units, with few anti-aircraft guns and no air cover, faced poor odds in battle, and had proposed delaying action until winter or even the following spring, when they might be better equipped. These worrisome views prompted Mao on the seventeenth to call Peng and Gao back to Beijing to canvas once again the precise time for moving into Korea and to hear Zhou's report on the details of his talks with the Soviets. Now, with the Americans about to take Pyongyang and the North Koreans in a panic, Mao thrust aside hesitations and made what proved to be the final decision for intervention. As the sun set on 19 October the first major body of Chinese troops advanced into Korea.

While Beijing edged toward intervention, it also moved to consolidate the homefront. On 10 October the party center responded to an upsurge in inter-

8. On 4 December China and Korea created a joint command under Peng Dehuai, and Mao hosted the first of several meetings with Kim held before armistice talks began in July 1951.

9. Zhou did receive assurances that the Soviets would immediately begin supplying weaponry for twenty Chinese divisions, and in November 1950 Soviet airmen operating incognito out of China's northeast did begin to provide air cover along the border. They later expanded their support south to the thirty-ninth parallel. Soviet mobile anti-aircraft units also operated in North Korea.

nal resistance with a hard-line directive. It called for an end to a policy too accommodating toward enemies of the new regime and ordered local authorities to step up internal security measures. At the same time both Mao and Zhou moved to win the middle-roaders by making patriotic appeals and issuing warnings against being deluded by American propaganda or daunted by the perils of war. The party-controlled media went into high gear, mobilizing popular support for the war effort.

The first three Chinese campaigns, beginning in late October and running to early January, scored great and unanticipated successes. Deeply engaged in daily, detailed direction of the operations, Mao watched his limited probes of the first campaign fail to produce any evident shift in Washington's thinking (Document 26). He thus proceeded with the second, all-out attack in late November (Documents 31 and 33). On 4 December he ordered reconnaissance in force against the clearly panicked UN army now retreating back into South Korea. The next day Pyongyang fell amid hints that the Americans might altogether abandon Korea. On 13 December he ordered the advance to continue *beyond* the thirty-eighth parallel. Determined to exploit the vulnerability of the disorganized, demoralized, and outnumbered enemy, Mao had launched his forces on their third campaign in three months. Having gotten on the roller coaster, he now was beginning to enjoy the ride (Document 36).

*   *   *

While the first limited Chinese campaign in late October raised a few unsettling questions on the American side, the second campaign begun in late November left no room for ambiguity or wishful thinking. MacArthur, stunned by the magnitude of his miscalculation, reported that Chinese forces had fundamentally changed the nature of the war (Document 32).

Washington went into shock. In private Truman warned his cabinet that Korea might envelop the United States in "total war."[10] Sobered by military reverses, his administration moved toward a pessimistic assessment of the Korean situation—and, however grudgingly, back to the original, limited goal of rescuing South Korea.

The most pressing task was to hold on in Korea and maintain support for the UN effort. On the military front, the outlook gradually improved despite enemy numerical superiority. At the end of the year some 250,000 UN troops (mainly South Korean) faced Chinese and North Korean forces totaling 442,000 (with some 315,000 additional Chinese troops being readied for battle). After taking charge in mid-January MacArthur's subordinate in Korea, General Matthew Ridgway, began to pull together the demoralized UN com-

10. Notes on cabinet meeting, 28 November 1950, Connelly Papers, Truman Library.

mand, thus assuring that the military reverse would not end in a complete rout.

On the diplomatic front, Washington had softened its stance in December. It was then prepared to accept a UN-promoted cease-fire that would win time to recover on the battlefield. But Zhou's public response to UN overtures asked the United States to pay a humiliatingly high price for the failed military gamble (Document 38). When the UN again in January proposed a cease-fire to be followed by talks on the broader issues of concern to China, Zhou reiterated China's determination to get a comprehensive settlement as the price for peace. Frustrated on this front, Washington strongly supported a UN resolution passed by the General Assembly on 1 February charging the PRC with aggression and laying the groundwork for possible UN retaliation.

Almost as important to the Truman administration was calming the American public and allies after the shocking appearance of the Chinese. Truman's admission during a press conference statement on 30 November that he was considering the use of nuclear weapons to meet the threat had only added to the agitation (Document 34). British prime minister Clement Attlee hurried to Washington to press long-standing complaints about U.S. policy (Document 35). No sooner had Truman emerged from an extended round of meetings with the British than he declared a state of emergency intended to rally the public (Document 37).

Truman's effort did not prevent critics of the now blatant costs of containment, such as former president Herbert Hoover and Republican senator Robert Taft, from going on the attack, nor did it stop the erosion of support for limited war. While an early February poll showed opposition to "an all-out war with Communist China" by a 77 to 14 percent margin, 50 percent of the respondents also thought that "the United States made a mistake in going into the war in Korea" in the first place, and only 39 percent still approved the decision.[11]

The most difficult person Truman now had to handle was MacArthur. The general had earlier rewarded Washington's trust with a dramatic military success. But following full-scale Chinese intervention, he became a thorn in Truman's side, calling for diverting resources from Europe to Asia and for bolder measures to win the war in Korea. MacArthur first posed his challenge privately, but the president held his ground (Document 39). MacArthur then made his dissatisfactions public in late March and early April. This open challenge still found Truman reluctant to act against a military figure whom he held in some awe. However, George C. Marshall, who had come out of retirement in the fall of 1950 to serve as secretary of defense, was a general whom

11. Gallup, *Gallup Poll*, 2:968.

Truman held no less in awe. After getting the backing of Marshall as well as the Joint Chiefs of Staff, Truman abruptly sacked his commander on 10 April and put Ridgway in his place.

MacArthur's dismissal set off a firestorm of criticism of presidential "indecision" and a war strategy that promised not victory but an open-ended conflict. MacArthur enjoyed a hero's welcome on his return home, but Truman again took his case to the public (Document 42). Senior administration officials followed up with extended testimony before Congress, defending limited war and highlighting the dangers of MacArthur's recommended course. Ironically, even though MacArthur was gone, some of the very proposals that he had made to widen or intensify the war continued to mire the Truman administration in internal debate (Document 43).

Beijing's views were also undergoing a critical transformation as difficulties on the battlefield began to puncture the initial euphoria. In late November and early December Peng Dehuai had already urged a halt at the thirty-eighth parallel. He wanted to give his forces a rest through the winter and prepare for a spring offensive. The Chinese commander continued to draw attention to supply and morale problems, and in late December Nie, from his post as army chief of staff, endorsed a pause in the campaigning. When Mao insisted on launching the third offensive (begun on 31 December), Peng loyally drove forward his exhausted, bone-chilled peasant army. In late January Peng proposed a cease-fire and a pull-back so that his forces could rest and prepare for renewed operations. An American offensive, launched at just that moment, exacerbated the difficulties of supply and morale. Mao, denying Peng's proposal, ordered the launching of the fourth campaign (Document 40).

With his troops at the end of their tether and hopes for a sweeping victory gone, Mao withdrew from daily direction of military affairs. Although troubled by ill health and absorbed in the campaign against counterrevolutionaries at home, he nonetheless continued to exercise a guiding hand. At last, in early February, he conceded that he had become entangled in an unwanted and costly war of attrition. Left with forces battered by almost four months of sustained campaigning, Mao decided to shift to a new strategy of "rotational warfare." Chinese armies would be trained, sent to Korea for a time, and then withdrawn in favor of a fresh force. In a prolonged series of meetings with Peng in late February and early March, Mao worked out the details of this new strategy. To Stalin Mao explained that rotational warfare was a way of continuing his contest of wills with the United States (Document 41).

In May the antagonists moved to get off the roller coaster. The Truman administration, the first to discover the dangers of an expanded war, had the recently retired Soviet specialist George F. Kennan propose to Jacob Malik, the Soviet ambassador to the UN, a cease-fire on the basis of the status quo ante without dragging in the broader issues raised by China. Malik responded on 5 June, conveying Soviet hopes for early peace on the peninsula and urging the United States to talk to the Chinese and North Koreans. At the same time Acheson emphasized in public testimony before a congressional committee that the administration was ready to accept a restoration of the prewar division of Korea along the thirty-eighth parallel.

Beijing was moving simultaneously toward a settlement. By late May the fifth major Chinese offensive had ground to a halt, confirming the military stalemate that Mao had perceived earlier and revealing the fragility of Chinese units. By contrast, the Americans, Mao observed on 26 May, remained determined and confident. This realization undermined his strategy, which had consistently turned on China's capacity to win a test of wills by imposing heavy casualties that would demoralize the enemy. While urging Peng to stabilize the battle lines, he began high-level discussions with his colleagues, and on 3 June Mao and Zhou received Kim to coordinate policy (Document 44).

This flurry of activity produced agreement on trying for a negotiated end to the conflict, with the thirty-eighth parallel to serve once again as the dividing line between the two Koreas. On 23 June Malik publicly proposed talks, and an editorial in China's official *People's Daily* offered an immediate endorsement. With negotiations looming, Mao resumed daily oversight of Korean policy and dispatched foreign ministry officials to Korea to ensure direct control of the joint Sino-Korean negotiating team.

The talks that opened in Kaesong on 10 July (later continued at Panmunjom) encountered serious obstacles. None was more disruptive than reaching terms for repatriating prisoners of war. Truman rejected the counsel of his chief advisers in favor of compulsory repatriation and instead insisted on the right of UN-held Koreans and Chinese to opt for "freedom" in South Korea or Taiwan. Beijing and Pyongyang demanded the return of all their prisoners. It would take two years of talks, mounting public impatience in the United States with the war, threats emanating from Washington, and Stalin's death before the combatants could devise a compromise on this issue. At last, in July 1953, the fighting came to a halt. To the end South Korea's Rhee tried to break up the negotiations and save his dream of a united Korea. Eisenhower considered a coup but instead silenced Rhee with the offer of a defense treaty.

*   *   *

The Sino-American collision in Korea has long stood as an example of how limited and distorted communications between deeply suspicious powers can set the stage for war. The two countries had no diplomatic contact. Even with some avenue of direct communications, diplomats would still have encountered considerable mistrust and misunderstanding. What limited information one side received about the other was often outdated when it arrived and mangled in the transmission.

Resolution or management of the crisis, once begun in June, was rendered difficult by the complex and shifting attitudes toward the conflict of the two opposing leaders. Mao would have been surprised and perhaps disconcerted to discover the generally aloof but also spasmodically disruptive role that the American president played in the policy process and the confusion and drift that as a result afflicted U.S. policy. The rational calculus that Mao supposed guided the American ruling class was hard to find. Rather, a poorly defined U.S. policy directed against a dimly imagined foe gyrated in response to developments on the battlefield—from caution and pessimism in late June and July, to optimistic opportunism in mid-September with the successful Inchon landing, to anxiety in November, near panic in December, and ultimately to a greater equilibrium in the new year.

American leaders, given a privileged look into Zhongnanhai, would have been similarly disconcerted. Mao was no Soviet puppet but rather a confident figure, pushing his close associates toward intervention for reasons that bring to mind nothing so strongly as the concerns that drew Washington into war. Like the Truman administration, Mao was guided by one part "national security" and another part "new world order." Taken together, China's policy toward Korea was every bit as complicated and unstable as Washington's. Once China was engaged in the fighting, Mao fell victim to the same military opportunism that characterized U.S. policy, in no small measure because he too suffered from a highly schematic view of the enemy. The American ruling class would not bear the high cost of aggression. As the American people, the British Commonwealth troops, and the South Korean puppet forces suffered casualties, they would lose their will to fight. Beleaguered at home and isolated internationally, Washington would then have to abandon Korea or seek a comprehensive solution of East Asian questions with China. At least so Mao thought.

Perhaps this crisis is best characterized as a process of armed interrogation. With the two parties ill-informed and out of synch, the crisis was difficult to stabilize until each had realized through a painful exchange of blows and counterblows how wrong its initial estimate of the enemy's intentions and will had been. Given the ambiguity of perception on both sides, the complexity of the interaction, and the instability of policy all around, it is hard to imagine the crisis developing otherwise. But armed interrogation requires the expenditure of lives and treasure. This costly "conversation" finally killed or wounded 382,000 Chinese (with Mao's own son among the dead). Nearly 34,000 Americans died and another 100,000 were wounded. Some three to four million Koreans fell victim as the fighting ravaged the peninsula.

Though fought on Korean soil, the war had profound effects on both intervening powers. On the U.S. side, the Korean War served as the catalyst for the first major Cold War arms buildup, undermined congressional war powers when Truman claimed that his intervention was only a "police action," and fueled popular fears of "subversives" at home and revolutionaries abroad all controlled by strings running back to the Kremlin. Though military leaders swore "never again" to get sucked into a land war in Asia, Korea nonetheless made the defense of Taiwan and Indochina more important, while confirming the view of the PRC as an international pariah.

The Korean War had for China an equally deep and pervasive impact. Intervention complicated the tasks of economic reconstruction and drained away scarce resources needed domestically. The mobilization campaign at home made the urban population and especially American-trained intellectuals the targets of reeducation, raised alarms over "subversives," and trumpeted the heinous deeds of American imperialism, not least germ warfare directed at China. And though intervention helped establish China's international credibility, there was a price. The war set Taiwan well beyond reach, highlighted the limits of the Sino-Soviet alliance, and left Washington determined to keep up the pressure at critical points along China's border. Thus one Sino-American crisis planted the seeds for others.

The Korean case prompts some unsettling questions about the alternative ways it might have unfolded. How might this crisis, with its high human cost, have been avoided or better managed? What made U.S. leaders tone deaf to Chinese warnings? What, if anything, might Beijing have done to command Washington's attention and perhaps thereby avoid a conflict? Conversely, what might Washington have done to reassure Beijing and thereby fend off Chinese intervention? These counterfactual questions are difficult to answer, but they direct our attention to the deep and sturdy roots of this costly collision.

FOR FURTHER READING

The literature on the Korean War has been undergoing some dramatic changes. A recent wave of work, notable for its fresh details on U.S. policy and on Anglo-American relations, has swept over an older generation of scholarship best represented by David Rees's synthesis, *Korea: The Limited War* (1964). This new literature is surveyed in Rosemary Foot, "Making Known the Unknown War: Policy Analysis of the Korean Conflict in the Last Decade," *Diplomatic History* 15 (Summer 1991). Burton I. Kaufman, *The Korean War: Challenges in Crisis, Credibility, and Command* (1986), and Callum A. MacDonald, *Korea: The War Before Vietnam* (1986), offer an up-to-date synthesis. Rosemary Foot, *The Wrong War: American Policy and the Dimensions of the Korean Con-*

flict, 1950–1953 (1985), and Foot, *A Substitute for Victory: The Politics of Peace-making at the Korean Armistice Talks* (1990), cover the same ground in more detail. On the role of American nuclear weapons, see Roger Dingman, "Atomic Diplomacy during the Korean War," *International Security* 13 (Winter 1988/89); Rosemary Foot, "Nuclear Coercion and the Ending of the Korean Conflict," *International Security* 13 (Winter 1988/89); and Mark A. Ryan, *Chinese Attitudes toward Nuclear Weapons: China and the United States during the Korean War* (1989).

New material coming out of China has begun to complicate and at points transform the older picture of Chinese intervention first reconstructed in Allen S. Whiting's classic *China Crosses the Yalu: The Decision to Enter the Korean War* (1960). The most detailed and up-to-date of the new accounts is Chen Jian, *China's Road to the Korean War: The Making of the Sino-American Confrontation* (1994).

Treatment of Sino-Soviet relations during the initial phase of the Korean War has until recently been sharply limited by the lack of documentation. Robert R. Simmons, *The Strained Alliance: Peking, Pyongyang, Moscow and the Politics of the Korean War* (1975); Wilbur A. Chaffee, "Two Hypotheses of Sino-Soviet Relations as Concerns the Instigation of the Korean War," *Journal of Korean Affairs*, vol. 6, nos. 3–4 (1976–77); and Nakajima Mineo, "The Sino-Soviet Confrontation: Its Roots in the International Background of the Korean War," *Australian Journal of Chinese Affairs*, no. 1 (January 1979), were early efforts to explore that topic and especially the ways the war may have intensified strains that would eventually bring about the Sino-Soviet split. The most recent entries drawing on new materials are Kathryn Weathersby, "The Soviet Role in the Early Phase of the Korean War: New Documentary Evidence," *Journal of American-East Asian Relations* 2 (Winter 1993), and Sergei N. Goncharov, John W. Lewis, and Xue Litai, *Uncertain Partners: Stalin, Mao, and the Korean War* (1993).

Background to the Korean crisis can be found both in the civil conflict within Korea and in the troubled state of Sino-American relations in the late 1940s. On these topics, see William W. Stueck, Jr., *The Road to Confrontation: American Policy toward China and Korea, 1947–1950* (1981); Bruce Cumings, *The Origins of the Korean War* (2 vols.; 1981 and 1990); John Merrill, *Korea: The Peninsular Origins of the War* (1989); Dorothy Borg and Waldo Heinrichs, eds., *Uncertain Years: Chinese-American Relations, 1947–1950* (1980); Nancy Bernkopf Tucker, *Patterns in the Dust: Chinese-American Relations and the Recognition Controversy, 1949–1950* (1983); and David McLean, "American Nationalism, the China Myth, and the Truman Doctrine: The Question of Accommodation with Peking, 1949–50," *Diplomatic History* 10 (Winter 1986).

DOCUMENTS

**I   President Harry S. Truman, press conference comments,
I I March 1948, offering his views on the political scene in civil-
war China.**[12]

The United States . . . is already on friendly relations with the [National-
ist] Government of China. . . . We have been trying to help the recognized
Government of China to maintain peace in the Far East.

. . .

. . . We don't want a Communist government in China, or anywhere else, if
we can help it.

. . .

. . . There is a very great difference between the liberal element in China and
the Communists. The Chinese Communists are those people who believe in
government from the top—the totalitarian state. There are a great many liberals in China. I talked to one of them just the day before yesterday. There are a
great many of them who have been educated in this country, and they are the
intelligentsia, really, of China. They are the people in whom we are interested
principally. We would like to see them included in the broadening of the base
of the Chinese Government.

**2   National Security Council study 8, 2 April 1948, limiting the U.S.
commitment to defend Korea.**[13]

The efforts of the U.S. to foster the establishment of a democratic and
sovereign government in Korea are handicapped by the political immaturity of
the Korean people. The tendency of Korean political elements to polarize into
extremes of right and left and to pursue their ends through the use of violence
acts as a serious deterrent to the achievement of political stability on a democratic basis in Korea.

The limited economy of south Korea, cut off as it is from its normal sources

12. *PPP: HST, 1948* (Washington: GPO, 1964), 180–81.

13. President Truman approved this report on "the Position of the United States with
Respect to Korea" on 8 April 1948. *FRUS, 1948*, vol. 6 (Washington: GPO, 1974), 1166–69. A
year later, on 23 March 1949, Truman approved NSC 8/2, which affirmed the decision to
withdraw U.S. forces while shoring up the new government in Seoul with diplomatic
support and economic and military assistance. *FRUS, 1949*, vol. 7 (Washington: GPO, 1976),
969–78.

of supply in the northern part of the country, is more than ever dependent upon the importation of raw materials—particularly coal and food. . . .

. . .

The persistent refusal of the Soviet Union to cooperate in good faith with the U.S. in formulating a just and mutually acceptable solution to the Korean problem and its further refusal to collaborate with the UN in its efforts to bring about the creation of a united, independent, and sovereign Korea, have made inescapable the conclusion that the predominant aim of Soviet policy in Korea is to achieve eventual Soviet domination of the entire country. Clearly indicative of this aim is the action of the Soviet occupation authorities . . . in fostering the establishment in north Korea of a satellite regime claiming authority over the entire country and backed by the arms of a Soviet-trained and equipped army.

The extension of Soviet control over all of Korea would enhance the political and strategic position of the Soviet Union with respect to both China and Japan, and adversely affect the position of the U.S. in those areas and throughout the Far East. Unless the U.S., upon withdrawal, left sufficient indigenous military strength to enable south Korea to defend itself against any but an overt act of aggression, U.S. withdrawal could be interpreted as a betrayal by the U.S. of its friends and allies in the Far East and might well lead to a fundamental realignment of forces in favor of the Soviet Union throughout that part of the world.

. . .

[Conclusions:]

a. It should be the effort of the U.S. Government through all proper means to effect a settlement of the Korean problem which would enable the U.S. to withdraw from Korea as soon as possible with the minimum of bad effects.

b. As a means to this end, the U.S. should pursue . . . the following steps:

(1) Expeditious completion of existing plans for expanding, training, and equipping the south Korean constabulary as a means of providing, so far as practicable, effective protection for the security of south Korea against any but an overt act of aggression by north Korean or other forces.

(2) Completion of the presently planned . . . programs for fiscal year 1949 to aid in forestalling the economic collapse of south Korea. . . .

c. The U.S. should be prepared to proceed with the implementation of withdrawal, following the formation of a government in south Korea. . . . Every effort should be made to create conditions for the withdrawal of occupation forces by 31 December 1948.

d. There should be established, following the withdrawal of occupation forces, a U.S. diplomatic mission to represent U.S. interests in Korea and to make recommendations . . . [on] economic and military aid. . . .

e. The U.S. should encourage continued UN interest and participation in the Korean problem and should continue to cooperate with the UN in the solution of that problem.

f. The U.S. should not become so irrevocably involved in the Korean situation that any action taken by any faction in Korea or by any other power in Korea could be considered a *casus belli* for the U.S.

3   CCP Central Committee directive (drafted by its chair, Mao Zedong), approved by the Political Bureau, 8 January 1949, evaluating the threat from the Nationalists and the United States as the civil war comes to a close.[14]

Once we have fought a few more battles, then not only in a military sense but also in a political and economic sense we will have fundamentally overturned the Nationalist regime. To overturn the Nationalists fundamentally is not the same as overturning the Nationalists completely. China still has many enemy forces that need to be eliminated. And there are still many regions that await our occupation and work. Regarding the enemy lightly is not at any time advisable. . . .

. . .

We have previously had to take as a possibility that the Americans might send troops directly to several cities along China's coast and do battle with us. These calculations had to be included in our battle plans. This kind of calculation even now cannot be put aside. We don't want to be caught unprepared in case something unexpected were to happen as the situation unfolds.[15] But as the strength of the Chinese people's revolution gets ever more powerful and ever more resolute, it becomes ever less likely that the United States will carry out a direct military intervention. . . . The mistaken view prevailing among some Chinese people as well as some of our party members that exaggerates the strength of American imperialism must be constantly watched and overcome.

U.S. imperialist policy toward China has already begun to shift away from exclusive support for the Nationalists' armed opposition to the Communist

14. My translation from *Mao Zedong junshi wenxuan* (A selection of Mao Zedong works on military affairs), comp. Zhongguo renmin jiefangjun junshi kexueyuan (Beijing: Zhongguo renmin jiefangjun zhanshi, 1981; "internal circulation"; reprint Tokyo: Sososha, 1985), 326–27, 328–29.

15. As late as 23 May 1949 Mao was still worried enough about an American invasion that he drafted orders designating the second field army as a reserve against that possibility. *Mao junshi wenxuan*, 337.

Party and toward a dualistic policy. This means, on the one hand, supporting remnants of Nationalist military power along with local warlords to continue resistance to the People's Liberation Army and, on the other hand, sending its running dogs to infiltrate the revolutionary camp and organizing so-called oppositionists in order to destroy the revolution from within. As the time approaches for the country-wide victory of the People's Liberation Army, it might come to pass that [the United States] would even resort to the technique of recognizing the People's Republic in order to legitimate its position and carry out a policy of "destruction from within." We must raise our vigilance against this imperialist scheme. . . .

4   CCP Central Committee chair Mao Zedong, statement to the second plenum of the seventh Central Committee, 5 March 1949, outlining the general approach to foreign relations.[16]

Old China was a semi-colonial country under imperialist domination. Thoroughly anti-imperialist in character, the Chinese people's democratic revolution has incurred the bitter hatred of the imperialists who have done their utmost to help the [Nationalist Party]. . . . In each city or place where the [Nationalist] troops are wiped out and the [Nationalist] government is overthrown, imperialist political domination is overthrown with it, and so is imperialist economic and cultural domination. But the economic and cultural establishments run directly by the imperialists are still there, and so are the diplomatic personnel and the journalists recognized by the [Nationalists]. We must deal with all these properly in their order of urgency. Refuse to recognize the legal status of any foreign diplomatic establishments and personnel of the [Nationalist] period, refuse to recognize all the treasonable treaties of the [Nationalist] period, abolish all imperialist propaganda agencies in China, take immediate control of foreign trade and reform the customs system—these are the first steps we must take upon entering the big cities. When they have acted thus, the Chinese people will have stood up in the face of imperialism. As for the remaining imperialist economic and cultural establishments, they can be allowed to exist for the time being, subject to our supervision and control, to be dealt with by us after country-wide victory. As for ordinary foreign nationals, their legitimate interests will be protected and not encroached upon.

16. *Selected Works of Mao Tse-tung* (5 vols. to date; Beijing: Foreign Languages Press, 1961–), 4:370–71. Mao subjected this speech to editing after its delivery. There is to date no copy of the original available for comparison.

As for the question of the recognition of our country by the imperialist countries, we should not be in a hurry to solve it now and need not be in a hurry to solve it even for a fairly long period after country-wide victory. We are willing to establish diplomatic relations with all countries on the principle of equality, but the imperialists, who have always been hostile to the Chinese people, will definitely not be in a hurry to treat us as equals. As long as the imperialist countries do not change their hostile attitude, we shall not grant them legal status in China. As for doing business with foreigners, there is no question; wherever there is business to do, we shall do it and we have already started; the businessmen of several capitalist countries are competing for such business. So far as possible, we must first of all trade with the socialist and people's democratic countries; at the same time we will also trade with capitalist countries.

5   U.S. Ambassador to China John Leighton Stuart to the State Department, telegram of 30 June 1949, urging a positive response to confidential CCP overtures.[17]

Huang Hua [official in charge of foreign affairs in Nanjing] called on me by appointment June 28. He reported that he had received message from Mao Tse-tung and Chou En-lai assuring me that they would welcome me to Peiping.[18] . . .

. . .

. . . To accept would undoubtedly be gratifying to [Mao and Zhou], would give me chance to describe American policy; its anxieties regarding Communism and world revolution; its desires for China's future; and would enable me to carry to Washington most authoritative information regarding CCP intentions. Such trip would be step toward better mutual understanding and should strengthen more liberal anti-Soviet element in CCP. It would provide unique opportunity for American official to talk to top Chinese Communists in informal manner which may not again present itself. It would be imaginative, adventurous indication of US open-minded attitude towards changing political trends in China and would probably have beneficial effect on future Sino-American relations.[19]

17. *FRUS, 1949,* vol. 8 (Washington: GPO, 1974), 766.

18. The designation for Beijing (Peking) before it became the capital of the PRC. This designation was consistently used by U.S. policymakers to indicate their refusal to recognize the Communist government located there.

19. Acheson responded on 1 July 1949: "Following highest level consideration [by the president] . . . , you are instructed under no condition to make visit to Peiping." *FRUS, 1949,* 8:769.

6 Chairman Mao, speech "On the People's Democratic Dictatorship," 30 June 1949, publicly affirming the CCP's foreign policy line.[20]

"You Lean to One Side." Precisely. . . . The Chinese people either lean to the side of imperialism or to the side of socialism. There is no exception. It is not possible to sit on the fence, and there is no third road. . . .

. . .

"Victory is . . . possible without international assistance." This is a mistaken idea. In the era when imperialism exists, it is impossible for the true people's revolution of any country to win its own victory without assistance in various forms from the international revolutionary forces. It is also impossible to consolidate the victory when it is won. . . .

"We need assistance from the British and American governments." At present this is also a childish idea. At present the rulers in Britain and the United States are still imperialists. Would they extend assistance to a people's state? If we do business with these countries or suppose these countries would be willing in the future to lend us money on terms of mutual benefit, what would be the reason for it? It would be because the capitalists of these countries want to make money and the bankers want to earn interest to relieve their own crises. . . . Internationally we belong to the anti-imperialist front headed by the Soviet Union, and we can look for genuine, friendly assistance only from that front, and not from the imperialist front.

7 Secretary of State Dean Acheson to President Truman, public letter, 30 July 1949, summarizing the China White Paper's defense against charges that the Truman administration had "lost China."[21]

The reasons for the failures of the Chinese National Government . . . do not stem from any inadequacy of American aid. . . . Its leaders had proved incapable of meeting the crisis confronting them, its troops had lost the will to

20. This speech was given on the twenty-eighth anniversary of the founding of the CCP. Translation in Conrad Brandt et al., *A Documentary History of Chinese Communism* (Cambridge: Harvard University Press, 1952), 453–56, revised on the basis of the original in *Mao Zedong ji* (Collected writings of Mao Zedong), ed. Takeuchi Minoru (10 vols.; Tokyo: Hokobosha, 1971–72; reprint Hong Kong, 1975), 10:296–99. The translation in *Selected Works of Mao Tse-tung*, 4:415–17, diverges somewhat from the original.

21. U.S. Department of State, *United States Relations with China with Special Reference to the Period 1944–1949* (The China White Paper) (Washington: GPO, 1949), xiv–xvi.

fight, and its Government had lost popular support. The Communists, on the other hand, through a ruthless discipline and fanatical zeal, attempted to sell themselves as guardians and liberators of the people. The Nationalist armies did not have to be defeated; they disintegrated. . . .

. . .

The historic policy of the United States of friendship and aid toward the people of China was, however, maintained in both peace and war. Since [the end of the Pacific War], the United States Government has authorized aid to Nationalist China in the form of grants and credits totaling approximately 2 billion dollars. . . . In addition to these grants and credits, the United States Government has sold the Chinese Government large quantities of military and civilian war surplus property with a total procurement cost of over 1 billion dollars. . . . A large proportion of the military supplies furnished the Chinese armies by the United States since [the end of the Pacific War] has, however, fallen into the hands of the Chinese Communists through the military ineptitude of the Nationalist leaders, their defections and surrenders, and the absence among their forces of the will to fight.

. . .

. . . [T]he only alternative open to the United States was full-scale intervention in behalf of a Government which had lost the confidence of its own troops and its own people. Such intervention would have required the expenditure of even greater sums than have been fruitlessly spent thus far, the command of Nationalist armies by American officers, and the probable participation of American armed forces—land, sea, and air—in the resulting war. Intervention of such a scope and magnitude would have been resented by the mass of the Chinese people, would have diametrically reversed our historic policy, and would have been condemned by the American people.

It must be admitted frankly that the American policy of assisting the Chinese people in resisting domination by any foreign power or powers is now confronted with the gravest difficulties. The heart of China is in Communist hands. The Communist leaders have foresworn their Chinese heritage and have publicly announced their subservience to a foreign power, Russia, which during the last 50 years, under czars and Communists alike, has been most assiduous in its efforts to extend its control in the Far East. In the recent past, attempts at foreign domination have appeared quite clearly to the Chinese people as external aggression and as such have been bitterly and in the long run successfully resisted. Our aid and encouragement have helped them to resist. In this case, however, the foreign domination has been masked behind the facade of a vast crusading movement which apparently has seemed to many Chinese to be wholly indigenous and national. Under these circumstances, our aid has been unavailing.

. . .

. . . [H]owever tragic may be the immediate future of China and however ruthlessly a major portion of this great people may be exploited by a party in the interest of a foreign imperialism, ultimately the profound civilization and the democratic individualism of China will reassert themselves and she will throw off the foreign yoke. I consider that we should encourage all developments in China which now and in the future work toward this end.

8　Chairman Mao, anonymously published criticism of Acheson and the White Paper, mid-August 1949.

—"Cast Away Illusions, Prepare for Struggle," 14 August:[22]

Part of the intellectuals still want to wait and see. They think: the Kuomintang [Nationalist Party] is no good and the Communist Party is not necessarily good either, so we had better wait and see. Some support the Communist Party in words, but in their hearts they are waiting to see. They are the very people who have illusions about the United States. They are unwilling to draw a distinction between the U.S. imperialists, who are in power, and the American people, who are not. They are easily duped by the honeyed words of the U.S. imperialists, as though these imperialists would deal with People's China on the basis of equality and mutual benefit without a stern, long struggle. They still have many reactionary, that is to say, anti-popular, ideas in their heads, but they are not Kuomintang [Nationalist] reactionaries. They are the middle-of-the-roaders or the right-wingers in People's China. They are the supporters of what Acheson calls "democratic individualism". The deceptive manoeuvres of the Achesons still have a flimsy social base in China.

Acheson's White Paper admits that the U.S. imperialists are at a complete loss as to what to do about the present situation in China. The Kuomintang [Nationalist Party] is so impotent that no amount of help can save it from inevitable doom; the U.S. imperialists are losing grip over things and feel helpless. . . .

—"Farewell, Leighton Stuart!" 18 August:[23]

The three main targets [of the U.S. policy of aggression] are Europe, Asia and the Americas. China, the centre of gravity in Asia, is a large country with a population of 475 million; by seizing China, the United States would possess all

22. The translation in *Selected Works of Mao Tse-tung*, 4:427, closely follows the original in *Mao Zedong ji*, 10:319–20.

23. The translation in *Selected Works of Mao Tse-tung*, 4:433–34, 436–37, closely follows the original in *Mao Zedong ji*, 10:326, 329–30.

of Asia. With its Asian front consolidated, U.S. imperialism could concentrate its forces on attacking Europe. U.S. imperialism considers its front in the Americas relatively secure. These are the smug over-all calculations of the U.S. aggressors.

. . .

. . . The United States refrained from dispatching large forces to attack China, not because the U.S. government didn't want to, but because it had worries. First worry: the Chinese people would oppose it, and the U.S. government was afraid of getting hopelessly bogged down in a quagmire. Second worry: the American people would oppose it, and so the U.S. government dared not order mobilization. Third worry: the people of the Soviet Union, of Europe and of the rest of the world would oppose it, and the U.S. government would face universal condemnation. . . .

Let those Chinese who are short-sighted, muddle-headed liberals or democratic individualists listen. Acheson is giving you a lesson; he is a good teacher for you. He has made a clean sweep of your fancied U.S. humanity, justice and virtue. . . .

True, the United States has science and technology. But unfortunately they are in the grip of the capitalists, not in the hands of the people, and are used to exploit and oppress the people at home and to perpetrate aggression and to slaughter people abroad. There is also "democracy" in the United States. But unfortunately it is only another name for the dictatorship of the bourgeoisie by itself. The United States has plenty of money. But unfortunately it is willing to give money only to the Chiang Kai-shek reactionaries, who are rotten to the core. The United States, it is said, is and will be quite willing to give money to its fifth column in China, but is unwilling to give it to the ordinary run of liberals or democratic individualists, who are much too bookish and do not know how to appreciate favours, and naturally it is even more unwilling to give money to the Communists. Money may be given, but only conditionally. What is the condition? Follow the United States. . . . But he who swallows food handed out in contempt will get a bellyache.

9   National Security Council study 48/2, 30 December 1949, defining U.S. policy toward China.[24]

The United States should continue to recognize the National Government of China until the situation is further clarified. The United States should

24. On 30 December Truman approved the recommendations of this top-secret study

avoid recognizing the Chinese Communist regime until it is clearly in the United States interest to do so. The United States should continue to express to friendly governments its own views concerning the dangers of hasty recognition of the Chinese Communist regime. . . . [I]t would be inappropriate for the United States to adopt a posture more hostile or policies more harsh towards a Communist China than towards the USSR itself. . . .

The United States should continue the policies of avoiding military and political support of any non-Communist elements in China unless such elements are willing actively to resist Communism with or without United States aid and unless such support would mean reasonable resistance to the Communists and contribute to the over-all national interests of the United States. . . . The United States should maintain so far as feasible active contact with all elements in China and maintain our cultural and informational program at the most active feasible level.

The United States should exploit, through appropriate political, psychological and economic means, any rifts between the Chinese Communists and the USSR and between the Stalinists and other elements in China, while scrupulously avoiding the appearance of intervention. Where appropriate, covert as well as overt means should be utilized to achieve these objectives.

. . .

The United States should continue the policy . . . of attempting to deny Formosa [Taiwan] and the Pescadores [an island group just off Taiwan] to the Chinese Communists through diplomatic and economic means. . . .

Since the United States may not be able to achieve its objectives through political and economic means, and in view of the opinion of the Joint Chiefs of Staff . . . that, while Formosa is strategically important to the United States, "the strategic importance of Formosa does not justify overt military action... so long as the present disparity between our military strength and our global obligations exists," the United States should make every effort to strengthen the over-all U.S. position with respect to the Philippines, the Ryukyus, and Japan. . . .

. . .

The sum of $75,000,000 for assistance to the general area of China . . . should be programmed as a matter of urgency.[25]

("The Position of the United States with Respect to Asia") and directed their implementation, with the one exception noted below. *FRUS, 1949*, 7:1218–20.

25. To this proposal Truman responded: "A program will be all right, but whether we implement it depends on circumstances." *FRUS, 1949*, 7:1215.

10 Chairman Mao (in Moscow) to the CCP Central Committee, early January 1950, describing progress in negotiations for a Sino-Soviet treaty.[26]

—Telegram of 2 January (11 p.m.):

This evening at eight o'clock Comrades [Vyacheslav] Molotov and [Anastas] Mikoyan[27] came to my place to talk, asking my views on a Sino-Soviet treaty and other matters. I at once laid out in detail three approaches: First, to conclude and sign a new Sino-Soviet treaty of alliance and friendship [replacing the treaty that the USSR had concluded with the Nationalists in August 1945]. This way of handling the matter would be of the greatest advantage. If Sino-Soviet relations are consolidated on the foundation of a new treaty, then China's workers, peasants, intellectuals, and the left wing of the national bourgeoisie will all feel a great thrill, and it will be possible to isolate the right wing of the national bourgeoisie. Internationally, thanks to the greater political capital which we will have to confront imperialist countries, we will be able to scrutinize all the past treaties between China and the imperialist countries. Second, to put out a simple announcement by our two countries' press agencies simply saying that the authorities of our two countries have exchanged views. . . . Third, to conclude and sign a declaration, the contents of which would speak to the main points in relations between the two countries. But this would not be a treaty. . . . After I analyzed in detail the pros and cons of the above three approaches, Comrade Molotov then said that the first approach was good. . . .

—Telegram of 3 January (4 p.m.):

[In informal briefings on the treaty for government officials in Beijing] you should point out that this initiative will put the PRC in an even more advantageous position. The capitalist countries cannot but accommodate us. It will be advantageous in compelling all countries to grant China unconditional recognition, to abrogate the old [unequal] treaties, and to conclude new treaties. And it will hold each of the capitalist countries back from rash action.

---

26. My translation from *Jianguo yilai Mao Zedong wengao* (Mao Zedong manuscripts for the period following the establishment of the country), comp. Zhonggong zhongyang wenxian yanjiushi (8 vols. to date; Beijing: Zhongyang wenxian, 1987–; "internal circulation"), 1:211–13. Alternative translation: Sergei N. Goncharov et al., *Uncertain Partners: Stalin, Mao, and the Korean War* (Stanford: Stanford University Press, 1993), 242–44.

27. Both Molotov and Mikoyan were members of the Politburo of the Communist Party of the Soviet Union and vice-chairmen of the USSR Council of Ministers.

11 Secretary of State Acheson, speech, 12 January 1950, "Crisis in Asia—An Examination of U.S. Policy."[28]

We are interested in stopping the spread of communism because communism is a doctrine that we don't happen to like. Communism is the most subtle instrument of Soviet foreign policy that has ever been devised, and it is really the spearhead of Russian imperialism which would, if it could, take from these people [of Asia] what they have won, what we want them to keep and develop, which is their own national independence, their own individual independence, their own development of their own resources for their own good and not as mere tributary states to this great Soviet Union.

. . .

. . . [T]he Soviet Union is detaching the northern provinces of China from China and is attaching them to the Soviet Union. This process is complete in outer Mongolia. It is nearly complete in Manchuria, and I am sure that in inner Mongolia and in Sinkiang there are very happy reports coming from Soviet agents to Moscow. . . .

. . .

The consequences of this Russian attitude and this Russian action in China are perfectly enormous. They are saddling all those in China who are proclaiming their loyalty to Moscow, and who are allowing themselves to be used as puppets of Moscow, with the most awful responsibility which they must pay for. . . .

. . .

[The U.S. defensive perimeter essential to military security in the Pacific] runs along the Aleutians to Japan and then goes to the Ryukyus. . . .

The defensive perimeter [then] runs from the Ryukyus to the Philippine Islands. . . .

So far as the military security of other areas in the Pacific is concerned, it must be clear that no person can guarantee these areas against military attack. But it must also be clear that such a guarantee is hardly sensible or necessary within the realm of practical relationship.

Should such an attack occur . . . the initial reliance must be on the people attacked to resist it and then upon the commitments of the entire civilized world under the Charter of the United Nations which so far has not proved a weak reed to lean on by any people who are determined to protect their independence against outside aggression. . . .

28. This speech was given before the National Press Club in Washington. *Department of State Bulletin* 22 (23 January 1950): 114–16.

12 President Truman, meetings with advisers at Blair House, late June 1950, discussing a response to the invasion of South Korea.

—Meeting of 25 June:[29]

After dinner the discussion began around the table. The President called on the Secretary of State to open the discussion.

MR. ACHESON summarized the various problems which he thought the President should consider [including stepped-up supply of matériel as well as air cover for South Korean forces, UN opposition to the invasion, neutralization of the Taiwan Strait, and increased aid to French Indochina]. . . .

. . .

[Chair of the Joint Chiefs of Staff] GENERAL [Omar N.] BRADLEY said that we must draw the line somewhere.

THE PRESIDENT stated he agreed on that.

GENERAL BRADLEY said that Russia is not yet ready for war. The Korean situation offered as good an occasion for action in drawing the line as anywhere else. . . . He questioned the advisability of putting in [U.S.] ground units particularly if large numbers were involved.

. . .

[Chief of Naval Operations] ADMIRAL [Forrest P.] SHERMAN said that the Russians do not want war now but if they do they will have it. The present situation in Korea offers a valuable opportunity for us to act. Korea is a strategic threat to Japan. . . .

. . .

[Air Force Chief of Staff] GENERAL [Hoyt S.] VANDENBERG agreed that we must stop the North Koreans but he would not base our action on the assumption that the Russians would not fight. . . .

. . .

[Secretary of the Army] MR. [Frank] PACE expressed doubts about the advisability of putting ground forces into Korea. He stressed the need for speed and for encouraging General MacArthur[30] to take action.

[Secretary of the Navy] MR. [Francis P.] MATTHEWS also stressed the need for prompt action and said that we would get popular approval.

[Secretary of the Air Force] MR. [Thomas K.] FINLETTER . . . said our forces in the Far East were sufficient if the Russians do not come in. . . . He stressed the analogy to the situation between the two world wars. He thought we should take calculated risks hoping that our action will keep the peace.

[Secretary of Defense] MR. [Louis A.] JOHNSON . . . thought there should

29. Meeting record by Philip Jessup, in *FRUS, 1950*, 7:157–60.
30. General Douglas MacArthur, Commander in Chief, Far East.

not be a real delegation of Presidential authority to General MacArthur. . . . He was opposed to committing ground troops in Korea.

. . .

THE PRESIDENT confirmed his decision that the following orders should be sent:

1. General MacArthur was to send the suggested supplies to the Koreans.

2. General MacArthur was to send a survey group to Korea.

3. The indicated elements of the fleet were to be sent to Japan.

4. The Air Force should prepare plans to wipe out all Soviet air bases in the Far East. This was not an order for action but an order to make the plans.

5. Careful calculation should be made of the next probable place in which Soviet action might take place. A complete survey should be made by State and Defense Departments.

He stressed that we are working entirely for the United Nations.

—Meeting of 26 June:[31]

MR. ACHESON suggested that an all-out order be issued to the Navy and Air Force to waive all restrictions on their operations in Korea and to offer the fullest possible support to the South Korean forces, attacking tanks, guns, columns, etc., of the North Korean forces in order to give a chance to the South Koreans to reform.

THE PRESIDENT said he approved this.

MR. PACE inquired whether this meant action only south of the 38th parallel.

MR. ACHESON said this was correct. He was making no suggestion for any action across the line.

GENERAL VANDENBERG asked whether this meant also that they should not fly over the line.

MR. ACHESON said they should not.

THE PRESIDENT said this was correct; that no action should be taken north of the 38th parallel. He added "not yet."

. . .

[Acheson] suggested that . . . [on the neutralization of the Taiwan Strait and increased aid to the Philippines and French Indochina] if orders were issued tonight it would be desirable for the President to make a statement tomorrow. He handed the President a rough draft of the type of statement which might be issued.

. . .

[Army Chief of Staff] GENERAL [J. Lawton] COLLINS stated that the military situation in Korea was bad. . . .

31. Meeting record by Philip Jessup, in *FRUS, 1950,* 7:179–80, 182–83.

MR. ACHESON stated that it was important for us to do something even if the effort were not successful.

. . .

THE PRESIDENT said he had done everything he could for five years to prevent this kind of situation. Now the situation is here and we must do what we can to meet it. . . . He repeated we must do everything we can for the Korean situation—"for the United Nations."

13 President Truman, public statement, 27 June 1950, ordering the defense of South Korea and Taiwan.[32]

In Korea the Government forces, which were armed to prevent border raids and to preserve internal security, were attacked by invading forces from North Korea. The Security Council of the United Nations called upon the invading troops to cease hostilities and to withdraw to the 38th parallel. This they have not done, but on the contrary have pressed the attack. The Security Council called upon all members of the United Nations to render every assistance to the United Nations in the execution of this resolution. In these circumstances I have ordered United States air and sea forces to give the Korean Government troops cover and support.

The attack upon Korea makes it plain beyond all doubt that Communism has passed beyond the use of subversion to conquer independent nations and will now use armed invasion and war. . . . [T]he occupation of Formosa [Taiwan] by Communist forces would be a direct threat to the security of the Pacific area and to United States forces performing their lawful and necessary functions in that area.

Accordingly I have ordered the Seventh Fleet to prevent any attack on Formosa. As a corollary of this action, I am calling upon the Chinese Government on Formosa to cease all air and sea operations against the mainland. The Seventh Fleet will see that this is done. . . .

I have also directed that United States Forces in the Philippines be strengthened and that military assistance to the Philippine Government be accelerated.

I have similarly directed acceleration in the furnishing of military assistance to the forces of France . . . in Indo China and the dispatch of a military mission to provide close working relations with those forces.

I know that all members of the United Nations will consider carefully the consequences of this latest aggression in Korea in defiance of the Charter of the United Nations. A return to the rule of force in international affairs would

32. *FRUS, 1950,* 7:202–3.

have far reaching effects. The United States will continue to uphold the rule of law.

14 Chairman Mao, speech to the Government Council, 28 June 1950, denouncing Truman's intervention in Korea and Taiwan.[33]

[T]he affairs of Asia should be managed by the peoples of Asia themselves, not by the United States. American aggression against Asia can only arouse widespread and resolute resistance by the peoples of Asia. In a statement made on 5 January of this year Truman even said that the United States would not intervene in Taiwan. Now he himself has proved it false, and moreover, he has torn to shreds all international agreements regarding the nonintervention of the United States in the internal affairs of China. This exposure by the United States of its own imperialist face is of great benefit to the people of China and the peoples of Asia. U.S. intervention in the internal affairs of countries such as Korea, the Philippines, and Vietnam is completely unreasonable. The sympathy of the entire Chinese people and the broad masses of the people throughout the world will be on the side of those subject to aggression and certainly not on the side of American imperialism. They will neither be enticed by the imperialists' bribes nor cowed by their threats. Imperialism is outwardly strong but inwardly withered because it does not have the support of the people. People throughout the country and the world unite and make ample preparations to defeat any provocations by American imperialism.

15 The Joint Chiefs of Staff to General Douglas MacArthur, telegram of 29 June 1950, stressing the limits of U.S. troop commitment in Korea.[34]

The decision to commit United States air and naval forces and limited army forces to provide cover and support for South Korean troops does not constitute a decision to engage in war with the Soviet Union if Soviet forces intervene in Korea. The decision regarding Korea, however, was taken in full realization of the risks involved. If Soviet forces actively oppose our operations

33. The Government Council served in effect as a cabinet, bringing together officials from the highest echelons of the central government. Mao's remarks appeared in *People's Daily* (Renmin ribao) on 29 June. Translation from Michael M. Kau and John K. Leung, *The Writings of Mao Zedong, 1949–1976* (2 vols. to date; Armonk, N.Y.: M. E. Sharpe, 1986–), 1:118, revised on the basis of *Jianguo yilai*, 1:423.

34. *FRUS, 1950*, 7:241.

in Korea, your forces should defend themselves, should take no action to aggravate the situation, and you should report the situation to Washington.

16 Indian prime minister Jawaharlal Nehru to Secretary of State Acheson, 30 July 1950, outlining views on communism in Asia and need to work with the PRC.[35]

Our recognition [of the PRC] is not based either on approval of Communism or all the policies of the Peiping Government; it conforms to our views of the facts of authority over Continental China, which is far the greater part of China, and to our appraisal of the psychology of the majority of the peoples of Southeast Asia. A process of revolution is at work in most of these countries; Indonesia, Indo-China, Malaya and Burma offer abundant proof of this. . . . Communists have found an ally in nationalism especially in those countries where the resistance of Colonialism to nationalist aspirations has proved obdurate. The political evil of Communist totalitarianism has not proved an obstacle to this alliance so far nor is it likely to prove so in future as long as a people's natural longing for freedom from foreign domination is not satisfied. Moreover since all the countries that I have mentioned have a predominantly agricultural economy and land reform is their crying need, any regime which carries out such reforms successfully is bound to make a sympathetic appeal. . . . Our latest effort to seat China in the Security Council . . . was prompted by the honest conviction that such a step was necessary to preserve the United Nations as a representative organisation and to maintain world peace. I think you will agree that so long as a nation of 450 million people remains outside the organisation, the organisation cannot be regarded as fully representative. . . . [G]iven the chance[,] the New China will take a line of its own and work for peace so vital to its economic and social reconstruction rather than try the hazards of war, of its own will or at someone else's behest. But that chance can scarcely come if she is for whatever reasons kept out of the Community of Nations. . . .

17 Central Intelligence Agency appraisal, 18 August 1950, warning of dangers of carrying war into North Korea.[36]

Although an invasion of North Korea by UN forces could, if successful, bring several important advantages to the US, it appears at present that grave

35. Nehru offered his views "on a strictly personal and confidential basis." *FRUS, 1950,* 7:500–501.
36. *FRUS, 1950,* 7:600, 602–3.

risks would be involved in such a course of action. The military success of the operation is by no means assured because the US cannot count on the cooperation of all the non-Communist UN members and might also become involved in hostilities with Chinese Communist and Soviet troops. Under such circumstances there would, moreover, be grave risk of general war.

. . .

The conquest of North Korea would not provide assurance of peace throughout the country or of true unification. The Soviet high command would almost certainly attempt to withdraw into Manchuria or into the USSR a large portion of the North Korean forces. From these areas the USSR might continue to threaten aggression and infiltration and thus produce such instability as to require the continuing presence of large numbers of US or UN forces. Moreover, Syngman Rhee and his regime are unpopular among many— if not a majority—of non-Communist Koreans. To re-establish his regime and extend its authority and its base of popular support to all of Korea would be difficult, if not impossible. Even if this could be done, the regime would be so unstable as to require continuing US or UN military and economic support. If, as one alternative, a new government should be formed consequent to a UN-supervised free election, there is no assurance that the Communists would not win either control of or a powerful voice in such a government. If, as another alternative, a prolonged trusteeship under UN control and with US participation were established, instability would nevertheless continue, with probably even the non-Communist Koreans reacting against the substitution of outside control for independence. Furthermore, Korea once more would become the catspaw of international politics, and its ultimate status would be dependent upon the comparative strength and ambitions of the countries whose representatives supervised the trust administration.

18 The Joint Chiefs of Staff, directive to General MacArthur, 27 September 1950, providing guidance on crossing the thirty-eighth parallel to unify Korea.[37]

Your military objective is the destruction of the North Korean armed forces. In attaining this objective you are authorized to conduct military oper-

37. *FRUS, 1950*, 7:781. This directive was based on NSC report 81/1, 9 September 1950, "United States Courses of Action With Respect to Korea." The conclusions, including a qualified approval for "roll-back" of Korean Communist forces north of the thirty-eighth parallel and unification of Korea under UN auspices, received Truman's endorsement on 11 September. Ibid., 712–21. Guided by this report, the Joint Chiefs drafted a directive, including the critical portions that appear here. They presented their draft to Truman on 26

ations, including amphibious and airborne landings or ground operations north of the 38° parallel in Korea, provided that at the time of such operation there has been no entry into North Korea by major Soviet or Chinese Communist forces, no announcement of intended entry, nor a threat to counter our operations militarily in North Korea. Under no circumstances, however, will your forces cross the Manchurian or USSR borders of Korea and, as a matter of policy, no non-Korean ground forces will be used in the northeast provinces bordering the Soviet Union or in the area along the Manchurian border. Furthermore, support of your operations north or south of the 38° parallel will not include air or naval action against Manchuria or against USSR territory.

In the event of the open or covert employment of major Soviet units south of the 38° parallel, you will assume the defense, make no move to aggravate the situation and report to Washington. You should take the same action in the event your forces are operating north of the 38° parallel and major Soviet units are openly employed. You will not discontinue air and naval operations north of the 38° parallel merely because the presence of Soviet or Chinese Communist troops is detected in a target area[,] but if the Soviet Union or the Chinese Communists should announce in advance their intention to reoccupy North Korea and give warning, either explicitly or implicitly, that their forces should not be attacked, you should refer the matter immediately to Washington.

19 Premier Zhou Enlai, statement of 30 September 1950, expressing publicly concerns over the U.S. role in Korea.[38]

The People's Republic of China resolutely stands on the side of the world camp of peace and democracy headed by the Soviet Union and has, moreover, established the closest fraternal relations with the Soviet Union. During Chairman Mao's visit to the Soviet Union, China and the USSR concluded a Sino-Soviet treaty of friendship, alliance, and mutual assistance which has enormous significance for world history.

September, and he approved it the next day. Ibid., 792–93. The point of the directive was clouded somewhat by Secretary of Defense George Marshall's reassuring follow-up message to MacArthur on 29 September: "We want you to feel unhampered tactically and strategically to proceed north of 38th parallel." Ibid., 826.

38. This statement, made before the Chinese People's Political Consultative Conference, was published in *People's Daily* on 1 October 1950. My translation from *Zhou Enlai waijiao wenxuan* (Selected diplomatic writings of Zhou Enlai), comp. Zhonghua renmin gongheguo waijiaobu and Zhonggong zhongyang wenxian yanjiushi (Beijing: Zhongyang wenxian, 1990), 21, 23–24.

. . . It is very clear that the Chinese people, having liberated the territory of their own land, want to rehabilitate and develop their own industrial and agricultural production and their cultural and educational work in a peaceful environment, free from threats. But if the American aggressors take this as an indication of the Chinese people's weakness, they will repeat the same serious mistake made by the Nationalist reactionaries. The Chinese people ardently love peace, but in order to defend peace they never have been and never will be afraid to oppose aggressive war. The Chinese people absolutely can not tolerate foreign aggression, nor can they stand idly aside while their own neighbors are outrageously invaded by imperialists. Whoever attempts to exclude the nearly 500 million Chinese people from the United Nations and whoever tries to blot out and violate the interests of this fourth of humankind and vainly thinks about an arbitrary solution to any Eastern issue of direct concern to China will certainly bloody their skulls.

20 Chairman Mao to Premier Joseph Stalin, telegram of 2 October 1950, announcing Beijing's decision to send troops to Korea.[39]

We have decided to send a part of [China's] armed forces into Korea, calling them a "volunteer army," to do battle with the forces of America and its running dog Syngman Rhee and to assist our Korean comrades. We consider this course necessary. The reason is that if we allow the United States to occupy all of Korea and Korean revolutionary strength suffers a fundamental defeat, then the American invaders will run more rampant to the detriment of the entire East.

Since we have decided to dispatch Chinese troops to do battle in Korea, we recognize: First, they must be able to solve the problem—that is, they must be prepared to destroy and expel the invading armies of the United States and other countries in Korea. Second, because Chinese troops will be fighting American troops in Korea (even though we will be using the title Volunteer Army), we must be prepared for the United States declaring and entering a state of war with China, and we must be prepared for the United States at least

39. This telegram reflects the decision made by the CCP leadership earlier, on 2 October. My translation from *Jianguo yilai*, 1:539–41. Alternative translations: Li Xiaobing, Wang Xi, and Chen Jian, "Mao's Dispatch of Chinese Troops to Korea: Forty-Six Telegrams, July–October 1950," *Chinese Historians* 5 (Spring 1992): 67–68, and Goncharov et al., *Uncertain Partners*, 275–76.

using its air force to bomb a good number of major cities and industrial centers in China and using its navy to assault [China's] coastal region.

Of these two problems, the primary problem is whether the Chinese army can destroy the American forces within Korea, and effectively resolve the Korean question. If our forces can destroy the American forces within Korea . . . , the seriousness of the second problem (i.e., the United States declaring war on China) will still be there, but the situation will have already turned in favor of the [world] revolutionary front and China. In other words, if the American forces are defeated, the Korean problem is for all practical purposes resolved. (It is possible that formally it may not be over, and the United States might not recognize Korea's victory for a relatively long time.) So [in this case], even if the Americans have already openly declared war on China, this war then will probably not be on a broad scale nor last long. We recognize that the least advantageous situation would be for the Chinese forces in Korea not to be able to destroy lots of American troops and for the two armies to become mutually deadlocked, while in the meantime the United States, having already entered an open state of war with China, would demolish the economic construction plans we have already begun and would moreover arouse dissatisfaction toward us among [China's] national bourgeoisie and other segments of the people. (They are very afraid of war.)

Under current conditions we have decided that on 15 October we will begin dispatching the twelve divisions previously transferred to southern Manchuria. They will locate themselves in suitable areas of North Korea (not necessarily down to the thirty-eighth parallel). On the one hand, [these troops] will fight the enemy that ventures north of the thirty-eighth parallel. In the first period [they] will only fight a defensive war, wiping out the enemy in small detachments and clarifying the situation in its various aspects. On the other hand, [these troops] will await the arrival of Soviet weapons to equip our army, and then in coordination with the Korean comrades carry out a counterattack and destroy the American army of aggression.

According to our information, one American corps (two infantry divisions and one mechanized division) has fifteen-hundred artillery pieces of various types . . . , while each of our corps (three divisions) is equipped with only thirty-six comparable pieces. The enemy has the power to control the air, and our air force, which has just begun training, will not be combat-ready until February 1951, with three-hundred plus planes. As a result, our forces still lack the means to destroy an entire American corps in one blow. Having decided to fight the Americans, we should be prepared with a troop strength four times that of the enemy . . . and firepower one and a half to two times that of the enemy. . . . Thus, we can confidently, completely, and thoroughly annihilate one enemy corps.

Besides the twelve divisions mentioned above, we are also transferring twenty-four divisions from south of the Yangzi River and from [the northwest] . . . to form the second and third batch of troops to assist Korea. We anticipate gradually employing them next spring and summer depending on the circumstances at the time.

21 Secretary of State Acheson, comments to the British UN delegation in New York, 4 October 1950, trying to calm worries about MacArthur's northward advance.[40]

[W]hile [Acheson] agreed there was a risk in going ahead in view of the Chinese Communists['] position as conveyed to the Indian Ambassador in Peiping,[41] nevertheless there had been risk from the beginning[,] and at present he believed a greater risk would be incurred by showing hesitation and timidity. The Secretary pointed out that the Chinese Communists were themselves taking no risk in as much as their private talks to the Indian Ambassador could be disavowed, that they had not made any statement directly to the United Nations or to [MacArthur's] Command and if they wanted to take part in the "poker game" they would have to put more on the table than they had up to the present. The Secretary further explained that . . . [MacArthur's] Command after a period of regrouping would be advancing into North Korea and that it was too late now to stop this process. In the Secretary's opinion the only proper course to take was a firm and courageous one and that we should not be unduly frightened at what was probably a Chinese Communist bluff.

22 The Joint Chiefs of Staff to General MacArthur, telegram of 9 October 1950, anticipating possible Chinese intervention.[42]

Hereafter in the event of the open or covert employment anywhere in Korea of major Chinese Communist units, without prior announcement, you should continue the action as long as, in your judgment, action by forces now under your control offers a reasonable chance of success. In any case you will obtain authorization from Washington prior to taking any military action against objectives in Chinese territory.

40. *FRUS, 1950*, 7:868–69.
41. Acheson refers here to a 3 October interview between Zhou and Indian ambassador K. M. Panikkar. Zhou had again emphatically warned against MacArthur's drive north.
42. *FRUS, 1950*, 7:915. Truman approved this directive on 8 October 1950. Ibid., 911.

**23 Central Intelligence Agency, memorandum of 12 October 1950,
downplaying prospects of Chinese or Soviet intervention.[43]**

[Capabilities:] The Chinese Communist ground forces, currently lacking requisite air and naval support, are capable of intervening effectively, but not necessarily decisively, in the Korean conflict.

. . .

[Intentions:] Despite statements by Chou En-lai, troop movements to Manchuria, and propaganda charges of atrocities and border violations, there are no convincing indications of an actual Chinese Communist intention to resort to full-scale intervention in Korea.

. . .

[Overall estimate:] While full-scale Chinese Communist intervention in Korea must be regarded as a continuing possibility, a consideration of all known factors leads to the conclusion that barring a Soviet decision for global war, such action is not probable in 1950. During this period, intervention will probably be confined to continued covert assistance to the North Koreans.

**24 Chairman Mao to Premier Zhou (in Moscow), mid-October 1950,
confirming the decision to intervene in Korea and laying out the
details of deployment.[44]**

—Telegram of 13 October:[45]

As a result of discussions with the comrades in the Political Bureau, there is a general recognition that dispatching our troops to Korea would still be beneficial to us. In the first phase, we can concentrate on fighting the puppet [South Korean] army. By dealing successfully with the puppet army, our forces can open up a base area in the mountainous region north of the Wonsan-Pyongyang line and raise the spirits of the Korean people. If we can eliminate several divisions of the puppet army in the first phase, the Korean situation may then evolve favorably for us.

Our adoption of the positive policy laid out above will be extremely favor-

43. Truman received this appraisal just before leaving for his Wake Island meeting with MacArthur. *FRUS, 1950,* 7:933–34.

44. Zhou was in Moscow seeking commitments of military support. Soon after his arrival he learned from Stalin that the Soviet air support that Beijing appears to have expected for its forces going into Korea would be delayed. This news made the CCP leadership hesitate before confirming the decision in favor of intervention.

45. My translation from *Jianguo yilai,* 1:556. Alternative translations: Li et al., "Mao's Dispatch of Chinese Troops to Korea," 71–72, and Goncharov et al., *Uncertain Partners,* 281–82.

able to China, Korea, the East, and the whole world. If we do not send troops, allow the enemy to press to the banks of the Yalu River, and let the reactionary bluster at home and internationally mount higher, then this would in all respects be unfavorable. It would above all be unfavorable for the northeast, tying down the whole Northeast Border Defense Army and subjecting the electric power in southern Manchuria to [enemy] control.

In short, we believe that we should and must enter the war. The gains from entering the war are enormous; so are the losses from not entering the war.

—Telegram of 14 October:[46]

I have already told Peng Dehuai [commander of the Chinese "Volunteers"] . . . to set up two or three defensive lines. . . . During the next six months, our troops will not initiate an attack on Pyongyang or Wonsan if the enemy becomes firmly entrenched in Pyongyang and Wonsan and does not take the offensive. After our forces are fully equipped and well trained and have achieved an overwhelming air and land superiority over the enemy forces, then we will launch attacks on Pyongyang, Wonsan, and other areas. This means that after six months we will once more discuss the question of an offensive. Our proceeding in this way allows for certainty and is very advantageous.

. . .

It has been decided that our troops will advance on 19 October. . . . It will take ten days for the whole army of 260,000 to cross the Yalu River, which means that the army will not have completely crossed the river until 28 October.

. . .

While our forces are deploying and are still engaged in the construction of defensive works, it would be good for the Korean People's Army to continue resistance and do everything possible to delay the advance of the American and puppet forces.

25 General MacArthur and President Truman, meeting on Wake Island, 15 October 1950, discussing prospects for an early victory.[47]

[MACARTHUR:] I believe that formal resistance will end throughout North and

46. My translation from *Jianguo yilai*, 1:560–61. Alternative translations: Li et al., "Mao's Dispatch of Chinese Troops to Korea," 73–74, and Goncharov et al., *Uncertain Partners*, 283–84.

47. Record constructed from the notes of seven present at the meeting, in *FRUS, 1950*, 7:949, 953–54.

South Korea by Thanksgiving. There is little resistance left in South Korea—only about 15,000 men—and those we do not destroy, the winter will. . . .

In North Korea, unfortunately, they are pursuing a forlorn hope. They have about 100,000 men who were trained as replacements. They are poorly trained, led and equipped, but they are obstinate and it goes against my grain to have to destroy them. They are only fighting to save face. Orientals prefer to die rather than to lose face.

. . .

It is my hope to be able to withdraw the Eighth Army to Japan by Christmas. That will leave the X Corps. . . . I hope the United Nations will hold elections by the first of the year. . . .

. . .

THE PRESIDENT: What are the chances for Chinese or Soviet interference?

GENERAL MACARTHUR: Very little. Had they interfered in the first or second months it would have been decisive. We are no longer fearful of their intervention. We no longer stand hat in hand. The Chinese have 300,000 men in Manchuria. Of these probably not more than 100/125,000 are distributed along the Yalu River. Only 50/60,000 could be gotten across the Yalu River. They have no Air Force. Now that we have bases for our Air Force in Korea, if the Chinese tried to get down to Pyongyang there would be the greatest slaughter.

With the Russians it is a little different. They have an Air Force in Siberia and a fairly good one. . . . The Russians have no ground troops available for North Korea. They would have difficulty in putting troops into the field. It would take six weeks to get a division across and six weeks brings the winter. The only other combination would be Russian air support of Chinese ground troops. . . .

26 Chairman Mao to General Peng Dehuai, late October 1950, offering guidance on the first major campaign.

—Telegram of 21 October (2:30 a.m.):[48]

Right up to the present time, neither the Americans nor the puppets anticipate our Volunteer Army entering the war, and thus they dare to break up into an eastern and western route and boldly advance. . . . This time we have

48. Telegram sent through the Chinese embassy in North Korea. My translation from *Jianguo yilai*, 1:575–76. Alternative translation in Li et al., "Mao's Dispatch of Chinese Troops to Korea," 76–77.

an exceedingly good opportunity to gain our first victory since leaving China by eliminating some three divisions of the puppet forces and to begin changing the war situation in Korea. . . . This campaign may take seven to ten days (including mopping up) before it can be concluded. Are our troops carrying adequate field rations? Hope you will encourage the entire army to neither spare sacrifice nor fear hardship and to fight for a total victory. . . .

—Telegram of 23 October:[49]

If we can use the night time to deploy our forces for battle with great skillfulness, then even the enemy, despite having a large number of airplanes, will still not be able to impose too great casualties or hindrance. Then our troops can continue field campaigns as well as attack many isolated strongpoints. . . . Even if the United States again reenforces with several divisions, we can wipe them out one by one. In this way it is possible to press the United States to enter into diplomatic talks with us, and perhaps after having our air and artillery requirements met to take [the] major cities one by one. If the casualties and hindrance caused by enemy air raids become so great that we cannot carry out combat operations to our advantage, then our troops will be placed in a very difficult position for the half or full year during which we have not yet been equipped with aircraft. . . . [T]he United States may again transfer five to ten divisions to Korea before our troops, engaging in mobile warfare and attacking isolated strongpoints, are able to eliminate several American divisions as well as several puppet divisions. In that case the situation would also become unfavorable to us. . . . [W]e must do all we can to gain a satisfactory victory in this campaign . . . and we must do all we can to eliminate as many enemy forces as possible before the enemy can transfer more forces to Korea from the United States or other places so that their reenforcements do not keep up with their losses. . . .

—Telegram of 30 October (8 p.m.):[50]

The enemy numbers, their deployment, fighting strength, morale, etc. are all already clear to us. All of our force is well deployed with morale high, while the enemy is right down to the moment in the dark about our situation

49. Mao concluded this telegram with melodramatic instructions to "burn after reading." My translation from *Jianguo yilai*, 1:588–89. Alternative translation in Li et al., "Mao's Dispatch of Chinese Troops to Korea," 80–81.

50. My translation from *Jianguo yilai*, 1:632. Alternative translation in Li Xiaobing and Glenn Tracy, "Mao's Telegrams during the Korean War, October–December 1950," *Chinese Historians* 5 (Fall 1992): 67.

(only thinking in their confusion that our army has forty to sixty thousand men). . . .

27 Director of the Central Intelligence Agency Walter B. Smith, memorandum of I November 1950, evaluating the Chinese troop presence in Korea.[51]

Fresh, newly-equipped North Korean troops have appeared in the Korean fighting, and it has been clearly established that Chinese Communist troops are also opposing UN forces. Present field estimates are that between 15,000 and 20,000 Chinese Communist troops organized in task force units are operating in North Korea while the parent units remain in Manchuria. . . .

. . . Although the possibility can not be excluded that the Chinese Communists, under Soviet direction, are committing themselves to full-scale intervention in Korea, their main motivation at present appears to be to establish a limited "cordon sanitaire" south of the Yalu River. . . .

The Chinese Communists probably genuinely fear an invasion of Manchuria despite the clear-cut definition of UN objectives. . . .

28 Secretary of State Acheson to British foreign minister Ernest Bevin, telegram of 6 November 1950, arguing for continued military effort to unify Korea.[52]

[I]f Peiping discovers that nothing at all happens in the face of its intervention it will be emboldened to act even more aggressively by what it might consider proof of weakness or nervousness on our part. On [the] other hand we do not wish to extend the fighting in Korea to China. . . .

. . .

. . . We can see that Peiping has an interest in having a neighbor in Korea whose intentions are peaceful, with whom any border problems can be worked out with the help of [the] UN, and in whose territory there are not established foreign military bases or installations constituting a threat to contiguous areas of Chi[na]. We do not believe however that we should concede to Peiping any interest whatever in the internal affairs of Korea or in the unification and rehabilitation work to be carried out by the UN. . . .

51. *FRUS, 1950,* 7:1025–26.
52. *FRUS, 1950,* 7:1053.

29 General MacArthur to the Joint Chiefs of Staff, telegram of 9 November 1950 (3:19 p.m.), announcing his final drive to unite Korea.[53]

I plan to launch my attack . . . on or about November 15 with the mission of driving to the border and securing all of North Korea. Any program short of this would completely destroy the morale of my forces and its psychological consequence would be inestimable. It would condemn us to an indefinite retention of our military forces along difficult defense lines in North Korea and would unquestionably arouse such resentment among the South Koreans that their forces would collapse or might even turn against us. . . .

The widely reported British desire to appease the Chinese Communists by giving them a strip of Northern Korea finds its historic precedent in the action taken at Munich on 29 Sept 1938 by Great Britain, France and Italy. . . .

. . .

To give up any portion of North Korea to the aggression of the Chinese Communists would be the greatest defeat of the free world in recent times. Indeed, to yield to so immoral a proposition would bankrupt our leadership and influence in Asia and render untenable our position both politically and militarily. . . .

30 President Truman, press conference statement, 16 November 1950, reacting to the appearance of Chinese forces in Korea.[54]

The United Nations forces now are being attacked from the safety of a privileged sanctuary. Planes operating from bases in China cross over into Korea to attack United Nations ground and air forces, and then flee back across the border. The Chinese Communist and North Korean Communist forces are being reinforced, supplied, and equipped from bases behind the safety of the Sino-Korean border.

. . .

. . . Speaking for the United States Government and people, I can give assurance that we support and are acting within the limits of United Nations policy in Korea, and that we have never at any time entertained any intention to carry hostilities into China. So far as the United States is concerned, I wish to state unequivocally that because of our deep devotion to the cause of world peace and our longstanding friendship for the people of China we will take every honorable step to prevent any extension of the hostilities in the Far East.

53. *FRUS, 1950*, 7:1108–9.
54. *PPP: HST, 1950*, 712.

If the Chinese Communist authorities or people believe otherwise, it can only be because they are being deceived by those whose advantage it is to prolong and extend hostilities in the Far East against the interests of all Far Eastern people.

31 Chairman Mao to General Peng, telegram of 18 November 1950, noting confusion among the enemy as Chinese forces prepare their second campaign.[55]

The enemy side still believes our forces are sixty to seventy thousand men, "by no means an imposing force." This point is favorable to us. America, Britain, and France have absolutely no idea what to do about us, and a feeling of pessimism is settling over each of those countries. Our army has only to fight a few more successful campaigns and wipe out several tens of thousands of the enemy's troops in order to change the whole international situation.

32 General MacArthur to the Joint Chiefs of Staff, telegram of 28 November 1950 (4:45 p.m.), announcing a fundamental change in the nature of the war.[56]

The Chinese military forces are committed in North Korea in great and ever increasing strength. No pretext of minor support under the guise of volunteerism or other subterfuge now has the slightest validity. We face an entirely new war. . . .

. . . At the present moment the freezing of the Yalu River increasingly opens up avenues of reinforcement and supply which it is impossible for our air potential to interdict. It is quite evident that our present strength of force is not sufficient to meet this undeclared war by the Chinese with the inherent advantages which accrue thereby to them. . . . This command . . . is now faced with conditions beyond its control and its strength.

33 Mao to Peng, late November 1950, ordering a third campaign against surprised UN forces.

—Telegram of 28 November (12 p.m.):[57]

55. My translation from *Jianguo yilai*, 1:672. Alternative translation in Li and Tracy, "Mao's Telegrams during the Korean War," 73.

56. *FRUS, 1950,* 7:1237–38.

57. My translation from *Jianguo yilai*, 1:689. Alternative translation in Li and Tracy, "Mao's Telegrams during the Korean War," 75–76.

We have now an extremely opportune moment for our army to destroy the enemy on a large scale and fundamentally to resolve the Korean problem. Forces on the western front should strive to eliminate five American and British divisions as well as four South Korean divisions. Forces on the eastern front should strive to eliminate two American divisions as well as one South Korean division. . . . [By pressing our forces forward] we may lessen our losses somewhat and lower the cost a bit. Hope you will encourage morale and strive for a great victory.

—Telegram of 30 November:[58]

Please do not raise the slogan of passing the winter at rest. . . . This time we will battle on a very large scale. The casualties on the eastern front and on the western front may exceed forty thousand men. It is requested that comrade Gao Gang hasten the recruitment and training of new troops and strive to fill out the ranks by several tens of thousands by mid-December. Awaiting your report on the conscripting and training of new troops.

34   President Truman, formal statement and comments at a press conference, 30 November 1950, responding to the military setback in Korea.[59]

[Prepared statement:] The Chinese Communist leaders have sent their troops from Manchuria to launch a strong and well-organized attack against the United Nations forces in North Korea. This has been done despite prolonged and earnest efforts to bring home to the Communist leaders of China the plain fact that neither the United Nations nor the United States has any aggressive intentions toward China. Because of the historic friendship between the people of the United States and China, it is particularly shocking to us to think that Chinese are being forced into battle against our troops in the United Nations command.

The Chinese attack was made in great force, and it still continues. It has resulted in the forced withdrawal of large parts of the United Nations command. The battlefield situation is uncertain at this time. . . . But the forces of the United Nations have no intention of abandoning their mission in Korea.

If the United Nations yields to the forces of aggression, no nation will be safe or secure. If aggression is successful in Korea, we can expect it to spread

58. My translation from *Jianguo yilai*, 1:692. Alternative translation in Li and Tracy, "Mao's Telegrams during the Korean War," 76.

59. *PPP: HST, 1950,* 724–27.

throughout Asia and Europe to this hemisphere. We are fighting in Korea for our own national security and survival.

. . .

Q. Mr. President, there has been some criticism of General MacArthur in the European press—

THE PRESIDENT. Some in the American press, too, if I'm not mistaken.

Q.—particularly in the British press—

THE PRESIDENT. They are always for a man when he is winning, but when he is in a little trouble, they all jump on him with what ought to be done, which they didn't tell him before. He has done a good job, and he is continuing to do a good job.

Go ahead with your question.

Q. The particular criticism is that he exceeded his authority and went beyond the point he was supposed to go?

THE PRESIDENT. He did nothing of the kind.

⟨Slight pause⟩

Well, what's the matter with you?

. . .

THE PRESIDENT. We will take whatever steps are necessary to meet the military situation, just as we always have.

Q. Will that include the atomic bomb?

THE PRESIDENT. That includes every weapon that we have.

Q. . . . Does that mean that there is active consideration of the use of the atomic bomb?

THE PRESIDENT. There has always been active consideration of its use. I don't want to see it used. It is a terrible weapon, and it should not be used on innocent men, women, and children who have nothing whatever to do with this military aggression. That happens when it is used.

. . .

Q. . . . Did we understand you clearly that the use of the atomic bomb is under active consideration?

THE PRESIDENT. Always has been. It is one of our weapons.

Q. Does that mean, Mr. President, use against military objectives, or civilian—

THE PRESIDENT. It's a matter that the military people will have to decide. I'm not a military authority that passes on those things.

. . .

. . . The military commander in the field will have charge of the use of the weapons, as he always has.[60]

60. After the news conference the White House issued a "clarification" that only the

35 **Meetings between the Truman administration and a British delegation led by Prime Minister Clement Attlee, early December 1950, discussing differences over Korean War strategy and China policy.**

—Meeting in the White House, 4 December (4-5:35 p.m.):[61]

THE PRIME MINISTER said that . . . we wish the Korean business to be limited to asserting the authority of the United Nations against aggression in Korea. We all realize that other forces might come in and might bring on another world war. We are very eager to avoid the extension of the conflict. If our forces become engaged in China, it will weaken us elsewhere. (The President agreed.) . . .

. . .

. . . [W]e must not get so involved in the East as to lay ourselves open to attack in the West. The West is, after all, the vital part in our line against communism. . . .

SECRETARY ACHESON, at the request of the President, commented . . . that the central enemy is not the Chinese but the Soviet Union. All the inspiration for the present action comes from there. . . .

. . . There would be some political advantage in suggesting a cease-fire, but if you go into negotiations, the question arises what price will be asked. The Chinese would probably ask for the recognition of their government and seating in the United Nations. They would also ask for concessions on Formosa and might well insist that any Japanese Peace Treaty must be concluded with their assent. . . .

. . . The Chinese Communists were not looking at the matter as Chinese but as communists who are subservient to Moscow. All they do is based on the Moscow pattern, and they are better pupils even than the Eastern European satellites. The Russians are no doubt pleased with the idea that we might be fully engaged in war with the Chinese Communists who are acting as their satellites. . . . It is hard to believe that this is merely a burst of Chinese military fervor; and if we give them Formosa and make other concessions, they would then become calm and peaceful. On the contrary, if we give concessions, they will become increasingly aggressive. . . .

. . . This moment for negotiations with the communist movement is the worst since [the Bolshevik revolution of] 1917. If we do not negotiate and do

---

president could authorize the use of the atomic bomb and that he had not issued any authorization. *PPP: HST, 1950, 727.*

61. U.S. delegation minutes, in *FRUS, 1950,* 7:1364–68, 1371.

not have a settlement, what do we do? We may fight as hard as we can in Korea, keeping going as long as possible, punishing the enemy as much as we can. Our negotiating position would be no worse then. If we are pushed out later and cannot hold Korea, we are still on the islands. We must refuse to recognize their gains. We could make as much trouble for the Chinese Communists as possible and hold Formosa. . . .

. . .

THE PRIME MINISTER inquired what the reaction of people would be if we continued to hold the beachhead with continuing losses. Wouldn't there be a demand for all-out war against China?

THE PRESIDENT said that such demands are now being made. . . .

THE PRIME MINISTER said opinions differ on the extent to which Chinese Communists are satellites. . . .

THE PRESIDENT believes that they are satellites of Russia and will be satellites so long as the present Peiping regime is in power. He thought they were complete satellites. The only way to meet communism is to eliminate it. After Korea, it would be Indochina, then Hong Kong, then Malaya. . . .

. . .

THE PRESIDENT then said he wished to read to the Prime Minister certain points as follows:

"1. It would be militarily advantageous in the immediate situation if a cease-fire order could be arranged provided that considerations offered were not so great as to be unacceptable. . . .

"2. If a cease-fire should be effected which permits a stabilization of the situation, United Nations should proceed with the political, military and economic stabilization of the Republic of Korea while continuing efforts to seek an independent and unified Korea by political means.

"3. . . . [A]ny United Nations evacuation [of South Korea] must be clearly the result of military necessity only."

THE PRESIDENT here interposed that we cannot get out voluntarily. All the Koreans left behind would be murdered. The communists care nothing about human life. . . .

—Meeting on board the presidential yacht, 5 December (2:45–4:45 p.m.):[62]
THE PRIME MINISTER . . . agreed that it was quite true that Chinese are hard-shelled Marxist-Leninists but it was quite possible that they were not Soviet imperialists. There was a chance of Titoism [a Chinese split with the Soviets]. . . . The Russians have not given very much help to China. The Chinese do not

62. U.S. delegation minutes, in *FRUS, 1950,* 7:1397, 1399, 1401–3.

owe them very much. There is a strong mixture of Chinese nationalism in their communist attitude. . . .

. . .

THE PRIME MINISTER wondered whether it was wise to follow a policy which without being effective against China leaves her with Russia as her only friend. . . .

. . .

SECRETARY ACHESON . . . As the President said yesterday no Administration in the United States could possibly urge the American people to take vigorous action in its foreign policy on one ocean front while on the other ocean front they seemed to be rolled back and to accept a position of isolation. The public mind was not delicate enough to understand such opposing attitudes and even if it were that difference would be wrong. . . . In common with other members of the UN we went out after a smaller aggressor. We are now faced by a big aggressor and we have been licked in this campaign. If we face that by saying that we adjust ourselves to it[,] it affects the whole stand of the people. In that case we must adjust ourselves to power and aggression everywhere. . . .

. . .

. . . For fifty years we have tried to be friends with the Chinese. They have now attacked us with their armies and have denounced us violently. They have done great harm to the work of the fifty years. It may be a decade before the American people are ready to forget it, and to take the attitude that they will overlook this conduct just as if it were a question of the Chinese Communists not having learned to have good table manners. If the Chinese Communists take an attitude of hostility to the United States they will suffer more than we do. Instead of our making an effort to prove that we are their friends we ask them to prove that they are ours. Formosa is too dangerous a thing for them to have to play with. We must hold the islands. We must also proceed with vigor to our armament efforts in Europe. . . .

THE PRESIDENT remarked that we could not separate our discussion from the political problems we face. Mr. Acheson had brought out the need to carry our people with us. Our interest in the Pacific is too great to desert Japan, the Philippines, Canada or Alaska and to run out on it because we have been licked in a campaign in Korea.

—Conversation after dinner at the British ambassador's residence, 6 December (9:30–12:00 p.m.):[63]
Prime Minister Attlee then said he wanted to raise a difficult and a

63. Memo by Lucius D. Battle based on Acheson's recollections, in *FRUS, 1950,* 7:1431–32.

delicate question. . . . He said that there was a feeling in Europe that General MacArthur was running the show and also a feeling that the other participating countries had little to say in what was done. General Bradley and General Marshall . . . said that General MacArthur was doing what he was required to do by the United Nations which had given him direction to hold Korea and get elections there. . . .

The British then proposed some sort of committee to direct the war. General Bradley said that a war could not be run by a committee. . . . He said that if others did not like what was going on, they should say so and they would be given assistance in withdrawing. . . .

The President then said that the United Nations had asked the United States to set up a unified command. He said that he was in charge and would run it as long as the United Nations wanted him to. . . . He said the orders to General MacArthur now were only concerned with the safety of his command. He said that if others came over to bomb the troops there, the President said that every airfield in sight would be bombed in order to protect our troops.

. . .

During the conversation the President said again that his attitude was that we stay in Korea and fight. If we have support from the others, fine; but if not, he said we would stay on anyway.

—Meeting in the White House, 7 December (3:45–5:10 p.m.):[64]

THE PRIME MINISTER remarked that the President had thrown out the idea that there might be some continuation of warfare against the Chinese. . . . [T]he Government of the United Kingdom does not approve of limited warfare against the Chinese if this were not directed to the immediate terrain of Korea but become a kind of war around the perimeter of China. If the Chinese were in the United Nations, there might be a possibility of reaching some settlement by discussion. He realized that this might seem distasteful since it might look as if we were climbing down. But if there were to be a settlement, it was better to have it in the United Nations than to have it forced on any one of us individually. . . .

. . .

THE PRESIDENT said it was political dynamite in the United States.

SECRETARY ACHESON said this was true. . . .

. . .

THE PRESIDENT . . . said that he wanted peace just as Mr. Attlee did. He was not, however, in any mood for an unnecessary surrender to give in to China which is actually the Russian government. He hoped that time would bring

64. U.S. delegation minutes, in *FRUS, 1950*, 7:1451, 1456–57.

them [the Chinese] to realize that their friends are not in Siberia but in London and in Washington.

THE PRIME MINISTER said that he didn't think we would make them realize that by continuing military action against them.

THE PRESIDENT said he quite agreed, but we couldn't leave the Koreans to be murdered.

. . .

GENERAL MARSHALL said they had not drawn up any detailed preparations for [direct action against China]. One suggestion had been for a blockade of the ports and possible air action against critical points. Another suggestion had been for undercover action in South China to make greater difficulties for them than they now have. This was not a proposal to hold the place but to make it harder for the Chinese. . . .

. . .

FIELD MARSHAL [Sir William] SLIM [Chief of the Imperial General Staff] inquired whether this kind of action against the Chinese Communists would not lead the Soviet Union to invoke their treaty with China.

GENERAL MARSHALL said it probably would.

THE PRESIDENT said that was what we were worried about.

SECRETARY [of the Treasury John W.] SNYDER said he could not understand why they could fight us and we could not fight them.

GENERAL BRADLEY said they were actually sending military forces against us and did not call it war, and yet if we drop one bomb across the Yalu they say we are making war against them. . . .

THE PRESIDENT remarked that there were also some Republicans who talked that way.

36 Mao to Peng, mid-December 1950, ordering a third military campaign to exploit China's battlefield advantage.

—Telegram of 11 December (10 a.m.):[65]

According to secret information, [U.S. Army Chief of Staff J. Lawton Collins, after visiting Japan and the Korean front,] has recognized that UN and U.S. forces in Korea are already in a hopeless situation. Given the speed and scale with which the Korean People's Army and the Chinese Volunteeers have attacked, and given the very heavy losses in men and matériel suffered by the American army as well as the extreme deterioration of morale, Collins recog-

---

65. My translation from *Jianguo yilai*, 1:719–20. Alternative translation in Li and Tracy, "Mao's Telegrams during the Korean War," 81.

nizes that the U.S. army cannot organize a long-term defense. Collins has already reported the situation described above and his opinion to the Chiefs of Staff. . . . To judge from the reports of foreign news agencies, Seoul is being prepared for evacuation. . . . Many news agencies report that the Chinese troops fought heroically and that American forces were in a terrible plight with very heavy losses.

—Telegram of 13 December:[66]

At present, America, Britain, and other countries are asking that our army stop north of the 38th parallel in order to facilitate reorganizing their army to do battle again. For this reason our army must cross the 38th parallel. It will be most unfavorable in political terms to arrive north of the 38th parallel and then stop. . . . It is extremely important to fill out [our forces] with a large batch of new troops by mid-January of next year. Request that Gao [Gang] speed up preparations. . . .

37 President Truman, speech of 15 December 1950, limiting goals in Korea and declaring a state of national emergency.[67]

[T]he rulers of the Soviet Union have been waging a relentless attack. They have tried to undermine or overwhelm the free nations one by one. They have used threats and treachery and violence.

. . .

Though the present situation is highly dangerous, we do not believe that war is inevitable. There is no conflict between the legitimate interests of the free world and those of the Soviet Union that cannot be settled by peaceful means. We will continue to take every honorable step we can to avoid general war.

But we will not engage in appeasement.

The world learned from Munich that security cannot be bought by appeasement.

We are ready, as we always have been, to take part in efforts to reach a peaceful solution of the conflict in Korea. In fact, our [UN] representatives . . . are taking part in just such efforts today.

We do not yet know whether the Chinese Communists are willing to enter into honest negotiations to settle the conflict in Korea. If negotiations are

---

66. My translation from *Jianguo yilai*, 1:722. Alternative translation in Li and Tracy, "Mao's Telegrams during the Korean War," 82.

67. *PPP: HST, 1950*, 741–42.

possible, we shall strive for a settlement that will make Korea a united, independent, and democratic country. That is what the Korean people want, and that is what the United Nations has decided they are entitled to have.

Meanwhile, our troops in Korea are continuing to do their best to uphold the United Nations.

38 Premier Zhou, statement of 22 December 1950, outlining China's terms for a cease-fire.[68]

We firmly insist that, as a basis for negotiating for a peaceful settlement of the Korean problem, all foreign troops must be withdrawn from Korea, and Korea's domestic affairs must be settled by the Korean people themselves. The American aggression forces must be withdrawn from Taiwan, and the representatives of the People[']s Republic of China must obtain a legitimate status in the United Nations. These points are not only the justified demands of the Chinese people and the Korean people; they are also the urgent desire of all progressive public opinion throughout the world. To put aside these points would make it impossible to settle peacefully the Korean problem and the important problems of Asia.

39 General MacArthur and President Truman, exchange of views, late December 1950–mid-January 1951, dividing over the limited-war policy in Korea.

—MacArthur to the Joint Chiefs of Staff, telegram of 30 December 1950:[69]

[Recommended retaliatory measures against China:] (1) Blockade the coast of China; (2) Destroy through naval gun fire and air bombardment China's industrial capacity to wage war; (3) Secure reinforcements from the Nationalist garrison on Formosa to strengthen our position in Korea if we decided to continue the fight for that peninsula; and (4) Release existing restrictions upon the Formosan garrison for diversionary action (possibly leading to counter-invasion) against vulnerable areas of the Chinese Mainland. I believe that by the foregoing measures we could severely cripple and largely

68. Zhou was responding to UN efforts to find a basis for cease-fire talks. The translation in *FRUS, 1950*, 7:1598, is faithful to the Chinese version in *Zhonghua renmin gongheguo duiwai guanxi wenjian ji* (A documentary collection on PRC foreign relations), comp. Shijie zhishi chubanshe (10 vols.; Beijing: Shijie zhishi, 1957–65), 1:192.

69. *FRUS, 1950*, 7:1631–32.

neutralize China's capability to wage aggressive war and thus save Asia from the engulfment otherwise facing it. . . . There is no slightest doubt but that this action would at once release the pressure upon our forces in Korea. . . .

. . .

I understand thoroughly the demand for European security and fully concur in doing everything possible in that sector, but not to the point of accepting defeat anywhere else—an acceptance which I am sure could not fail to insure later defeat in Europe itself. . . .

—Truman to General MacArthur, telegram of 13 January 1951:[70]

Our course of action at this time should be such as to consolidate the great majority of the United Nations. This majority is not merely part of the organization but is also the nations whom we would desperately need to count on as allies in the event the Soviet Union moves against us. Further, pending the build-up of our national strength, we must act with great prudence in so far as extending the area of hostilities is concerned. . . .

We recognize, of course, that continued resistance might not be militarily possible with the limited forces with which you are being called upon to meet large Chinese armies. Further, in the present world situation, your forces must be preserved as an effective instrument for the defense of Japan and elsewhere. . . .

. . .

The entire nation is grateful for your splendid leadership in the difficult struggle in Korea and for the superb performance of your forces under the most difficult circumstances.

40 Peng and Mao, exchange of late January 1951, disagreeing over whether to seek a temporary respite from fighting or to start the fourth campaign.

—Peng to Mao, telegram of 27 January:[71]

In order to intensify the contradictions within the imperialist camp, could the Chinese and Korean armies endorse a temporary cease-fire and pull back the [North Korean] People's Army and the [Chinese] Volunteer Army fifteen to thirty kilometers[?] . . .

70. MacArthur replied to Truman on 14 January 1951, "We shall do our best." *FRUS, 1951*, vol. 7, pt. 1 (Washington: GPO, 1983), 78–79.

71. My translation from the document reprinted in extenso in Ye Yumeng, *Chubing Chaoxian: kangMei yuanChao lishi jishi* (Sending troops to Korea: A historical record of the resistance to America and assistance to Korea) (Beijing: Beijing shiyue wenyi, 1990), 339.

The enemy steadily attacks northward. If we don't sally forth at full strength, then it will be very difficult to wipe out anything over a division and to hold our bridgeheads. The result will be the destruction of our plan for troop consolidation and training and the delay of the spring offensive. Moreover, at the moment we have absolutely no resupply of ammunition and rations. At the soonest it would not be until early next month that we could with difficulty move out. Would it be permissible in the light of domestic and foreign political conditions to abandon temporarily the positions from Inchon to the bridge-heads?... If politically it is not possible to let go of Seoul and Inchon, then we will be compelled to deploy for the counter-attack. But considered from every angle, it will be very difficult. I await your instructions as to what is correct.

—Mao to Peng, telegram of 28 January:[72]

It is inappropriate that Chinese and Korean forces pull north fifteen to thirty kilometers and put out information endorsing a temporary cease-fire. For our forces to withdraw from one sector of the area blocking the Han River is exactly what the enemy wants before a cease-fire.

It is possible that after the fourth campaign the enemy will enter into peace talks with us to resolve the Korean problem. . . . China and Korea would be put in a disadvantageous position if Seoul falls under the threat of enemy fire and we then stop fighting and talk peace. This is absolutely unacceptable to us.

That our forces are not being resupplied with sufficient troops, ammunition, and medicines is indeed a very great difficulty. But we still have the strength to annihilate an American corps in part and four to five South Korean divisions if we concentrate our main forces. . . .

After occupying areas north of Taejon and Andong, the Chinese and Korean troops can spend two or three months on preparatory work, and then conduct the fifth and what we intend as the final campaign. Taken from whatever perspective, this is rather more favorable.

41   Chairman Mao to Premier Stalin, telegram of 1 March 1951, explaining the shift to a new strategy of rotational warfare.[73]

First, it is clear from the most recently conducted campaigns of the Korean War that the greater part of the enemy has not suffered destruction and

72. My translation from Ye, *Chubing Chaoxian,* 340–41. Alternative translation: Chen Jian, "China's Changing Aims during the Korean War," *Journal of American–East Asian Relations* 1 (Spring 1992): 32–33.

73. My translation from *Jianguo yilai,* 2:151–53.

therefore is not going to abandon Korea. If we are going to destroy the enemy in any large numbers, then we need time. . . . We ought to make preparations for at least two years. The enemy's current plan is to conduct a war of attrition against us. Just within the past month the enemy forces held in the rear areas have been set in order and reenforced with an eye to carrying out probing attacks against us. Their intention is, on the one hand, to deprive essential rest and resupply to our front lines and, on the other hand, to use their technological advantage to wear down our forces. At the same time the enemy has been most active in carrying out harassing attacks on the Korean coast and constantly bombing transport lines. Only sixty to seventy percent of the resupply matériel for our forces are reaching the front lines, and the remaining thirty to forty percent is being destroyed. . . .

Second, in order to destroy the enemy's plan, to support a long-term conflict, and to realize our goal of progressively annihilating the enemy, our Chinese Volunteer Army is adopting a plan of rotational warfare [by which forces would serve for a time on the front line and then fall back in favor of fresh new forces]. . . . Over the past four campaigns the Chinese Volunteer Army has already suffered over a hundred thousand battle and non-battle casualties. . . . This year and next we are preparing for an additional three hundred thousand casualties. . . .

. . .

In sum, under conditions in which the United States fights constantly and with determination and the U.S. forces constantly obtain great quantities of resupply in preparation for a long-term war of attrition against our forces, our forces will have to prepare for a prolonged conflict. After losing several hundred thousand Americans over a period of several years, they will have to recognize the difficulty that they are in and pull back. Then we can settle the Korean question.

42   President Truman, national radio report of 11 April 1950, defending his limited-war strategy and his dismissal of MacArthur.[74]

The Communists in the Kremlin are engaged in a monstrous conspiracy to stamp out freedom all over the world. If they were to succeed, the United States would be numbered among their principal victims. It must be clear to everyone that the United States cannot—and will not—sit idly by and await foreign conquest. . . .

74. *PPP: HST, 1951* (Washington: GPO, 1965), 223, 225–26.

. . .

So far, by fighting a limited war in Korea, we have prevented aggression from succeeding, and bringing on a general war. And the ability of the whole free world to resist Communist aggression has been greatly improved.

We have taught the enemy a lesson. He has found that aggression is not cheap or easy. . . .

. . .

But you may ask why can't we take other steps to punish the aggressor. Why don't we bomb Manchuria and China itself? Why don't we assist the Chinese Nationalist troops to land on the mainland of China?

If we were to do these things we would be running a very grave risk of starting a general war. If that were to happen, we would have brought about the exact situation we are trying to prevent.

If we were to do these things, we would become entangled in a vast conflict on the continent of Asia and our task would become immeasurably more difficult all over the world.

. . .

A number of events have made it evident that General MacArthur did not agree with that policy. I have therefore considered it essential to relieve General MacArthur so that there would be no doubt or confusion as to the real purpose and aim of our policy.

It was with the deepest personal regret that I found myself compelled to take this action. General MacArthur is one of our greatest military commanders. But the cause of world peace is much more important than any individual.

. . .

We are ready, at any time, to negotiate for a restoration of peace in the area. But we will not engage in appeasement. We are only interested in real peace.

43 National Security Council study 48/5, 17 May 1951, confirming a policy of pressure against China while seeking peace in Korea.[75]

In view of the threat to United States security interests resulting from communist aggression in Asia, it should be the policy of the United States to:

a. Detach China as an effective ally of the USSR and support the development of an independent China which has renounced aggression.

. . .

75. Truman gave his approval to this study, titled "United States Objectives, Policies and Courses of Action in Asia," on 17 May 1951. *FRUS, 1951*, vol. 6, pt. 1 (Washington: GPO, 1977), 35–37.

e. Continue as an ultimate objective to seek by political, as distinguished from military means, a solution of the Korean problem which would provide for a united, independent and democratic Korea. Seek, through appropriate UN machinery, as a current objective a settlement acceptable to the United States, of the Korean conflict which would, as a minimum (1) terminate hostilities under appropriate armistice arrangements; (2) establish the authority of the Republic of Korea [ROK] . . . [at least up to] the 38th Parallel[;] (3) provide for the withdrawal by appropriate stages of non-Korean armed forces from Korea; (4) permit the building of sufficient ROK military power to deter or repel a renewed North Korean aggression. Until the above current objective is attainable, continue to oppose and penalize the aggressor.

f. Consistent with *e.* above and the protection of the security of U.S. and UN forces, seek to avoid the extension of hostilities in Korea into a general war with the Soviet Union, and seek to avoid the extension beyond Korea of hostilities with Communist China, particularly without the support of our major allies.

. . .

While continuing to recognize the National Government [on Taiwan] as the legal government of China, the United States, with respect to Communist China, should now:

a. Continue strong efforts to deflate Chinese Communist political and military strength and prestige by inflicting heavy losses on Chinese forces in Korea through the present UN operation.

b. Expand and intensify, by all available means, efforts to develop noncommunist leadership and to influence the leaders and people in China to oppose the present Peiping regime and to seek its reorientation or replacement.

c. Foster and support anti-communist Chinese elements both outside and within China with a view to developing and expanding resistance in China to the Peiping regime's control, particularly in South China.

d. Stimulate differences between the Peiping and Moscow regimes and create cleavages within the Peiping regime itself by every practicable means.

e. Continue United States economic restrictions against China, continue to oppose seating Communist China in the UN, intensify efforts to persuade other nations to adopt similar positions, and foster the imposition of United Nations political and economic sanctions as related to developments in Korea.

f. . . . [E]xpedite the development of plans for the following courses of action, if such action should later be deemed necessary:

(1) Imposing a blockade of the China coast by naval and air forces.

(2) Military action against selected targets held by Communist China outside of Korea.

(3) Participation defensively or offensively of the Chinese Nationalist forces, and the necessary operational assistance to make them effective.

44 Mao to Peng, late May–early June 1951, urging Chinese forces to hold firm while consultations on peace talks begin.

—Telegram of 26 May:[76]

[I]n every respect we have had difficulty in carrying out our task [of destroying American forces]. This is because American forces at present still have quite a strong combat determination and confidence. . . . If in carrying out three or four more campaigns we can completely wipe out three or four entire battalions from each of the American and British divisions, then their morale has to fall and their confidence has to quake. Then we can plan on possibly destroying an entire enemy division or two or three entire divisions. . . . We still need several campaigns to complete the process of moving from the stage of destroying small units to the stage of large-scale field campaigns. . . .

—Telegram of 2 June:[77]

Comrade Kim Il Sung will probably arrive in Beijing late on 3 June. He may offer views on the conduct of the war. . . . Right now it is extremely important to raise the fighting spirit, halt the enemy advance, and stabilize the situation. . . .

76. My translation from *Jianguo yilai,* 2:331–32.
77. My translation from *Jianguo yilai,* 2:350.

5

Managing the Cuban Missile Crisis, 1961–1963

MODEL OR MUDDLE?

The confrontation in October 1962 between the United States and the Soviet Union is well established as a classic foreign policy crisis. It summoned up in the minds of participants the nightmare of all-out nuclear war, and forced both sides to make life-and-death decisions quickly and under conditions of psychological wear and tear that grew greater as the crisis consumed one week and extended into another. Then with the same suddenness that it had appeared, the crisis came to a resolution—to the relief of tension-wracked policymakers in Moscow and Washington.

*   *   *

In the United States the Cuban missile crisis has figured as the golden hour in the Camelot drama staged by the administration of President John F. Kennedy. The drama began with Kennedy entering office after a slim election victory over Dwight Eisenhower's vice president, Richard Nixon. During the election Kennedy had attacked the political torpor of the Eisenhower years and promised to get the country "moving again." His inaugural address continued that activist theme. "In the long history of the world, only a few generations have been granted the role of defending freedom in its hour of maximum danger. I do not shrink from this responsibility—I welcome it."[1] He singled out Latin America as a critical front in this battle for freedom (Document 1).

1. *Public Papers of the Presidents: John F. Kennedy* [hereafter *PPP: JFK*], *1961* (Washington: Government Printing Office, 1962), 2–3.

But in fact the world proved more obdurate than Kennedy had expected. And so, rather than getting the nation going again, JFK almost at once suffered foreign policy failures that left the young president's skill and resolution in doubt and his administration vulnerable to criticism.

His first fiasco was an attempt to overthrow Fidel Castro's new revolutionary regime in Cuba by dispatching a force of Cuban exiles trained and supported by the Central Intelligence Agency (CIA). Eisenhower had approved planning for Castro's overthrow in January 1960, only a year after the latter's triumph over the dictator Fulgencio Batista. The goal was to put in place a Cuban government "more devoted to the true interests of the Cuban people and more acceptable to the U.S." while avoiding "any appearance of U.S. intervention."[2] By the time Kennedy entered the White House, plans for an invasion by Cuban exiles were well advanced, and Kennedy agreed to let the invasion go forward.

The landing at the Bay of Pigs on 17 April 1961 went all wrong. Kennedy cut back on the already limited air support for the landing. Castro, having correctly concluded that the United States would not tolerate a revolutionary regime nearby, had his army at the ready. And the Cuban people, defying the planners' predictions, did not rise up to support the landing. The setback was galling to Kennedy. He had electioneered against the Republican failure to hold Cuba, and now he had failed to redeem the loss.

Kennedy's initial dealings with Nikita Khrushchev, premier of the USSR and chairman of its Communist Party, was also a cause for chagrin. The two leaders had met for the first time in Vienna in June 1961. For three years Khrushchev had been challenging four-power occupation rights in Berlin, with the aim of extracting U.S., French, and British recognition of the eastern regime within a permanently divided Germany. His insistent, sometimes belligerent handling of this sensitive issue had raised tensions with the other three powers sharing control of the city. The Vienna meeting failed to open the doors to a diplomatic settlement. Indeed, the two leaders engaged in a bruising exchange that raised the possibility of war over Berlin. The two parted, with Khrushchev contending that he would act unilaterally by December and Kennedy muttering, "It will be a cold winter."[3] In August Khrushchev imposed his own dramatic and simple solution on Berlin: he constructed a wall blocking population movement out of the Communist-controlled eastern part of the city. Kennedy decided to acquiesce. But his earlier defense of the status quo made his response now look weak.

2. U.S. Department of State, *Foreign Relations of the United States, 1958–1960*, vol. 6 (Washington: GPO, 1991), 850.

3. Kennedy quoted in Arthur M. Schlesinger, Jr., *A Thousand Days: John F. Kennedy in the White House* (Boston: Houghton Mifflin, 1965), 374.

Castro also helped set the stage for the crisis. He was determined not only to defend his revolution but also to take his country out of the tight U.S. orbit in which it had moved for half a century. Castro rejected the view commonplace among North Americans of a benevolent relationship between teacher and student. He instead saw the United States intent on subordinating the island nation to mainland political and economic interests beginning formally with the U.S. intervention in 1898 to end Spanish colonial control. After a three-year military occupation Washington had maintained its own control by military interventions, the backing of a line of "responsible" Cuban leaders (most recently Batista), and the promotion and protection of private investments. Cuba could not shape its own destiny, whether revolutionary or even reformist, so long as this deep and complex pattern of Yanqui control continued.

Castro was thus defiant in the face of mounting American pressure (Document 3). As early as the spring of 1959 the CIA had begun small-scale operations including support for anti-Castro guerilla groups. In the summer of 1960, following the forging of Cuban diplomatic and trade ties with the USSR, Washington had retaliated by suspending Cuban sugar's favored access to the U.S. market, imposing a trade embargo, and setting in motion the first plot to assassinate Castro. In January 1961 the outgoing Eisenhower administration broke diplomatic relations in response to Cuba's nationalization of U.S. investments and Castro's tightening military and economic ties with the Soviet Union.

Kennedy came into office determined to keep up the pressure and bring Castro down. In November 1961 he authorized a covert operation whose code name, Mongoose, revealed Washington's hope to direct a fatal strike at Castro's regime. Run by Edward Lansdale, a veteran of counterinsurgency programs in the Philippines and Vietnam, Mongoose was one of the largest Cold War covert efforts. It included in its menu of options an invasion by U.S. forces, and military preparations for just such a contingency intensified through the summer and fall of 1962. Reflecting the priority Mongoose enjoyed, the president assigned his brother, Attorney General Robert Kennedy, and Chairman of the Joint Chiefs of Staff Maxwell Taylor the responsibility for overseeing the project. Impatient for results, the oversight group pressed Lansdale forward into the fall and even into the first day of the missile crisis (Documents 4, 6, and 8). Along with Mongoose, the CIA continued planning for Castro's assassination. Finally, in January 1962, the Kennedy administration secured Cuba's expulsion from the Organization of American States, a prelude to a program of intensified pressure on Castro's government.

Khrushchev watched the American campaign against Cuba with growing apprehension. He still wanted "peaceful coexistence" with the United States, a position he had first laid out in 1956. In January 1961, just before Kennedy entered the White House, the Soviet leader repeated his call to compete with and overtake the capitalist economies. "The quicker we increase economic construction, the stronger we are economically and politically, the greater will be the influence of the Socialist camp on historical development, on the destiny of the world." At the same time, in remarks read nervously in Washington, he made clear that he endorsed wars of national liberation. Such wars "will continue to exist as long as imperialism exists, as long as colonialism exists. These are revolutionary wars. Such wars are not only admissible but inevitable, since the colonialists do not grant independence voluntarily." Cuba's "uprising against the internal tyrannical regime supported by U.S. imperialism" was a prime example of a trend in the "third world" that Khrushchev regarded as favorable to the USSR.[4] The Vienna summit conversations between the Russian and American leaders brought the divergence of views on the third world in general and Cuba in particular sharply into focus (Document 2).

Sometime during the spring of 1962 Khrushchev conceived his missile initiative. By then Cuban agents who had penetrated the exile groups had brought to light the invasion plans built into Operation Mongoose. U.S. military exercises in the Caribbean in April and May confirmed the possibility of an invasion. Khrushchev later recalled that he was then "haunted by the knowledge that the Americans could not stomach having Castro's Cuba right next to them. They would do something. They had the strength, and they had the means."[5] Khrushchev was also agitated by the placement of U.S. Jupiter intermediate-range missiles in Turkey right on the Soviet border and within easy reach of Soviet targets. Kennedy himself had made the decision, in 1961, to place these already obsolete missiles in Turkey, and they had become operational in March or April 1962 just as Khrushchev was vacationing nearby on the Black Sea.

After discussions with his advisers, the Soviet leader decided in May to deploy clandestinely to Cuba forty-eight SS-4s (medium-range ballistic missiles or MRBMs) and thirty-two SS-5s (intermediate-range ballistic missiles or IRBMs). The SS-5s, with a range of 2,200 miles, could reach virtually any part of the continental United States, while the SS-4s, with their 1,020 mile range, put under threat a broad arc extending as far north as Dallas, Saint Louis, Cincinnati, and Washington. These missiles were to be accompanied by forty-two

4. Khrushchev's speech, delivered on 6 January 1961 at the Institute of Marxism-Leninism, had as its general subject the sharpening Soviet differences with China. Copy in U.S. Congress, Senate Committee on the Judiciary, Subcommittee to Investigate the Administration of the Internal Security Act and Internal Security Laws, *Hearings* (June 16, 1961), 87th Cong., 1st sess. (Washington: GPO, 1961). Quotes from 57, 64–65, 76.

5. *Khrushchev Remembers: The Glasnost Tapes,* ed. and trans. Jerrold L. Schecter with Vyacheslav B. Luchkov (Boston: Little, Brown, 1990), 170.

light IL-28 bombers. Though outdated and vulnerable, they had a range of six hundred miles and thus could reach the southern United States. To protect the missiles and repel any invaders, surface-to-air missiles (SAMS), coastal defense missiles, and forty-two MIG-21 intercepters were also to go to Cuba. Khrushchev later recalled being assured by his security specialists that forests of palm trees would keep the missiles out of American sight before they were operational. Once they were ready, he would publicly announce the missiles' presence in order to deter an American attack. The Soviet leader put his defense minister, Marshal Rodion Ya. Malinovsky, in overall charge of the deployment, while directing General of the Army Issa A. Pliyev to proceed to Cuba to lay the groundwork.

Early in June Havana agreed in principle to the Soviet plan. But Castro and his chief associates engaged in negotiating terms were soon at odds with Moscow's approach. They did not like the secretive nature of the Soviet plan, preferring a more ostentatious display of outside support based on a forthright claim to self-defense. The Cubans appear to have thought that basing the missiles in Cuba was significantly if not primarily intended to right the nuclear imbalance and strengthen the position of the socialist world. Once in place, these missiles would surely stay as a deterrent to any American attack against either the Soviet Union or Cuba. Finally, Havana was prepared to call the missiles offensive since their purpose was to strike the United States in case of war.[6]

By August the CIA had begun to notice a major increase in Soviet personnel, equipment, and construction activity in Cuba. On 10 August John A. McCone, the agency's director, began to press for stepped-up use of high-altitude American reconnaissance aircraft (U-2s) on the suspicion that this buildup presaged the placement of surface-to-surface missiles aimed at the United States. By late in the month the president and his advisers were following developments closely, prompted in part by this unsettling intelligence and in part by Republican cries that the Soviets were creating a bastion right on the U.S. doorstep. But most of the leading figures in the Kennedy administration did not believe that Khrushchev would gamble with missiles, a view confirmed by a special intelligence review issued on 19 September. Thus with no sense of urgency in Washington, U-2 flights remained limited. Poor weather further slowed the pace of information gathering. In any case Kennedy wanted to keep Cuba out of the news so as not to inject "a new and more violent Cuban issue" into the

6. See Castro's lengthy comments offered in January 1992, reproduced in *The Cuban Missile Crisis, 1962: A National Security Archive Documents Reader,* ed. Laurence Chang and Peter Kornbluh (New York: New Press, 1992), 330–45.

Range of Soviet Missiles in Cuba

The map reproduced here was attached to a Central Intelligence Agency memorandum of 16 October 1962, in Mary S. McAuliffe, ed., *CIA Documents on the Cuban Missile Crisis* (Washington: History Staff, CIA, 1992), 144. Distances are given in nautical miles (1 nautical mile = 1.15 mile). The outer circle corresponds roughly to the range of Soviet Medium Range Ballistic Missiles (MRBMs). The next circle in (630 nautical miles) indicates the approximate striking distance of the Soviet IL-28 light bombers. "Psalm" was the CIA designation for special handling of intelligence on missiles in Cuba demanded by President Kennedy to prevent embarrassing leaks. Robert Kennedy prompted the addition to the map of Oxford, Mississippi, when he asked in jest if Soviet missiles could reach that university town, where the attorney general had become embroiled over desegregation.

congressional election campaign then in progress.[7] If Cuba was the president's chance to prove himself, he was slow to recognize or embrace the challenge.

To deter Moscow as well as to quiet Republicans, Kennedy resorted to public diplomacy. On 4 September he issued a warning against the introduction of offensive weapons, and he followed up at a press conference on 13 September (Document 5). Soviet officials including Khrushchev responded with denials that aid to Cuba involved "offensive" weapons, while insisting that Russia had the right to give Cuba military assistance as long as a threat of invasion hung over the island. They held to this position even into the first days of the crisis. For example, Soviet foreign minister Andrei Gromyko arrived at the White House on 18 October for a longstanding appointment. Questioned by Kennedy, he denied that any of the Soviet assistance to Cuba was offensive or meant to threaten the United States. It was intended, rather, to help Cuba stave off an American attack.

A u-2 flight over Cuba on 14 October finally captured the incriminating images—and plunged the Kennedy team into crisis. On the morning of the sixteenth Kennedy himself was informed and then given a briefing that quickly turned into a discussion of potential American responses (Document 7). Over the next several days the CIA filled out the alarming picture: Cuba held between sixteen and thirty-two missiles, which would probably be operational within a week and might be able to inflict as many as eighty million casualties on American cities. Neither then nor later in the crisis was American intelligence certain that nuclear warheads for these delivery systems had yet reached Cuba. (In fact, thirty-six warheads ultimately arrived and were placed some distance apart from their missile carriers.)

The next several days were marked by intense discussions as Kennedy and his aides met as an executive committee (ExComm) of the National Security Council. Three different responses—each geared to the ultimate removal of the missiles—came quickly to the fore and dominated the next five days of discussion: an air strike or invasion, negotiations, and a blockade (Documents 9–11). Finally, on 22 October, Kennedy went before television cameras to announce to the nation the discovery of Soviet missiles in Cuba and the implementation of a blockade. The U.S. navy would lay down a "quarantine" line to prevent threatening military hardware from reaching Cuba. He warned that an attack from Cuba would be regarded as coming from the USSR itself (Document 12).

The crisis now entered the period of greatest peril. On the twenty-third and twenty-fourth Khrushchev responded with letters condemning the quarantine

7. McCone memorandum of conversation with the President, 11 October 1962, in *CIA Documents on the Cuban Missile Crisis,* ed. Mary S. McAuliffe (Washington: History Staff, Central Intelligence Agency, 1992), 123.

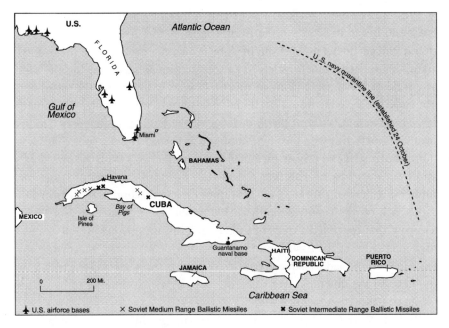

Cuba and the Caribbean, October 1962

as a gross violation of international law and an attempt to strip the USSR of its sovereign right to deal with another sovereign, Cuba, as the two saw fit. He contended that Soviet ships would not respect the blockade and warned that the United States "pushes mankind toward the abyss of a world nuclear-missile war."[8] All attention turned to the showdown at the quarantine line five hundred miles from Havana. On the morning of 24 October the Soviet ships halted short of the line. Some turned back, although tankers were allowed to continue to Cuba. As the tension building in Washington momentarily broke, Secretary of State Dean Rusk is supposed to have remarked, "We're eyeball to eyeball, and I think the other fellow just blinked."[9] The confrontation, however, remained serious. The construction on the missile sites continued, and already nine missiles had been assembled. American forces, including 140,000 troops, gathered in Florida in preparation for an invasion, while U.S. strategic nuclear forces went on high alert. The Cuban military also mobilized for war. By contrast, Soviet and allied east European forces made no dramatic preparations for the looming conflict.

8. "Back from the Brink: The Correspondence Between President John F. Kennedy and Chairman Nikita S. Khrushchev on the Cuban Missile Crisis of Autumn 1962," *Problems of Communism* 41 (special edition, Spring 1992): 33–36.

9. Robert A. Divine, ed., *The Cuban Missile Crisis* (rev. ed.; New York: Markus Wiener, 1988), 61.

Pressures on policymakers reached their height on 26–27 October. The ExComm began its work on the twenty-sixth by discussing possible courses that would get Soviet missiles out of Cuba (Document 13). Late on the twenty-sixth Khrushchev wrote privately to Kennedy, again condemning the blockade as a reckless act of aggression but this time offering to remove the missiles in exchange for a pledge from the United States not to invade Cuba (Document 15). That evening, without the knowledge of the ExComm, Kennedy had his brother Robert visit with the Soviet ambassador, Anatoly Dobrynin. (This was but one of a string of private meetings between the two.) With the president's approval, they began exploring a deal that included removal of American Jupiter missiles from Turkey. Perhaps responding to this initiative, Khrushchev came back on the twenty-seventh with a public letter, broadcast over Radio Moscow, that suggested a trade of Cuban and Turkish missiles as well as a no-invasion pledge as the basis for an agreement (Document 16). Meanwhile the ExComm continued to explore courses of action and then was electrified by the news of the downing over Cuba of a U-2 by a SAM thought to be under Soviet control (Documents 17–18).

By late on 27 October the ExComm was uncertain of Soviet intentions, unclear about the elements that might combine to produce a settlement, and fearful of losing control of the crisis. At the same time news came in that an Alaska-based U-2 had strayed into Soviet territory, thus adding to the edginess of both sides. An agitated Secretary of Defense Robert McNamara exclaimed, "This means war with the Soviet Union."[10] The participants continued to agree that removal of the missiles from Cuba was imperative, but they still divided on the best means and the degree of risk each course entailed (Document 19).

After prolonged discussions, Kennedy deferred a decision on military action, while embracing the first Soviet offer of an American no-invasion pledge in exchange for withdrawal of the Soviet missiles. He chose to ignore, at least in his direct communications with Khrushchev, the issue of the Jupiter missiles raised in the Dobrynin contacts and in Khrushchev's second letter (Document 20).

To push Khrushchev toward acceptance Kennedy used both carrot and stick. Between the afternoon and evening ExComm meetings on the twenty-seventh the president met with a small group from the ExComm that included his brother and his national security adviser, McGeorge Bundy, as well as Rusk and McNamara. The group quickly reached a consensus on putting the Jupiters on the table. Meeting secretly with Ambassador Dobrynin later that same day, Robert Kennedy promised that the missiles in Turkey would be withdrawn after the crisis was resolved. (Robert Kennedy later claimed that he also warned of military action if Moscow did not accept the trade offered in Khrushchev's

10. Chang and Kornbluh, *Cuban Missile Crisis,* 376.

first letter, but the Soviet ambassador has denied that any threats were made.) Just in case Khrushchev rejected the private deal and a formal trade of the Jupiters became necessary to avoid war, the president prepared a fallback without telling the ExComm. He had Rusk draft a proposal along the lines of Robert Kennedy's promise for possible delivery to U Thant, secretary general of the United Nations (UN).

The next morning (28 October) Khrushchev accepted Kennedy's offer of a settlement on the basis of the premier's own first letter. However, the Soviet leader supplemented the formal radio announcement with a private letter indicating that he regarded the Jupiter withdrawal as part of the overall bargain (Document 21). The worst of the crisis was over.

As the pieces of a settlement fell into place, a resentful, sullen Castro refused to cooperate. Ready to die fighting in defense of Cuba's independence, he had at the height of the crisis contemplated a Soviet first-strike against the United States (Document 14). Khrushchev had instead agreed to withdraw the missiles without consulting his ally. Castro learned of the deal over the telephone from a newspaper editor who had been following the Associated Press ticker. A betrayed Castro exploded, "Son of a bitch! Bastard! Asshole!"[11] Unwilling to compromise his country's sovereignty, Castro would not countenance UN or other international inspectors snooping about Cuban soil to verify the removal of the missiles, nor would he sanction overflights into Cuban airspace (Documents 23 and 25). Perhaps with the hope of disrupting the Soviet-American accord, he even advanced his own broader set of demands on 28 October, including surrender of the American base at Guantanamo (at the southeastern tip of the island) and an end to Washington's program of economic warfare and subversion.

Immediately after the settlement Khrushchev sought to calm Castro's anger. He personally responded to his ally with justifications for his bargain with Kennedy and earnest homilies on the dangers of nuclear war (Documents 22 and 24). Anastas Mikoyan, Moscow's main high-level contact with Cuba, arrived in Havana on 1 November for a three-week pacification campaign. (On 8 November, in the midst of this visit, a Mongoose team that Washington was not able to recall blew up a Cuban factory, heightening Castro's doubts about U.S. intentions and Soviet judgment.) Khrushchev capped his bridge-mending effort in late January 1963 with an ingratiating invitation to visit the Soviet Union, where generous trade agreements and credits awaited the Cuban leader (Document 27). Throughout, Khrushchev insisted that the missile gambit had made Cuba more secure and that the Soviet Union would continue with its

---

11. The editor, Carlos Franqui, reports Castro's surprise and anger in *Family Portrait with Fidel,* trans. Alfred MacAdams (New York: Random House, 1984), 194.

program of economic and military support. Khrushchev appears not to have revealed the concession on the Jupiters missiles that he had extracted from Kennedy until Castro's visit in 1963—and even then the information seems to have come out inadvertently.

Castro's resistance and American demands complicated the final resolution of the crisis and set off a round of sparring between Khrushchev and Kennedy on one side and Khrushchev and Castro on the other. Unable to monitor the dismantling of weapons on the ground, Kennedy was forced to rely on aerial surveillance. In this Khrushchev cooperated by having the launchers on board outbound Soviet ships bared for reconnaissance cameras. When Kennedy insisted that the IL-28 bombers be included in the list of offensive weapons to be removed, Khrushchev resisted on the grounds that they had been turned over to the Cubans for coastal defense duties and in any case were not covered by the bargain worked out in late October. Khrushchev for his part pressed a resistant Kennedy to formalize the no-invasion pledge.

On 19–20 November the two reached an accord that brought the crisis to a definitive conclusion. Having finally gotten Castro's grudging acquiescence, Khrushchev promised to remove the bombers within thirty days, and Kennedy lifted the blockade. The no-invasion pledge remained as Kennedy wanted it, a highly qualified commitment contingent above all on Castro's good behavior (Document 26). Khrushchev continued in early December to press for a more satisfactory American statement, but Kennedy would not budge. In April 1963 Kennedy finally delivered on the last, tacit element of the bargain by removing the Jupiter missiles from Turkey. On only two points did Castro get his way: no inspectors violated Cuban sovereignty, and one of the four Soviet combat regiments remained behind despite Washington's call for the withdrawal of all Soviet troops.

* * *

The appearance of a wide range of new evidence since the mid-1980s has done much to improve our understanding of the Cuban missile crisis. But new evidence can complicate as much as clarify. Historians are thus still grappling with the central interpretive issues that have long surrounded this crisis.

Why Khrushchev put the missiles in Cuba is a question that goes back to the days of the crisis itself. Some have offered a psychological explanation. Khrushchev was an opportunist at best or a reckless gambler at worst who was determined to test Kennedy's courage and resolve. The American leader had accepted a humiliating defeat at the Bay of Pigs and in Berlin. At Vienna the Soviet leader had talked tough. Even Kennedy himself came in the course of his first year in office to see the need to prove his determination. "That son of a bitch won't pay any attention to words," he is reported to have said of Khrushchev. "He has to see you move."[12]

A second interpretation (also American in origin) contends that it was not Kennedy's courage and commitment that were in question but rather Soviet leadership of the socialist bloc. China's Mao Zedong was challenging that leadership, charging that peaceful coexistence revealed Moscow's loss of resolve in the face of American imperialism. According to this view, as the Sino-Soviet split widened and erupted into public polemics in the early 1960s, Khrushchev reacted by placing missiles in Cuba to demonstrate that the USSR could lead and defend the socialist bloc. These first two explanations can be seen as complementary. While testing a weak Kennedy, Khrushchev could also turn back Chinese taunts.

A third, strategic interpretation, first suggested in the ExComm meetings, was that Khrushchev sought to close the missile gap that had developed to Soviet disadvantage. Kennedy had entered office charging that the Eisenhower administration had allowed the Soviets to pull ahead of the United States. But in the late summer of 1961 the Kennedy administration discovered from intelligence reports that the "missile gap" favored the United States rather than the USSR. Even so, Kennedy continued to expand his strategic arsenal, moving toward if not actually gaining a first-strike capability.[13] The loss of power to retaliate against an American attack threw in doubt the deterrent effect of the Soviets' main counterweapon, its intercontinental ballistic missiles (ICBMs). According to proponents of this strategic explanation, when Khrushchev read the administration's open boasts of its strategic superiority, he sought to restore the credibility of Soviet deterrence by shifting his shorter-range missiles to Cuba. Well out of reach of the United States when based in the Soviet Union, they could score a strike if placed off the American coast. Here was a quick, cheap, and effective solution to the dangers of inferiority and vulnerability.

A variant on this strategic explanation (suggested in Soviet accounts) is that Khrushchev saw the Cuban crisis as a chance to win greater reciprocity in the rules of the Cold War. If the United States could place missiles right on the Soviet border, then the USSR could do the same to the United States. Khrushchev thus wanted to serve notice that his country would no longer play the nuclear game in the one-sided way that Americans preferred.

Soviet obligations to members of the socialist bloc have provided the fourth major explanation. The placement of the missiles reflected above all a desire to

12. Schlesinger, *A Thousand Days*, 391.

13. A first-strike capability means one side can destroy so much of an opponent's nuclear force so quickly that a serious counterblow would not be possible.

protect a beleaguered Cuba. Havana calculated that a U.S. invasion could cost a country with a total population of eight million some 200,000 to 800,000 casualties. Khrushchev sought some means to deter that threat. The alternative, to leave Castro to his uncertain fate, would have betrayed repeated promises to help struggling, vulnerable new revolutionary governments and given the lie to Soviet doctrine on the importance of wars of national liberation.

How well did Kennedy and Khrushchev handle the crisis? The new documentation suggests that both leaders appear to have been determined to avoid a nuclear conflict. They recognized that developments might slip out of their control and thus each worried about missteps that might have pushed the crisis closer to the brink.

It is still difficult to reach a secure judgment on the Soviet performance without more primary documentation. For a time students of this crisis treated Khrushchev as an erratic and emotional leader seeking to wiggle out of the fix that his gamble had gotten him and his country into. Khrushchev's memoirs and his correspondence during the crisis, however, counter this impression. He professed to have been gravely concerned with keeping the crisis in hand and curbing the hotheaded Castro, who seemed eager to see Soviet missiles speeding their way to the United States. As insurance against provocation, Khrushchev kept the naval task force, the long-range missile and SAM sites, and the troops protecting those sites under Soviet command.

Much more controversy has surrounded the performance of the Kennedy administration. Critics have suggested that Kennedy overreacted and felt driven through the crisis to prove his mettle after his earlier foreign policy failures and to score political points at Soviet expense. When he made the confrontation a public affair with his speech on 22 October, he made it harder for Khrushchev to back down. Although the administration had issued warnings earlier, it did not use the hard photographic information to confront privately either Ambassador Dobrynin or Foreign Minister Gromyko or to communicate directly with Khrushchev with an eye to a private settlement. By drawing the line publicly, so the critics have argued, Kennedy sought to prove his resolve not only to the Soviets but also to the American public on the eve of a congressional election. He may have also wished to head off hard-liners within his own administration, who might themselves have gone public had Kennedy tried to confine missile discussions to secret diplomatic channels.

There is a good deal of evidence on which to make a judgment about the American performance, although the overall verdict is still open. The Kennedy administration seemed shocked by the missile challenge and by Soviet duplicity. Drawing the line openly and dramatically appeared the only reasonable response. The transcripts of the ExComm discussions suggest some concern with the public political effect of the crisis—before as well as after the 22

October public announcement. But on the whole, partisan political calculations and worry over the public reputation of the Kennedy administration seem to have played a minor role in the decision-making.

The more powerful and unexpected impression conveyed by the ExComm transcripts is of confusion. Faced by a host of unknowns, the participants wrestled with the consequences of their actions. (The proceedings degenerated at times into a babble that makes the ExComm seem more like a kindergarten than a crisis-management team.) While some in the group, notably McNamara, were strikingly thoughtful and articulate, others were reduced to near incoherence. Kennedy himself is the most conspicuous instance of this latter tendency. At times he struggled to put a clear, complete sentence together. Poor health and medication may have impaired the president's performance. He suffered from a severe back problem. Malfunctioning adrenal glands called for cortisone shots, and as an all-purpose pick-me-up Kennedy received injections of a New York doctor's home brew that included amphetamines and steroids. This mix of drugs entered his bloodstream without medical coordination.

However tangled his tongue, Kennedy seems to have been clear in his own mind on the need to avoid a belligerent course of action. He consistently held his ground even when on occasion most or even all of his advisers made the case for a more truculent course. Though Kennedy appears to have resolved against military action, he still regarded missiles in Cuba as intolerable. Thus he sought a middle way—getting the missiles out through a deal with Khrushchev while keeping up the military pressure applied through a naval quarantine.

Despite caution on both sides, decision-makers were plagued by misinformation that did lead to miscalculations but not, as it turned out, to any major miscues. A set of key events on 26 October illustrates this point. Alexander S. Fomin (an officer in the security services fronting as counselor in the Soviet embassy) suggested to a newsman, John Scali, removal of the missiles in exchange for a no-invasion pledge. The administration at once assumed that the offer came from Khrushchev himself. Khrushchev's first letter late on 26 October seemed to confirm this view because it proposed the same deal. Hence the administration's astonishment and confusion on the receipt of Khrushchev's second letter, which dragged American missiles in Turkey into the deal while putting the Soviet-American exchange in the public spotlight.

But new information indicates that Fomin's overture was not prompted by instructions from Khrushchev; nor did it even enjoy Kremlin authorization. It was rather Fomin's own idea, to which Ambassador Dobrynin had given his approval. Kennedy's response to the proposed deal did not get to Khrushchev in time to influence the dispatch of the first letter. Khrushchev was more likely moved to send that letter by an alarmist cable from Cuba and Soviet intelligence that an American attack was imminent. When Khrushchev took a tougher stance in his second letter, he may have been prompted above all by Kennedy's own offer on the Jupiters conveyed through Dobrynin. Fomin's initiative loomed large at the time, but in retrospect it appears irrelevant to Soviet decision-making.

The uneven quality of American intelligence offers another illustration of the fog in which the two sides operated. Initially, the intelligence community could not imagine that the USSR would take the unprecedented risk of putting missiles in Cuba. Later, Washington's belief that an American invasion would encounter an estimated eight thousand to ten thousand Soviet troops was dangerously wide of the mark. Soviet sources now claim that they had some forty-two thousand men in Cuba, half of them combat troops awaiting any invader. Those troops possessed, according to those sources, nine short-range (tactical) nuclear missiles, each with a destructive power equal to the bomb dropped on Hiroshima. Moreover, commanders on the ground had authority to decide on their use. They had, in other words, the power to begin a low-level nuclear conflict without even asking Moscow. Washington only belatedly realized that Soviet troops might be armed with these tactical nuclear weapons. American intelligence did somewhat better in estimating the number of Soviet nuclear weapons in Cuba—twenty, with another twenty thought to be en route. In fact Soviet sources have set the figure of MRBMs in Cuba at thirty-six, with more missiles on the way. (None of the longer-range SS-5s ever reached Cuba.)

Contemporary American estimates of the overall nuclear balance were perhaps the most accurate. The Soviets had no more than three hundred warheads targeted on the United States (including only twenty to forty ICBM-mounted warheads), a force that seemed paltry when compared with about three thousand warheads and some 170 ICBMs aimed at the USSR. Clearly the United States enjoyed a marked superiority, but policymakers did not know whether in case of nuclear war they would face only twenty ICBMs launched from Soviet soil or there would also be twenty MRBMs hurtling toward New York and Washington from Cuba. Not knowing whether the warheads for those missiles had yet arrived and, if so, whether they had been mounted on the missiles, the ExComm participants could not be certain what level of destruction the nation faced on the other side of the brink.

These crisis managers were also plagued by untoward events. Kennedy was unpleasantly surprised by the presence of American missiles still in Turkey, which he thought (incorrectly) he had ordered removed. In addition, a U-2 flight strayed into the Soviet Union at the tensest moment of the crisis. Khrushchev, despite his determination to control the military deployment in Cuba, still could not prevent two attacks on American aircraft on 27 October that agitated the ExComm and might have lit the fuse. The anti-aircraft that hit a U.S. reconnaissance plane was under Cuban rather than Soviet command, and the decision by a Soviet SAM missile commander to bring down a U-2 was not authorized by Moscow's rules of engagement but was in fact prompted by instructions from Castro.[14]

Who won the stand off? The answer hinges in the main on the motives assigned in the first place to Khrushchev's Cuban initiative. The long-established answer, at least in the American literature, takes as its point of departure the psychological interpretation of Khrushchev's motives and concludes that the Kennedy administration scored a decisive and dramatic victory. When the Soviet leader threw down the gauntlet, he did not expect the young, seemingly hesitant American to pick it up. When Kennedy did, Khrushchev could no longer persist in a nuclear showdown against superior American forces. He thus withdrew his missiles as the Americans had demanded.

Other verdicts follow if one assigns other motives to Khrushchev. If he was, as he himself claimed, moved by fear of Castro's overthrow, then the quid pro quo extracted from the Kennedy administration makes the outcome look like a draw. Though caught in mid-course, he was still able to secure from Washington a hedged promise of nonintervention as the price for removing his missiles, and so the trade of missiles for Cuban security gave each side what it most valued.

If on the other hand Khrushchev is credited with primarily strategic concerns, then the verdict veers toward the more negative. He secured the removal of American missiles in Turkey, but the preexisting, one-sided rules of the nuclear game survived. Soviet missiles alongside the American border, particularly in Cuba, were still unacceptable. Moreover, the MRBMs that had been returned from Cuba to Soviet territory were once again out of range of the continental United States and thus could no longer play a role in the strategic balance of terror.

Castro might be counted as the real winner. He had thumbed his nose at the Monroe Doctrine, had defied Eisenhower, and would remain a thorn in Kennedy's side. During his last year in the White House, Kennedy could not decide what to do about Castro's painful presence. He had suspended Mongoose operations against Cuba on 30 October and later disbanded the project altogether. In the new year he and his staff discussed some accommodation that might wean Castro from the USSR and began to explore hints that Castro wanted to talk. But in June 1963 the Kennedy administration revived the as-

14. For a fuller list of "near misses," see James A. Nathan, "The Heyday of the New Strategy: The Cuban Missile Crisis and the Confirmation of Coercive Diplomacy," in *The Cuban Missile Crisis Revisited*, ed. Nathan (New York: St. Martin's Press, 1992), 17–20.

sassination project, sabotage missions, and plans for a military strike. Despite continued U.S. pressure and Khrushchev's betrayal, Castro survived and watched both the American and the Soviet leader disappear from the scene. In November 1963, with his Cuba policy still in doubt, Kennedy ended up the victim rather than the beneficiary of an assassination plot. A year later Khrushchev fell from power, undermined chiefly by domestic issues, although his handling of the missile crisis may have weakened his position. Castro's regime remained a galling reminder to American policymakers of the limits of their power to contain revolution even in their backyard, and to Moscow Cuba continued to be an important but expensive and difficult ally.

What was the long-term consequence of the crisis? An answer to this question is the most difficult to formulate, involving as it does disentangling the aftereffects of the crisis from other developments. One plausible response is that the crisis created cross-cutting pressures on the nuclear arms race.

On the one side, the crisis promoted détente. Washington and Moscow agreed in June 1963 to install a hotline to facilitate rapid, direct communications between the leaders in future crises. They also moved with greater alacrity toward arms control. Almost two months after the crisis Khrushchev repeated his earlier warning against the nuclear danger. For his part Kennedy took to the public his concerns over a nuclear arms race and the Cold War fears that fueled it. He offered some statesmanlike and sober reflections in his commencement address at American University in June 1963. Henceforth arms negotiation, he contended, should enjoy high priority. True to his word, he took a first step, proposing a treaty banning tests in the atmosphere (Document 28). Such a treaty was in fact concluded the following August. What else Kennedy might have done to promote détente with the USSR and slow the arms race is difficult to judge.

On the other side, Kennedy bore responsibility for twice accelerating the arms race. His first contribution was direct. On coming to the White House, he had dramatically increased American outlays on nuclear forces. His second was indirect. During the missile crisis he administered a bitter lesson to the Soviets in the costs of nuclear inferiority. One Russian diplomat is said to have observed, "You Americans will never be able to do this to us again."[15] In the following years, while the United States preoccupied itself with Vietnam, Soviet leaders strengthened their own nuclear arsenal, with the goal of achieving a rough parity with the United States.

*   *   *

15. United Nations representative Vasily Kuznetsov quoted in Raymond L. Garthoff, *Reflections on the Cuban Missile Crisis* (rev. ed.; Washington: Brookings Institution, 1989), 133–34.

Dean Acheson, an elder statesman who was consulted briefly during the crisis, looked back at the Kennedy performance and saw little to praise. Although he judged the outcome satisfactory, he thought that it was "plain dumb luck" that had gotten the Kennedy administration there.[16] Acheson's memorable and pungent phrase—offered, to be sure, out of contempt for a government that had not responded as forcefully and quickly as he had wanted—is perhaps wiser than he knew. Plain dumb luck is what decision-makers in crisis need and, thankfully, in the Cuban crisis had.

Prisoners of contingent events and cut off from the intentions and calculations of the other side, American and Soviet leaders struggled to maintain control and a sense of perspective in the face of crossed diplomatic signals and military snafus. As it turned out, they were able to engage in a measured exchange of views and avoid a panic that might have deepened the crisis and brought the collision both sides feared. But under somewhat altered circumstances events might have unfolded less smoothly. In any case, neither side's performance deserves to be held up as a model, not least because each by its own aggressive behavior had helped set the stage for the dangerous confrontation. The Kennedy people could not see how pressure on Cuba might trigger Soviet measures to counter the invasion that seemed in the offing. Khrushchev for his part badly miscalculated when he assumed that Washington would reconcile itself to the missiles in Cuba and leave the island alone. But on the other hand, neither side can be fairly accused of falling into a muddle, oblivious to the need to find the most promising road away from danger.

Castro, the only survivor among the crisis leaders, reminds us that a picture of policymakers muddling through to safety may appeal more to defenders of the status quo, such as Kennedy's United States and Khrushchev's Soviet Union, than to those determined to change the world. The latter, understandably, have regarded warnings of nuclear danger as self-serving efforts to preserve the position of the powerful and to turn back the building of new political orders. As Castro's own 1965 reflections on the crisis make clear, revolutionaries must run potentially high risks that can make even their superpower supporters nervous. The wisdom of those risks, Castro also suggests, is best left to history to appraise (Document 29).

FOR FURTHER READING

A new wave of scholarship building since the mid-1980s has displaced earlier accounts of the Cuban missile crisis shaped by Kennedy administration mem-

16. Dean Acheson, "Dean Acheson's Version of Robert Kennedy's Version of the Cuban Missile Affair," *Esquire* 71 (February 1969): 76.

oirs. The process of interpretive renewal was first evident in the updating of two old standards—Robert A. Divine, ed., *The Cuban Missile Crisis* (rev. ed.; 1988), and Raymond L. Garthoff, *Reflections on the Cuban Missile Crisis* (rev. ed.; 1989). These works were soon followed by Michael R. Beschloss, *The Crisis Years: Kennedy and Khrushchev, 1960–1963* (1991), and the fine set of articles in James A. Nathan, ed., *The Cuban Missile Crisis Revisited* (1992). A series of recent conferences attended by former crisis participants produced insights recorded in James G. Blight and David A. Welch, *On the Brink: Americans and Soviets Reexamine the Cuban Missile Crisis* (1989); Bruce J. Allyn et al., *Back to the Brink: Proceedings of the Moscow Conference on the Cuban Missile Crisis, January 27–28, 1989* (1992); and James G. Blight et al., *Cuba on the Brink: Fidel Castro, the Missile Crisis, and the Collapse of Communism* (1993).

Jules R. Benjamin, *The United States and the Origins of the Cuban Revolution: An Empire of Liberty in an Age of National Liberation* (1990); Louis A. Pérez, Jr., *Cuba and the United States: Ties of Singular Intimacy* (1990); Richard E. Welch, Jr., *Response to Revolution: The United States and the Cuban Revolution, 1959–1961* (1985); and Thomas G. Paterson, *Contesting Castro: The United States and the Triumph of the Cuban Revolution* (1994), offer important perspective on the long-troubled U.S.-Cuban relationship.

The National Security Archive has put out a major microfiche collection of newly declassified documents, *The Cuban Missile Crisis, 1962* (1990), that will remain indispensable to researchers until the U.S. Department of State publishes the relevant volume of the series *Foreign Relations of the United States*. A condensation and updating of that collection—Laurence Chang and Peter Kornbluh, eds., *The Cuban Missile Crisis, 1962: A National Security Archive Documents Reader* (1992)—along with Mary S. McAuliffe, ed., *CIA Documents on the Cuban Missile Crisis* (1992); "Back from the Brink: The Correspondence between President John F. Kennedy and Chairman Nikita S. Khrushchev on the Cuban Missile Crisis of October 1962," *Problems of Communism* 41 (special ed., Spring 1992); and David L. Larson, ed., *The "Cuban Crisis" of 1962: Selected Documents, Chronology and Bibliography* (2d ed.; 1986), provide convenient access to an important sampling of the original sources.

Khrushchev Remembers, ed. and trans. Strobe Talbott and Jerrold L. Schecter with Vyacheslav B. Luchkov (3 vols.; 1970, 1974, 1990), is the most notable Soviet counterpart to the American insider accounts. Some of the still limited Soviet materials are conveniently brought together in Ronald R. Pope, ed., *Soviet Views on the Cuban Missile Crisis: Myth and Reality in Foreign Policy Analysis* (1982).

DOCUMENTS

1 President John F. Kennedy, inaugural address, 20 January 1961, calling for defense of freedom in the hemisphere as elsewhere around the world.[17]

Let the word go forth from this time and place, to friend and foe alike, that the torch has been passed to a new generation of Americans—born in this century, tempered by war, disciplined by a hard and bitter peace, proud of our ancient heritage—and unwilling to witness or permit the slow undoing of those human rights to which this nation has always been committed, and to which we are committed today at home and around the world.

Let every nation know, whether it wishes us well or ill, that we shall pay any price, bear any burden, meet any hardship, support any friend, oppose any foe to assure the survival and the success of liberty.

. . .

To our sister republics south of our border, we offer a special pledge—to convert our good words into good deeds—in a new alliance for progress—to assist free men and free governments in casting off the chains of poverty. But this peaceful revolution of hope cannot become the prey of hostile powers. Let all our neighbors know that we shall join with them to oppose aggression or subversion anywhere in the Americas. And let every other power know that this Hemisphere intends to remain the master of its own house.

2 President Kennedy and Premier Nikita Khrushchev, meeting in Vienna, 3 June 1961, sparring over third-world revolutions and the future of Cuba.[18]

The President then recalled Mr. Khrushchev's earlier reference to the death of feudalism. He said he understood this to mean that capitalism was to be succeeded by Communism. This was a disturbing situation because the French Revolution . . . had caused great disturbances and upheavals throughout Europe. Even earlier the struggle between Catholics and Protestants had caused the Hundred Year War. Thus it is obvious that when systems are in transition we should be careful, particularly today when modern weapons are at hand. . . .

17. *PPP: JFK, 1961,* 1.
18. Chang and Kornbluh, *Cuban Missile Crisis,* 10–13.

. . .

Even the Russian Revolution had produced convulsions, even intervention by other countries, the President continued. He then said that he wanted to explain what he meant by "miscalculation." In Washington, he has to attempt to make judgments of events, judgments which may be accurate or not; he made a misjudgment with regard to the Cuban situation. He has to attempt to make judgments as to what the USSR will do next, just as he is sure that Mr. Khrushchev has to make judgments as to the moves of the US. The President emphasized that the purpose of this meeting was to introduce greater precision in these judgments so that our two countries could survive this period of competition without endangering their national security.

Mr. Khrushchev responded [that] . . . the Soviet Union understood the situation differently. The US believes that when people want to improve their lot, this is a machination by others. . . . This is not so. Failure by the US to understand this generates danger. The USSR does not foment revolution but the United States always looks for outside forces whenever certain upheavals occur. [Long security deletion] . . . A mere handful of people, headed by Fidel Castro, overthrew the Batista regime because of its oppressive nature. During Castro's fight against Batista, US capitalist circles, as they are called in the USSR, supported Batista and this is why the anger of the Cuban people turned against the United States. The President's decision to launch a landing in Cuba only strengthened the revolutionary forces and Castro's own position, because the people of Cuba were afraid that they would get another Batista and lose the achievements of the revolution. Castro is not a Communist but US policy can make him one. US policy is grist on the mill of Communists, because US actions prove that Communists are right. Mr. Khrushchev said that he himself had not been born a Communist and that it was capitalists who had made him a Communist. He continued by saying that the President's concept was a dangerous one. The President had said that the US had attacked Cuba because it was a threat to American security. Can six million people really be a threat to the mighty US? The United States has stated that it is free to act, but what about Turkey and Iran? These two countries are US followers, they march in its wake, and they have US bases and rockets. If the US believes that it is free to act, then what should the USSR do? The US has set a precedent for intervention in internal affairs of other countries. The USSR is stronger than Turkey and Iran, just as the US is stronger than Cuba. This situation may cause miscalculation, to use the President's term. Both sides should agree to rule out miscalculation. This is why, Mr. Khrushchev said, he was happy that the President had said that Cuba was a mistake.

. . . [T]he President said . . . that he held no brief for Batista. . . . The main point is that Castro has announced his intention to act in that general area, using Cuba as a base. This could eventually create a peril to the United States. A further point is, the President said, that the United States recognizes that it has bases in Turkey and Iran. However, these two countries are so weak that they could be no threat to the USSR, no more than Cuba to the US. The President reminded Mr. Khrushchev of the announced policy of the USSR that it would not tolerate governments hostile to it in areas which it regards as being of national interest to it. He inquired what the USSR's reaction would be if a government associated with the West were established in Poland. The United States stands for the right of free choice for all peoples and if Castro had acted in that spirit, he might have obtained endorsement. . . . The President concluded by saying that it was critical to have the changes occurring in the world and affecting the balance of power take place in a way that would not involve the prestige or the treaty commitments of our two countries. The changes should be peaceful. Finally, the President said, if certain governments should fail . . . to give better education, higher standard of living, etc., to their people, and if they worked in the interest of only a small group, their days would be doomed. But in all these developments, the President reiterated, we should avoid direct contact between our two countries so as not to prejudice the interests of their national security.

. . . Mr. Khrushchev said, he agreed that the right of free choice should be ensured to all peoples but the question of choice should be solely up to the people themselves. If Castro has not held any elections, this is an internal affair and it grants no one the right to intervene. If Castro fails to give freedom to his people he will detach himself from them and he will be removed just as Batista was. It would be a different situation if our two countries took it upon themselves to decide this question. Mr. Khrushchev then said that he had noted some inconsistency in US policy. . . .

3   Prime Minister Fidel Castro, declaration issued in Havana, 4 February 1962, denouncing the U.S. program of pressure on Cuba and U.S. domination of the hemisphere.[19]

Cuba has lived three years of the Revolution under the incessant harassment of Yankee intervention in our internal affairs. Pirate airplanes coming

19. Castro issued "The Second Declaration of Havana" following the expulsion of Cuba from the Organization of American States. Martin Kenner and James Petras, eds., *Fidel Castro Speaks* (New York: Grove Press, 1969), 105, 115–16.

from the United States, dropping incendiaries, have burned millions of [pounds] of sugar cane; acts of international sabotage perpetrated by Yankee agents . . . have cost dozens of Cuban lives; thousands of North American weapons have been dropped by parachute by the U.S. military services onto our territory to promote subversion; hundreds of tons of explosive materials and bombs have been secretly landed on our coast from North American launches to promote sabotage and terrorism; . . . our sugar quota was abruptly cut and an embargo proclaimed on parts and raw materials for factories and North American construction machinery in order to ruin our economy. Cuban ports and installations have been surprise-attacked by armed ships and bombers from bases prepared by the United States. Mercenary troops, organized and trained in countries of Central America by the same government, have in a warlike manner invaded our territories, escorted by ships of the Yankee fleet and with aerial support from foreign bases, causing much loss of life as well as material wealth; counter-revolutionary Cubans are being trained in the U.S. army and new plans of aggression against Cuba are being made. . . .

. . .

Great as was the epic of Latin American Independence, heroic as was that struggle, today's generation of Latin Americans is called upon to engage in an epic which is even greater and more decisive for humanity. For that struggle was for liberation from Spanish colonial power, from a decadent Spain invaded by the armies of Napoleon. Today the call for struggle is for liberation from the most powerful world imperialist center. . . .

. . .

. . . [N]ow in the fields and mountains of America, on its slopes and prairies and in its jungles, in the wilderness or in the traffic of the cities, this world is beginning with full cause to erupt. Anxious hands are stretched forth, ready to die for what is theirs, to win those rights which were laughed at by one and all for 500 years. Yes, now history will have to take the poor of America into account, the exploited and spurned of Latin America, who have decided to begin writing history for themselves for all time. . . .

4 Special Group (Augmented), "Guidelines for Operation Mongoose," 14 March 1962, aiming at the overthrow of Castro.[20]

In undertaking to cause the overthrow of the target government, the U.S. will make maximum use of indigenous resources, internal and external, but recognizes that final success will require decisive U.S. military intervention.

20. President Kennedy was briefed on these guidelines on 16 March 1962. The Special Group (Augmented) was created in late November 1961 by the president to oversee Opera-

Such indigenous resources as are developed will be used to prepare for and justify this intervention, and thereafter to facilitate and support it.

The immediate priority objective of U.S. efforts during the coming months will be the acquisition of hard intelligence on the target area. Concurrently, all other political, economic and covert actions will be undertaken short of those reasonably calculated to inspire a revolt within the target area, or other development which would require U.S. armed intervention. These actions, insofar as possible, will be consistent with overt policies of isolating the [Cuban leader?] and of neutralizing his influence in the Western Hemisphere. [Security deletion] The JCS [Joint Chiefs of Staff] will continue the planning [security deletion]. . . .

5   President Kennedy, press conference statement, 13 September 1962, responding to charges of a Soviet arms buildup in Cuba.[21]

Mr. Castro and his supporters . . . are in trouble. In the last year his regime has been increasingly isolated from this hemisphere. His name no longer inspires the same fear or following in other Latin American countries. He has been condemned by the OAS [Organization of American States]. . . . By his own monumental economic mismanagement, supplemented by our refusal to trade with him, his economy has crumbled, and his pledges for economic progress have been discarded, along with his pledges for political freedom. His industries are stagnating, his harvests are declining, his own followers are beginning to see that their revolution has been betrayed.

So it is not surprising that in a frantic effort to bolster his regime he should try to arouse the Cuban people by charges of an imminent American invasion, and commit himself still further to a Soviet takeover in the hope of preventing his own collapse.

. . .

. . . If at any time the Communist buildup in Cuba were to endanger or interfere with our security in any way . . . or if Cuba should ever attempt to export its aggressive purposes by force or the threat of force against any nation in this hemisphere, or become an offensive military base of significant capacity for the Soviet Union, then this country will do whatever must be done to protect its own security and that of its allies.

---

tion Mongoose. It included Robert Kennedy and Maxwell Taylor. Chang and Kornbluh, *Cuban Missile Crisis*, 38.

21. *PPP: JFK, 1962* (Washington: GPO, 1963), 674.

6   Attorney General Robert F. Kennedy, meeting with Edward Lansdale, 4 October 1962, expressing impatience with lack of results from Mongoose.[22]

The Attorney General reported on discussions with the President on Cuba; dissatisfied with lack of action in sabotage field, went on to stress that nothing was moving forward, commented that one effort attempted had failed, expressed general concern over developing situation.

. . .

As a result, General Lansdale was instructed to give consideration to new and more dynamic approaches, the specific items of sabotage should be brought forward immediately and new ones conceived, that a plan for mining harbors should be developed and presented, and the possibility of capturing Castro forces for interrogation should be studied.

7   President Kennedy, first meetings with advisers making up the National Security Council Executive Committee (ExComm), 16 October 1962, reacting to evidence of Soviet missiles in Cuba.

—Meeting from 11:50 a.m. to 12:57 p.m.:[23]

[SECRETARY OF STATE] DEAN RUSK: . . . Mr. President, this is a, of course, a ⟨widely?⟩ serious development. It's one that we, all of us, had not really believed the Soviets could, uh, carry this far. . . . Now, uhm, I do think we have to set in motion a chain of events that will eliminate this base. I don't think we ⟨can?⟩ sit still. The questioning becomes whether we do it by sudden, unannounced strike of some sort, or we, uh, build up the crisis to the point where the other side has to consider very seriously about giving in, or, or even the Cubans themselves, uh, take some, take some action on this. . . .

. . .

I think also that we ought to consider getting some word to Castro . . . that Cuba is being victimized here, and that, uh, the Soviets are preparing Cuba for destruction or betrayal.

22. Brig. Gen. Edward F. Lansdale (USAF) was in charge of Operation Mongoose. Memorandum of meeting by CIA director John A. McCone, in McAuliffe, *CIA Documents*, 111–12.

23. This as well as the other transcripts reproduced below are based on tapes recorded secretly at the time of the meetings. John F. Kennedy Library, *Cuban Missile Crisis Meetings, October 16, 1962* (Boston: n.p., [1984]), 8–9, 11, 13–15, 17, 19–22, 27. Much of the 16 October transcript included here also appears in Marc Trachtenberg, ed., "White House Tapes and Minutes of the Cuban Missile Crisis," *International Security* 10 (Summer 1985): 171–94.

. . .

[SECRETARY OF DEFENSE] ROBERT MCNAMARA: . . . [I]f we are to conduct an air strike against these installations, or against any part of Cuba, we must agree now that we will schedule that prior to the time these missile sites become operational. . . . [I]f they're launched there is almost certain to be, uh, chaos in part of the east coast or the area, uh, in a radius of six hundred to a thousand miles from Cuba.

Uh, secondly, . . . any air strike must be directed . . . against the missile sites plus the airfields plus the aircraft which may not be on the airfields but hidden by that time plus all potential nuclear storage sites. Now, this is a fairly extensive air strike. . . . [T]here would be . . . potential casualties of Cubans in, at least in the hundreds, more likely in the low thousands, say two or three thousand. . . .

. . . In any event, we would be prepared, following the air strike, for an air, invasion, both by air and by sea. . . .

. . .

. . . We don't know what kinds of communications the Soviets have with those sites. We don't know what kinds of control they have over the warheads.

. . .

JFK: What is the, uh, advant—. . . . Must be some major reason for the Russians to, uh, set this up as a. . . . Must be that they're not satisfied with their ICBMs. What'd be the reason that they would, uh. . . .

[GENERAL MAXWELL TAYLOR, chair of the Joint Chiefs of Staff:] What it'd give 'em is primary, it makes the launching base, uh, for short range missiles against the United States to supplement their rather ⟨deceptive?⟩ ICBM system, for example. There's one reason.

. . .

RUSK: Still, about why the Soviets are doing this, uhm, Mr. McCone [CIA director John A. McCone] suggested some weeks ago that one thing Mr. Khrushchev may have in mind is that, uh, uh, he knows that we have a substantial nuclear superiority, but he also knows that we don't really live under fear of his nuclear weapons to the extent that, uh, he has to live under fear of ours. Also we have nuclear weapons nearby, in Turkey and places like that. Uhm. . . .

JFK: How many weapons do we have in Turkey?

TAYLOR?: We have Jupiter missiles...

[MCGEORGE] BUNDY? [special assistant to the president for national security affairs]: Yeah. We have how many?

MCNAMARA?: About fifteen, I believe it is.

. . .

RUSK: Uhm, and that Mr. McCone expresses the view that Khrushchev may feel that it's important for us to learn about living under medium-range missiles, and he's doing that to sort of balance that, uh, that political, psychological ⟨plank?⟩. I think also that, uh, Berlin is, uh, very much involved in this. Uhm, for the first time, I'm beginning really to wonder whether maybe Mr. Khrushchev is entirely rational about Berlin. . . . But, uh, they may be thinking that they can either bargain Berlin and Cuba against each other, or that they could provoke us into a kind of action in Cuba which would give an umbrella for them to take action with respect to Berlin. . . . But, uh, I must say I don't really see the rationality of, uh, the Soviets' pushing it this far unless they grossly misunderstand the importance of Cuba to this country.

. . .

. . . [I]f we go with the quick strike, then, in fact, they do back it up, then you've exposed all of your allies ⟨word unintelligible⟩, ourselves to all these great dangers without...

. . .

JFK: But, of course, warning them, uh, it seems to me, is warning everybody. And I, I, obviously you can't sort of announce that in four days from now you're going to take them out. They may announce within three days they're going to have warheads on 'em; if we come and attack, they're going to fire them. Then what'll, what'll we do? Then we don't take 'em out. Of course, we then announce, well, if they do that, then we're going to attack with nuclear weapons.

. . .

MCNAMARA: . . . And I, I doubt very much that we can keep this out of the hands of, uh, of members of Congress, for example, for more than a week.

RUSK: Well, Senator Keating[24] has already, in effect, announced it on the floor of the Senate.

. . .

[VICE PRESIDENT LYNDON] JOHNSON: . . . [T]he *fact* is the country's blood pressure *is* up and they are fearful, and they're insecure, and we're getting divided. . . . People are really concerned about this, in my opinion. Uh, I think we have to be prudent and cautious. . . . ⟨I'm⟩ not much for circularizing it over the Hill or our allies, even though I realize it's a breach of faith. . . . We're not going to get much help out of them.

. . .

JFK: Uh, eh, well, this, which.... What you're really talking about are two or three different, uh ⟨tense?⟩ operations. One is the strike just on this, these

24. Kenneth B. Keating, Republican of New York, who had begun sounding a warning in late August that the Soviets were engaged in an arms buildup in Cuba.

three bases. One, the second is the broader one that Secretary McNamara was talking about, which is on the airfields and on the SAM sites and on anything else connected with, uh, missiles. Third is doing both of those things and also at the same time launching a blockade, which requires really the, uh, the, uh, third and which is a larger step. And then, as I take it, the fourth question is the, uh, degree of consultation. [Security deletion]

. . .

[ATTORNEY GENERAL ROBERT F. KENNEDY]: We have the fifth one, really, which is the invasion. I would say that, uh, you're dropping bombs all over Cuba if you do the second, uh, air, the airports, knocking out their planes, dropping it on all their missiles. You're covering most of Cuba. You're going to kill an awful lot of people, and, uh, we're going to take an awful lot of heat on it...

. . .

MCNAMARA: . . . There's a real possibility you'd *have* to invade. If you carried out an air strike, this might lead to an uprising such that in order to prevent the slaughter of, of, uh, of the free Cubans, we would have to invade to, to, uh, reintroduce order into the country. And we would be prepared to do that.

. . .

JFK: I think we ought to, what we ought to do is, is, uh, after this meeting this afternoon, we ought to meet tonight again at six, consider these various, uh, proposals. In the meanwhile, we'll go ahead with this maximum, whatever is needed from the [reconnaissance] flights, and, in addition, we will.... I don't think we got much time on these missiles. They may be.... So it may be that we just have to, we can't wait two weeks while we're getting ready to, to roll. Maybe just have to just take *them out,* and continue our other preparations if we decide to do that. That may be where we end up. I think we ought to, beginning right now, be preparing to.... Because that's what we're going to do *anyway.* We're certainly going to do number one; we're going to take out these, uh, missiles. Uh, the questions will be whether, which, what I would describe as number two, which would be a general air strike. That we're not ready to say, but we should be in preparation for it. The third is the, is the, uh, the general invasion. At least we're going to do number one, so it seems to me that we don't have to wait very long. We, we ought to be making *those* preparations.

BUNDY: You want to be clear, Mr. President, whether we have *definitely* decided *against* a political track. . . .

—The meeting resumes at 6:30 p.m. and lasts until 7:55 p.m.:[25]

25. Kennedy Library, *Cuban Missile Crisis Meetings,* 9–15, 17–18, 24–27, 46–47.

MCNAMARA: Mr. President, could I outline three courses . . .

JFK?: ⟨Yes?⟩.

MCNAMARA: . . . of action we have considered and speak very briefly on each one? The first is what I would call the political course of action, in which we, uh, follow some of the possibilities that Secretary Rusk mentioned this morning by approaching Castro, by approaching Khrushchev, by discussing with our allies. An overt and open approach politically to the problem ⟨attempting, or in order?⟩ to solve it. This seemed to me likely to lead to no satisfactory result, and it almost *stops* subsequent military action. [Security deletion]

A second course of action we haven't discussed but lies in between the military course we began discussing a moment ago and the political course of action is a course of action that would involve declaration of open surveillance; a statement that we would immediately impose an, uh, a blockade against *offensive* weapons entering Cuba in the future; and an indication that with our open-surveillance reconnaissance which we would plan to maintain indefinitely for the future, [security deletion]

. . .

. . . [T]he third course of action is any one of these variants of military action directed against Cuba, starting with an air attack against the missiles. The [Joint] Chiefs are strongly opposed to so limited an air attack. But even so limited an air attack is a very extensive air attack. . . .

. . .

It seems to me almost certain that any one of these forms of direct military action will lead to a Soviet military response of some type some place in the world. It may well be worth the price. Perhaps we should pay that. But I think we should recognize that possibility . . . by trying to deter it, which means we probably should alert SAC [Strategic Air Command], probably put on an airborne alert, perhaps take other s—, alert measures. These bring risks of their own. . . . Almost certainly, we should accompany the initial air strike with at least a partial mobilization. We should accompany an, an invasion following an air strike with a large-scale mobilization, a *very* large-scale mobilization, certainly exceeding the limits of the authority we have from Congress requiring a declaration therefore of a national emergency. We should be prepared, in the event of even a small air strike and certainly in the event of a larger air strike, for the possibility of a Cuban uprising, which would force our hand in some way. Either force u—, us to accept a, a, uh, an unsatisfactory uprising, with all of the adverse comment that result; or would, would force an invasion to support the uprising.

. . .

JFK: . . . [T]here isn't any doubt that if we announced that there were MRBM sites going up that that would change, uh, we would secure a good deal of political support, uh, after my statement; and, uh, the fact that we indicated our desire to restrain, this really would put the burden on the Soviet[s]. On the other hand, the very fact of doing that makes the military.... We lose all the advantages of our strike. Because if we announce that it's there, then it's quite obvious to them that we're gonna probably do something about it. I would *assume*. Now, I don't know, that, it seems to me what we ought to be thinking about tonight is if we made an announcement that the intelligence has revealed that there are, and if we ⟨did the note?⟩ message to Khrushchev.... I don't think, uh, that Castro has to know we've been paying much attention to it any more than.... Over a period of time, it might have some effect, ⟨have settled?⟩ back down, change. I don't think he plays it that way. So ⟨have?⟩ a note to Khrushchev.... I don't.... It seems to me, uh, my press statement was so *clear* about how we *wouldn't* do anything under these conditions and under the conditions that we *would*. He must know that we're going to find out, so it seems to me he just, uh...

. . .

He's initiated the danger really, hasn't he? He's the one that's playing ⟨his card, or God?⟩, not us. So we could, uh...

. . .

BUNDY: . . . What is the strategic impact on the position of the United States of MRBMs in *Cuba*? How gravely does this change the strategic balance?

McNAMARA: Mac, I asked the Chiefs that this afternoon, in effect. And they said, substantially. My own personal view is, not at all.

. . .

TAYLOR: . . . You're quite right in saying that these, these are just a few more missiles, uh, targetted on the United States. Uh, however, they *can* become a, a very, a rather important adjunct and reinforcement to the, to the strike capability of the Soviet Union. We have no idea how far they will go. But more than that, these are, uh, uh, to our nation it means, it means a great deal more. You all are aware of that, in Cuba and not over in the Soviet Union.

. . .

JFK: ... let's just say that, uh, they get, they get these in there and then you can't, uh, they get sufficient capacity so we can't, uh, with warheads. Then you don't want to knock 'em out ⟨'cause?⟩, uh, there's too much of a gamble. Then they just begin to build up those air bases there and then put more and more. I suppose they really.... Then they start getting ready to squeeze us in Berlin, doesn't that.... You may say it doesn't make any difference if you get blown up by an ICBM flying from the Soviet Union or one that was ninety miles away. Geography doesn't mean that much.

TAYLOR: We'd have to target then [them?] with our missiles and have the same kind of, of pistol-pointed-at-the-head situation as we have in the Soviet Union at the present time.

BUNDY: [security deletion]

JFK: That's why it shows the Bay of Pigs was really right. ⟨We've, or We'd?⟩ got it right. . . .

. . .

ROBERT F. KENNEDY: Of course, the other problem is, uh, in South America a year from now. And the fact that you got, uh, *these* things in the hands of Cubans, here, and then you, say your, some problem arises in Venezuela, er, you've got Castro saying, You move troops down in to that part of Venezuela, we're going to fire these missiles.

. . .

JFK: It makes them look like they're coequal with us and that...

DILLON [Secretary of the Treasury Douglas Dillon]: We're scared of the Cubans.

. . .

JFK: . . . What difference does it make? They've got enough to blow us up now anyway. I think it's just a question of.... After all this is a political struggle as much as military. Well, uh, so where are we now? Where is the.... Don't think the message to Castro's got much in it. Uh, let's just, uh, let's try to get an answer to this question. How much.... It's quite obviously to our advantage to surface this thing to a degree before.... First to inform these governments in Latin America, as the secretary suggests; secondly to, uh, the rest of NATO [North Atlantic Treaty Organization] [security deletion] Uh, how much does this diminish.... Not that we're going to do anything, but the existence of them, without any say about what we're gonna do. Let's say we, twenty-four hours ahead of our doing something about it, [security deletion] we make a public statement that these have been found on the island. That would, that would be notification in a sense that, uh, of their existence, and everybody could draw whatever conclusion they wanted to.

. . .

I'm not completely, uh, I don't think we ought to abandon just knocking out these missile bases as opposed to, that's much more, uh, defensible, explicable, politically or satisfactory-in-every-way action than the general strike which takes us...

SPEAKER?: Move down...

JFK: ... us into the city of Havana...

SPEAKER?: ... those two.

JFK: ... and ⟨it is plain to me?⟩ takes us into much more...

. . .

BUNDY: Their bombers take off against us, then *they* have made a general war against Cuba of it, which is a, it then becomes much more *their* decision. We move *this* way.... The political advantages are, are *very* strong, it seems to me, of the small strike. Uh, it corresponds to the, the punishment fits the crime in political terms, the[n] we are doing only what we *warned* repeatedly and publicly we would *have* to do. Uh, we are *not* generalizing the attack. The things that we've already recognized and said that we have *not* found it necessary to attack and said we would not find it necessary to attack...

. . .

RFK: . . . Assume that we go in and knock these sites out, uh, I don't know what's gonna stop them from saying, We're gonna build the sites six months from now, bring 'em in...

TAYLOR: Noth—, nothing permanent about it.

. . .

MCNAMARA: You have to put a blockade in following any...

SPEAKER?: Sure.

MCNAMARA: ... limited action.

RFK: Then we're gonna have to sink Russian ships.

MCNAMARA?: Right.

RFK: Then we're gonna have to sink...

MCNAMARA?: Right.

RFK: ... Russian submarines. Now whether it wouldn't be, uh, the argument, if you're going to get into it at all, uh, whether we should just get into it and get it over with and say that, uh, take our losses, and if we're gonna.... If he wants to get into a war over *this*, uh.... Hell, if it's war that's gonna come on this thing, or if he sticks those kinds of missiles in, it's after the warning, and he's gonna, and he's gonna get into a war for, six months from now or a year from now, so....

MCNAMARA: Mr. President, this is why I think tonight we ought to put on paper the alternative plans and the probable, possible consequences thereof. . . . Because the consequences of these actions have *not* been thought through clearly. The one that the attorney general just mentioned is illustrative of that.

JFK: If the, uh, it doesn't increase very much their strategic, uh, strength, why is it, uh, can any Russian expert tell us why they .... After all Khrushchev demonstrated a sense of caution ⟨thousands?⟩...

SPEAKER?: Well, there are several, several possible...

JFK: ... Berlin, he's been cautious, I mean, he hasn't been, uh...

[UNDER SECRETARY OF STATE GEORGE] BALL?: Several possibilities, Mr. President. One of them is that he has given us word now that he's coming over in

November to, to the UN. . . . [W]hen he comes over this is something he can do, a ploy. That here is Cuba armed against the United States, or possibly use it to try to trade something in Berlin, saying he'll disarm Cuba if, uh, if we'll, uh, yield some of our interests in Berlin and some arrangement for it. I mean, that this is a, it's a trading ploy.

BUNDY: I would think one thing that I would still cling to is that he's not likely to give Fidel Castro nuclear warheads. I don't believe that has happened or is likely to happen.

JFK: Why does he put these in there though?

. . .

. . . It's just as if we suddenly began to put a major number of MRBMS in Turkey. Now that'd be goddam dangerous, I would think.

BUNDY?: Well, we *did*, Mr. President.

. . .

JFK: Yeah, but that was five years ago.

. . .

[DEPUTY UNDER SECRETARY OF STATE U. ALEXIS] JOHNSON?: But doesn't he realize he has a deficiency of ICBMS. . . . He's got lots of MRBMS and this is a way to balance it out a bit?

BUNDY?: I'm sure his generals have been telling him for a year and a half that he had, was missing a golden opportunity to add to his strategic capability.

. . .

RFK: . . . one other thing is whether, uh, we should also think of, uh, uh, whether there is some *other* way we can get involved in this through, uh, Guantanamo Bay, or something, er, or whether there's some ship that, you know, sink the *Maine*[26] again or something.

. . .

MCNAMARA: . . . this, this is a domestic, political problem. . . .

BUNDY: Yeah.

MCNAMARA: . . . Now, how do we pre—, act to prevent their use? Well, first place, we carry out open surveillance, so we know what they're doing. All times. Twenty-four hours a day from now and forever, in a sense indefinitely. What else do we do? We prevent any further offensive weapons coming in. In other words we blockade offensive weapons.

BUNDY: How do we do that?

MCNAMARA: We search every ship.

. . .

26. The *Maine* was an American battleship whose sinking in Havana harbor in 1898 increased popular pressure for war with Spain.

MCNAMARA: . . . And then an ul—, I call it an ultimatum associated with these two actions is a statement to the world, particularly to Khrushchev, that we have located these offensive weapons; we're maintaining a constant surveillance over them; if there is ever any indication that they're to be launched against this country, we will respond not only against Cuba, but we will respond directly against the Soviet Union with, with a full nuclear strike. Now this alternative doesn't seem to be a very acceptable one, but wait until you work on the others.

8   Attorney General Robert Kennedy, meeting with the Operation Mongoose oversight group, 16 October 1962 (2:30 p.m.), relaying the president's impatience with the lack of results.[27]

The Attorney General opened the meeting by expressing the "general dissatisfaction of the President" with Operation MONGOOSE. He pointed out that the Operation had been under way for a year, that the results were discouraging, that there had been no acts of sabotage, and that even the one which had been attempted had failed twice. He indicated that there had been noticeable improvement during the year in the collection of intelligence but that other actions had failed to influence significantly the course of events in Cuba. He spoke of the weekly meetings of top officials on this problem and again noted the small accomplishments despite the fact that Secretaries Rusk and McNamara, General Taylor, McGeorge Bundy, and he personally had all been charged by the President with finding a solution. . . . The Attorney General then stated that in view of this lack of progress, he was going to give Operation MONGOOSE more personal attention. . . .

. . .

. . . I [Helms] pointed out . . . that the objective of Operation MONGOOSE would have to be determined at some point since the Cubans with whom we have to work were seeking a reason for risking their lives in these operations. I retailed my conversation with the young Cuban . . . who pointed out that they were willing to commit their people only on operations which they regarded as sensible. I defined "sensible" in Cuban terminology these days as meaning an action which would contribute to the liberation of their country, another way of saying that the United States, perhaps in conjunction with other Latin countries, would bail them out militarily. . . . The Attorney General's rejoinder

27. Memorandum of meeting by Richard Helms, CIA deputy director for plans and future CIA director, in McAuliffe, CIA Documents, 153–54.

was a plea for new ideas of things that could be done against Cuba. In passing, he made reference to the change in atmosphere in the United States Government during the last twenty-four hours, and asked some questions about the percentage of Cubans whom we thought would fight for the regime if the country were invaded.

9   President Kennedy, meeting with the ExComm, 18 October 1962 (11 a.m.), continuing discussions of a response to the missiles in Cuba.[28]

President Kennedy was non-committal, however he seemed to continually raise questions of reactions of our allies, NATO, South America, public opinion and others. Raised the question whether we should not move the missiles out of Turkey. All readily agreed they were not much use but a political question was involved. . . .

McNamara . . . agreed that we could move [missiles] out of Turkey and Italy; pointed out the political complications. At this point McNamara seemed to be reconsidering his prior position of advocating military action and laid special emphasis on the fact that the price of Soviet retaliation, whether in Berlin or elsewhere, would be very high and we would not be able to control it.

Secretary Ball throughout the conversation maintained the position that strike without warning was not acceptable and that we should not proceed without discussion with Khrushchev. President Kennedy then said that he thought at some point Khrushchev would say that if we made a move against Cuba, he would take Berlin. McNamara surmised perhaps that was the price we must pay and perhaps we'd lose Berlin anyway. . . .

President Kennedy rather summed up the dilemma stating that action of a type contemplated would be opposed by the alliance—on the other hand, lack of action will create disunity, lack of confidence and disintegration of our several alliances and friendly relations with countries who have confidence in us.

. . .

Meeting adjourned with the President requesting that we organize into two groups. One to study the advantages of what might be called a slow course of action which would involve a blockade to be followed by such further actions as appeared necessary as the situation evolved. Second would be referred to as a fast dynamic action which would involve the strike of substantial proportions with or without notice.

28. McCone memorandum of the meeting, in McAuliffe, CIA Documents, 184–86.

10   ExComm meeting, 19 October 1962 (11 a.m.), continuing discussions of a response to the missiles in Cuba.[29]

[Former secretary of state and crisis consultant Dean Acheson] said that Khrushchev had presented the United States with a direct challenge, we were involved in a test of wills, and that [the] sooner we got to a showdown the better. He favored cleaning the missile bases out decisively with an air strike. There was something else to remember. This wasn't just another instance of Soviet missiles aimed at the United States. Here they were in the hands of a madman whose actions would be perfectly irresponsible; the usual restraints operating on the Soviets would not apply. We had better act, and act quickly. So far as questions of international law might be involved, Mr. Acheson agreed ... that self-defense was and [*sic*] entirely sufficient justification. ...

Secretary Dillon said he agreed there should be a quick air strike. Mr. McCone was of the same opinion.

General Taylor ... favored a strike. ...

Secretary McNamara ... did not, however, advocate an air strike, and favored the alternative of blockade.

. . .

The Attorney General ... thought it would be very, very difficult indeed for the President if the decision were to be for an air strike, with all the memory of Pearl Harbor and with all the implications this would have for us in whatever world there would be afterward. For 175 years we had not been that kind of country. A sneak attack was not in our traditions. Thousands of Cubans would be killed without warning, and a lot of Russians too. He favored *action,* to make known unmistakably the seriousness of United States determination to get the missiles out of Cuba, but he thought the action should allow the Soviets some room for maneuver to pull back from their over-extended position in Cuba.

Mr. Bundy, addressing himself to the Attorney General, said this was very well but a blockade would not eliminate the bases; an air strike would.

... Others expressed the view that we might have to proceed with invasion following a strike. Still another suggestion was that US armed forces seize the base areas alone in order to eliminate the missiles. Secretary McNamara thought this a very unattractive kind of undertaking from the military point of view.

. . .

29. President Kennedy was not present at this meeting. Memorandum of meeting by Leonard Meeker, State Department legal adviser, in Chang and Kornbluh, *Cuban Missile Crisis,* 124–27.

More than once during the afternoon Secretary McNamara voiced the opinion that the US would have to pay a price to get the Soviet missiles out of Cuba. He thought we would at least have to give up our missile bases in Italy and Turkey and would probably have to pay more besides. At different times the possibility of nuclear conflict breaking out was referred to. The point was made that once the Cuban missile installations were complete and operational, a new strategic situation would exist, with the United States more directly and immediately under the gun than ever before. A striking Soviet military push into the Western Hemisphere would have succeeded and become effective. The clock could not be turned back, and things would never be the same again. During this discussion, the Attorney General said that in looking forward into the future it would be better for our children and grandchildren if we decided to face the Soviet threat, stand up to it, and eliminate it, now. The circumstances for doing so at some future time were bound to be more unfavorable, the risks would be greater, the chances of success less good.

. . .

. . . [T]oward the end of the day [Robert Kennedy] made clear that he firmly favored blockade as the first step; other steps subsequently were not precluded and could be considered; he thought it was now pretty clear what the decision should be.

I I President Kennedy, meeting with military advisers, 21 October 1962 (11:30 a.m.), discussing air strikes against missiles in Cuba.[30]

The President directed that we be prepared to carry out the air strike Monday morning [29 October] or any time thereafter during the remainder of the week. . . .

The Attorney General stated he was opposed to such a strike because:

(1) "It would be a Pearl Harbor type of attack."

(2) It would lead to unpredictable military responses by the Soviet Union which could be so serious as to lead to general nuclear war.

He stated we should start with the initiation of the blockade and thereafter "play for the breaks."

30. The advisers included McNamara, Taylor, and Walter C. Sweeney, Jr., commander of the Air Force Tactical Air Command. Memorandum of meeting by McNamara, in Chang and Kornbluh, *Cuban Missile Crisis*, 145.

12 President Kennedy, speech to the nation, 22 October 1962, outlining his response to the Soviet missiles.[31]

Within the past week, unmistakable evidence has established the fact that a series of offensive missile sites is now in preparation on that imprisoned island [Cuba]. The purpose of these bases can be none other than to provide a nuclear strike capability against the Western Hemisphere.

. . .

For many years, both the Soviet Union and the United States . . . have deployed strategic nuclear weapons with great care, never upsetting the precarious status quo which insured that these weapons would not be used in the absence of some vital challenge. Our own strategic missiles have never been transferred to the territory of any other nation under a cloak of secrecy and deception; and our history—unlike that of the Soviets since the end of World War II—demonstrates that we have no desire to dominate or conquer any other nation or impose our system upon its people. . . .

. . .

But this secret, swift, and extraordinary buildup of Communist missiles—in an area well known to have a special and historical relationship to the United States and the nations of the Western Hemisphere, in violation of Soviet assurances, and in defiance of American and hemispheric policy—this sudden, clandestine decision to station strategic weapons for the first time outside of Soviet soil—is a deliberately provocative and unjustified change in the status quo which cannot be accepted by this country, if our courage and our commitments are ever to be trusted again by either friend or foe.

The 1930s taught us a clear lesson: aggressive conduct, if allowed to go unchecked and unchallenged, ultimately leads to war. . . .

. . . We will not prematurely or unnecessarily risk the costs of worldwide nuclear war in which even the fruits of victory would be ashes in our mouth—but neither will we shrink from that risk at any time it must be faced.

. . . I have directed that the following *initial* steps be taken immediately:

First: To halt this offensive buildup, a strict quarantine on all offensive military equipment under shipment to Cuba is being initiated. All ships of any kind bound for Cuba from whatever nation or port will, if found to contain cargoes of offensive weapons, be turned back. . . .

31. Theodore Sorensen, one of the President's close advisers, drafted this speech. *PPP: JFK, 1962,* 806–9. Shortly before delivering the speech, Kennedy sent a copy to Khrushchev along with a letter stressing American determination to defend its security and urging caution on the Soviet side. "Back from the Brink," 30.

Second: I have directed the continued and increased close surveillance of Cuba and its military buildup. . . . I have directed the Armed Forces to prepare for any eventualities. . . .

Third: It shall be the policy of this Nation to regard any nuclear missile launched from Cuba against any nation in the Western Hemisphere as an attack by the Soviet Union on the United States, requiring a full retaliatory response upon the Soviet Union.

Fourth: As a necessary military precaution, I have reinforced our base at Guantanamo. . . .

Fifth: We are calling tonight for an immediate meeting of . . . the Organization of American States, to consider this threat to hemispheric security. . . . Our other allies around the world have also been alerted.

Sixth: Under the Charter of the United Nations, we are asking tonight that an emergency meeting of the Security Council be convoked without delay to take action against this latest Soviet threat to world peace. Our resolution will call for the prompt dismantling and withdrawal of all offensive weapons in Cuba, under the supervision of U.N. observers, before the quarantine can be lifted.

Seventh and finally: I call upon Chairman Khrushchev to halt and eliminate this clandestine, reckless, and provocative threat to world peace and to stable relations between our two nations. I call upon him further to abandon this course of world domination, and to join in an historic effort to end the perilous arms race and to transform the history of man. . . .

. . . We have in the past made strenuous efforts to limit the spread of nuclear weapons. We have proposed the elimination of all arms and military bases in a fair and effective disarmament treaty. We are prepared to discuss new proposals for the removal of tensions on both sides—including the possibilities of a genuinely independent Cuba, free to determine its own destiny. We have no wish to war with the Soviet Union—for we are a peaceful people who desire to live in peace with all other peoples.

. . .

Finally I want to say a few words to the captive people of Cuba. . . . I have watched and the American people have watched with deep sorrow how your nationalist revolution was betrayed—and how your fatherland fell under foreign domination. Now your leaders are no longer Cuban leaders inspired by Cuban ideals. They are puppets and agents of an international conspiracy which has turned Cuba against your friends and neighbors in the Americas—and turned it into the first Latin American country to become a target for nuclear war—the first Latin American country to have these weapons on its soil.

These new weapons are not in your interest. They contribute nothing to your peace and well-being. They can only undermine it. But this country has no wish to cause you to suffer or to impose any system upon you. We know that your lives and land are being used as pawns by those who deny your freedom.

Many times in the past, the Cuban people have risen to throw out tyrants who destroyed their liberty. And I have no doubt that most Cubans today look forward to the time when they will be truly free—free from foreign domination, free to choose their own leaders, free to select their own system, free to own their own land, free to speak and write and worship without fear or degradation. And then shall Cuba be welcomed back to the society of free nations and to the associations of this hemisphere.

13 President Kennedy, meeting with the ExComm, 26 October 1962 (10 a.m.), discussing ways to get missiles out of Cuba.[32]

[Rusk] said the object of the talks with U Thant [secretary general of the United Nations] today was to set up some form of negotiations with the Russians in New York. The objective would be to obtain a commitment from the Russians that there would be no further construction at the missiles sites in Cuba, no further Soviet military shipments, the defuzing [sic] of existing weapons in Cuba, UN inspection of all nuclear-capable missiles, and an observer corps on the ground in Cuba of 350 technically able inspectors. The U.S. quarantine would continue until a UN quarantine is in place. . . .

. . .

The President said we will get the Soviet strategic missiles out of Cuba only by invading Cuba or by trading. He doubted that the quarantine alone would produce a withdrawal of the weapons. He said our objective should be to prevent further military shipments, further construction at missile sites, and to get some means of inspection.

. . .

Secretary Dillon said we could not negotiate for two weeks under the missile threat which now exists in Cuba.

. . . [The president asked:] If the quarantine would not result in the Soviets withdrawing the missiles, what will we do if negotiations break down?

Mr. Bundy said when the interim 24–48-hour talks fail, then our choice would be to expand the blockade or remove the missiles by air attack.

32. Summary prepared by Bromley Smith, in Trachtenberg, "White House Tapes and Minutes," 194–96. Alternative source: Chang and Kornbluh, *Cuban Missile Crisis,* 179, 182–83.

. . .

. . . The President decided that a presentation of the current situation should be made to the Congressional Leaders.

14 Prime Minister Castro to Premier Khrushchev, cable of 26 October 1962 (evening), urging a first-strike against the United States in case of an invasion attempt.[33]

I consider that the aggression is almost imminent within the next 24 or 72 hours.

. . .

If . . . the imperialists invade Cuba with the goal of occupying it, the danger that that aggressive policy poses for humanity is so great that following that event the Soviet Union must never allow the circumstances in which the imperialists could launch the first nuclear strike against it.

. . . [I]f they actually carry out the brutal act of invading Cuba in violation of international law and morality, that would be the moment to eliminate such danger forever through an act of clear legitimate defense, however harsh and terrible the solution would be, for there is no other.

15 Premier Khrushchev to President Kennedy, private letter, 26 October 1962, offering to trade missiles in Cuba for a no-invasion pledge.[34]

You are threatening us with war. But you well know that the very least which you would receive in reply would be that you would experience the same

33. Castro wrote this message in the bomb shelter of the Soviet embassy in Havana. It was translated and forwarded to Moscow by the embassy, but communications delays prevented Khrushchev from receiving it until early on 28 October. Chang and Kornbluh, *Cuban Missile Crisis*, 189. Castro later claimed that Khrushchev misunderstood his message. He was calling for a nuclear strike only in case of a U.S. invasion and occupation but not in case of an air strike alone.

34. Washington had a full version of this letter by 9 p.m. National Security Archive, *The Cuban Missile Crisis, 1962* (Alexandria, Va.: Chadwyck-Healey, 1990), microfiche no. 01388. Translation corrected on the basis of William H. Brubeck (executive secretary, Department of State), memorandum to McGeorge Bundy, 27 October 1962, in ibid., fiche 25, catalog no. 01521. Alternative sources: *Department of State Bulletin* 69 (19 November 1973): 640–43; and Chang and Kornbluh, *Cuban Missile Crisis*, 185–88.

consequences as those which you sent us. And that must be clear to us, people invested with authority, trust, and responsibility. We must not succumb to intoxication and petty passions, regardless of whether elections are impending in this or that country. . . . [I]f indeed war should break out, then it would not be in our power to stop it, for such is the logic of war. I have participated in two wars and know that war ends when it has rolled through cities and villages, everywhat [everywhere] sowing death and destruction.

. . .

You have now proclaimed piratical measures, which were employed in the Middle Ages, when ships proceeding in international waters were attacked, and you have called this "a quarantine" around Cuba. Our vessels, apparently, will soon enter the zone which your Navy is patrolling. . . .

. . . I assure you that on those ships, which are bound for Cuba, there are no weapons at all. The weapons which were necessary for the defense of Cuba are already there. . . . Cuba has already received the necessary means of defense.

. . . If you stop the vessels, then, as you yourself know, that would be piracy. . . . We should then be forced to put into effect the necessary measures of a defensive character to protect our interests in accordance with international law. . . . To what would all this lead?

. . . You have asked what happened, what evoked the delivery of weapons to Cuba? . . .

We were very grieved by the fact—I spoke about it in Vienna—. . . that an attack on Cuba was committed, as a result of which many Cubans perished. You yourself told me then that this had been a mistake. I respected that explanation. You repeated it to me several times. . . .

. . .

We know how difficult it is to accomplish a revolution and how difficult it is to reconstruct a country on new foundations. We sincerely sympathize with Cuba and the Cuban people. . . . The Soviet Union desires to help the Cubans build their life as they themselves wish, and that others should not hinder them.

You once said that the United States was not preparing an invasion. But you also declared that you sympathized with the Cuban counter-revolutionary emigrants, that you support them and would help them to realize their plans against the present government of Cuba. It is also not a secret to anyone that the threat of armed attack, aggression, has constantly hung, and continues to hang over Cuba. It was only this which impelled us to respond to the request of the Cuban government to furnish it aid for the strengthening of the defensive capacity of this country.

. . .

Let us therefore show statesmanlike wisdom. I propose: we for our part, will declare that our ships, bound for Cuba, will not carry any kind of armaments. You would declare that the United States will not invade Cuba with its forces and will not support any sort of forces which might intend to carry out an invasion of Cuba. Then the necessity for the presence of our military specialists in Cuba would disappear.

. . .

. . . If . . . you have not lost your self-control and sensibly conceive what this [naval quarantine] might lead to, then, Mr. President, we and you ought not now to pull on the ends of the rope in which you have tied the knot of war, because the more the two of us pull, the tighter that knot will be tied. And a moment may come when that knot will be tied so tight that even he who tied it will not have the strength to untie it, and then it will be necessary to cut that knot, and what that would mean is not for me to explain to you, because you yourself understand perfectly of what terrible forces our countries dispose.

16 Premier Khrushchev to President Kennedy, broadcast message ("second letter"), 27 October 1962, introducing missiles in Turkey into the bargain.[35]

Our aim has been and is to help Cuba, and no one can dispute the humanity of our motives, which are oriented toward enabling Cuba to live peacefully and develop in the way its people desire.

You wish to ensure the security of your country, and this is understandable. But Cuba, too, wants the same thing; all countries want to maintain their security. But how are we, the Soviet Union, our Government, to assess your actions which are expressed in the fact that you have surrounded the Soviet Union with military bases; surrounded our allies with military bases; placed military bases literally around our country; and stationed your missile armaments there? . . .

You are disturbed over Cuba. You say that this disturbs you because it is 90 miles by sea from the coast of the United States of America. But Turkey adjoins us; our sentries patrol back and forth and see each other. Do you consider, then, that you have the right to demand security for your own country and the removal of the weapons you call offensive, but do not accord the same right to us? . . .

. . .

I therefore make this proposal: We are willing to remove from Cuba the means which you regard as offensive. We are willing to carry this out and to

35. Chang and Kornbluh, *Cuban Missile Crisis,* 197–98. Alternative sources: "Back from the Brink," 45–50; and *Department of State Bulletin* 47 (12 November 1962): 742–43.

make this pledge in the United Nations. Your representatives will make a declaration to the effect that the United States, for its part, considering the uneasiness and anxiety of the Soviet State, will remove its analogous means from Turkey. . . .

We . . . will make a statement within the framework of the Security Council to the effect that the Soviet Government gives a solemn promise to respect the inviolability of the borders and sovereignty of Turkey, not to interfere in its internal affairs, not to invade Turkey, not to make available our territory as a bridgehead for such an invasion, and that it will also restrain those who contemplate committing aggression against Turkey, either from the territory of the Soviet Union or from the territory of Turkey's other neighboring states.

The United States Government will make a similar statement within the framework of the Security Council regarding Cuba. It will declare that the United States will respect the inviolability of Cuba's borders and its sovereignty, will pledge not to interfere in its internal affairs, not to invade Cuba itself or make its territory available as a bridgehead for such an invasion, and will also restrain those who might contemplate committing aggression against Cuba, either from the territory of the United States or from the territory of Cuba's other neighboring states.

. . .

The means situated in Cuba, of which you speak and which disturb you, as you have stated, are in the hands of Soviet officers. Therefore, any accidental use of them to the detriment of the United States is excluded. These means are situated in Cuba at the request of the Cuban Government and are only for defense purposes. Therefore, if there is no invasion of Cuba, or attack on the Soviet Union or any of our other allies, then of course these means are not and will not be a threat to anyone. For they are not for purposes of attack.

. . .

. . . The greatest joy for all peoples would be the announcement of our agreement and of the eradication of the controversy that has arisen. I attach great importance to this agreement in so far as it could serve as a good beginning and could in particular make it easier to reach agreement on banning nuclear weapons tests.

17 President Kennedy, meeting with ExComm, 27 October 1962 (10 a.m.), discussing a reply to Khrushchev.

—Summary record of the first part of this meeting:[36]

36. Prepared by Bromley Smith, in Trachtenberg, "White House Tapes and Minutes," 196–99.

Secretary McNamara reported on the positions of Soviet Bloc ships moving toward Cuba. He said we do not know yet whether any such ships will enter the interception area. He recommended that we be prepared to board the Graznyy, which is now out about 600 miles. . . . [security deletion]

Under Secretary Ball pointed out that the Soviets did not know the extent of our quarantine zone.

The President agreed that we should ask U Thant to tell the Russians in New York where we are drawing the quarantine line. The Russians would then be in a position to decide whether to turn back their tanker or allow her to enter the quarantine zone sometime later today.

. . .

At this point in the meeting the partial text of a Soviet public statement [Khrushchev's second offer] was read by the President as it was received in the room. The President commented that the statement was a very tough position and varied considerably from the tone of Khrushchev's personal letter to the President received last night. The President felt that the Soviet position would get wide support and said we should consider making public the Khrushchev [earlier] private letter.

Secretary Rusk returned to the question of U.S. missiles in Turkey and pointed out that this subject must be kept separate from Soviet missiles in Cuba. . . .

. . .

Mr. Bundy said we cannot get into the position of appearing to sell out an ally, i.e. Turkey, to serve our own interests, i.e. getting the Soviet missiles out of Cuba.

The President commented that the Russians had made the Turkish missile withdrawal proposal in the most difficult possible way. Now that their proposal is public, we have no chance to talk privately to the Turks about the missiles, which, for a long time, we have considered to be obsolete.

. . .

. . . [President Kennedy] said we must ensure that the construction work on the missile sites in Cuba be stopped at once. He suggested that we talk to the Turks about the missiles, pointing out to them the great peril facing them during the next week. . . .

. . .

. . . [Bundy suggested:] one explanation for the varying Soviet proposals is that the hard line Russians wanted to make public their preferred demands in order to make impossible progress toward the Khrushchev private offer which may have been drafted by those who are less hard-nosed.

The President noted that it appeared to him that the Russians were making various proposals so fast, one after the other, that they were creating a kind of shield behind which work on the missile sites in Cuba continued. . . .

Mr. Bundy suggested that we tell Khrushchev privately that the position in their public statement was impossible for us, but that the position Khrushchev took in his private letter was different and we were studying these proposals. In the meantime, however, time is running out.

. . .

The Attorney General . . . desired that we make doubly clear that Turkish NATO missiles were one problem and that Cuba was an entirely separate problem.

. . .

The President recalled that over a year ago we wanted to get the Jupiter missiles out of Turkey because they had become obsolete and of little military value. If the missiles in Cuba added 50% to Soviet nuclear capability, then to trade these missiles for those in Turkey would be of great military value. But we are now in the position of risking war in Cuba and in Berlin over missiles in Turkey which are of little military value. From the political point of view, it would be hard to get support on an airstrike against Cuba because many would think that we would make a good trade if we offered to take the missiles out of Turkey in the event the Russians would agree to remove the missiles from Cuba. We are in a bad position if we appear to be attacking Cuba for the purpose of keeping useless missiles in Turkey. We cannot propose to withdraw the missiles from Turkey, but the Turks could offer to do so. The Turks must be informed of the great danger in which they will live during the next week and we have to face up to the possibility of some kind of a trade over missiles.

—Transcript of the meeting picks up the discussion at this point:[37]

JFK: It seems to me what we ought to—to be reasonable. We're not going to get these weapons out of Cuba, probably, anyway. But I mean—by negotiation—we're going to have to take our weapons out of Turkey. I don't think there's any doubt he's not going to ⟨retreat?⟩ now that he made that public, Tommy [Llewellyn Thompson, special adviser for Soviet affairs], he's not going to take them out of Cuba if we—

THOMPSON: I don't agree, Mr. President, I think there's still a chance that we can get this line going.

JFK: He'll back down?

. . .

37. McGeorge Bundy and James G. Blight, "October 27, 1962: Transcripts of the Meetings of the ExComm," *International Security* 12 (Winter 1987/88): 59–60.

THOMPSON: The important thing for Khrushchev, it seems to me, is to be able to say "I saved Cuba, I stopped an invasion," and he can get *away* with this, if he wants to, and he's had a go at this Turkey thing, and that we'll discuss later. . . .

. . .

[PRESIDENTIAL COUNSEL THEODORE C.] SORENSEN: In other words, Mr. President, your position is that once he meets this condition of the—uh—halting of the work and the inoperability, you're then prepared to go ahead on either the specific Cuban track or what we call the general détente track.

JFK: Yeah, now it all comes down—I think it's a substantive question, because it really depends on whether we believe that we can get a deal on just the Cuban—or whether we have to agree to his position of tying. Tommy doesn't think we do. I think that having made it public how can he take these missiles out of Cuba . . . if we just do nothing about Turkey.

. . .

THOMPSON: The position, even in the public statement, is that this is all started by our threat to Cuba. Now he's removed that threat.

RFK: He *must* be a *little* shaken up or he wouldn't have sent the message to you in the first place.

JFK: That's last night.

—Summary record of the 10 a.m. meeting describes the outcome:[38]

A draft message to Khrushchev, which had been prepared by Ambassador Thompson, was read and a final version was to be completed for the President's consideration later in the day. . . .

18 President Kennedy, meeting with the ExComm, 27 October 1962 (4 p.m.), receiving news of U-2 mishaps while reviewing a possible resolution of the crisis.

—Summary record:[39]

Secretary Rusk reported that one of our U-2 planes had overflown the Soviet Union by accident due to navigational error. Soviet fighters were scrambled from a base near Wrangel Island. . . .

. . .

38. Prepared by Bromley Smith, in Trachtenberg, "White House Tapes and Minutes," 200.

39. Prepared by Bromley Smith, in Trachtenberg, "White House Tapes and Minutes," 200–203.

The President asked whether we wanted to continue to say that we would talk only about the missiles in Cuba. He believed that for the next few hours we should emphasize our position that if the Russians will halt missile activity in Cuba we would be prepared to discuss NATO problems with the Russians. He felt that we would not be in a position to offer any trade for several days. He did feel that if we could succeed in freezing the situation in Cuba and rendering the strategic missiles inoperable, then we would be in a position to negotiate with the Russians.

Mr. Bundy pointed out that there would be a serious reaction in NATO countries if we appeared to be trading withdrawal of missiles in Turkey for withdrawal of missiles from Cuba. The President responded that if we refuse to discuss such a trade and then take military action in Cuba, we would also be in a difficult position.

. . .

The President expressed his concern that the alternatives we are facing have not been presented to NATO. NATO does not realize what may be coming and the Europeans do not realize that we may face a choice of invading Cuba or taking the missiles out of Turkey.

. . .

The President suggested that we talk immediately to the Turks, explaining to them what we were planning to do with our missiles and then explain the entire situation to the North Atlantic Council.

. . .

The President said that the key to any letter to Khrushchev was the demand that work cease on the missile sites in Cuba. He predicted that if we make no mention of Turkey in our letter, Khrushchev will write back to us saying that if we include Turkey, then he would be prepared to settle the Cuban situation. The President said this would mean that we would lose twenty-four hours while they would continue to work on the bases and achieve an operational status for more of their missiles. He suggested that we would be willing to guarantee not to invade Cuba if the Soviet missiles were taken out.

. . .

General Taylor summarized the conclusions of the Joint Chiefs. Unless the missiles are defused immediately, the Chiefs recommended implementation on Monday [security deletion].

Secretary McNamara asked what we should do about air surveillance tomorrow. He stated his recommendation, i.e. if our reconnaissance planes are fired on, we will attack the attackers. General Taylor noted that in order to be ready to invade on Monday, we must continue intensive air surveillance.

The President directed that our air reconnaissance missions be flown tomorrow without fighter escort. If our planes are fired on, we must be prepared for a general response or an attack on the SAM site which fired on our planes. We will decide tomorrow how we return fire after we know if they continue their attacks on our planes and after we hear from U Thant the Russian reply to our offer.

The President considered a draft message to the Turks about their missiles. His objective was to persuade the Turks to suggest to us that we withdraw our missiles. . . .

—Transcript recording the balance of the meeting:[40]

VOICE: The U-2.

MCNAMARA: The U-2 is shot down [over Cuba]—the fire against our low-altitude surveillance—

RFK: U-2 shot down?

MCNAMARA: Yes.... it was found shot down.

. . .

JFK: This is much of an escalation by them, isn't it?

MCNAMARA: Yes, exactly, and this—this relates to the timing. I think we can defer an air attack on Cuba until Wednesday or Thursday, but *only* if we continue our surveillance and—and—uh—fire against anything that fires against the surveillance aircraft, and only if we maintain a tight blockade in this interim period. If we're willing to do these two things, I think we can defer the air attack until Wednesday or Thursday and *take* time to go to NATO—

JFK: How do we explain the effect—uh—this Khrushchev message of last night and their decision, in view of their previous orders, the change of orders? We've both had flak and a SAM-site operation. How do we—I mean that's a—

MCNAMARA: How do we interpret this? I know—I don't know how to interpret—

. . .

JFK: How can we put a U-2 fellow over there tomorrow unless we take out *all* the SAM-sites?

MCNAMARA: That's just exactly—in fact, I don't think we can.

. . .

TAYLOR: .... It's on the ground—the wreckage is on the ground. The pilot's dead.

40. Bundy and Blight, "October 27, 1962: Transcripts of the Meetings of the ExComm," 66–67, 71, 74–80, 82–83.

. . .

MCCONE: I wonder if this shouldn't cause a most violent protest .... a letter right to Khrushchev. Here's, here's an action they've taken against—against us, a new order in defiance of—of public statements he made. I think that—

VOICE: I think we ought—

VOICE: They've fired the first shot.

MCCONE: If there's any continuation of this, we just take those SAM-sites out of there.

. . .

VOICE: We assume these SAM-sites are manned by Soviets.

. . .

[U. A.] JOHNSON: . . . You could have an undisciplined anti-aircraft—Cuban anti-aircraft outfit fire, but to have a SAM-site and a Russian crew fire is not any accident.

. . .

DILLON: I think we're going to have such pressure internally in the United States too, to act quickly ....

. . .

MCNAMARA: . . . We must be in a position to attack, quickly. We've been fired on today. We're going to send surveillance aircraft in tomorrow. Those are going to be fired on without question. We're going to respond. You can't do this very long. We're going to lose airplanes, and we'll be shooting up Cuba quite a bit, but we're going to lose airplanes every day. So you just can't maintain this position very long. So we must be prepared to attack Cuba— quickly. That's the first proposition. Now the second proposition. When we attack Cuba we're going to have to attack with an all-out attack, and that means [security deletion] sorties at a minimum the first day, and it means sorties every day thereafter, and I personally believe that this is almost certain to lead to an invasion. . . .

. . .

MCNAMARA: The third proposition is that if we do this, and leave those missiles in Turkey the Soviet Union *may*, and I think probably will, attack the Turkish missiles. Now the fourth proposition is, *if* the Soviet Union attacks the Turkish missiles, we *must* respond. We *cannot* allow a Soviet attack on the—on the Jupiter missiles in Turkey without a military response by NATO.

. . .

. . . Now the minimum military response by NATO to a Soviet attack on the Turkish Jupiter missiles would be a response with conventional weapons by NATO forces in Turkey, that is to say Turkish and U.S. aircraft, against Soviet warships and/or naval bases in the Black Sea area. Now that to me is the absolute minimum, and I would say that it is *damned dangerous* to—to have had a Soviet attack on Turkey and a NATO response on the Soviet Union. This is extremely dangerous. Now I'm not sure we can avoid anything like that, if we attack Cuba, but I think we should make every effort to avoid it, and one way to avoid it is to defuse the Turkish missiles *before* we attack Cuba. . . .

. . .

VOICE: Why you don't make the trade then?

. . .

BALL: I would say that in the assumption that if you defuse the Turkish missiles that saves you from a reprisal, it may—may mean a reprisal *elsewhere.*

MCNAMARA: Oh, I think it doesn't save you from a reprisal.

. . .

BALL: I think you're in a position where you've gotten rid of your missiles for *nothing.*

MCNAMARA: Well, wait a minute. I didn't say it saved you from a reprisal. I simply said it reduced the chances of military action against Turkey.

BALL: Well, but what good does that do you ⟨in the event of?⟩ action against Berlin, or somewhere else⟨?⟩

. . .

MCNAMARA: You have to go back in my proposition and say if there aren't Jupiter missiles in Turkey to attack, they're going to employ military force elsewhere. I'm not—I'm not at all certain of that.

BALL: Oh, I am.

LBJ: Bob, if you're willing to give up your missiles in Turkey, you think you ought to.... why don't you say that to him and say we're cutting a trade—make the trade there?.... save all the invasion, lives ....

. . .

MCNAMARA: . . . [A]ll I'm suggesting is, don't push us into a position where we *haven't* traded it and we *are* forced to attack Cuba, and the missiles remain in Turkey. That's all I'm suggesting. Let's avoid that position. We're fast moving into that.

. . .

BALL: Well. I would far rather—if we're going to get the damned missiles out of Turkey *anyway*, say, we'll trade you the missiles, we're going to put . . . [submarine-launched] Polaris [missiles] in there, you're not going to benefit by this—but *we will*, if this is a matter of *real* concern to you, to have these on your borders, all right, we'll get rid of them, you get rid of them . . . in Cuba. These things are obsolete anyway—I mean.... you're not going to reduce the retaliatory power of the NATO Alliance.

. . .

BUNDY: And what's left of NATO?

BALL: I don't think NATO is going to be wrecked, and if NATO isn't any better than that, it isn't that good to us.

. . .

MCCONE: . . . I think that we ought to take this case to—send directly to Khrushchev by fast wire the most violent protest, and demand that he—that he stop this business and stop it right away, or we're going to take those SAM-sites out *immediately*. . . . I'd trade these Turkish things out right now. I wouldn't even talk to anybody about it. . . .

. . .

MCNAMARA: . . . [L]et me go back a second. When I read that message of last night this morning, I thought, *My God* I'd never sell—I'd never base a transaction on *that contract*. Hell, that's no offer. There's not a damned thing in it that's an offer. You read that message carefully. He didn't propose to take the missiles out. Not once—there isn't a single word in it that proposes to take the missiles out. It's twelve pages of—of fluff.

. . .

. . . All of which leads me to conclude that the *probabilities* are that nothing's going to be signed quickly. Now my question is, *assuming* nothing is signed quickly, what do we do. (Pause.) Well, I don't think attack is the only answer. I think we ought to be *prepared* for attack, all-out attack, but I think we ought to know how far we can postpone that. . . .

. . .

[McNamara agrees to draft a message to NATO for ExComm consideration.]

LBJ: I've been afraid of these damned flyers ever since they mentioned them. Just an ordinary plane goin' in there at two or three hundred feet without arms or an announcement.... Imagine some crazy Russian captain.... He might just pull a trigger. Looks like we're playing Fourth of July over there or something. I'm scared of that, and I don't see—I don't see what you get for that photograph that's so much more important than what you—you know they're working at night; you see them working at night. Now what do you do? Psychologically you scare them. Well, Hell, it's like the fellow telling me in Congress, "Go on and put the monkey on his back." Every time I tried to put a monkey on somebody else's back I *got* one. If you're going to try to psychologically scare them with a flare you're liable to get your bottom shot at.

. . .

[JFK returns to the meeting.]

THOMPSON: . . . It seems to me there are many indications that—uh—they suddenly thought they could get—uh—up the price. They've upped the price, and they've upped the action. And I think that we have to bring them back by upping our action and by getting them back to this other thing without any mention of Turkey. . . . It seems to me the public will be pretty solid on that, and that we ought to keep the heat on him [Khrushchev] and get him back on the line which he obviously was on the night before. That message was almost incoherent and showed that they were quite worried. . . .

. . .

JFK: Well, I think we ought to—just a second—I'll just say, of *course* we ought to try to go the first route which you suggest. Get him back—that's what our letter's doing—that's what we're going to do by one means or another. But it seems to me we *ought* to have this discussion with NATO about these Turkish missiles, but more generally about sort of an up-to-date briefing about where we're going.

[The ExComm briefly discusses trading Turkish for Cuban missiles.]

JFK: We can't very well invade Cuba with all its toil, and long as it's going to be, when we could have gotten them out by making a deal on the same missiles in Turkey. If that's part of the record I don't see how we'll have a very good war.

[The meeting ends with the president asking the ExComm to reassemble at 9:00 p.m.]

19 President Kennedy, meeting with the ExComm, 27 October 1962 (9 p.m.), continuing work on a reply to Khrushchev.[41]

TAYLOR: . . . The problem of low-level surveillance is becoming difficult because in all the flights today around the SAM-sites, the—uh.... missile sites, there's low-level ack-ack.... Quite a bit. . . . We think, however, the Chiefs would recommend, that we still go back with about six planes tomorrow, picking out targets which we don't know have this kind of flack around, to verify that the work is still going ahead, and also to prove we're still on the job. But we're approaching the point, I think, Mr. President, where low-level reconnaissance will be entirely impossible. . . .

MCNAMARA: I would add to that I don't believe we should carry out tomorrow's U-2 mission.... but I do believe we should carry out the low-level reconnais-

41. Transcript record, in Bundy and Blight, "October 27, 1962: Transcripts of the Meetings of the ExComm," 86–89, 91–92.

sance with the necessary fighter escorts and preparations for following our reconnaissance, if it's attacked, with attack on the attackers.

. . .

JFK: Let me say, I think we ought to wait till tomorrow afternoon, to see whether we get any answer. . . . I think we ought to figure that Monday [29 October]—if tomorrow they fire at us, and we don't have any answer from the Russians, then Monday, it seems to me, we ought to—we can consider making a statement tomorrow about the fire and that we're going to take action now any place in Cuba, on those areas which can fire, and then go in and take all the SAM-sites out. I'd rather take—I don't think that it does any good to take out—to try to fire at a twenty millimeter on the ground. You just hazard our planes, and the people on the ground have the advantage. On the other hand, I don't want to—I don't think we do any good to begin to sort of *half* do it. I think we ought to keep tomorrow clean, do the best we can with the surveillance. If they still fire, and we haven't got a satisfactory answer back from the Russians[,] then I think we ought to put a statement out tomorrow that we were fired upon, and we are therefore considering the island of Cuba as an open territory, and then take out all these SAM-sites. . . . What do you think?

MCNAMARA: .... I would say only that we ought to keep some kind of pressure on.... tomorrow night, that indicates we're ⟨serious?⟩. . . . I believe we should issue an order tonight calling up the twenty-four air reserve squadrons, roughly 300 troop carrier transports, which are required for an invasion, and this would both be a preparatory move, and also a strong indication of what lies ahead—

JFK: I think we ought to do it.

. . .

JFK: Well now, will the introduction of Turkey, we think that if we take an action which we may have to take, I don't think we ought to say—which we may well have to take the way it's escalating, if they hit Turkey and they hit Berlin, we want them—if they want to get off, now's the time to speak up.

. . .

RFK: How are you doing, Bob?

MCNAMARA: Well, hard to tell. You have any doubts?

RFK: Well, I think we're doing the only thing we can do and well, you know.

. . .

MCNAMARA: I think.... Bobby.... we need to have two things ready, a government for Cuba, because we're going to need one.... and secondly, plans for how to respond to the Soviet Union in Europe, because sure as hell they're going to do something there.

. . .

VOICE: Suppose we make Bobby mayor of Havana.

20 President Kennedy to Premier Khrushchev, letter, 27 October 1962, proposing a settlement on the basis of Khrushchev's 26 October letter.[42]

The first thing that needs to be done . . . is for work to cease on offensive missile bases in Cuba and for all weapons systems in Cuba capable of offensive use to be rendered inoperable, under effective United Nations arrangements.

Assuming this is done promptly, I have given my representatives in New York instructions that will permit them to work out this weekend—in cooperation with the Acting Secretary General and your representative—an arrangement for a permanent solution to the Cuban problem along the lines suggested in your letter of October 26th. As I read your letter, the key elements of your proposals—which seem generally acceptable as I understand them—are as follows:

1. You would agree to remove these weapons systems from Cuba under appropriate United Nations observation and supervision; and undertake, with suitable safeguards, to halt the further introduction of such weapons systems into Cuba.

2. We, on our part, would agree—upon the establishment of adequate arrangements through the United Nations to ensure the carrying out and continuation of these commitments—(a) to remove promptly the quarantine measures now in effect and (b) to give assurances against an invasion of Cuba. I am confident that other nations of the Western Hemisphere would be prepared to do likewise.

If you will give your representative similar instructions, there is no reason why we should not be able to complete these arrangements and announce them to the world within a couple of days. The effect of such a settlement on easing world tensions would enable us to work toward a more general arrangement regarding "other armaments," as proposed in your second letter which you made public. . . .

But the first ingredient, let me emphasize, is the cessation of work on missile sites in Cuba and measures to render such weapons inoperable, under effective international guarantees. The continuation of this threat, or a prolonging of this discussion concerning Cuba by linking these problems to the broader questions of European and world security, would surely lead to an intensification of the Cuban crisis and a grave risk to the peace of the world. . . .

42. *PPP: JFK*, 1962, 813–14.

21 Premier Khrushchev to President Kennedy, letters of 28 October 1962, confirming the bargain settling the crisis.

—Public letter, stressing removal of the missiles in Cuba for a no-invasion pledge:[43]

[T]he Soviet Government, in addition to previously issued instructions on the cessation of further work at building sites for the weapons, has issued a new order on the dismantling of the weapons which you describe as "offensive," and their crating and return to the Soviet Union.

. . .

I regard with respect and trust your statement in your message of October 27, 1962 that no attack will be made on Cuba—that no invasion will take place—not only by the United States, but also by other countries of the Western Hemisphere, as your message pointed out. Then the motives which promoted us to give aid of this nature to Cuba cease. . . .

As I already told you in my letter of October 27, we both agree to come to an agreement that United Nations rapresentative [sic] could verify the dismantling of these means.

In this way . . . all necessary conditions for liquidation of the conflict which has arisen appear to exist.

. . .

. . . I also wish to continue an exchange of opinions on the prohibition of atomic and thermonuclear weapons, general disarmament, and other questions concerning the lessening of international tension.

. . .

I should like, Mr. President, to remind you that military aircraft of a reconnaissance character have violated the frontier of the Soviet Union [including the u-2 shot down in 1960]. . . .

However, during the period of your tenure of office as president, a second instance of the violation of our frontier by an American u-2 aircraft took place in the Sakhalin area. . . .

. . .

An even more dangerous case occurred on October 28, when your reconnaissance aircraft intruded into the territory of the Soviet Union in the north, in the area of the Chukotka Peninsula, and flew over our territory.

One asks, Mr. President, how should we regard this? What is it? A provocation? Your aircraft violates our frontier and at times as anxious as those which we are now experiencing when everything has been placed in a state of combat

43. Chang and Kornbluh, *Cuban Missile Crisis*, 226–29. Slightly variant translations: "Back from the Brink," 52–58; and *Department of State Bulletin* 47 (12 November 1962): 743–45.

readiness. For an intruding American aircraft can easily be taken for a bomber with nuclear weapons, and this could push us toward a fatal step—all the more so because both the United States government and Pentagon have long been saying that bombers with atomic bombs are constantly on duty in your country.

. . .

I would like to ask you, Mr. President, to bear in mind that a violation of Cuban airspace by American aircraft may also have dangerous consequences. If you do not want this, then no pretext should be given for the creation of a dangerous situation.

—Private letter, stressing Jupiter missiles in Turkey as part of the deal:[44]

Ambassador [Anatoly] Dobrynin has apprised me of his conversation with Robert Kennedy which took place on October 27. In this conversation Robert Kennedy said that it is somewhat difficult for you at the present time to publicly discuss the question of eliminating the US missile bases in Turkey because of the fact that the stationing of those bases in Turkey was formalized through a NATO Council decision.

. . .

. . . I do understand the delicacy involved for you in an open consideration of the issue of eliminating the US missile bases in Turkey. . . . You may have noticed that in my message to you on October 28 [directly above], which was to be published immediately, I did not raise this question—precisely because I was mindful of your wish conveyed through Robert Kennedy. But all the proposals that I presented in that message took into account the fact that you had agreed to resolve, [sic] the matter of your missile bases in Turkey consistent with what I had said in my message of October 27 and what you stated through Robert Kennedy in his meeting with Ambassador Dobrynin on the same day.

22   Premier Khrushchev to Prime Minister Castro, letter, 28 October 1962, urging acceptance of the Soviet-American bargain.[45]

Our October 27 message to President Kennedy allows for the question to be settled in your favor, to defend Cuba from an invasion and prevent war from breaking out. Kennedy's reply . . . offers assurances that the United States will not invade Cuba with its own forces, nor will it permit its allies to carry out an invasion. . . .

44. "Back from the Brink," 60–61.
45. Chang and Kornbluh, *Cuban Missile Crisis*, 239.

. . .

. . . Now that an agreement is within sight, the Pentagon is searching for a pretext to frustrate this agreement. This is why it is organizing the provocative flights. Yesterday you shot down one of these, while earlier you didn't shoot them down when they overflew your territory. The aggressors will take advantage of such a step for their own purposes.

Therefore, I would like to advise you in a friendly manner to show patience, firmness and even more firmness. Naturally, if there's an invasion it will be necessary to repulse it by every means. But we mustn't allow ourselves to be carried away by provocations. . . .

On our part, we will do everything possible to stabilize the situation in Cuba, defend Cuba against invasion and assure you the possibilities for peacefully building a socialist society.

23 Prime Minister Castro to Premier Khrushchev, letter, 28 October 1962, defending the downing of the U.S. reconnaissance plane and rebuffing inspections.[46]

There was the danger of a surprise attack on certain military installations. We decided not to sit back and wait for a surprise attack, with our detection radar turned off, when the potentially aggressive planes flying with impunity over the targets could destroy them totally. . . .

Earlier, airspace violations were carried out de facto and furtively. Yesterday the American government tried to make official the privilege of violating our airspace at any hour of the day and night. We cannot accept that, as it would be tantamount to giving up a sovereign prerogative. However, we agree that we must avoid an incident at this precise moment that could seriously harm the negotiations. . . .

I also wish to inform you that we are in principle opposed to an inspection of our territory.

24 Premier Khrushchev to Prime Minister Castro, letter, 30 October 1962, defending the deal with Kennedy and warning against nuclear recklessness.[47]

Had we . . . allowed ourselves to be carried away by certain passionate sectors of the population and refused to come to a reasonable agreement with

46. Chang and Kornbluh, *Cuban Missile Crisis*, 240.
47. Chang and Kornbluh, *Cuban Missile Crisis*, 243.

the U.S. government, then a war could have broken out, in the course of which millions of people would have died and the survivors would have pinned the blame on the leaders for not having taken all the necessary measures to prevent that war of annihilation.

. . .

In addition, there are opinions that you and we, as they say, failed to engage in consultations concerning these questions before adopting the decision known to you.

. . . [We] believe that we consulted with you, dear Comrade Fidel Castro, receiving the cables, each one more alarming than the next, and finally your cable of October 27, saying you were nearly certain that an attack on Cuba would be launched. . . .

. . .

In your cable of October 27 you proposed that we be the first to launch a nuclear strike against the territory of the enemy. You, of course, realize where that would have led. Rather than a simple strike, it would have been the start of a thermonuclear world war.

Dear Comrade Fidel Castro, I consider this proposal of yours incorrect, although I understand your motivation.

We have lived through the most serious moment when a nuclear world war could have broken out. Obviously, in that case, the United States would have sustained huge losses, but the Soviet Union and the whole socialist camp would have also suffered greatly. . . . Cuba would have been burned in the fire of war. There is no doubt that the Cuban people would have fought courageously or that they would have died heroically. But we are not struggling against imperialism in order to die. . . .

Now, as a result of the measures taken, we reached the goal sought when we agreed with you to send the missiles to Cuba. We have wrested from the United States the commitment not to invade Cuba and not to permit their Latin American allies to do so. We have wrested all this from them without a nuclear strike.

. . .

Naturally, in defending Cuba as well as the other socialist countries, we can't rely on a U.S. government veto. We have adopted and will continue to adopt in the future all the measures necessary to strengthen our defense and build up our forces, so that we can strike back if needed. At present, as a result of our weapons supplies, Cuba is stronger than ever. Even after the dismantling of the missile installations you will have powerful weapons to throw back the enemy, on land, in the air and on the sea, in the approaches to the island. . . .

. . .

We feel that the aggressor came out the loser. He made preparations to attack Cuba but we stopped him and forced him to recognize before world public opinion that he won't do it at the current stage. We view this as a great victory. The Imperialists, of course, will not stop their struggle against communism. . . . This process of struggle will continue as long as there are two political and social systems in the world, until one of these—and we know it will be our communist system—wins and triumphs throughout the world.

25 Prime Minister Castro to Premier Khrushchev, letter, 31 October 1962, rebutting Khrushchev's arguments.[48]

Few times in history, and it could even be said that never before, because no people had ever faced such a tremendous danger, was a people so willing to fight and die with such a universal sense of duty.

We knew, and do not presume that we ignored it, that we would have been annihilated, as you insinuate in your letter, in the event of nuclear war. However, that didn't prompt us to ask you to withdraw the missiles, that didn't prompt us to ask you to yield. Do you believe that we wanted that war? But how could we prevent it if the invasion finally took place? . . .

. . .

I understand that once aggression is unleashed, one shouldn't concede to the aggressor the privilege of deciding, moreover, when to use nuclear weapons. The destructive power of this weaponry is so great and the speed of its delivery so great that the aggressor would have a considerable initial advantage.

And I did not suggest to you, Comrade Khrushchev, that the USSR should be the aggressor, because that would be more than incorrect, it would be immoral and contemptible on my part. But from the instant the imperialists attack Cuba and while there are Soviet armed forces stationed in Cuba to help in our defense in case of an attack from abroad, the imperialists would by this act become aggressors against Cuba and against the USSR, and we would respond with a strike that would annihilate them.

. . . I did not suggest, Comrade Khrushchev, that in the midst of this crisis the Soviet Union should attack, which is what your letter seems to say; rather, that following an imperialist attack, the USSR should act without vacillation and should never make the mistake of allowing circumstances to develop in which the enemy makes the first nuclear strike against the USSR. . . .

. . .

I do not see how you can state that we were consulted in the decision you took.

48. Chang and Kornbluh, *Cuban Missile Crisis*, 244.

...

There are not just a few Cubans, as has been reported to you, but in fact many Cubans who are experiencing at this moment unspeakable bitterness and sadness.

The imperialists are talking once again of invading our country, which is proof of how ephemeral and untrustworthy their promises are. Our people, however, maintain their indestructible will to resist the aggressors and perhaps more than ever need to trust in themselves and in that will to struggle.

26 President Kennedy, press conference statement, 20 November 1962, making a qualified no-invasion pledge.[49]

[I]f all offensive weapons systems are removed from Cuba and kept out of the hemisphere in the future, under adequate verification and safeguards, and if Cuba is not used for the export of aggressive Communist purposes, there will be peace in the Caribbean. And as I said in September, "we shall neither initiate nor permit aggression in this hemisphere."

We will not, of course, abandon the political, economic, and other efforts of this hemisphere to halt subversion from Cuba nor our purpose and hope that the Cuban people shall some day be truly free. But these policies are very different from any intent to launch a military invasion of the island.

27 Premier Khrushchev to Prime Minister Castro, letter, 31 January 1963, seeking to repair a frayed relationship.[50]

Now, on my way to Moscow from Berlin, . . . I write to you. Our train is crossing the fields and forests of Soviet Byelorussia and it occurs to me how wonderful it would be if you could see, on a sunny day like this, the ground covered with snow and the forests silvery with frost.

Perhaps you, a southern man, have seen this only in paintings. It must surely be fairly difficult for you to imagine the ground carpeted with snow and the forests covered with white frost. It would be good if you could visit our

---

49. *PPP: JFK, 1962*, 831. Kennedy wrote to Khrushchev the next day, expressing regret that Castro was obstructing "a suitable form of inspection or verification in Cuba" while also offering assurances that "there need be no fear of any invasion of Cuba while matters take their present favorable course." Chang and Kornbluh, *Cuban Missile Crisis*, 296.

50. Chang and Kornbluh, *Cuban Missile Crisis*, 319–21, 323, 326–28.

country each season of the year; every one of them, spring, summer, fall, and winter, has its delights.

Cuba is a country of eternal summer. I remember that during our talk in New York, we reacted differently to the weather of that city: I was choking with heat, but you told me you felt chilly.

. . .

The gravity of the crisis created by North American imperialism in the Caribbean has ended. But it seems to me that this crisis has left a mark, although barely visible, in the relations between our states . . . and in our own personal relationship. Speaking frankly, these relations are not what they were before the crisis. I will not conceal the fact that this troubles and worries us. . . .

. . .

That is why we want to meet—to even out, to close the gaps in our relations, whatever their extent; even if they are only small, we would try to smooth them out. . . .

. . .

. . . [T]he United States of North America will never resign itself to the existence of a socialist Cuba. We knew that they would do all they could to eliminate socialist Cuba and to maintain the capitalist system in all the countries of the western hemisphere. Precisely with this end in mind they went to the archives, and dusted off the Monroe Doctrine, which they had practically renounced.

. . .

. . . As a Byelorussian proverb says: You can insult the master, but with that he only gets fatter. And so it is effect [in fact?]. You can insult imperialism as much as you like, but that won't make it wither, it won't make it weaker, nor will it diminish its insolence. Imperialism takes into account only real forces. It does not recognize anything else. . . .

. . .

In conditions of peace, socialism deploys to the fullest its forces and demonstrates its advantages in all fields, even in fields as decisive as the powerful growth of the economy, worker productivity, and the material and cultural level of the masses.

On the other hand, peaceful coexistence does not free capitalism from its insoluble contradictions—it contributes to sharpening the workers' class struggle, of the workers against the exploiters, and contributes to the rise of the national liberation movement.

. . .

. . . [T]oday, after the acute crisis in the area of the Caribbean Sea, there are reasons to believe that you have won a truce and that you will take advantage of it for peaceful construction. One must use this truce, above all, to expand the economy and agricultural production: this will allow you to improve the people's living standards. It is precisely this revolutionary example of Cuba's that the North American monopolists and imperialists most fear. That is why they want to strangle Cuba.

. . . When we help to strengthen the economy and defense of Cuba, we consider it to be a contribution to the common cause of developing and strengthening revolutionary forces, of strengthening the unity of socialist countries. With joint efforts we open in the new continent the road to anew [sic] world, the world of socialism.

28 President Kennedy, commencement address at the American University, 10 June 1963, calling for a lessening of tensions between the United States and the Soviet Union.[51]

Today, should total war ever break out again—no matter how—our two countries would become the primary targets. It is an ironic but accurate fact that the two strongest powers are the two in the most danger of devastation. All we have built, all we have worked for, would be destroyed in the first 24 hours. And even in the cold war, which brings burdens and dangers to so many countries, including this Nation's closest allies—our two countries bear the heaviest burdens. For we are both devoting massive sums of money to weapons that could be better devoted to combating ignorance, poverty, and disease. We are both caught up in a vicious and dangerous cycle in which suspicion on one side breeds suspicion on the other, and new weapons beget counterweapons.

. . .

. . . [I]f we cannot end now our differences, at least we can help make the world safe for diversity. For, in the final analysis, our most basic common link is that we all inhabit this small planet. We all breathe the same air. We all cherish our children's future. And we are all mortal.

. . .

. . . It is our hope . . . to convince the Soviet Union . . . [to] let each nation choose its own future, so long as that choice does not interfere with the choices of others. The Communist drive to impose their political and economic system on others is the primary cause of world tension today. . . .

. . .

. . . Chairman Khrushchev, [British] Prime Minister Macmillan, and I have

51. *PPP: JFK, 1963* (Washington: GPO, 1964), 462–64.

agreed that high-level discussions will shortly begin in Moscow looking toward early agreement on a comprehensive test ban treaty. . . .

. . . To make clear our good faith and solemn convictions on the matter, I now declare that the United States does not propose to conduct nuclear tests in the atmosphere so long as other states do not do so. We will not be the first to resume. . . .

29 Prime Minister Castro, speech at the University of Havana, 13 March 1965, looking back on the missile crisis.[52]

We speak in the name of a people who, for the sake of the strength of the revolutionary movement, for the sake of the strength of the socialist camp, for the sake of the firmness and the determination to defend the Revolution against the imperialists, did not hesitate. We are a people who did not hesitate to risk the danger of thermonuclear war, of a nuclear attack, when in our country and on our territory—with the full and absolute right that we have never abjured, an absolutely legitimate act that we will never regret—we agreed to the installation of thermonuclear strategic missiles on our territory. And, not only did we agree that they should be brought here, but we disagreed that they should be taken away. And I think that this is no secret to anyone.

. . .

Let us leave the papers and files and documents to history, let history be the one to say who acted well or badly, to say who was right and who was wrong, let history show what each thought, what each did, what each said—but let it be history. . . .

52. Kenner and Petras, *Fidel Castro Speaks,* 122–24.

6

Going to War in Vietnam, 1950–1965

A TEST OF WILLS

Vietnam was not one crisis but a string of crises that plagued American presidents for twenty-five years. Each crisis was provoked by the relentless Vietnamese pursuit of national liberation. Each forced on Washington a fresh appraisal of its commitment to resist "communism" in the region. And each ended with more territory and population slipping away from the "free world." Step by step forces led by Ho Chi Minh closed off the easy choices for American policymakers caught between a strong aversion to fighting another war on the Asian mainland and an equally strong aversion to suffering a humiliating retreat. It finally fell to Lyndon Baines Johnson to embark on the long delayed direct test of wills. The dispatch of American combat forces in 1965 began the bloodiest phase of a war that would prove both destructive to the country Ho had dedicated his life to liberating and corrosive to the liberal ideals Johnson was bent on vindicating.

*   *   *

For American policymakers entering the postwar era, Vietnam no less than the rest of French Indochina was like the other side of the moon—beyond their vision and far from their daily thoughts. During World War II Franklin D. Roosevelt had expressed support for Indochina's independence from what he regarded as exploitative and irresponsible French rule. But his concerns were tempered by a paternalistic conviction that the Vietnamese, unprepared to rule themselves, would need a period of foreign tutelage, perhaps by Nationalist China or some combination of powers serving as trustee (Document 5). His views were also tempered by his broader goal of sustaining cooperation among U.S. allies into the postwar period. Any attempt to strip the French or for that matter the British of their colonial empires was sure to strain that cooperation. Roosevelt quietly set the nettlesome Indochina question aside, clearing the way for the French return at the end of the war.

The new Truman administration regarded with distaste the French effort to regain control. But increasingly Washington saw Indochina not as a colonial issue but as part of the global anticommunist struggle. Hints of movement in that direction were already evident in a June 1945 State Department position paper that characterized the French presence as a check against instability in the region (Document 6).

In early 1950, even before the outbreak of the Korean War, Washington decided to prop up an embattled colonial regime in order to block a communist victory but also to insure Paris's cooperation on the European Cold War front. In February Washington granted diplomatic recognition to a puppet government headed by the former emperor, Bao Dai. At the same time a National Security Council study approved by the president identified Indochina as an important front on the containment line (Document 9). In May Washington made the first major grant of aid. The alarm created by the Korean War at mid-year and the fear of the new communist regime in China opening a second front in Indochina and taking all mainland Southeast Asia kept the funds flowing. As paymaster for French forces, the United States would give a total of $2 billion and bear three-fourths of the cost of the last years of the war.

By the summer of 1954 France had failed as a U.S. proxy. French-led forces had become snared in a remote outpost in the northwest, Dien Bien Phu. Paris called urgently for rescue by American bombers or even American troops. President Dwight Eisenhower strongly sympathized with the French struggle as an extension of the American Cold War effort (Document 10). But he hesitated to use U.S. air and naval power. With the Korean War just ended, neither Eisenhower nor the congressional leaders whom he consulted (including the Democratic majority leader in the Senate, Lyndon Johnson) wanted to risk entanglement in another Asian land war. France wanted prompt assistance without making the concessions to Vietnamese independence that Washington thought necessary. And the British refused to endorse armed action, thus leaving the Americans isolated. The fall of the French garrison in early May not only settled the issue in Washington but also convinced the French government to abandon its colonial war. In July diplomats meeting in Geneva fashioned a peace agreement. France would give up Indochina; Vietnam would be temporarily partitioned at the seventeenth parallel; and elections would be held within two years to effect unification.

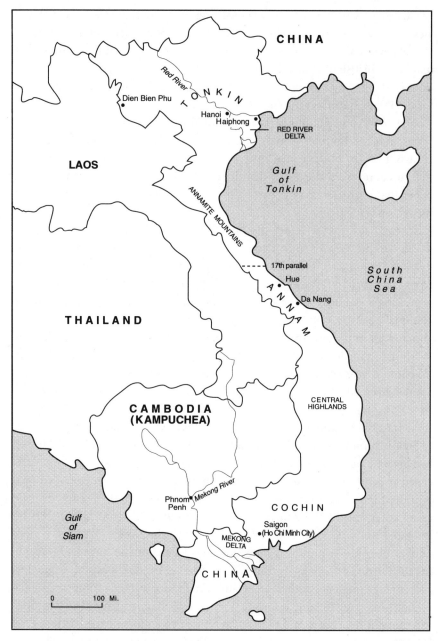

Vietnam

In responding to this breach in the containment line American policy-makers were guided by a set of simple verities worked out over the previous decade. Containment remained their compass, and the prospects that communist expansion might send dominoes tumbling across Southeast Asia and even beyond was still their worst fear. The loss of North Vietnam, coming on the heels of the loss of China, stiffened Washington's resolve. Although the Eisenhower administration was not prepared to fight partition, it refused to sign a Geneva conference agreement that Secretary of State John Foster Dulles described as a "Far Eastern Munich."

The Eisenhower administration turned at once to creating an anticommunist state in the south, formally throwing its support to Ngo Dinh Diem, an exiled Catholic with a clear anticommunist record and with influential admirers in the United States. The president offered formal backing in October; military assistance followed (Document 12). To protect the "free" people of the south from aggression, Dulles organized a loose regional defense agreement, the Southeast Asia Treaty Organization (SEATO), which had as members the United States, Britain, France, Australia, New Zealand, Thailand, Pakistan, and the Philippines.

* * *

The sweeping abstractions driving U.S. policy could accommodate only the most superficial and simple conceptions of the "communist" enemy. Its leaders were seen as politically immature and slavishly devoted to Moscow's false faith. To advance their cause those leaders were thought to rely on terror and coercion, thus bending to their will a peasantry American observers regarded as passive and apolitical. These perceptions blinded Washington to the concerns of politically engaged intellectuals arrayed against French domination and soon to rally against the United States. Their concerns, formed well before Washington began to notice Vietnam, did not fit neatly into the stark, alternative American categories of communism and nationalism.

Perhaps the single most powerful idea sustaining the Vietnamese cause was the commitment to resisting foreign intervention. Patriots drew inspiration from the centuries-long struggle against Chinese invaders. They were determined to win vindication for their humiliating nineteenth-century conquest by the French, who with their superior technology and civilizing zeal had subdued armed resistance in the 1890s. Some of the Vietnamese elite turned their back on the failed monarchy, rallied to the French cause, and collaborated with the colonial administration. But others saw themselves as the descendants of patriots who had fought and died for independence. An 1864 poem that concluded with a call for sacrifice to expel the French sounded a familiar theme with an appeal that remained powerful long into the twentieth century: "Life has fame, death too has fame. Act in such a way that your life and your death will be a fragrant ointment to your families and to your country."[1] Americans would find themselves confronting a generation of Vietnamese schooled in a national literature of struggle and sacrifice (Documents 1 and 2).

A second element critical to Vietnamese resistance was a faith in Leninist party organization. French conquest had discredited the imperial state, so patriots had to begin a search for a replacement to which they could attach themselves and entrust the formidable task of restoring indigenous political authority against a well-entrenched colonial power. By the 1920s a new generation had found an answer in the disciplined, centralized party with a mass base and ideological coherence built on the Soviet model. With the help of the Communist International (Comintern) in Moscow, the Indochinese Communist Party was formally established in Hong Kong in 1930 by uniting rival communist groups. In 1941 the party took the lead in setting up the Viet Minh, the chief wartime anti-French and anti-Japanese resistance force (Document 4).[2] Its successes confirmed the faith in party organization as the most effective vehicle for Vietnam's speedy liberation.

The third element on the Vietnamese side was a populist program that would bring the peasantry into the resistance. Communist organizers searching for a proletarian spearhead for their movement learned early that urban centers were not only short on workers but also inhospitable and dangerous. Forced to take refuge in the countryside, where four-fifths of their countrymen lived, they had to make a virtue of necessity—winning the support of peasants. They also had to learn that the most palpable, pressing enemy of the peasantry was less the humiliating foreign occupation than the oppression and poverty of everyday life. Beginning in the 1940s the Viet Minh promised a new rural order and made some down payments toward its realization, above all by redistributing land and ending exploitatively high interest rates on loans and high rents on land. Ho's forces thus secured their base in the mountains of northernmost Vietnam during World War II and gradually penetrated the populous Red River delta in the final months of the war. Their effectiveness in combatting famine by directing relief efforts and seizing grain held by the wealthy did much to win over peasants (Document 8).

1. Quoted in Truong Buu Lam, ed. and trans., *Patterns of Vietnamese Response to Foreign Intervention, 1858–1900* (New Haven, Conn.: Yale Southeast Asia Studies, 1967), 79.

2. The party was disbanded nominally at least in the fall of 1945. Membership, no more than twenty thousand in 1946, increased to 700,000 by 1950. In 1951 the party was renamed the Vietnamese Workers' Party to allow room for the development of separate Cambodian and Laotian Communist parties.

This mix of elements sustaining Vietnam's liberation movement is reflected in the life of its leader, Ho Chi Minh. Born in 1890 in the northern part of Vietnam, Ho had grown up steeped in the patriotic tradition. His classically educated father had briefly served the emperor but could not accommodate the French colonial system. The locale in which Ho came to maturity (Nghe An province, south of the Red River delta) was noted for its stubborn hostility to the French even after organized resistance had collapsed. Exposed to both Chinese classical and western eduction, Ho decided in his late teens to travel to France. He had first sought support for his country's cause from the victors of World War I, with their liberal peace program and paper commitment to self-determination. Ignored by them, he turned to the French Socialist Party, only to discover it tainted by colonial ambitions. Even the French Communist Party, which Ho helped found, did not extend its solicitude for the downtrodden to the colonies. Ho at last discovered in the Comintern an unmatched commitment to colonial liberation (Document 3). He served the Comintern in the 1920s and 1930s, working chiefly in Thailand and China. Only in 1941 did he return home to head the Viet Minh.

When the Japanese surrendered suddenly in August 1945, the Viet Minh seized power. In what is known as the August revolution, Viet Minh forces marched into Hanoi and established the Democratic Republic of Vietnam (DRV), headed by Ho and run by a coalition government (Document 7). Ho failed to convince the French to withdraw gradually from Vietnam. He also failed again in his appeals to the victorious allies for support on the basis of a presumed common commitment to self-determination. The U.S. intelligence teams dispatched by the Office of Strategic Services during the war had been impressed by Ho and the Viet Minh. But President Harry Truman, to whom Ho wrote directly, did not respond.

By December 1946 negotiations with the French had collapsed and armed conflict began in earnest. Ho abandoned Hanoi, returned to the countryside, and resumed the war of resistance. The Viet Minh went back to work on the political mobilization of the peasantry. The rural program had to be adjusted to the different conditions within the country. In the north, where most peasants clung to small plots of land, the party attacked usury, while in the south, where peasants were more often tenants to French and wealthy Vietnamese landlords, the emphasis was on land redistribution. This program helped to consolidate the Viet Minh hold in the north and to bring more than half of the south under its control.

Paralleling Ho's success in the countryside was his success in securing the support of the new Communist government in China. Stalin made Asia Beijing's revolutionary beat, and Mao Zedong was quick to do his "glorious internationalist duty" when Ho called for help in early 1950.[3] China as well as the USSR granted the DRV diplomatic recognition then, and by August a Chinese military advisory team had arrived to help with training and planning operations. Chinese supplies were soon flowing across the border, with the quantity increasing with the end of China's war in Korea in 1953 and the beginning of the diplomatically critical attack on the French garrison at Dien Bien Phu in early 1954.

By then the Viet Minh had worn the French down; the victory at Dien Bien Phu capped its success. Under pressure from his Soviet and Chinese patrons, Ho agreed to accept a temporary partition and wait for the promised national elections to unify the country. In the meantime he would concentrate on strengthening the DRV and avoid provocations that might draw the Americans deeper into the contested south (Document 11).

*   *   *

Hanoi and Washington now faced a showdown over the future of South Vietnam that neither was prepared to lose but that neither was eager to precipitate. Ngo Dinh Diem proved the catalyst by spurring first Hanoi and later Washington into action. For a time Diem appeared a successful nation-builder. He moved to crush his opposition (including the remaining Viet Minh in the southern countryside) and began to consolidate his political position. He also brushed aside countrywide elections stipulated by the Geneva accords. Washington supported him in this decision and, encouraged by his strong performance, stepped up aid.

But Diem's very success put Ho in a difficult position. The cancellation of elections seemed to rule out peaceful unification, while Saigon's repressive policy threatened the survival of the cadres who had stayed behind after the 1954 partition. Isolated and vulnerable, they complained of a lack of support from Hanoi and restrictions on armed resistance. Continued passivity, they warned, might cost Hanoi organizational networks and experienced personnel that would be essential in winning the south. At the same time peasant animosity toward Diem rose as landlords returned to the countryside to reclaim land previously distributed by the Viet Minh. To neutralize the Viet Minh's rural influence, the Diem government created agrovilles (the precursors of "strategic hamlets"), uprooting, resettling, and thereby further antagonizing the peasantry (Document 13).

In 1959–1960 the leaders of the DRV finally responded by turning toward a significantly more active southern strategy. Hanoi first gave cadres in the south

3. Quoted in Chen Jian, "China and the First Indo-China War, 1950–54," *China Quarterly*, no. 133 (March 1993): 92.

greater latitude to use force to protect themselves and strike at Saigon's authority. It then moved to put the southern resistance on a sustainable, organized basis by launching the National Liberation Front (NLF) in late 1960. This communist-dominated government-in-embryo (pejoratively referred to by its enemies as the Viet Cong, short for Vietnamese communists) brought under its organizational umbrella religious leaders and politicians resentful of the Ngo family's political oppression, dependence on the Americans, and regressive land policy (Document 14).

In the countryside the NLF built on the earlier successes of the Viet Minh and on a campaign of assassination to drive out Saigon officials. From what we know of one Mekong delta province strategically located athwart the supply road to Saigon, the NLF's appeal to the peasantry and assault on the government presence had already secured local administrative control by the early 1960s. When Saigon's forces fought back with bombing, military sweeps, and arrests, they further alienated the peasantry. By the fall of 1961 Hanoi saw signs that Diem was in trouble (Document 16). Saigon countered in the spring of 1962 with a "strategic hamlet" program intended to reclaim the countryside. Hastily implemented and badly managed, it deepened the resentment of peasants forced to resettle away from their land and to work on government projects.

The Hanoi-backed initiatives in turn triggered an American response that raised the stakes and the level of conflict. The initial successes of the NLF commanded the attention of the incoming Kennedy administration in 1961, and Nikita Khrushchev's speech of January 1961 endorsing wars of national liberation stirred fears that Vietnam might become a model for Soviet-sponsored takeovers around the world. Kennedy had to prove that he was tough and efficient to veteran cold warriors such as Dean Acheson, Robert Lovett, and Douglas Dillon and to Republican partisans ready to exploit Democratic weakness in foreign policy. The pressure on the young president mounted in 1961 following his failure at the Bay of Pigs, Khrushchev's unilateral settlement of the Berlin issue, and the neutralization of Laos.

Kennedy's advisers reenforced his resolve. Maxwell D. Taylor, an experienced military man working in the White House, regarded Vietnam as a place to test the techniques of limited war. Robert McNamara, the secretary of defense, saw a chance to fight a programmed conflict drawing on the efficient management methods that he had brought to the automobile industry. Dean Rusk, the secretary of state, wanted to press the anticommunist crusade in which he had enlisted in the late 1940s and early 1950s under Acheson. Walt Rostow, an MIT economic historian who worked for a year in the White House before taking charge of long-term policy planning in the State Department, sought to prove the tenets of nation-building against the challenge of communists, the "scavengers of the modernization process." He articulated widely accepted premises about the nature of the conflict in Vietnam (Document 15). McGeorge Bundy, a Harvard academic brought into the White House as Kennedy's national security adviser, was convinced that the United States could not accept defeat. Some within the administration, such as John Kenneth Galbraith, the ambassador to India, did warn of dangers looming ahead (Document 19). But these voices were faint and at odds with sentiment among the president's closest advisers.

Kennedy predictably devoted himself to shoring up the containment line in defense of South Vietnam. In May 1961 he formally affirmed the U.S. commitment to block the communist advance. To that end the new president implemented a broad program of support for Diem while also asking Saigon to improve its popularity. Washington held to its course into the fall even as the situation in the south deteriorated. Kennedy urged the U.S. military to introduce counterinsurgency techniques and new equipment suited to jungle combat. In November he finally agreed to a proposal formulated jointly by McNamara and Rusk to press Diem harder for reform, to increase the number of advisers, and even to contemplate a large-scale American military presence in case the situation became desperate. A formal public assurance to Diem followed (Documents 17 and 18). The American military presence steadily grew. By 1963 twenty-five thousand Americans were in Vietnam, and fifty of the sixteen thousand military "advisers" had died.

By then Diem had again emerged as a catalyst for intensified conflict. The stepped-up American support had only temporarily checked NLF gains, and Hanoi doubted that the United States could save the situation (Document 20). Diem's own base of political support steadily narrowed to his family and Catholic co-religionists. Conflict with Buddhists and other opposition groups deepened his isolation. Distracted and unpopular, the Diem government was immobilized. At the same time Diem and his brother and chief adviser, Ngo Dinh Nhu, were growing resentful of American pressure for a shake up of the government and army. Patriots in their own way, both feared that American assistance was leading to American control. Nhu talked of cutting a deal with Hanoi, thus setting off alarm bells in Washington.

During his last months in the White House Kennedy may have questioned the Vietnam commitment, though his public statements did not reflect it (Document 21). Policy discussions of Vietnam turned him into a brooding, silent presence, cool to recommendations for sharply increased aid. Confronted with reports that Diem had become a liability and that the NLF was making great strides in the countryside and the cities, Kennedy wavered over whether to support a military coup. Henry Cabot Lodge, Jr., the new American ambassador in Saigon, vigorously pushed for such an effort (Document 22). Kennedy's indecision finally came to an end when South Vietnam's army, prodded by threats of U.S. aid cuts, struck on 1 November. Diem's overthrow was followed at once by his and Nhu's murder. The news left Kennedy shaken and somber. Whatever ambivalence he may have felt about Vietnam, he had little time to resolve it. Three weeks later Kennedy himself lay dead in Dallas.

* * *

Suddenly thrust into the presidency, Lyndon Johnson seemed to have little latitude on policy toward Vietnam. He had inherited Kennedy's advisers as well as his policy, and in his first Vietnam meeting in late November demanded that Americans in Vietnam stop their "bickering," pull together to "win the war," and worry less about reform programs.[4] But the rapid deterioration of Saigon's authority made victory less and less likely without a major investment of American resources in the conflict. A December 1963 visit to South Vietnam by McNamara provided an early warning, and it was emphatically confirmed a year later by Taylor, Lodge's replacement in Saigon (Documents 24 and 26).

What made Johnson's position particularly difficult was that for the first time the middle option was missing. The French and then Diem had failed to hold on despite U.S. money, equipment, advice, and encouragement. The generals who had toppled Diem played musical chairs in Saigon, leading Hanoi to glimpse an early victory (Document 23). Now Johnson had to chose between a retreat (covered by an international agreement neutralizing South Vietnam) and a full-scale American commitment to the war. As early as January 1964 the Joint Chiefs made their preference clear by recommending a dramatic escalation of the conflict directed and executed by American forces (Document 25).

Hanoi tried to make the neutralization option attractive to Washington. Ho and his colleagues feared a full-fledged American military intervention, which they assumed would take the form of an invasion of the north along with a buildup of American forces in the south. To avoid this worst-case scenario Hanoi was not prepared to abandon the struggle in the south (as Washington demanded). As a middle way, however, Hanoi was willing to accept a negotiated settlement that would in the short term remove the staunchly anticommunist government in Saigon and set in motion the U.S. withdrawal. With the south effectively neutralized and with the NLF playing a prominent (but not necessarily the dominant) role in Saigon, Hanoi could wait patiently for a

---

4. U.S. Department of State, *Foreign Relations of the United States* [hereafter *FRUS*], *1961–1963*, vol. 4 (Washington: Government Printing Office, 1991), 636.

propitious time to reunite the country. The August 1962 international agreement neutralizing Laos won praise from North Vietnamese leaders as one model.

Consistent with this policy, Hanoi responded in a restrained fashion to the seemingly promising developments of 1963—the collapse of the "strategic hamlets" early in the year, the Buddhist crisis in the major southern cities beginning in April, and the coup in November. Although Hanoi did send increased numbers of cadres down the Ho Chi Minh Trail (running through parts of Laos and Cambodia) in early 1963 to help southern forces, it remained committed to avoiding provocation to the United States and to promoting political neutralization in the south. For example, there is some evidence that Ho responded positively to Diem's overtures for talks in the weeks before the coup.

The uncertain trend of events in the south following Diem's fall prompted a major policy reassessment in Hanoi. In December 1963 leaders of the Workers' Party agreed to widen the Ho Chi Minh Trail to accommodate heavier weapons, to increase northern military forces, and to step up aid to the NLF. In April 1964 units began training in the north for possible combat in the south. At the same time, however, Ho endorsed a neutralization proposal by French president Charles de Gaulle. A few months later Hanoi endorsed the idea of a neutralized Indochina bloc put forward by the Cambodian leader, Norodom Sihanouk, and Premier Pham Van Dong asked a Canadian diplomat to tell Washington of Hanoi's continued interest in neutralization of the south. As late as April 1965 the premier was still laying down peace terms that sought to breath life into the 1954 Geneva accords and thereby to eliminate the Americans as a force in a neutralized South Vietnam (Document 28).

The proud, determined American president slowly made his choice. In August 1964 Johnson used what appeared to be two separate North Vietnamese attacks on U.S. destroyers in the Gulf of Tonkin to get from Congress a broad grant of authority to use force in the region (the Tonkin Gulf resolution). At the same time, by way of reprisal, he sent American warplanes against the nearby coast. He then ran in the November election as the peace candidate and easily disposed of the conservative Republican Barry Goldwater.

Now commanding the powers of the presidency in his own right, Johnson began steadily raising the pressure on Hanoi. December marked the beginning of bombing of supply routes running through Laos. In February, provoked by repeated NLF attacks on American facilities in the south, Johnson launched a program of bombing raids against the north itself. The escalating air offensive was intended (as Johnson put it) to seduce, not rape, the north while somehow giving hope to a Saigon government rendered ineffectual by incessant plotting. Early in March he sent 3,500 marines to protect the air base at Da Nang. Soon he let them go on patrol beyond the base, authorized the dispatch of several additional combat units, and gave the Pentagon permission to prepare two divisions for Vietnam.

In early April, against this deepening commitment, Johnson delivered a nationally televised address at Johns Hopkins University. Drawing in equal measure from Woodrow Wilson and from his Texas Hill Country roots, Johnson justified the defense of Vietnam, sought to infuse it with a humanitarian spirit, and vowed a resolute American effort. But now, as in his other public comments since the election, he carefully obscured the importance of the measures he had already taken and gave no hint of even more important measures to come (Document 27).

In May and June the president faced dramatic NLF gains and urgent requests from his commander in the field, William Westmoreland, for more American troops (already at fifty thousand) to take up the slack left by a crumbling South Vietnamese army. The debate in Washington on the next step reached its climax in July. Johnson formally took up a recommendation from McNamara for a major infusion of American combat troops (Document 31). He also received a sharp warning from George Ball, a State Department official, that the dispatch of troops was a trap, not a solution (Document 29).

As he had in the past when making critical decisions concerning Vietnam, Johnson summoned his advisers for an extended examination of war aims and in a variety of settings listened carefully to skeptics such as Ball as well as Clark Clifford and Senator Mike Mansfield (both prominent Democrats respected by Johnson). Although the president and his advisers did not know their enemy well, they did at least recognize that the foe was determined as well as resourceful. But the ultimate decision turned not on an understanding of the enemy but on the question central to earlier Vietnam decisions: In a Cold War contest of wills, could the United States afford to back down? The meetings not only served as an elaborate ratification of all the earlier incremental decisions on use of U.S. air and ground forces but also provided the basis for the major deployment contemplated since November 1961 (Documents 32–34).

Johnson emerged from the July meetings to make public what may have been a foregone conclusion—an immediate increase of American forces to 125,000 (Document 35). The Joint Chiefs indicated that they wanted 210,000 by the end of the year, and more requests would follow. By 1967 half a million American troops were in Vietnam and the war was thoroughly Americanized. Even so, Johnson sought to keep the war low-key. As the new initiatives began to devour the defense budget, he at first tried to hide the problem so that Congress would not be tempted to cut his "Great Society" domestic programs. He also avoided a dramatic mobilization in order to keep the USSR and China calm and to prevent an anti-Red rampage by the American right.

The appearance in 1965 first of strategic bombers and then of American combat units raised the stakes in ways Hanoi had already anticipated following the Tonkin Gulf collision in August the year before. The U.S. retaliatory bombing raids along the coast, coming on the heels of U.S.-backed covert operations against the north begun earlier in the year, convinced the leaders in the north that Washington had decided on intervention. Meeting a week after the bombing, they concluded that the United States was shifting from "special war" (fighting through southern forces) to "limited war" (putting U.S. combat units directly into the fray). It was thus in their view time to put northern forces in the field before U.S. forces began to arrive. In September or October the first regiment left on the six-week march down the Ho Chi Minh Trail, soon followed by two others. (These units, probably based along the border, were not discovered by U.S. intelligence until late April 1965, after the first U.S. combat units had been committed.) Even while the Johnson administration entered its July debate, Le Duan (the head of the Workers' Party) contemplated the various levels to which the United States might escalate the struggle, and contended that the DRV could handle them all (Document 30).

A cycle of escalation had set in, with each step further raising the destructiveness of the conflict while denying Washington victory. The first North Vietnamese units to go south were far smaller than the first American forces to arrive early in 1965. Johnson's July troop decision dramatically raised the U.S. commitment, and Hanoi responded with reenforcements that did not catch up with the Americans but still posed a worrisome threat. And so not surprisingly, a November 1965 inspection trip to Vietnam revealed to McNamara that still more American forces would be needed to make headway on the battlefield (Document 36).

As the conflict mounted in Vietnam, the USSR and China, despite the Sino-Soviet split, threw their weight behind Hanoi. In June 1964 Mao had offered authoritative, sweeping assurances of support, and the Tonkin Gulf encounter the following August confirmed his view of an imminent U.S. threat to the region. By mid-1965 Chinese engineering and anti-aircraft units as well as supplies were beginning to arrive as part of a large-scale aid effort that would last until 1972. Moreover, Chinese troops stood ready just north of the border to counter any American invasion of the north. Hanoi was further reassured in 1965 when the post-Khrushchev leadership stepped up the Soviet Union's material contribution to the DRV.

While the increasing intensity of warfare inflicted damage throughout all of Vietnam, the Saigon regime may have lost the most. Extensive bombing and defoliation, free-fire zones, and search-and-destroy missions swelled the ranks of refugees in the south. The result was social disruption and economic hardship that posed a challenge beyond Saigon's capacity. Only American imports staved off economic collapse. Though by the close of 1967 the president and

Westmoreland reported seeing "a light at the end of the tunnel," the war looked more like a dead end.

At home trends were even less favorable. By 1967 Johnson faced antiwar sentiment of formidable proportions. Reputable critics had begun to ask as early as 1965 why the United States was fighting in Vietnam. They contended that Hanoi was less a tool of international communism than a traditional enemy of China. In any case Vietnam was peripheral to American Cold War interests, and its defense was hobbled by a weak, unpopular ally. Finally, they noted that massive application of American firepower was morally suspect as well as ineffective. It was destroying Vietnam but not the resistance. These arguments, together with the loss of American lives and higher taxes, belatedly drew attention to the war and fed discontent, which was soon reflected in public opinion polls. In the spring of 1964 two-thirds of the public had paid little or no attention to Vietnam. By October 1967, 46 percent of the public regarded sending American troops as a mistake, while only 44 percent approved.[5] Public demonstrations against the war dramatized the discontent.

Johnson was taking a personal beating. He waited anxiously for reports on air missions to reach the White House, and the daily tallies of American losses tore him up. Vietnam began to intrude into his dreams, inspiring scenes of personal paralysis played out on the contested paddy fields of a distant country. But Johnson fought back, blaming public opposition on the journalists, the Kennedy crowd (especially Robert Kennedy), and dissident professors. He reminded doubters of the lessons of Munich and of the communists' global ambitions.

The Tet offensive in February 1968 finally broke Johnson. In a surprise move the NLF mobilized its forces at Tet (the Vietnamese new year) and seized cities all over the south, including parts of Saigon (Document 37). Though beaten back with heavy losses, the offensive sent shock waves across the United States that reached both policymakers and the public. More than two years of direct action by the American military seemed to have brought victory not an inch nearer.

For Clark Clifford, successor to the spent McNamara as secretary of defense, Tet confirmed his earlier skepticism of a full-scale commitment. He pursued a review of Vietnam policy as he entered office in March 1968. Clifford later recalled, "I could not find out when the war was going to end; I could not find out the manner in which it was going to end; I could not find out whether the new requests for men and equipment were going to be enough, or whether

---

5. George H. Gallup, *The Gallup Poll: Public Opinion, 1935–1971* (3 vols.; New York: Random House, 1972), 3:1882 (survey of 24–29 April 1964) and 3:2087 (survey of 6–11 October 1967).

it would take more and, if more, when and how much; I could not find out how soon the South Vietnamese forces would be ready to take over."[6]

Doubt now became contagious. The veterans of the Cold War (the so-called "wise men" whom Johnson had been consulting) reacted to Tet by withdrawing their support from what had become "Johnson's war." Even the stalwart Rusk revealed privately and for the first time a faltering resolve. With American casualties climbing to 130,000, public disapproval of Johnson's handling of the presidency rose to 52 percent. Only 33 percent thought the war effort was "making progress," while 61 percent felt the United States and its allies were "losing" or "standing still."[7]

At first defiant in the wake of Tet, Johnson watched his support crumble, and in March he decided to modify his policy. He refused Westmoreland an additional 200,000 men and sharply restricted air and sea attacks against the north in hopes of drawing Hanoi into talks that would bring peace and preserve South Vietnam. At the same time he withdrew from the presidential race to spare himself the humiliation of a possible defeat but also to remove his peace initiative as an issue in the coming campaign (Document 38). Johnson's agony was coming to an end; Indochina's was just beginning.

* * *

Richard Nixon directed the dirty and demoralizing disengagement phase of America's Vietnam War. He had come into the White House in 1969 with a "secret plan" to bring "a peace with honor," meaning one that would give the government in the south a reasonable chance to survive. Nixon calculated that a new campaign of bombing and an expansion of the ground war into North Vietnamese sanctuaries in Cambodia and Laos, together with Chinese and Soviet pressure, would force Hanoi to accept a peace agreement favorable to the United States and Saigon. Hanoi, as implacable as ever, would not bow to pressure. The peace talks begun by Johnson remained deadlocked until October 1972, when the two sides reached a compromise. Washington dropped its insistence on North Vietnamese troop withdrawal from the south, and Hanoi gave up its demand for the end of the southern government headed by Nguyen Van Thieu.

To reach that compromise, Nixon had had to hold at bay mounting public and congressional opposition to the war. He began by extricating American soldiers from the fighting. A force level of 543,000 when he came into office

6. Clark M. Clifford, "A Viet Nam Reappraisal: The Personal History of One Man's View and How It Evolved," *Foreign Affairs* 47 (July 1969): 611–12.

7. Gallup, *Gallup Poll,* 3:2109 (survey of 22–27 February 1968) and 3:2113 (survey of 15–20 March 1968).

was by January 1973 down to 24,000 (mostly advisers and support personnel). He dramatically reduced the demand for young men to serve in Vietnam, a sedative to unrest on college campuses and to anxious parents. When he decided to bomb in Cambodia in 1969, he kept the decision a secret. His April 1970 ground attack into Cambodia did stir up intense nationwide protest, but he weathered the storm.

Nixon also had to neutralize Saigon's objections. Parallel with the reduction of American troop levels, he implemented a strategy of Vietnamization. Strengthened by a major infusion of U.S. money and equipment, the South Vietnamese army and air force were supposed to take over the war. The Thieu government had nonetheless resisted the October 1972 peace agreement, and even arm-twisting by the presidential aide Henry Kissinger during a visit to Saigon failed to win assent. Saigon's intransigence had denied Nixon a diplomatic victory on the eve of his November reelection bid, so he turned a necessity into a virtue by demanding extensive changes in the accord. When Hanoi proved unyielding, the talks collapsed, and Nixon retaliated with heavy bombing in late December, only to agree to a settlement in January that was virtually the same as the one in October. Nixon now forced a still resistant Thieu to submit, with the only balm a promise of assistance in case of a renewed North Vietnamese threat.

Thieu's time was running out. Vietnamization had not overcome the corruption and inept leadership that hobbled his army. The North Vietnamese spring 1975 offensive revealed how fragile was Saigon's fighting force and how empty were Nixon's assurances of support. Gerald Ford, who in August 1974 had succeeded a Nixon disgraced by the Watergate scandal, could not answer Saigon's desperate appeals because Congress, which had already cut Saigon's aid in half (to $700 million), tied his hands. The rapid collapse of the South Vietnamese forces, climaxing in the fall of Saigon in late April, forced the remaining Americans to scramble out in disarray—the dismal finale to a twenty-five-year effort. Hanoi for its part savored victory in a struggle begun decades earlier, well before the first American "advisers" had even appeared on the scene.

*   *   *

The confrontation between Ho Chi Minh and Lyndon Baines Johnson was a test of wills that carried a high price for winners, losers, and bystanders. Ho and his colleagues brought a stubborn determination to the cause of liberation. In pursuit of that goal they could tap a capacity for struggle and sacrifice whose strength Washington never understood. Ho closed his life with an almost lyrical celebration of the mountains and streams that he had devoted virtually the whole of his life to liberating (Document 39). But he had only to look around him in his last years to see some of the costs to his land and people, and others would become evident only at the end of the war. An estimated 1.4 million of his countrymen—civilians as well as combatants on one side or the other—died during the U.S. combat phase of the war (1965 to early 1973), and another 300,000 fell in the subsequent period, to April 1975. The environment in the south suffered lasting harm from heavy bombing and from the extensive use of herbicides that damaged human genes as well as plants holding down fragile tropical soil. More than ten million Vietnamese became refugees between 1965 and 1973, and by the war's end Vietnam had some 1.4 million disabled and half a million orphans to care for, as well as schools, hospitals, and other public facilities to rebuild.

Johnson for his part was but the most recent of a line of foreigners who had sought to deprive Ho of his dreams and the Vietnamese of their country. Following the French and the Japanese, American presidents had sought to bend Vietnam to their will. When Johnson at last took up the challenge, it took only three years of war to prove that neither he nor his fellow Americans had the stomach to go on. In exile on his Texas Hill Country ranch he died in 1973 with the American war he had begun mercifully at an end. But some fifty-eight thousand American soldiers had died, and American taxpayers faced a bill of $141 billion for military outlays between 1961 and the end of the war in 1975. Long-term costs would push the figure into the range of $350 billion. What Americans did not pay for directly in taxes they paid for indirectly through double-digit inflation or passed on as a debt for their children and grand-children to pay. The war crushed the Great Society programs—and the hopes of many Americans. It left a country with bitter, deep, and lasting divisions.

Cambodia may have suffered even more than Vietnam and certainly far more than the United States. Norodom Sihanouk had tried to stand aside from the destructive American-Vietnamese contest. But Hanoi wanted his country as a sanctuary and supply route, and Nixon wanted an anticommunist in Sihanouk's place. Both got what they wanted, and the result was to plunge Cambodia into the maelstrom. Rural conflict and carpet bombing by B-52s combined between 1970 and 1975 to kill half a million Cambodians, to send the rural population fleeing to overburdened cities, and to reduce agricultural production. After the Khmer Rouge came to power (1975–1979) one million people died from revolutionary violence and starvation and a second million fled abroad for safety. The turmoil unleashed in Cambodia began to ease in the early 1990s, but the long-term costs and consequences are still difficult to determine.

Trying to understand, not to mention evaluate, what happened in the Viet-nam crisis is equally difficult—and it gets even more difficult as we make Vietnam more than a "quagmire" and the Vietnamese more than failed objects of "hearts and minds" or heroic but shadowy jungle figures. What brought on the 1965 crisis? Do we look essentially to individual leaders to understand its unfolding, or should we see it as a problem of divergent cultures and national values? Was there a failure of perception or miscalculation, and did it afflict Hanoi and Washington equally? Was there a point when the looming collision might have been averted? Why did the crisis develop such destructive inertia? What lessons emerge from an examination of this case? Putting Vietnamese on an equal historical plane with Americans may make simple, morally satisfying answers to these questions more elusive. But this more international conception of the crisis makes for richer history.

FOR FURTHER READING

The Vietnam War boasts a large literature, and the release of new materials in Washington, Hanoi, and other capitals is bound to give rise to new studies with fresh insights. The recommendations that follow are thus highly selective and distinctly provisional.

Among general accounts Marilyn B. Young, *The Vietnam Wars, 1945–1990* (1991), and Gabriel Kolko, *Anatomy of a War: Vietnam, the United States, and the Modern Historical Experience* (1985), are both notable for seeking to give Vietnamese equal attention alongside Americans, and both are sharply critical of U.S. policy. George McT. Kahin's dispassionate *Intervention: How America Became Involved in Vietnam* (1986) brings a special sensitivity to the U.S. role in Saigon politics between 1954 and 1965. Stanley Karnow, *Vietnam: A History* (rev. ed.; 1991), a popular account enriched by the author's experience in reporting on the war, puts more emphasis on the American role. Gareth Porter, ed., *Vietnam: A History in Documents* (1981), offers a good sampling of Vietnamese as well as American materials. A wide range of critical issues is examined in Jayne S. Werner and Luu Doan Huynh, eds., *The Vietnam War: Vietnamese and American Perspectives* (1993).

George C. Herring, *The Longest War: The United States and Vietnam, 1950–1975* (rev. ed.; 1986), provides a thoughtful overview of U.S. policy that still holds up despite the large number of policy studies that have come into print since the last revision. For details on the critical decision-making between 1963 and 1965, see Ellen Hammer, *A Death in November: America in Vietnam, 1963* (1987); Brian VanDeMark, *Into the Quagmire: Lyndon Johnson and the Escalation of the Vietnam War* (1991); David M. Barrett, *Uncertain Warriors: Lyndon Johnson and His Vietnam Advisers* (1993); Mark Clodfelter, *The Limits of Airpower: The American Bombing of North Vietnam* (1989); Larry Berman, *Lyndon Johnson's War: The Road to Stalemate in Vietnam* (1989); and George C. Herring, *LBJ and Vietnam: A Different Kind of War* (1994). Domestic dimensions of the Vietnam commitment are dealt with in the synthesis by David W. Levy, *The Debate over Vietnam* (1991), which contains a full, up-to-date guide to the literature on the war at home.

The general Vietnamese perspective on the war emerges from Frances Fitz-Gerald, *Fire in the Lake: The Vietnamese and the Americans in Vietnam* (1972), a pioneering and prize-winning attempt by a nonspecialist to give life to the "other side," and William J. Duiker, *Sacred War: Nationalism and Revolution in a Divided Vietnam* (1995), with its helpful, current survey of the writings on the Vietnamese side of the war. Huynh Kim Khanh, *Vietnamese Communism, 1925–1945* (1982), is perhaps the single most important treatment of the roots of the Vietnamese revolution; but see also Alexander Woodside, *Community and Revolution in Modern Vietnam* (1976), for its rich insights. Jeffrey Race, *War Comes to Long An: Revolutionary Conflict in a Vietnamese Province* (1972); James W. Trullinger, Jr., *Village at War: An Account of Revolution in Vietnam* (1980); and Eric M. Bergerud, *The Dynamics of Defeat: The Vietnam War in Hau Nghia Province* (1991), are invaluable on rural conflict. David P. Chandler, *The Tragedy of Cambodian History: Politics, War, and Revolution since 1945* (1991), helps fill out the Indochina picture.

DOCUMENTS

1   Tran Hung Dao, proclamation of 1285, urging his army to resist the Mongol invasion.[8]

What can I now say about you and me who are born into an age of adversity? We have all grown up in difficult times. We have seen the enemy's ambassadors stroll about in our streets with conceit, using their owls' and crows' tongues to abuse our court, flexing their goats' and dogs' bodies to threaten our ministers. . . .

. . .

. . . [T]he invaders and we are enemies who cannot live under the same sky. If you do not care to wash away the stains of humiliation, if you do not trouble to weed out the seeds of violence, if you are not anxious to train your soldiers, . . . [then] when the enemy is expelled, shame shall descend upon you for thousands of generations. How will you be able to face Heaven and Earth?

2   Nguyen Dinh Chieu, funeral oration in 1861, honoring peasant soldiers who died fighting the French.[9]

The only things you knew were ricefields and water buffaloes. You lived according to the village's customs.
Digging, plowing, harrowing, replanting were your usual occupations.
. . .
You were not professional soldiers . . . experienced in military life and training. You were but inhabitants of villages and hamlets turned partisans to serve the cause of righteousness.
. . .
In your hands, a pointed stick; you did not ask for knives or helmets.
The match for your gunpowder was made of straw; but this did not prevent you from successfully burning the missionary house.
For a sword, you used your kitchen knife; yet you were able to behead the enemies' lieutenant.
Your officers were not compelled to beat the drums in order to urge you

8. Tran Hung Dao was a Vietnamese prince and army commander. Truong, *Patterns of Vietnamese Response*, 50, 53.

9. Nguyen Dinh Chieu was a well-known southern Vietnamese writer who supported the resistance. Truong, *Patterns of Vietnamese Response*, 68–70.

forward. You advanced on your own, clambering onto the barricades. You looked upon the enemy as if he did not exist.

You were not frightened by the French who shot large and small bullets at you. You forced your way into their camp, risking your life as if you had no material body.

Some of you stabbed, some struck so eagerly that the French soldiers and their mercenaries lost heart.

You screamed in the forefront, you shouted at the rear regardless of the enemies' gunboats, their ships, or their rifles.

. . .

You preferred to die fighting the enemy, and return to our ancestors in glory rather than survive in submission to the Occidentals and share your miserable life with barbarians.

. . .

O, the smoke of your battle has already dissipated, but your right conduct shall be recorded for a thousand years.

3   Ho Chi Minh recalling his discovery of communist anticolonialism.[10]

After World War One, I made my living in Paris, at one time as an employee at a photographer's, at another as painter of "Chinese antiques" (turned out by a French shop). I often distributed leaflets denouncing the crimes committed by the French colonialists in Viet Nam.

At that time, I supported the October Revolution[11] only spontaneously. I did not yet grasp all its historic importance. I loved and respected Lenin because he was a great patriot who had liberated his fellow-countrymen; until then, I had read none of his books.

. . .

Heated discussions were then taking place in the cells of the Socialist Party, about whether one should remain in the [Socialist] Second International, found a "Second-and-a-half" International or join Lenin's Third [Moscow-based Communist] International[.] I attended the meetings regularly, two or three times a week, and attentively listened to the speakers. . . .

10. Ho Chi Minh, "The Path Which Led Me to Leninism," April 1960, in Ho, *Selected Writings (1920–1969)* (Hanoi: Foreign Languages Publishing House, 1973), 251–52. Ho wrote this article for the Soviet review *Problems of the East* on the occasion of Lenin's ninetieth birthday.

11. The 1917 seizure of power by the Bolsheviks in Russia.

What I wanted most to know—and what was not debated in the meetings—was: which International sided with the peoples of the colonial countries?

I raised this question—the most important for me—at a meeting. Some comrades answered: it was the Third, not the Second International. One gave me to read Lenin's "Theses on the national and colonial questions" [1920]. . . .

In those Theses, there were political terms that were difficult to understand. But by reading them again and again finally I was able to grasp the essential part. What emotion, enthusiasm, enlightenment and confidence they communicated to me! I wept for joy. Sitting by myself in my room, I would shout as if I were addressing large crowds: "Dear martyr compatriots! This is what we need, this is our path to liberation!"

. . .

. . . [F]rom then on, I . . . plunged into the debates and participated with fervour in the discussions. Though my French was still too weak to express all my thoughts, I hit hard at the allegations attacking Lenin and the Third International. My only argument was: "If you do not condemn colonialism, if you do not side with the colonial peoples, what kind of revolution are you then waging?"

4   Ho Chi Minh, appeal on behalf of the Viet Minh (issued from South China), 6 June 1941, calling for an independence struggle against the Japanese and the French.[12]

Now, the opportunity has come for our liberation. France itself is unable to help the French colonialists rule over our country. As for the Japanese, on the one hand bogged down in China, on the other hampered by the British and American forces, they certainly cannot use all their strength against us. If our entire people are solidly united we can certainly get the better of the best-trained armies of the French and the Japanese.

. . .

Dear fellow-countrymen! A few hundred years ago . . . when our country faced the great danger of invasion by Yuan [Mongol-led Chinese] armies the elders ardently called on their sons and daughters throughout the country to stand up as one man to kill the enemy. Finally they saved their people, and their glorious memory will live forever. Let our elders and patriotic personalities follow the illustrious example set by our forefathers.

. . .

12. Ho, *Selected Writings,* 45–46.

Dear fellow-countrymen!

National salvation is the common cause of our entire people. Every Vietnamese must take part in it. He who has money will contribute his money, he who has strength will contribute his strength, he who has talent will contribute his talent. For my part I pledge to follow in your steps and devote all my modest abilities to the service of the country and am ready for the supreme sacrifice.

5   President Franklin D. Roosevelt and Premier Joseph Stalin, discussion at the Tehran conference, 28 November 1943, calling for an end of French control over Indochina.[13]

STALIN . . . said, in his opinion, [the French ruling classes] should not be entitled to share in any of the benefits of the peace, in view of their past record of collaboration with Germany.

THE PRESIDENT said that . . . he felt that many years of honest labor would be necessary before France would be re-established. He said the first necessity for the French, not only for the Government but the people as well, was to become honest citizens.

[STALIN] agreed and went on to say that he did not propose to have the Allies shed blood to restore Indochina, for example, to the old French colonial rule. . . .

THE PRESIDENT said he was 100% in agreement with Marshal Stalin and remarked that after 100 years of French rule in Indochina, the inhabitants were worse off than they had been before. . . . He added that he had discussed with [China's leader] Chiang Kai-shek the possibility of a system of trusteeship for Indochina which would have the task of preparing the people for independence within a definite period of time, perhaps 20 to 30 years.

6   State Department policy paper on postwar Asia, 22 June 1945, recognizing French sovereignty over Indochina.[14]

At the end of the war, political conditions in Indochina, and especially in the north, will probably be particularly unstable. The Indochinese indepen-

13. Minutes by Roosevelt's interpreter Charles E. Bohlen, in *FRUS: The Conferences at Cairo and Tehran, 1943* (Washington: GPO, 1961), 485.

14. Secretary of War Henry L. Stimson asked the State Department to formulate a position on Indochina. On 28 June Acting Secretary of State Joseph C. Grew transmitted

dence groups, which may have been working against the Japanese, will quite possibly oppose the restoration of French control. Independence sentiment in the area is believed to be increasingly strong. . . .

. . .

French policy toward Indochina will be dominated by the desire to re-establish control in order to reassert her prestige in the world as a great power. This purpose will be augmented by the potent influence of the Banque de l'Indochine and other economic interests. Many French appear to recognize that it may be necessary for them to make further concessions to Indochinese self-government and autonomy primarily to assure native support but also to avoid unfriendly United States opinion. . . .

. . .

The United States recognizes French sovereignty over Indochina. It is, how-ever, the general policy of the United States to favor a policy which would allow colonial peoples an opportunity to prepare themselves for increased participa-tion in their own government with eventual self-government as the goal.

**7   President Ho Chi Minh, statement read in Hanoi,
2 September 1945, declaring Vietnam independent of France.[15]**

"All men are created equal. They are endowed by their Creator with certain unalienable Rights; among these are Life, Liberty and the pursuit of Happiness."

. . .

Those are undeniable truths.

Nevertheless, for more than eighty years, the French imperialists, abusing the standard of Liberty, Equality and Fraternity, have violated our Fatherland and oppressed our fellow-citizens. They have acted contrary to the ideals of humanity and justice.

Politically, they have deprived our people of every democratic liberty.

They have enforced inhuman laws; they have set up three different political regimes in the North, the Centre and the South of Viet Nam in order to wreck our country's oneness and prevent our people from being united.

They have built more prisons than schools. They have mercilessly mas-sacred our patriots. They have drowned our uprisings in seas of blood.

---

this paper to Stimson, characterizing it as "representing the considered views of the Depart-ment of State as a whole." *FRUS, 1945*, vol. 6 (Washington: GPO, 1969), 556, 567–68.

15. Ho, *Selected Writings*, 53–56. Alternative source: Gareth Porter, ed., *Vietnam: A History in Documents* (New York: New American Library, 1981), 29–30.

They have fettered public opinion and practised obscurantism.

They have weakened our race with opium and alcohol.

In the field of economics, they have sucked us dry, driven our people to destitution and devastated our land.

. . .

We, the Provisional Government of the new Viet Nam, representing the entire Vietnamese people, hereby declare that from now on we break off all relations of a colonial character with France; cancel all treaties signed by France on Viet Nam, and abolish all privileges held by France in our country.

The entire Vietnamese people are of one mind in their determination to oppose all wicked schemes by the French colonialists.

We are convinced that the Allies . . . cannot fail to recognize the right of the Vietnamese people to independence.

A people who have courageously opposed French enslavement for more than eighty years, a people who have resolutely sided with the Allies against the fascists during these last years, such a people must be free, such a people must be independent.

8   Political activists in Hung Yen province in the Red River delta near Hanoi, recalling in 1967 the rural conditions and anti-French resistance of the 1940s.[16]

—Tuan Doanh (a member of the provincial committee of the Workers' Party):[17]

The province was so poor that it used to be known as Beggars' Province. . . .

. . .

Historically, our province has been a battlefield ever since . . . the second and third centuries. The marshes and reeds provided an excellent terrain for guerrilla warfare in the lowlands, and the dense vegetation stopped the enemy from advancing. There were also major battles against the Mongols in the thirteenth century. It is fair to say that the peasants of Hung Yen have had to withstand continual attempts at invasion throughout their history, in addition to long periods of drought and flooding. They've had the French to contend with, too! It was the Scholars who organized a resistance movement in the villages. There is not a single village in these parts which did not play a part in

16. Interviews conducted by Gérard Chaliand in October–November 1967 and published in his *The Peasants of North Vietnam*, trans. Peter Wiles (Baltimore: Penguin, 1969).

17. Chaliand, *Peasants of North Vietnam*, 71–75.

the resistance. That was in my grandfather's day, and he did his share. It was a peasant uprising on a really large scale, and even the women fought.

. . . All in all, the resistance against the French was kept up for over twenty years. . . .

The first [Communist] Party cell in the province was set up in 1930. . . . Between 1933 and 1940 they established contact with the general population and began to build up a mass following. . . . By 1940, repression or no repression, we were able to get on with our propaganda work and agitation. Each militant was required to establish contact with several villages . . . and do his best to establish nests of sympathizers. This went on from 1940 until 1944. There were very few professional revolutionaries in the area—no more than four or five in the entire province; the rest did ordinary jobs as well as working for the Party. And then, round about 1943 or 44, we started making military preparations. On a very small scale, mind: we had no arms and ammunition as yet. . . .

On 9 March 1945 came the Japanese *coup* toppling the colonial administration. . . . The French were in such disarray that they could do nothing to stop us. Side by side with the armed conflict, the masses were incited to lay hands on the stocks of rice held by the Japanese. . . . The communal rice-stocks in the possession of the village elders . . . were shared out, together with the supplies appropriated by the Japanese. In addition, all taxes were withheld. As a result of these steps, starvation was averted in the province. . . . This seizure of rice for public use finally removed the peasants' uncertainties about the revolution. . . .

In August 1945, we took over every district in the land. . . . Suddenly we found ourselves enjoying independence and freedom. The mood of the country was unbelievable: people were burning with enthusiasm. I shall never forget those times.

And then, in December, the French invaded us again. . . .

After 1949 the people living in the delta became [the target of French forces]. . . . [O]ur army and cadres could not be dislodged; the peasants continued to hide them. A complete network of underground shelters and communication trenches was established, stretching for tens of miles, with exits in or on the outskirts of villages. As the war dragged on, it became possible to conceal and accommodate whole regiments and, eventually, whole divisions.

The French set up puppet municipal councils, staffed with collaborators. It was our task to smash these councils. So we turned the villages into military strongholds, barricading them and digging underground passages. Sometimes a guerrilla platoon was able to withstand a siege by an enemy regiment. After dark, parties of our men would go and harass enemy posts defended by entire battalions. . . .

—Phan Van Ha (a thirty-six-year-old commune party secretary):[18]

My own family were landless peasants: all they had was a house and a small yard. They were hired labourers, working for landowners. . . .

I was eleven when my father died, after an illness, at the age of fifty-four. My mother died of starvation during the great famine of 1945. I was fourteen at the time. We were a family of six. . . . My little sister and I took jobs, looking after landowners' children. . . . At that time, I ate one meal a day: rice with fig-leaves, and usually a soup made from rice and bran. There were no vegetables: all we had was rice and salt. One of my sisters died of starvation in 1945; another was killed during a bombardment in 1948. And one of my brothers was killed in the army in 1953. That leaves three of us. . . .

. . . The landowners used to hold huge feasts and make the villagers contribute. Some of them had three wives. They ate meat or chicken every day. When you were working for them, you got a few sweet potatoes in the morning and some rice at midday. That was for heavy labour. . . . If they wanted to grab a peasant's land, they would plant some liquor in his home (the colonial administration had exclusive rights to liquor) and tip off the authorities. The peasant was duly prosecuted and had to sell his plot. That is how my uncle was dispossessed. And another thing: peasants would run into debt whenever the taxes fell due. The interest rate was 50 per cent for a period of six months. They would just manage to pay off the interest. The debt itself was never disposed of. . . . The poorer a family was, the greater the attempts to make it sell its land, fall into debt and move to another part of the country. . . . In 1943 the village notables decided to put pressure on my family. At their bidding a man came to my uncle's house, feigned insanity and set fire to the place. . . . [M]y two uncles were arrested for laying hands on the notables. There was pandemonium at the district court. In the end, my uncles had to sell all they owned to pay for the trial and were sentenced to three months' imprisonment. We had already lost three saos[19] as a result of the liquor incident, and now the last four saos had to be sold. We had nothing left. In 1945, the young uncle to whom all this had happened was the first person in Quoc Tri to join the self-defence forces; afterwards, the whole family served in the Resistance.

—Doan Van Hoc (a forty-five-year-old peasant):[20]

My parents used to peddle rice. They owned two and a half saos, but that wasn't enough to keep them going so they took to trade. My father did the

18. Chaliand, *Peasants of North Vietnam*, 93–95.
19. One sao is equal to about a tenth of an acre.
20. Chaliand, *Peasants of North Vietnam*, 141–43.

husking and my mother did the selling. . . . We were poor, and I had to help my parents with the jobs. . . .

. . . On ordinary days, we only ate one meal: rice soup with bran.

. . . Our family was in debt: we borrowed from this landowner at an interest rate of 10 per cent per month. From time to time we also borrowed rice at an interest rate of 50 per cent. . . . On one occasion my father had to give up two saos of his land, which left us with only half a sao; and since we had no money to repay the debt, we were compelled to leave the two saos in the hands of the landowner. . . .

. . .

. . . [During the famine] the Revolution started, and the Vietminh arrived in the district to take over the stocks of rice which the Japanese had built up. They seized the rice and shared it out among the neediest. . . .

I didn't really know what the Vietminh was. Also, I was scared: I was chary of joining them because I couldn't see what good they would do us. But we weren't afraid of them, for they weren't out to harm us.

By 1947 I had seen the light, and I did my bit by becoming a village security agent, checking people's papers, tracking down poultry thieves, that kind of thing. I wasn't treated to a lot of propaganda: I just noticed how different they were from the Japanese, who used to grab our rice or else make us pull it up and plant jute instead. We gradually came to realize that our army had our interests at heart. Also, I heard of the victories which our troops had won in this province and others besides.

9 National Security Council report 64, "The Position of the United States With Respect to Indochina," 27 February 1950, calling for containment of communism in the region.[21]

[T]he threat of communist aggression against Indochina is only one phase of anticipated communist plans to seize all of Southeast Asia. . . .

A large segment of the Indochinese nationalist movement was seized in 1945 by Ho Chi Minh, a Vietnamese who under various aliases has served as a communist agent for thirty years. . . . In 1946, he attempted, but failed to secure French agreement to his recognition as the head of a government of Vietnam.

21. President Truman approved this report on 24 April. *FRUS, 1950*, vol. 6 (Washington: GPO, 1976), 744–47. Alternative source: The Senator Gravel Edition, *The Pentagon Papers: The Defense Department History of United States Decisionmaking in Vietnam* (4 vols.; Boston: Beacon Press, 1971), 1:361–62.

Since then he has directed a guerrilla army in raids against French installations and lines of communication. French forces which have been attempting to restore law and order found themselves pitted against a determined adversary who manufactures effective arms locally, who received supplies of arms from outside sources, who maintained no capital or permanent headquarters and who was, and is able, to disrupt and harass almost any area within Vietnam (Tonkin, Annam and Cochinchina) at will.

The United States has, since the Japanese surrender, pointed out to the French Government that the legitimate nationalist aspirations of the people of Indochina must be satisfied, and that a return to the prewar colonial rule is not possible. The Department of State has pointed out to the French Government that it was and is necessary to establish and support governments in Indochina particularly in Vietnam, under leaders who are capable of attracting to their causes the non-communist nationalist followers who had drifted to the Ho Chi Minh communist movement in the absence of any non-communist nationalist movement around which to plan their aspirations.

. . .

CONCLUSIONS

It is important to United States security interests that all practicable measures be taken to prevent further communist expansion in Southeast Asia. Indochina is a key area of Southeast Asia and is under immediate threat.

. . .

Accordingly, the Departments of State and Defense should prepare as a matter of priority a program of all practicable measures designed to protect United States security interests in Indochina.

10 President Dwight Eisenhower to British prime minister Winston Churchill, 4 April 1954, calling for an international coalition to back the French.[22]

I am sure that like me you are following with the deepest interest and anxiety the daily reports of the gallant fight being put up by the French at Dien Bien Phu. . . .

But regardless of the outcome of this particular battle, I fear that the French cannot alone see the thing through, this despite the very substantial assistance

---

22. *FRUS, 1952–1954*, vol. 13, pt. 1 (Washington: GPO, 1982), 1239–40. Alternative source: Peter G. Boyle, ed., *The Churchill-Eisenhower Correspondence, 1953–1955* (Chapel Hill: University of North Carolina Press, 1990), 136–38.

in money and matériel that we are giving them. It is no solution simply to urge the French to intensify their efforts, and if they do not see it through, and Indochina passes into the hands of the Communists, the ultimate effect on our and your global strategic position with the consequent shift in the power ratio throughout Asia and the Pacific could be disastrous. . . . It is difficult to see how Thailand, Burma and Indonesia could be kept out of Communist hands. This we cannot afford. The threat to Malaya, Australia and New Zealand would be direct. The offshore island chain would be broken. The economic pressures on Japan which would be deprived of non-Communist markets and sources of food and raw materials would be such, over a period of time, that it is difficult to see how Japan could be prevented from reaching an accommodation with the Communist world which would combine the manpower and natural resources of Asia with the industrial potential of Japan. . . .

. . .

I believe that the best way . . . to bring greater moral and material resources to the support of the French effort is through the establishment of a new, *ad hoc* grouping or coalition composed of nations which have a vital concern in the checking of Communist expansion in the area. I have in mind in addition to our two countries, France, the Associated States [of Indochina], Australia, New Zealand, Thailand and the Philippines. The United States Government would expect to play its full part in such a coalition. . . .

. . .

. . . [W]e failed to halt Hirohito, Mussolini and Hitler by not acting in unity and in time. That marked the beginning of many years of stark tragedy and desperate peril. May it not be that our nations have learned something from that lesson?

11 President Ho, report to the sixth plenum of the Workers' Party Central Committee, 15 July 1954, adjusting policy to the Geneva conference decisions ending the French war and to the greater U.S. role in South Vietnam.[23]

[N]ow the French are having talks with us while the American imperialists are becoming our main and direct enemy; so our spearhead must be directed at the latter. Until peace is restored, we shall keep fighting the French; but the brunt of our attack and that of the world's peoples should be focused on the United States. US policy is to expand and internationalize the Indochina war. Ours is to struggle for peace and oppose the US war policy. . . .

23. Ho, *Selected Writings*, 177–79.

. . . We must take firm hold of the banner of peace to oppose the US imperialists' policy of direct interference in, and prolongation and expansion of, the war in Indochina. Our policy must change in consequence: formerly we confiscated the French imperialists' properties; now, as negotiations are going on, we may, in accordance with the principle of equality and mutual benefit, allow French economic and cultural interests to be preserved in Indochina. Negotiations entail reasonable mutual concessions. Formerly we said we would drive out and wipe out all French aggressive forces; now, in the talks held, we have demanded and the French have accepted, that a date be set for the withdrawal of their troops. In the past, our aim was to wipe out the puppet administration and army with a view to national reunification; now we practise a policy of leniency and seek reunification of the country through nation-wide elections.

Peace calls for an end to the war; and to end the war one must agree on a cease-fire. A cease-fire requires regrouping zones, that is, enemy troops should be regrouped in a zone with a view to their gradual withdrawal, and ours in another. We must secure a vast area where we would have ample means for building, consolidating and developing our forces so as to exert influence over other regions and thereby advance towards reunification. The setting up of regrouping zones does not mean partition of the country; it is a temporary measure leading to reunification. Owing to the delimitation and exchange of zones, some previously free areas will be temporarily occupied by the enemy; their inhabitants will be dissatisfied; some people might fall prey to discouragement and to enemy deception. We should make it clear to our compatriots that the trials they are going to endure for the sake of the interests of the whole country, for the sake of our long-range interests, will be a cause for glory and will earn them the gratitude of the whole nation. We should keep everyone free from pessimism and negativism and urge all to continue a vigorous struggle for the complete withdrawal of French forces and for independence.

12 President Eisenhower to Premier Ngo Dinh Diem, 25 October 1954, promising American assistance conditioned on reform.[24]

We have been exploring ways and means to permit our aid to Viet-Nam to be more effective and to make a greater contribution to the welfare and

24. *Public Papers of the Presidents* [hereafter *PPP*]: *Dwight D. Eisenhower, 1954* (Washington: GPO, 1969), 949.

stability of the Government of Viet-Nam. I am, accordingly, instructing the American Ambassador to Viet-Nam to examine with you in your capacity as Chief of Government, how an intelligent program of American aid given directly to your Government can serve to assist Viet-Nam in its present hour of trial. . . .

. . . The Government of the United States expects that this aid will be met by performance on the part of the Government of Viet-Nam in undertaking needed reforms. It hopes that such aid, combined with your own continuing efforts, will contribute effectively toward an independent Viet-Nam endowed with a strong government. Such a government would, I hope, be so responsive to the nationalist aspirations of its people, so enlightened in purpose and effective in performance, that it will be respected both at home and abroad and discourage any who might wish to impose a foreign ideology on your free people.

13   Le Van Chan (former Communist cadre), interview on the development of resistance in South Vietnam in the late 1950s.[25]

—on the Communist forces put on the defensive by Diem:[26]

[T]he years 1954–1956 were a period of faith in the general elections, but toward the end of 1956 the communists were most pessimistic. . . .

. . .

During 1957 and 1958 the Party was able to recover its apparatus and its mass organizations, and it counted on contradictions within the government to produce a coup. Thus it emphasized troop proselytizing activities with the hope that in the event of a coup it could seize power. Because the Party judged that it had a sufficient chance to seize power in a coup through its mass organizations and its apparatus, it did not allow the armed forces it was still maintaining in the South to appear.

However, by 1959 the situation in the South had passed into a stage the communists considered the darkest in their lives: almost all their apparatus had been smashed [by the Diem government], the population no longer dared to provide support, families no longer dared to communicate with their relatives in the movement, and village chapters which previously had one or two

25. Le Van Chan (a pseudonym created to hide the interviewee's identity) had been a party member since 1947 and had climbed into the upper echelon of the southern branch of the party organization. He was captured in 1962 and subsequently interviewed by Jeffrey Race. Race, *War Comes to Long An: Revolutionary Conflict in a Vietnamese Province* (Berkeley: University of California Press, 1972), 74n.

26. Race, *War Comes to Long An*, 99, 110–11.

hundred members were now reduced to five or ten who had to flee into the jungle. Because of this situation Party members were angry at the Central Committee, and demanded armed action. The southern branch of the Party demanded of the Central Committee a reasonable policy in dealing with the southern regime, in order to preserve its own existence. If not, it would be completely destroyed.

In the face of this situation the Central Committee saw that it was no longer possible to seize power in the South by means of a peaceful struggle line, since the southern regime, with American assistance, was becoming stronger and not collapsing as had been predicted. Not only had the southern regime not been destroyed, it was instead destroying the Party.... As a result, the Fifteenth Conference of the Central Committee developed a decision permitting the southern organization . . . to develop armed forces with the mission of supporting the political struggle line. These forces were not to fight a conventional war, nor were they intended merely for a guerrilla conflict. Their mission was to sap the strength of the government's village and hamlet forces, or what they called the "tyrannical elements." They were only to attack such units as entered their own base areas, in order to preserve the existence of the apparatus and to develop forces for a new line which the Central Committee would develop. Only in November of 1959 did this policy reach the village level, and it was from this decision that the guerrilla movement and the current armed forces in the South sprang into existence.

—on winning peasant support on the land issue:[27]

In 1957 the Party began to recover, because of a number of not very intelligent actions and policies on the part of the government, which the Party exploited. Among these actions and policies the most deserving of attention were [Saigon's] land-reform program, which automatically restored to the landlords who had followed the French all the lands granted to the peasants during the [anti-French] Resistance....

This land-reform program had a great impact in the countryside, making the majority of the peasantry angry at the government. The peasants felt that they had spilled their blood to drive the French from the country, while the landlords sided with the French and fought against the peasants. Thus at the very least the peasants' rights to the land should have been confirmed. Instead, they were forced to buy the land, and thus they felt they were being victimized by the government. At the same time the Party apparatus took advantage of this situation to propagandize on how bad the government was, how it was the

27. Race, *War Comes to Long An*, 97–98, 129–30.

government of the landlords, stealing the land from the peasants. Added to this were the issues of corruption and abuses by officials. These things all made the people agree with the Party's propaganda on the land issue. After all, the peasants are 90 percent of the population of Vietnam, and land is their life-blood. If Diem took their land away, how could they be free, no matter how else he helped them? . . .

. . .

The peasants in the rural areas have a very limited outlook. Some have never in their lives left their village to visit Saigon or even their own provincial capital. They live close to the land and are concerned with nothing else. . . . Their concern is to see that their immediate interests are protected, and that they are treated reasonably and fairly.

In this situation, the communists are extremely clever. They never propagandize communism, which teaches that the land must be collectivized. If they did, how would the peasantry ever listen to them? Instead, they say: the peasants are the main force of the revolution; if they follow the Party, they will become masters of the countryside and owners of their land, and that scratches the peasants right where they itch. . . .

. . .

. . . Previously the peasantry felt that it was the most despised class, with no standing at all, particularly the landless and the poor peasants. For example, at a celebration they could just stand in a corner and look, not sit at the table like the village notables. Now the communists have returned and the peasants have power. The land has been taken from the landlords and turned over to the peasants, just as have all the local offices. Now the peasants can open their eyes and look up to the sky: they have prestige and social position. The landlords and other classes must fear them because they have power: most of the cadres are peasants, most of the Party members are peasants, most of the military commanders are peasants. Only now do the peasants feel that they have proper rights: materially they have land and are no longer oppressed by the landlords; spiritually they have a position in society, ruling the landlords instead of being ruled by them. This the peasants like. But if the communists were to go and the government to come back, the peasants would return to their former status as slaves. Consequently they must fight to preserve their interests and their lives, as well as their political power.

On the other hand, there are some, particularly the middle and rich peasants, who do not like the communists, because the communists hurt their interests: they are not permitted to charge interest and rentals as before, and if they want to hire laborers they are accused of exploitation. Thus they don't like the communists, but they don't dare oppose them. . . .

14 National Liberation Front of South Vietnam, manifesto, December 1960, rallying opposition to the U.S.-backed Diem regime.[28]

[T]he American imperialists, who had in the past helped the French colonialists to massacre our people, have now replaced the French in enslaving the southern part of our country through a disguised colonial regime. They have been using their stooge—the Ngo Dinh Diem administration—in their downright repression and exploitation of our compatriots, in their manoeuvres to permanently divide our country and to turn its southern part into a military base in preparation for war in Southeast Asia.

The aggressors and traitors, working hand in glove with each other, have set up an extremely cruel dictatorial rule. They persecute and massacre democratic and patriotic people, and abolish all human liberties. They ruthlessly exploit the workers, peasants and other labouring people, strangle the local industry and trade, poison the minds of our people with a depraved foreign culture, thus degrading our national culture, traditions and ethics. They feverishly increase their military forces, build military bases, use the army as an instrument for repressing the people and serving the US imperialists' scheme to prepare an aggressive war.

. . .

At present, our people are urgently demanding an end to the cruel dictatorial rule; they are demanding independence and democracy, enough food and clothing, and peaceful reunification of the country.

To meet the aspirations of our compatriots, the *South Viet Nam National Front for Liberation* came into being, pledging itself to shoulder the historic task of liberating our people from the present yoke of slavery.

The *South Viet Nam National Front for Liberation* undertakes to unite all sections of the people, all social classes, nationalities, political parties, organizations, religious communities and patriotic personalities, without distinction of their political tendencies, in order to struggle for the overthrow of the rule of the US imperialists and their stooges—the Ngo Dinh Diem clique—and for the realization of independence, democracy, peace and neutrality pending the peaceful reunification of the fatherland.

28. Gareth Porter, ed., *Vietnam: The Definitive Documentation of Human Decisions* (2 vols.; Stanfordville, N.Y.: Earl M. Coleman Enterprises, 1979), 2:87–88. Original source: *Vietnamese Studies* (Hanoi), no. 23 (1970): 247–54.

15 **Walt W. Rostow (deputy special assistant to President John F. Kennedy for national security affairs), speech at the U.S. Army Special Warfare School, Fort Bragg, North Carolina, 28 June 1961, describing the revolution of modernization and the scavenger role of communist insurgents.**[29]

What is happening throughout Latin America, Africa, the Middle East, and Asia is this: Old societies are changing their ways in order to create and maintain a national personality on the world scene and to bring to their peoples the benefits modern technology can offer. This process is truly revolutionary. . . .

Like all revolutions, the revolution of modernization is disturbing. Individual men are torn between the commitment to the old familiar way of life and the attractions of a modern way of life. The power of old social groups—notably the landlord, who usually dominates the traditional society—is reduced. Power moves toward those who can command the tools of modern technology, including modern weapons. Men and women in the villages and the cities, feeling that the old ways of life are shaken and that new possibilities are open to them, express old resentments and new hopes.

This is the grand arena of revolutionary change which the Communists are exploiting with great energy. They believe that their techniques of organization—based on small disciplined cadres of conspirators—are ideally suited to grasp and to hold power in these turbulent settings. They believe that the weak transitional governments that one is likely to find during this modernization process are highly vulnerable to subversion and to guerrilla warfare. And whatever Communist doctrines of historical inevitability may be, Communists know that their time to seize power in the underdeveloped areas is limited. They know that, as momentum takes hold in an underdeveloped area—and the fundamental social problems inherited from the traditional society are solved—their chances to seize power decline.

It is on the weakest nations, facing their most difficult transitional moments, that the Communists concentrate their attention. They are the scavengers of the modernization process. They believe that the techniques of political centralization under dictatorial control—and the projected image of Soviet and Chinese Communist economic progress—will persuade hesitant

29. Rostow cleared this speech, "Guerrilla Warfare in the Underdeveloped Areas," in advance with President Kennedy. *Department of State Bulletin* 45 (7 August 1961): 234–37. Alternative source: T. N. Greene, ed., *The Guerilla—And How to Fight Him* (New York: Praeger, 1962), 54–61.

men, faced by great transitional problems, that the Communist model should be adopted for modernization, even at the cost of surrendering human liberty. They believe that they can exploit effectively the resentments built up in many of these areas against colonial rule and that they can associate themselves effectively with the desire of the emerging nations for independence, for status on the world scene, and for material progress.

. . . Communism is best understood as a disease of the transition to modernization.

. . . We are dedicated to the proposition that this revolutionary process of modernization shall be permitted to go forward in independence, with increasing degrees of human freedom. . . . Moreover, we Americans are confident that, if the independence of this process can be maintained over the coming years and decades, these societies will choose their own version of what we would recognize as a democratic, open society.

. . .

. . . [T]he primary responsibility for dealing with guerrilla warfare in the underdeveloped areas cannot be American. . . . [A] guerrilla war must be fought primarily by those on the spot. This is so for a quite particular reason. A guerrilla war is an intimate affair, fought not merely with weapons but fought in the minds of the men who live in the villages and in the hills, fought by the spirit and policy of those who run the local government. An outsider cannot, by himself, win a guerrilla war. He can help create conditions in which it can be won, and he can directly assist those prepared to fight for their independence. We are determined to help destroy this international disease; that is, guerrilla war designed, initiated, supplied, and led from outside an independent nation.

. . . [T]he operation run from Hanoi against Viet-Nam is as clear a form of aggression as the violation of the 38th parallel by the north Korean armies in June, 1950.

. . . [G]uerrilla warfare, mounted from external bases—with rights of sanctuary—is a terrible burden to carry for any government in a society making its way toward modernization. As you know, it takes somewhere between 10 and 20 soldiers to control 1 guerrilla in an organized operation. Moreover, the guerrilla force has this advantage: its task is merely to destroy, while the government must build, and protect what it is building. A guerrilla war mounted from outside a transitional nation is a crude act of international vandalism. There will be no peace in the world if the international community accepts the outcome of a guerrilla war, mounted from outside a nation, as tantamount to a free election.

. . .

When Communists speak of wars of national liberation and of their support for "progressive forces," I think of the systematic program of assassination now going forward in which the principal victims are the health, agriculture, and education officers in Viet-Nam villages. The Viet Cong are not trying to persuade the peasants of Viet-Nam that communism is good; they are trying to persuade them that their lives are insecure unless they cooperate with them. . . .

16 North Vietnam's Workers' Party, Central Committee guidelines, circa October 1961, anticipating intensified political-military struggle in the south as the Diem regime weakens.[30]

The period of temporary stabilization of the U.S.-Diem regime has passed and the period of continuous crisis and serious decline has begun.

. . . [T]he enemy's forces and government will continue to disintegrate, the revolutionary forces will be rapidly built and developed and forms of revolutionary government will appear in localities everywhere. A general all-sided crisis of the U.S.-Diem regime will appear, and a general offensive and general uprising of the people will break out, overthrow the U.S.-Diem regime and liberate the South. Also during that process, the enemy will experience increasingly deep internal contradictions and the revolutionary movement will rise higher everyday. Coups or military revolts could occur, in which the revolution must seize the opportune moment in order to turn it into a situation favorable to the revolution. At the same time, the possibility of armed intervention by bringing troops of U.S. imperialism and its lackeys into the South . . . is also a complex problem which we must follow and find ways to limit, guard against and be prepared to cope with in a timely fashion.

17 Secretary of Defense Robert McNamara and Secretary of State Dean Rusk, memorandum to President Kennedy, 11 November 1961, contemplating an expanded commitment to South Vietnam.[31]

It seems, on the face of it, absurd to think that a nation of 20 million people can be subverted by 15–20 thousand active guerillas if the Government

30. Extract from Central Office for South Vietnam, conference resolution of October 1961, in Porter, *Vietnam: A History in Documents*, 217. Porter translation from a captured document.

31. After a discussion with his advisers on 11 November, Kennedy approved the memorandum's proposal for planning for the use of American forces and for at once stepping up the level of advisory and matériel support for the Diem government. U.S. Department of Defense, *United States–Vietnam Relations, 1945–1967* [Pentagon Papers] (12 books; Wash-

and people of that country do not wish to be subverted. South Viet-Nam is not, however, a highly organized society with an effective governing apparatus and a population accustomed to carrying civic responsibility. Public apathy is encouraged by the inability of most citizens to act directly as well as by the tactics of terror employed by the guerillas throughout the countryside. . . .

. . .

The United States should commit itself to the clear objective of preventing the fall of South Viet-Nam to Communism. The basic means for accomplishing this objective must be to put the Government of South Viet-Nam into a position to win its own war against the guerillas. We must insist that that Government itself take the measures necessary for that purpose in exchange for large-scale United States assistance in the military, economic and political fields. At the same time we must recognize that it will probably not be possible for the GVN [Government of Vietnam] to win this war as long as the flow of men and supplies from North Viet-Nam continues unchecked and the guerillas enjoy a safe sanctuary in neighboring territory.

We should be prepared to introduce United States combat forces if that should become necessary for success. Dependent upon the circumstances, it may also be necessary for United States forces to strike at the source of the aggression in North Viet-Nam.

. . .

The commitment of United States forces to South Viet-Nam involves two different categories: (A) Units of modest size required for the direct support of South Viet-Namese military effort, such as communications, helicopter and other forms of airlift, reconnaissance aircraft, naval patrols, intelligence units, etc., and (B) larger organized units with actual or potential direct military missions. *Category (A) should be introduced as speedily as possible.* Category (B) units pose a more serious problem in that they are much more significant from the point of view of domestic and international political factors and greatly increase the probabilities of Communist bloc escalation. Further, the employment of United States combat forces (in the absence of Communist bloc escalation) involves a certain dilemma: if there is a strong South Viet-Namese effort, they may not be needed; if there is not such an effort, United States forces could not accomplish their mission in the midst of an apathetic or hostile population. Under present circumstances, therefore, the question of injecting United States and SEATO combat forces should in large part be considered as a contribution to the morale of the South Viet-Namese in their own effort to do the principal job themselves.

---

ington: GPO, 1971), book 11, pp. 359–61. For a brief record of Kennedy's meeting with his advisers, see *FRUS, 1961–1963*, vol. 1 (Washington: GPO, 1988), 577–78.

. . .

If we commit Category (B) forces to South Viet-Nam, the ultimate possible extent of our military commitment in Southeast Asia must be faced. The struggle may be prolonged, and Hanoi and Peiping may overtly intervene. It is the view of the Secretary of Defense and the Joint Chiefs of Staff that, in the light of the logistic difficulties faced by the other side, we can assume that the maximum United States forces required on the ground in Southeast Asia would not exceed six divisions, or about 205,000 men. . . .

18 President Kennedy to President Diem, 14 December 1961, publicly affirming American support.[32]

The situation in your embattled country is well known to me and to the American people. We have been deeply disturbed by the assault on your country. Our indignation has mounted as the deliberate savagery of the Communist program of assassination, kidnapping and wanton violence became clear.

. . . [T]he campaign of force and terror now being waged against your people and your Government is supported and directed from the outside by the authorities at Hanoi. They have thus violated the provisions of the Geneva Accords designed to ensure peace in Viet-Nam and to which they bound themselves in 1954.

. . .

. . . [W]e are prepared to help the Republic of Viet-Nam to protect its people and to preserve its independence. We shall promptly increase our assistance to your defense effort. . . .

19 Ambassador to India John Kenneth Galbraith, memorandum to President Kennedy, 4 April 1962, arguing for a neutralized South Vietnam.[33]

1. We have a growing military commitment. This could expand step by step into a major, long-drawn out indecisive military involvement.

2. We are backing a weak and, on the record, ineffectual government and a leader who as a politician may be beyond the point of no return.

32. *PPP: John F. Kennedy, 1961* (Washington: GPO, 1962), 801. Alternative source: Senator Gravel Edition, *Pentagon Papers*, 2:805–6.

33. Galbraith was a Harvard economist brought into government service by Kennedy. *FRUS, 1961–1963*, vol. 2 (Washington: GPO, 1990), 297. Alternative source: Senator Gravel Edition, *Pentagon Papers*, 2:670–71.

3. There is consequent danger we shall replace the French as the colonial force in the area and bleed as the French did.

4. The political effects of some of the measures which pacification requires or is believed to require, including the concentration of population, relocation of villages, and the burning of old villages, may be damaging to those and especially to Westerners associated with it.

5. We fear that at some point in the involvement there will be a major [domestic] political outburst [in the United States] about the new Korea and the new war into which the Democrats as so often before have precipitated us.

6. It seems at least possible that the Soviets are not particularly desirous of trouble in this part of the world and that our military reaction with the need to fall back on Chinese protection may be causing concern in Hanoi.

In the light of the foregoing we urge the following:

1. That it be our policy to keep open the door for political solution. We should welcome as a solution any broadly based non-Communist government that is free from external interference. It should have the requisites for internal law and order. We should not require that it be militarily identified with the United States.

2. We shall find it useful in achieving this result if we seize any good opportunity to involve other countries and world opinion in [a] settlement and its guarantee. This is a useful exposure and pressure on the Communist bloc countries and a useful antidote for the argument that this is a private American military adventure.

3. We should measurably reduce our commitment to the particular present leadership of the Government of South Viet-Nam.

20 **Nguyen Chi Thanh (member of the Political Bureau of the Workers' Party), article of July 1963, "Who Will Win in South Vietnam?" arguing that a frustrated and divided United States was vulnerable to defeat.[34]**

The United States thought that, with its numerous arms, dollars, rich political and military experience and a faithful lackey Ngo Dinh Diem, it could

34. The forty-nine-year-old Thanh came from a poor peasant family in central Vietnam. This staunch supporter of the southern struggle would serve as his party's senior member in the south down to his death in 1967. He was reportedly killed by U.S. bombing. Porter, *Vietnam: The Definitive Documentation*, 2:184, 186. Alternative version: *Vietnamese Studies*, no. 1 (1964): 14–23.

solve all the problems in south Viet Nam in a very short time. Events, however, have proved this to be sheer wishful thinking.

Nine years have elapsed and the U.S. imperialists are still unable to come to any definite conclusion as regards their plans for aggression.

Much discussion on the situation in south Viet Nam has been going on in the American press and radio, and opinions are varied. U.S. politicians and generals, who agree on invading south Viet Nam, are widely divided over the line of action. Some of them stand for kicking out Ngo Dinh Diem because he has dirtied the showcase of American "democracy." Others are against "changing the horse in the middle of the stream." Militarily, U.S. generals have so far failed to work out a single, consistent strategic and tactical line for aggression in south Viet Nam. Some of them hold that the anti-guerrilla tactics employed in Malaya should be applied *in toto* in south Viet Nam, while others say that this would be an inflexible approach. Some of them advocate using large mobile forces in "spectacular" campaigns to wipe out the armed forces of the National Liberation Front, while others believe that victory can be obtained only through the use of smaller units in surprise attacks since their opponents, appearing and disappearing mysteriously, are difficult to deal with.

. . .

We do not have any illusions about the United States. We do not underestimate our opponent—the strong and cunning U.S. imperialism. But we are not afraid of the United States. . . . If . . . one is afraid of the United States and thinks that to offend it would court failure, and that firm opposition to U.S. imperialism would touch off a nuclear war, then the only course left would be to compromise with and surrender to U.S. imperialism.

21   President Kennedy, press conference comments, 17 July 1963, reacting to the Buddhist demonstrations against the Diem regime.[35]

Viet-Nam has been in war for 20 years. The Japanese came in, the war with the French, the civil war which has gone on for 10 years, and this is very difficult for any society to stand. It is a country which has got a good many problems and it is divided, and there is guerrilla activity and murder and all of the rest. Compounding this, however, now is a religious dispute. I would hope this would be settled, because we want to see a stable government there, carrying on a struggle to maintain its national independence.

35. *PPP: John F. Kennedy, 1963* (Washington: GPO, 1964), 569. Alternative source: Senator Gravel Edition, *Pentagon Papers*, 2:824.

We believe strongly in that. We are not going to withdraw from that effort. In my opinion, for us to withdraw from that effort would mean a collapse not only of South Viet-Nam, but Southeast Asia. So we are going to stay there. . . .

22 Kennedy administration officials in Washington and Ambassador Henry Cabot Lodge, Jr., in South Vietnam, cables, 24 August–6 October 1963, discussing Diem's overthrow.

—Under Secretary of State George W. Ball to Lodge, 24 August:[36]

US Government cannot tolerate situation in which power lies in [Ngo Dinh] Nhu's hands. Diem must be given chance to rid himself of Nhu and his coterie and replace them with best military and political personalities available.

If, in spite of all your efforts, Diem remains obdurate and refuses, then we must face the possibility that Diem himself cannot be preserved.

—Lodge to Secretary of State Rusk, 29 August:[37]

We are launched on a course from which there is no respectable turning back: The overthrow of the Diem government. There is no turning back in part because U.S. prestige is already publicly committed to this end in large measure and will become more so as facts leak out. In a more fundamental sense, there is no turning back because there is no possibility, in my view, that the war can be won under a Diem administration, still less that Diem or any member of the family can govern the country in a way to gain the support of the people who count, i.e., the educated class in and out of government service, civil and military—not to mention the American people. In the last few months (and especially days), they have in fact positively alienated these people to an incalculable degree. . . .

. . .

I realize that this course involves a very substantial risk of losing Vietnam. It also involves some additional risk to American lives. I would never propose it if I felt there was a reasonable chance of holding Vietnam with Diem.

36. This cable was drafted by Roger Hilsman (assistant secretary of state for far eastern affairs) and cleared by Averell Harriman (under secretary of state for political affairs), Michael Forrestal (of the National Security Council staff), and George Ball. It was presented to President Kennedy while he was on vacation at Hyannis Port, Massachusetts. Kennedy gave his approval with a casualness that he may soon have regretted. *FRUS, 1961–1963*, vol. 3 (Washington: GPO, 1991), 628.

37. Copies of this cable went to the White House, the Defense Department, and the CIA. *FRUS, 1961–1963*, 4:21–22.

—White House to Lodge, 17 September:[38]

We see no good opportunity for action to remove present government in immediate future. Therefore . . . we must for the present apply such pressures as are available to secure whatever modest improvements on the scene may be possible. . . .

—McGeorge Bundy to Lodge, 5 October:[39]

President today approved recommendation that no initiative should now be taken to give any active covert encouragement to a coup. There should, however, be urgent covert effort with closest security under broad guidance of Ambassador to identify and build contacts with possible alternative leadership as and when it appears. . . .

—Central Intelligence Agency (for the White House?) to Lodge, 9 October:[40]

We have following additional general thoughts which have been discussed with President. While we do not wish to stimulate coup, we also do not wish to leave impression that U.S. would thwart a change of government or deny economic and military assistance to a new regime if it appeared capable of increasing effectiveness of military effort, ensuring popular support to win war and improving working relations with U.S. . . .

23 Central Committee of the Workers' Party, secret resolution of December 1963, offering an optimistic appraisal of the situation in South Vietnam following Diem's overthrow.[41]

We have sufficient conditions to quickly change the balance of forces in our favor. And whether the U.S. maintains its combat strength at the present level or increases it, she must still use her henchmen's army as a main force. However, this army becomes weaker day by day due to the serious decline of its quality, the demoralization of its troops and the disgust of the latter for the Americans and their lackeys. These are the factors that cause the collapse of Americans' and their lackeys' troops. No U.S. financial assistance or weapons can prevent this collapse.

As for us, we become more confident in the victory of our armed forces. Our

38. This cable was drafted by McGeorge Bundy, Kennedy's special assistant for national security affairs, and sent via the State Department. *FRUS, 1961–1963,* 4:252.

39. Sent via the CIA. *FRUS, 1961–1963,* 4:379.

40. *FRUS, 1961–1963,* 4:393.

41. Porter, *Vietnam: A History in Documents,* 256–57.

technical and tactical skills are improved and our fighting spirit is heightened. The people in South Viet-Nam have stood up against the imperialists for almost 20 years, so they have a high political enlightenment. At the present time, the more they fight, the bigger victories they win, the revolutionary movement has created favorable conditions for building up the armed forces. . . .

If the U.S. imperialists send more troops to Viet-Nam to save the situation after suffering a series of failures, *the Revolution in Viet-Nam will meet more difficulties, the struggle will be stronger and harder but it will certainly succeed in attaining the final victory.* . . . [T]he U.S. imperialists cannot win over 14 million Vietnamese people in the South who have taken arms to fight the imperialists for almost 20 years, and who, with all the compatriots throughout the country, have defeated the hundreds of thousands of troops of the French expeditionary force. Now the South Vietnamese people show themselves capable of beating the enemy in any situation. They certainly have the determination, talents, strength and patience to crush any U.S. imperialists' schemes and plans, and finally to force them to withdraw from Viet-Nam as the French imperialists did.

24 Secretary of Defense McNamara to President Lyndon B. Johnson, memorandum, 21 December 1963, reporting on problems identified during a two-day visit to Vietnam.[42]

Summary. The situation is very disturbing. Current trends, unless reversed in the next 2–3 months, will lead to neutralization at best and more likely to a Communist-controlled state.

The new government is the greatest source of concern. It is indecisive and drifting. Although [General Duong Van] Minh states that he, rather than the committee of Generals, is making decisions, it is not clear that this is actually so. In any event, neither he nor the Committee are experienced in political administration and so far they show little talent for it. There is no clear concept on how to re-shape or conduct the strategic hamlet program; the Province Chiefs, most of whom are new and inexperienced, are receiving little or no direction; military operations, too, are not being effectively directed because the generals are so preoccupied with essentially political affairs. . . .

The Country Team is the second major weakness. It lacks leadership, has been poorly informed, and is not working to a common plan. . . . Lodge simply does not know how to conduct a coordinated administration. . . . [H]e has just operated as a loner all his life and cannot readily change now.

42. *FRUS, 1961–1963,* 4:732–35.

...

Viet Cong progress has been great during the period since the coup, with my best guess being that the situation has in fact been deteriorating in the countryside since July to a far greater extent than we realized because of our undue dependence on distorted Vietnamese reporting. The Viet Cong now control very high proportions of the people in certain key provinces, particularly those directly south and west of Saigon. The Strategic Hamlet Program was seriously over-extended in these provinces, and the Viet Cong has been able to destroy many hamlets, while others have been abandoned or in some cases betrayed or pillaged by the government's own Self Defense Corps. In these key provinces, the Viet Cong have destroyed almost all major roads, and are collecting taxes at will.

...

Infiltration of men and equipment from North Vietnam continues using (a) land corridors through Laos and Cambodia; (b) the Mekong River waterways from Cambodia; (c) some possible entry from the sea and the tip of the [Mekong] Delta. The best guess is that 1000–1500 Viet Cong cadres entered South Vietnam from Laos in the first nine months of 1963. The Mekong route (and also the possible sea entry) is apparently used for heavier weapons and ammunition and raw materials which have been turning up in increasing numbers in the south and of which we have captured a few shipments.

...

Plans for Covert Action into North Vietnam were prepared as we had requested and were an excellent job. . . .

...

Conclusion. . . . We should watch the situation very carefully, running scared, hoping for the best, but preparing for more forceful moves if the situation does not show early signs of improvement.

25 Joint Chiefs of Staff to Secretary of Defense McNamara, memorandum, 22 January 1964, urging a widening of the war and a greater American role.[43]

Currently we and the South Vietnamese are fighting the war on the enemy's terms. He has determined the locale, the timing, and the tactics of the battle while our actions are essentially reactive. One reason for this is the fact that we have obliged ourselves to labor under self-imposed restrictions with respect to impeding external aid to the Viet Cong. These restrictions include

43. Senator Gravel Edition, *Pentagon Papers*, 3:497–98.

keeping the war within the boundaries of South Vietnam, avoiding the direct use of US combat forces, and limiting US direction of the campaign to rendering advice to the Government of Vietnam. These restrictions, while they may make our international position more readily defensible, all tend to make the task in Vietnam more complex, time consuming, and in the end, more costly. In addition to complicating our own problem, these self-imposed restrictions may well now be conveying signals of irresolution to our enemies—encouraging them to higher levels of vigor and greater risks. A reversal of attitude and the adoption of a more aggressive program would enhance greatly our ability to control the degree to which escalation will occur. It appears probable that the economic and agricultural disappointments suffered by Communist China, plus the current rift with the Soviets, could cause the communists to think twice about undertaking a large-scale military adventure in Southeast Asia.

. . . [T]he Joint Chiefs of Staff are aware that the focus of the counterinsurgency battle lies in South Vietnam itself, and that the war must certainly be fought and won primarily in the minds of the Vietnamese people. At the same time, the aid now coming to the Viet Cong from outside the country in men, resources, advice, and direction is sufficiently great in the aggregate to be significant—both as help and as encouragement to the Viet Cong. . . .

Accordingly, the Joint Chiefs of Staff consider that the United States must make ready to conduct increasingly bolder actions in Southeast Asia; specifically as to Vietnam to:

a. Assign to the US military commander responsibilities for the total US program in Vietnam.

b. Induce the Government of Vietnam to turn over to the United States military commander, temporarily, the actual tactical direction of the war.

c. Charge the United States military commander with complete responsibility for conduct of the program against North Vietnam.

d. Overfly Laos and Cambodia to whatever extent is necessary for acquisition of operational intelligence.

e. Induce the Government of Vietnam to conduct overt ground operations in Laos of sufficient scope to impede the flow of personnel and material southward.

f. Arm, equip, advise, and support the Government of Vietnam in its conduct of aerial bombing of critical targets in North Vietnam and in mining the sea approaches to that country.

g. Advise and support the Government of Vietnam in its conduct of large-scale commando raids against critical targets in North Vietnam.[44]

44. President Johnson had already, earlier in January, authorized a program of covert

h. Conduct aerial bombing of key North Vietnam targets, using US resources under Vietnamese cover, and with the Vietnamese openly assuming responsibility for the actions.

i. Commit additional US forces, as necessary, in support of the combat action within South Vietnam.

j. Commit US forces as necessary in direct actions against North Vietnam.

26 General Maxwell D. Taylor (ambassador in Saigon), briefing, "The Current Situation in South Vietnam," undated [late November 1964], recommending action to halt the continuing decline of the Saigon government.[45]

After a year of changing and ineffective government, the counter-insurgency program country-wide is bogged down and will require heroic treatment to assure revival. . . .

. . .

. . . While the most critical governmental weaknesses are in Saigon, they are duplicated to a degree in the provinces. It is most difficult to find adequate provincial chiefs and supporting administrative personnel to carry forward the complex programs which are required in the field for successful pacification. . . .

As the past history of this country shows, there seems to be a national attribute which makes for factionalism and limits the development of a truly national spirit. . . . [T]here is no national tendency toward team play or mutual loyalty to be found among many of the leaders and political groups within South Viet-Nam. . . .

The ability of the Viet-Cong continuously to rebuild their units and to make good their losses is one of the mysteries of this guerilla war. We are aware of the recruiting methods by which local boys are induced or compelled to join the Viet-Cong ranks and have some general appreciation of the amount of infiltration of personnel from the outside. Yet taking both of these sources into account, we still find no plausible explanation of the continued strength of the Viet-Cong if our data on Viet-Cong losses are even approximately correct. Not only do the Viet-Cong units have the recuperative powers of the phoenix, but they have an amazing ability to maintain morale. . . .

Undoubtedly one cause for the growing strength of the Viet-Cong is the

operations against the north intended to pressure Hanoi to end its "aggression" in the south. *FRUS, 1964–1968*, vol. 1 (Washington: GPO, 1992), 4–5, 27n.

45. *FRUS, 1964–1968*, 1:948–50, 952–54.

increased direction and support of their campaign by the government of North Viet-Nam. This direction and support take the form of endless radioed orders and instructions, and the continuous dispatch to South Viet-Nam of trained cadre and military equipment, over infiltration routes by land and by water. While in the aggregate, this contribution to the guerilla campaign over the years must represent a serious drain on the resources of the DRV [Democratic Republic of Vietnam], that government shows no sign of relaxing its support of the Viet-Cong. . . .

. . .

In bringing military pressure to bear on North Viet-Nam, there are a number of variations which are possible. At the bottom of the ladder of escalation, we have the initiation of intensified covert operations, anti-infiltration attacks in Laos, and reprisal bombings. . . . From this level of operations, we could begin to escalate progressively by attacking appropriate targets in North Viet-Nam. . . . In its final forms, this kind of attack could extend to the destruction of all important fixed targets in North Viet-Nam and to the interdiction of movement on all lines of communication.

. . .

. . . [W]e are tired of standing by and seeing the unabashed efforts of the DRV to absorb South Viet-Nam into the Communist orbit against its will. We know that Hanoi is responsible and that we are going to punish it until it desists from this behavior.

27 President Johnson, speech at Johns Hopkins University, Baltimore, 7 April 1965, justifying the U.S. commitment to Vietnam.[46]

Why must this Nation hazard its ease, and its interest, and its power for the sake of a people so far away?

We fight because we must fight if we are to live in a world where every country can shape its own destiny, and only in such a world will our own freedom be finally secure.

. . .

The world as it is in Asia is not a serene or peaceful place.

The first reality is that North Viet-Nam has attacked the independent na-

46. *PPP: Lyndon B. Johnson, 1965* (Washington: GPO, 1966), 1:394–99. This speech was the product of a two-week effort to which White House staffers McGeorge Bundy, Richard Goodwin, and Jack Valenti all contributed, with Johnson playing an important role in the last stage of the drafting.

tion of South Viet-Nam. Its object is total conquest. Of course, some of the people of South Viet-Nam are participating in attack on their own government. But trained men and supplies, orders and arms, flow in a constant stream from north to south.

This support is the heartbeat of the war.

And it is a war of unparalleled brutality. Simple farmers are the targets of assassination and kidnapping. Women and children are strangled in the night because their men are loyal to their government. And helpless villages are ravaged by sneak attacks. Large-scale raids are conducted on towns, and terror strikes in the heart of cities.

. . .

Over this war—and all Asia—is another reality: the deepening shadow of Communist China. The rulers in Hanoi are urged on by Peking. This is a regime which has destroyed freedom in Tibet, which has attacked India, and has been condemned by the United Nations for aggression in Korea. It is a nation which is helping the forces of violence in almost every continent. The contest in Viet-Nam is part of a wider pattern of aggressive purposes.

Why are these realities our concern? Why are we in South Viet-Nam?

We are there because we have a promise to keep. Since 1954 every American President has offered support to the people of South Viet-Nam. . . .

. . .

We are also there to strengthen world order. Around the globe, from Berlin to Thailand, are people whose well-being rests, in part, on the belief that they can count on us if they are attacked. To leave Viet-Nam to its fate would shake the confidence of all these people in the value of an American commitment and in the value of America's word. The result would be increased unrest and instability, and even wider war.

We are also there because there are great stakes in the balance. Let no one think for a moment that retreat from Viet-Nam would bring an end to conflict. The battle would be renewed in one country and then another. The central lesson of our time is that the appetite of aggression is never satisfied. To withdraw from one battlefield means only to prepare for the next. . . .

. . .

In recent months attacks on South Viet-Nam were stepped up. Thus, it became necessary for us to increase our response and to make attacks by air. This is not a change of purpose. It is a change in what we believe that purpose requires.

We do this in order to slow down aggression.

We do this to increase the confidence of the brave people of South Viet-Nam who have bravely borne this brutal battle for many years with so many casualties.

And we do this to convince the leaders of North Viet-Nam—and all who seek to share their conquest—of a very simple fact:

We will not be defeated.

We will not grow tired.

We will not withdraw, either openly or under the cloak of a meaningless agreement.

. . .

. . . We have no desire to see thousands die in battle—Asians or Americans. We have no desire to devastate that which the people of North Viet-Nam have built with toil and sacrifice. We will use our power with restraint and with all the wisdom that we can command.

But we will use it.

. . .

. . . [O]ur generation has a dream. It is a very old dream. But we have the power, and now we have the opportunity to make that dream come true.

For centuries nations have struggled among each other. But we dream of a world where disputes are settled by law and reason. And we will try to make it so.

For most of history men have hated and killed one another in battle. But we dream of an end to war. And we will try to make it so.

For all existence most men have lived in poverty, threatened by hunger. But we dream of a world where all are fed and charged with hope. And we will help to make it so.

. . .

This generation of the world must choose: destroy or build, kill or aid, hate or understand.

We can do all these things on a scale never dreamed of before.

Well, we will choose life. In so doing we will prevail over the enemies within man, and over the natural enemies of all mankind.

28 DRV premier Pham Van Dong, statement to the national assembly in Hanoi, 8 April 1965, outlining a settlement based on a revival of the 1954 Geneva agreement.[47]

1. Recognition of the basic national rights of the Vietnamese people: peace, independence, sovereignty, unity and territorial integrity. According to the Geneva Agreements, the U.S. government must withdraw from South

47. U.S. Department of State, *American Foreign Policy: Current Documents, 1965* (Washington: GPO, 1968), 852. This statement was broadcast by Radio Hanoi on 13 April 1965, and it was printed in the *New York Times,* 14 April 1965, A-17.

Vietnam all U.S. troops, military personnel and weapons of all kinds, dismantle all U.S. military bases there, [and] cancel its "military alliance" with South Vietnam. It must end its policy of intervention and aggression in South Vietnam. According to the Geneva Agreements, the U.S. government must stop its acts of war against North Vietnam, [and] completely cease all encroachments on the territory and sovereignty of the Democratic Republic of Vietnam.

2. Pending the peaceful reunificiation of Vietnam, while Vietnam is still temporarily divided into two zones the military provisions of the 1954 Geneva Agreements on Vietnam must be strictly respected: the two zones must refrain from joining any military alliance with foreign countries, [and] there must be no foreign military bases, troops [or] military personnel in their respective territory.

3. The internal affairs of South Vietnam must be settled by the South Vietnamese people themselves, in accordance with the programme of the South Vietnam National Front for Liberation, without any foreign interference.

4. The peaceful reunification of Vietnam is to be settled by the Vietnamese people in both zones, without any foreign interference.

29 Under Secretary of State George Ball to President Johnson, memorandum, I July 1965, proposing "A Compromise Solution in Vietnam."[48]

The South Vietnamese are losing the war to the Viet Cong. No one can assure you that we can beat the Viet Cong or even force them to the conference table on our terms, no matter how many hundred thousand *white, foreign* (U.S.) troops we deploy.

No one has demonstrated that a white ground force of whatever size can win a guerilla war—which is at the same time a civil war between Asians—in jungle terrain in the midst of a population that refuses cooperation to the white forces (and the South Vietnamese) and thus provides a great intelligence advantage to the other side. Three recent incidents vividly illustrate this point: (a) the sneak attack on the Da Nang Air Base which involved penetration of a defense perimeter guarded by 9,000 Marines. This raid was possible only because of the cooperation of the local inhabitants; (b) the B-52 raid that failed to hit the Viet Cong who had obviously been tipped off; (c) the search and destroy mission of the 173rd Air Borne Brigade which spent three days looking for the Viet Cong, suffered 23 casualties, and never made contact with the enemy who had obviously gotten advance word of their assignment.

48. Senator Gravel Edition, *Pentagon Papers,* 4:615–16.

. . .

. . . So long as our forces are restricted to advising and assisting the South Vietnamese, the struggle will remain a civil war between Asian peoples. Once we deploy substantial numbers of troops in combat it will become a war between the U.S. and a large part of the population of South Vietnam, organized and directed from North Vietnam and backed by the resources of both Moscow and Peiping.

The decision you face now, therefore, is crucial. Once large numbers of U.S. troops are committed to direct combat, they will begin to take heavy casualties in a war they are ill-equipped to fight in a non-cooperative if not downright hostile countryside.

Once we suffer large casualties, we will have started a well-nigh irreversible process. Our involvement will be so great that we cannot—without national humiliation—stop short of achieving our complete objectives. *Of the two possibilities I think humiliation would be more likely than the achievement of our objectives—even after we have paid terrible costs.*

. . . Should we commit U.S. manpower and prestige to a terrain so unfavorable as to give a very large advantage to the enemy—or should we seek a compromise settlement which achieves less than our stated objectives and thus cut our losses while we still have the freedom of manuever to do so?

. . . In my judgment, if we can act before we commit a substantial U.S. truce [troop force] to combat in South Vietnam we can, by accepting some short-term costs, avoid what may well be a long-term catastrophe. . . .

30 Le Duan (general secretary of the Workers' Party), speech to a cadre conference, 6–8 July 1965, contemplating a major confrontation with the United States.[49]

[T]he U.S. is still strong enough to enter into a limited war in Vietnam, by sending . . . 300,000–400,000 troops to South Vietnam. But if it switches to limited war, the U.S. still will have weaknesses which it cannot overcome. The U.S. rear area is very far away, and American soldiers are "soldiers in chains," who cannot fight like the French, cannot stand the weather conditions, and

49. Le Duan, born in central Vietnam the son of a railway worker, had played a leading role in the south during both the war against France and the first years of partition. He moved to Hanoi in 1957 to head the Workers' Party, and in party debates he proved a strong proponent of early efforts to reunite the country. Porter translation, in Porter, *Vietnam: The Definitive Documentation,* 2:383–85.

don't know the battlefield. . . . If the U.S. puts 300–400,000 troops into the South, it will have stripped away the face of its neocolonial policy and revealed the face of an old style colonial invader. . . . Thus, the U.S. will not be able to maintain its power with regard to influential sectors of the United States. If the U.S. itself directly enters the war in the South it will have to fight for a prolonged period with the people's army of the South, with the full assistance of the North and of the Socialist bloc. To fight for a prolonged period is a weakness of U.S. imperialism. The Southern revolution can fight a protracted war, while the U.S. can't, because American military, economic and political resources must be distributed throughout the world. . . .

With regard to the North, the U.S. still carries out its war of distruction [sic], primarily by its air force: Besides bombing military targets, bridges and roads to obstruct transport and communications, the U.S. could also indiscriminately bomb economic targets, markets[,] villages, schools, hospitals, dikes, etc., in order to create confusion and agitation among the people. . . . The North will not flinch for a moment before the destructive acts of the U.S., which could grow increasingly made [mad] with every passing day. The North will not count the cost. . . .

If the U.S. is still more adventurous and brings U.S. and puppet troops of all their vassal states to attack the North, broadening it into a direct war in the entire country, the situation will then be different. Then it will not be we alone who still fight the U.S. but our entire camp. First the U.S. will not only be doing battle with 17 million people in the North but will also have to battle with hundreds of millions of Chinese people. . . . [The DRV and China] would resist together. Could the American imperialists suppress hundreds of millions of people? Certainly they could not. If they reach a stage of desperation, would the U.S. use the atomic bomb? Our camp also has the atomic bomb. The Soviet Union has sufficient atomic strength to oppose any imperialists who wish to use the atomic bomb in order to attack a socialist country, and threaten mankind. If U.S. imperialism uses the atomic bomb in those circumstances they would be committing suicide. The American people themselves would be the ones to stand up and smash the U.S. government when that government used atomic bombs. Would the U.S. dare to provoke war between the two blocks [sic], because of the Vietnam problem; would it provoke a third world war in order to put an early end to the history of U.S. imperialism and of the entire imperialist system in general[?] Would other imperialist countries, factions in the U.S., and particularly the American people, agree to the U.S. warmongers throwing them into suicide? Certainly, the U.S. could not carry out their intention, because U.S. imperialism is in a weak position and not in a position of strength.

31 Secretary of Defense McNamara, memorandum for President Johnson, 20 July 1965, recommending a sharp increase in U.S. forces in Vietnam.[50]

The situation in South Vietnam is worse than a year ago (when it was worse than a year before that). After a few-months of stalemate, the tempo of the war has quickened. A hard VC [Viet Cong] push is now on to dismember the nation and to maul the army. The VC main and local forces, reinforced by by militia and guerillas, have the initiative and, with large attacks (some in regimental strength), are hurting ARVN [Army of the Republic of Vietnam] badly. . . . The central highlands could well be lost to the National Liberation Front during this monsoon season. Since June 1, the GVN [Government of Vietnam] has been forced to abandon six district capitals; only one has been retaken. US combat troop deployments and US/VNAF [Vietnamese Air Force] strikes against the North have put to rest most South Vietnamese fears that the United States will forsake them, and US/VNAF air strikes in-country have probably shaken VC morale somewhat. Yet the government is able to provide security to fewer and fewer people in less and less territory as terrorism increases. . . .

. . .

. . . Nor have our air attacks in North Vietnam produced tangible evidence of willingness on the part of Hanoi to come to the conference table in a reasonable mood. The DRV/VC seem to believe that South Vietnam is on the run and near collapse; they show no signs of settling for less than a complete take-over.

. . .

. . . There are now 15 US (and 1 Australian) combat battalions in Vietnam; they, together with other combat personnel and non-combat personnel, bring the total US personnel in Vietnam to approximately 75,000.

I recommend that the deployment of US ground troops in Vietnam be increased by October to 34 maneuver battalions. . . . The battalions—together with increases in helicopter lift, air squadrons, naval units, air defense, combat support and miscellaneous log[istical] support and advisory personnel which I also recommend—would bring the total US personnel in Vietnam to approximately 175,000. . . . It should be understood that the deployment of more men

50. McNamara presented this memorandum just after a hurried visit to Vietnam. National Security Council History, Deployment of Major Forces to Vietnam, July 1945, box 43, National Security File, Lyndon B. Johnson Papers, Johnson Library, Austin, Tex. Senator Gravel Edition, *Pentagon Papers*, 4:619–22, contains a draft version of this memorandum.

(perhaps 100,000) may be necessary in early 1966, and that the deployment of additional forces thereafter is possible but will depend on developments.

. . .

. . . The DRV, on the other hand, may well send up to several divisions of regular forces in South Vietnam to assist the VC if they see the tide turning and victory, once so near, being snatched away. This possible DRV action is the most ominous one, since it would lead to increased pressures on us to "counter-invade" North Vietnam and to extend air strikes to population targets in the North; acceding to these pressures could bring the Soviets and the Chinese in. The Viet Cong, especially if they continue to take high losses, can be expected to depend increasingly upon the PAVN [People's Army of (North) Vietnam] forces as the war moves into a more conventional phase; but they may find ways to continue almost indefinitely their present intensive military, guerilla and terror activities, particularly if reinforced by some regular PAVN units. . . .

32 President Johnson, meetings with advisers in the White House, 21–22 July 1965, discussing a large increase of U.S. forces in Vietnam.

—Meeting of 21 July (beginning 11:30 a.m.):[51]

[Secretary of Defense McNamara summarized his 20 July recommendations.]

PRESIDENT: What has happened in [the] recent past that requires this decision on my part? What are the alternatives? Also, I want more discussions on what we expect to flow from this decision. Discuss in detail.

Have we wrung every single soldier out of every country we can? Who else can help? Are we the sole defenders of freedom in the world? Have we done all we can in this direction? The reasons for the call up? The results we can expect? . . .

We know we can tell SVN [South Vietnam] "we're coming home." Is that the option we should take? What flows from that[?]

The negotiations, the [bombing] pause, all the other approaches—have all been explored. It makes us look weak—with cup in hand. We have tried.

. . .

[UNDER SECRETARY OF STATE GEORGE] BALL: Isn't it possible that the VC will do what they did against the French—stay away from confrontation and not accommodate us?

[CHAIRMAN OF THE JOINT CHIEFS OF STAFF EARLE G.] WHEELER: Yes, but by constantly harassing them, they will have to fight somewhere.

51. Meeting Notes File, box 1, Johnson Papers.

MCNAMARA: If VC doesn't fight in large units, it will give ARVN a chance to re-secure hostile areas.

We don't know what VC tactics will be when VC is confronted by 175,000 Americans.

[CENTRAL INTELLIGENCE AGENCY DIRECTOR ADMIRAL WILLIAM F.] RABORN: We agree—by 1965, we expect NVN [North Vietnam] will increase their forces. They will attempt to gain a substantial victory before our build-up is complete.

. . .

BALL: I can foresee a perilous voyage—very dangerous—great apprehensions that we can win under these conditions. . . .

PRESIDENT: But is there another course in the national interest that is better than the McNamara course? We know it's dangerous and perilous. But can it be avoided?

BALL: There is no course that will allow us to cut our losses. If we get bogged down, our cost might be substantially greater. The pressures to create a larger war would be irresistible. . . .

PRESIDENT: What other road can I go?

BALL: Take what precautions we can—take losses—let their government fall apart—negotiate—probable take over by Communists. This is disagreeable, I know.

. . .

PRESIDENT: I don't think we have made a full commitment. You have pointed out the danger, but you haven't proposed an alternative course. . . .

I feel we have very little alternative to what we are doing.

. . . We [should] look at all other courses carefully. Right now I feel it would be more dangerous for us to lose this now, than endanger a greater number of troops.

[SECRETARY OF STATE DEAN] RUSK: What we have done since 1954–61 has not been good enough. We should have probably committed ourselves heavier in 1961.

[U.S. INFORMATION AGENCY DIRECTOR CARL] ROWAN: What bothers me most is the weakness of the [Nguyen Cao] Ky government [in Saigon]. Unless we put the screws on the Ky government, 175,000 men will do us no good.

[AMBASSADOR TO SOUTH VIETNAM HENRY CABOT] LODGE [JR.]: There is no tradition of a national government in Saigon. There are no roots in the country. Not until there is tranquility can you have any stability. I don't think we ought to take this government seriously. There is no one who can do anything. We have to do what we think we ought to do regardless of what the Saigon government does.

As we move ahead on a new phase—it gives us the right and duty to do certain things with or without the government's approval.

. . .

[MCNAMARA and WHEELER on sending more troops:] 75,000 now just enough to protect bases—it will let us lose slowly instead of rapidly. The extra men will stabilize the situation and improve it. It will give ARVN breathing room. We limit it to another 100,000 because VN [Vietnam] can't absorb any more. There is no major risk of catastrophe.

PRESIDENT: But you will lose [a] greater number of men.

WHEELER: The more men we have the greater the likelihood of smaller losses.

PRESIDENT: What makes you think if we put in 100,000 men Ho Chi Minh won't put in another 100,000?

WHEELER: This means greater bodies of men—which will allow us to cream them.

PRESIDENT: What are the chances of more NVN men coming?

WHEELER: 50–50 chance. He would be foolhardy to put ¼ of his forces in SVN. It would expose him too greatly in NVN.

[The meeting ends at 1:00 p.m. and then resumes at 2:45 p.m.]

BALL: We can't win. Long protracted [conflict]. The most we can hope for is messy conclusion. There remains a great danger of intrusion by Chicoms [Chinese Communists].

Problem of long war in US:

1. . . . As casualties increase, pressure to strike at jugular of the NVN will become very great.

2. . . . [I]f long and protracted[,] we will suffer because a great power cannot beat guerilas.

3. . . . The enemy cannot even be seen; he is indigenous to the country.

Have serious doubt if an army of westerners can fight orientals in Asian jungle and succeed.

PRESIDENT: This is important—can westerners, in absence of intelligence, successfully fight orientals in jungle rice-paddies? I want McNamara and Wheeler to seriously ponder this question.

BALL: I think we have all underestimated the seriousness of this situation. Like giving cobalt treatment to a terminal cancer case. I think a long protracted war will disclose our weakness, not our strength.

The least harmful way to cut losses in SVN is to let the government decide it doesn't want us to stay there. Therefore, put such proposals to SVN government that they can't accept, then it would move into a neutralist position—and I have no illusions that after we were asked to leave, SVN would be under Hanoi control.

. . .

PRESIDENT: . . . [W]ouldn't we lose credibility breaking the word of three presidents[?] . . .

BALL: The worse blow would be that the mightiest power in the world is unable to defeat guerillas.

PRESIDENT: Then you are not basically troubled by what the world would say about pulling out?

BALL: If we were actively helping a country with a stable, viable government, it would be a vastly different story. Western Europeans look at us as if we got ourselves into an imprudent [situation].

PRESIDENT: But I believe that these people [the Vietnamese] are trying to fight. They're like Republicans who try to stay in power, but don't stay there long. (aside—amid laughter—"excuse me, Cabot")[52]

. . .

MCNAMARA: Ky will fall soon. He is weak. We can't have elections until there is physical security, and even then there will be no elections because as Cabot said, there is no democratic tradition. . . .

PRESIDENT: Two basic troublings:

1. That Westerners can ever win in Asia.

2. Don't see how you can fight a war under direction of other people whose government changes every month.

. . .

RUSK: If the Communist world finds out we will not pursue our commitment to the end, I don't know where they will stay their hand.

I am more optimistic than some of my colleagues. I don't believe the VC have made large advances among the VN [Vietnamese] people.

We can't worry about massive casualties when we say we can't find the enemy. I don't see great casualties unless the Chinese come in.

LODGE: There is a greater threat to [bringing on] World War III if we don't go in. Similarity to our indolence at Munich.

I can't be as pessimistic as Ball. We have great seaports in Vietnam. We don't need to fight on roads. We have the sea. Visualize our meeting VC on our own terms. We don't have to spend all our time in the jungles.

If we can secure their bases, the VN can secure, in time, a political movement to do (one) apprehend the terrorist and (two) give intelligence to the government[.]

. . .

The VN have been dealt more casualties than, per capita, we suffered in the

52. Henry Cabot Lodge, Jr., was a prominent Massachusetts Republican and sometime contender for his party's presidential nomination.

Civil War. The VN soldier is an uncomplaining soldier. He has ideas he will die for.

—Meeting with military advisers, 22 July (noon to 2:15 p.m.):[53]

PRESIDENT: I asked McNamara to invite you here to counsel with you. . . .

. . .

[CHIEF OF NAVAL OPERATIONS] ADM. [DAVID] MCDONALD: . . . If we continue the way we are it will be a slow, sure victory for the other side. By putting more men in it will turn the tide and let us know what further we need to do. I wish we had done this long before.

PRESIDENT: But you don't know if 100,000 will be enough. What makes you conclude that if you don't know where we are going—and what will happen —we shouldn't pause and find this out?

MCDONALD: Sooner or later we'll force them to the conference table. . . .

PRESIDENT: If we put in 100,000 won't they put in an equal number?

MCDONALD: No. If we step up our bombing—

PRESIDENT: Is this a chance we want to take?

MCDONALD: Yes, when I view the alternatives. Get out now or pour in more men.

PRESIDENT: Is that all?

MCDONALD: I think our allies will lose faith in us.

PRESIDENT: We have few allies really helping us.

. . .

PRESIDENT: What are our chances of success?

[NAVY SECRETARY PAUL] NITZE: If we want to turn the tide, by putting in more men, it would be about 60/40.

PRESIDENT: If we gave Westmoreland[54] all he asked for, what are our chances? I don't agree that NVN and China won't come in.

. . .

PRESIDENT: Why wouldn't NVN pour in more men? Also, call on volunteers from China and Russia[?]

WHEELER: First, they may decide they can't win by putting in forces they can't afford. At most would put in two more divisions. Beyond that they strip their country and invite a counter move on our part.

Secondly, on volunteers—the one thing all NVN fear is Chinese. For them to invite Chinese volunteers is to invite China's taking over NVN.

Weight of judgment is that NVN may re-inforce their forces, [but] they can't match us on a build-up.

53. Meeting Notes File, box 1, Johnson Papers.
54. General William Westmoreland, the commander of U.S. forces in Vietnam.

From military view, we can handle, if we are determined to do so, China and NVN.

. . .

PRESIDENT: Any ideas on cost . . . ?

MCNAMARA: Yes—$12 billion [in] 1966[.]

PRESIDENT: Any idea what effect this will have on our economy?

MCNAMARA: It would not require wage and price controls in my judgment. Price index ought not go up more than one point or two.

[AIR FORCE CHIEF OF STAFF GENERAL JOHN] MCCONNELL: If you put in these requested forces and increase air and sea effort—we can at least turn the tide where we are not losing anymore. . . .

PRESIDENT: Have results of bombing actions been as fruitful and productive as we anticipated?

MCCONNELL: No sir, they haven't been. Productive in SVN, but not as productive in NVN because we are not striking the targets that hurt them.

PRESIDENT: Are you seriously concerned when we change targets we escalate the war? They might send more fighters down. Can't be certain if it will escalate their efforts on the ground.

Would it hurt our chances at a conference if we started killing civilians?

. . .

PRESIDENT: Doesn't it really mean if we follow Westmoreland's requests we are in a new war—this going off the diving board[?]

MCNAMARA: This is a major change in US policy. We have relied on SVN to carry the brunt. Now we would be responsible for satisfactory military outcome.

PRESIDENT: Are we in agreement we would rather be out of there and make our stand somewhere else?

[ARMY CHIEF OF STAFF GENERAL HAROLD] JOHNSON: Least desirable alternative is getting out. Second least is doing what we are doing. Best is to get in and get the job done.

PRESIDENT: But I don't know how we are going to get that job done. There are millions of Chinese. I think they are going to put their stack in. Is this the best place to do this? We don't have the allies we had in Korea. Can we get our allies to cut off supplying the NVN?

MCNAMARA: No, we can't prevent Japan, Britain, etc to charter ships to [Haiphong].

PRESIDENT: Have we done anything to get them to stop?

MCNAMARA: We haven't put the pressure on them as we did in Cuba, but even if we did, it wouldn't stop the shipping.

[AIR FORCE SECRETARY HAROLD] BROWN: It seems that all of our alternatives are dark. I find myself in agreement with the others.

PRESIDENT: Is there anything to the argument this [South Vietnamese] government is likely to fail, and we will be asked to leave[?] If we try to match the enemy, we will be bogged down in protracted war and have the government ask us to leave[.]

. . .

PRESIDENT: Suppose we told Ky of requirements we need—he turns them down—and we have to get out and make our stand in Thailand.

BROWN: The Thais will go with the winner.

PRESIDENT: If we didn't stop in Thailand where would we stop?

MCNAMARA: Laos, Cambodia, Thailand, Burma, surely affect Malaysia. In 2–3 years Communist domination would stop there, but ripple effect would be great—Japan, India. We would have to give up some bases. Ayub [Khan, president of Pakistan] would move closer to China. Greece, Turkey would move to neutralist position. Communist agitation would increase in Africa.

. . .

[MARINE CORPS COMMANDANT WALLACE] GREENE: . . . I am convinced we are making progress with the SVN—in food and construction. We are getting evidence of intelligence from SVN.

In the North—we haven't been hitting the right targets. We should hit pol [petroleum, oil, lubricants] storage—essential to their transportation. Also airfields destroyed, MIGS, and IL28's. As soon as SAM installations are operable.

PRESIDENT: What would they do?

GREENE: Nothing. We can test it by attacking pol storage.

Then we should attack industrial complex in NVN. Also, they can be told by pamphlet drop why we are doing this. Then we ought to blockade Cambodia—and stop supplies from coming down.

How long will it take? 5 years—plus 500,000 troops. I think the US people will back you.

PRESIDENT: How would you tell the American people what the stakes are?

GREENE: The place where they will stick by you is the national security stake.

[GENERAL] JOHNSON: We are in a face-down. The solution, unfortunately, is long-term. Once the military solution is solved, the problem of political solution will be more difficult.

PRESIDENT: If we come in with hundreds of thousands of men and billions of dollars, won't this cause them to come in (China and Russia)?

[GENERAL] JOHNSON: No. I don't think they will.

PRESIDENT: MacArthur didn't think they would come in either.

[GENERAL] JOHNSON: Yes, but this is not comparable to Korea. . . .

PRESIDENT: But China has plenty of divisions to move in, don't they?

[GENERAL] JOHNSON: Yes, they do.

PRESIDENT: Then what would we do?

[GENERAL] JOHNSON: (long silence) If so, we have another ball game.

PRESIDENT: But I have to take into account they will.

. . .

PRESIDENT: But remember they're going to write stories about this like they did the Bay of Pigs—and about my advisors. That's why I want you to think very carefully about alternatives and plans. . . .

. . .

PRESIDENT: What is your reaction to Ho's statement he is ready to fight for 20 years?

[GENERAL] JOHNSON: I believe it.

PRESIDENT: What are Ho's problems?

[GENERAL] JOHNSON: His biggest problem is doubt about what our next move will be. He's walking a tightrope between the Reds [Soviet Union] & Chicoms. Also, he is worrying about the loss of caches of arms in SVN.

. . .

[ARMY SECRETARY STANLEY] RESOR: Of the three courses the one we should follow is the McNamara plan. We can't go back on our commitment. Our allies are watching carefully.

PRESIDENT: Do all of you think the Congress and the people will go along with 600,000 people and billions of dollars 10,000 miles away?

RESOR: Gallup poll shows people are basically behind our commitment.

PRESIDENT: But if you make a commitment to jump off a building, and you find out how high it is, you may withdraw the commitment.

I judge though that the big problem is one of national security. Is that right?

(murmured assent)

33 Clark Clifford, comments at a Camp David meeting with President Johnson, late afternoon of 25 July 1965, expressing opposition to escalation.[55]

Don't believe we can win in SVN. If we send in 100,000 more, the NVN will meet us. If the NVN run out of men, the Chinese will send in volunteers. Russia and China don't intend for us to win the war. If we don't win, it is a catastrophe. If we lose 50,000+ it will ruin us. Five years, billions of dollars, 50,000 men, it is not for us.

55. Clifford, a senior statesman in the Democratic Party, was at this time chair of the Foreign Intelligence Advisory Board and an adviser to President Johnson. Also attending this informal Camp David meeting were Arthur Goldberg (ambassador to the United Nations) and Robert McNamara. Meeting Notes File, box 1, Johnson Papers.

At end of monsoon, quietly probe and search out with other countries—by moderating our position—to allow us to get out. Can't see anything but catastrophe for my country. . . .

34 President Johnson and advisers, meeting with congressional leaders, 27 July 1965 (beginning at 6:35 p.m.), discussing new initiatives in Vietnam.[56]

[PRESIDENT:] . . . We don't know if this will be 2 years or 4 years or what. We didn't know World War I was going to be one year or five years.

RUSK: The attitude of the Communist world is the key question.

[Democratic senator from Florida GEORGE] SMATHERS: We are denying the VC the victory[,] aren't we? Is not our purpose not to be driven out—and avoid WW III by not bringing in China and Russia[?] Is this a change of policy?

PRESIDENT: As aid to the VC increases, our need to increase our forces goes up. There is no change in policy.

 . . .

[Democratic senator from Louisiana RUSSELL] LONG: If we back out, they'd move somewhere else. Ready to concede all Asia to Communists? Not ready to turn tail. If a nation with 14 million can make Uncle Sam run, what will China think?

SPEAKER [of the House and Massachusetts Democrat John W. McCormack]: I don't think we have any alternatives. Our military men tell us we need more and we should give it to them. The lesson of Hitler and Mussolini is clear. I can see five years from now a chain of events far more dangerous to our country.

 . . .

[Republican senator from Illinois EVERETT] DIRKSEN: . . . Tell the country we are engaged in very serious business. People are apathetic. . . .

 . . .

[Democratic senator from Montana and Senate majority leader MIKE] MANSFIELD: I agree with Dirksen [on] apathy in the country.

I would not be true to myself if I didn't speak. This position has certain inevitability. Whatever pledge we had was to *assist* SVN in its own defense. Since then there has been no government of legitimacy. . . . We owe this government nothing—no pledge of any kind.

We are going deeper into war. Even total victory would be vastly costly. Best hope for salvation is quick stalemate and negotiations[.]

56. Ball did not attend this meeting. Meeting Notes File, box 1, Johnson Papers.

We cannot expect our people to support a war for 3–5 years. What we are about is an anti-Communist crusade[.] . . . Escalation begets escalation.

35 President Johnson, statement at White House press conference, 28 July 1965, justifying the dispatch of fifty thousand fresh troops to Vietnam.[57]

We did not choose to be the guardians at the gate, but there is no one else.

Nor would surrender in Viet-Nam bring peace, because we learned from Hitler at Munich that success only feeds the appetite of aggression. The battle would be renewed in one country and then another country, bringing with it perhaps even larger and crueler conflict, as we have learned from the lessons of history.

Moreover, we are in Viet-Nam to fulfill one of the most solemn pledges of the American Nation. Three Presidents—President Eisenhower, President Kennedy, and your present President—over 11 years have committed themselves and have promised to help defend this small and valiant nation.

Strengthened by that promise, the people of South Viet-Nam have fought for many long years. Thousands of them have died. Thousands more have been crippled and scarred by war. We just cannot now dishonor our word, or abandon our commitment, or leave those who believed us and who trusted us to the terror and repression and murder that would follow.

. . .

Let me also add now a personal note. I do not find it easy to send the flower of our youth, our finest young men, into battle. . . . I have seen them in a thousand streets, of a hundred towns, in every State in this Union—working and laughing and building, and filled with hope and life. I think I know, too, how their mothers weep, and how their families sorrow.

This is the most agonizing and the most painful duty of your President.

There is something else, too. When I was young, poverty was so common that we didn't know it had a name. An education was something that you had to fight for, and water was really life itself. I have now been in public life 35 years, more than three decades, and in each of those 35 years I have seen good men, and wise leaders, struggle to bring the blessings of this land to all of our people.

And now I am the President. It is now my opportunity to help every child get an education, to help every Negro and every American citizen have an

57. *PPP: Lyndon B. Johnson, 1965*, 2:794–95, 797–98.

equal opportunity, to have every family get a decent home, and to help bring healing to the sick and dignity to the old.

As I have said before, that is what I have lived for, that is what I have wanted all my life since I was a little boy, and I do not want to see all those hopes and all those dreams of so many people for so many years now drowned in the wasteful ravages of cruel wars. I am going to do all I can to see that that never happens.

But I also know, as a realistic public servant, that as long as there are men who hate and destroy, we must have the courage to resist, or we will see it all, all that we have built, all that we hope to build, all of our dreams for freedom—all, *all* will be swept away on the flood of conquest.

So, too, this shall not happen. We will stand in Viet-Nam.

36 Secretary of Defense McNamara, report after a two-day visit to Vietnam, 30 November 1965, announcing lack of progress in the war and need for more troops and bombing.[58]

[T]he Ky "government of generals" is surviving, but not acquiring wide support . . . ; pacification is thoroughly stalled, with no guarantee that security anywhere is permanent and no indications that able and willing leadership will emerge in the absence of that permanent security. (Prime Minister Ky estimates that his government controls only 25% of the population today . . . .)

. . . The Communists appear to have decided to increase their forces in SVN both by heavy recruitment in the South (especially in the Delta) and by infiltration of regular NVN forces from the North. . . .

. . .

To meet this possible—and in my view likely—Communist buildup, the presently contemplated Phase I forces will not be enough (approx 220,000 Americans, almost all in place by end of 1965). . . .

. . . If it is decided not to move now toward a compromise, I recommend that the US both send a substantial number of additional troops and very gradually intensify the bombing of NVN. . . .

(recommend up to 74 battalions by end-66: total to approx 400,000 by end-66. And it should be understood that further deployments (perhaps exceeding 200,000) may be needed in 1967.)

Bombing of NVN. . . . over a period of the next six months we gradually enlarge the target system in the northeast (Hanoi-Haiphong) quadrant . . . .

58. Senator Gravel Edition, *Pentagon Papers*, 4:622–23.

Pause in bombing NVN. It is my belief that there should be a three- or four-week pause in the program of bombing the North before we either greatly increase our troop deployments to VN or intensify our strikes against the North. . . . [W]e must lay a foundation in the mind of the American public and in world opinion for such an enlarged phase of the war and, second, we should give NVN a face-saving chance to stop the aggression. . . .

. . . We should be aware that deployments of the kind I have recommended will not guarantee success. US killed-in-action can be expected to reach 1000 a month, and the odds are even that we will be faced in early 1967 with a "no-decision" at an even higher level. My overall evaluation, nevertheless, is that the best chance of achieving our stated objectives lies in a pause followed, if it fails, by the deployments mentioned above.

37 Province Party Standing Committee to district and local party committees, directive, 1 November 1967, summoning effort for forthcoming Tet offensive.[59]

Our victory is close at hand. The conditions are ripe. Our Party has carefully judged the situation. We must act and act fast. This is an opportunity to fulfill the aspirations of the entire people, of cadre, of each comrade and of our families. We have long suffered hardships, death and pain. We are looking for an opportunity to avenge evil done to our families, to pay our debt to the Fatherland, to display our loyalty to the country, affection for the people and love for our families. We cannot afford to miss this rare opportunity. All Party members and cadre must be willing to sacrifice their lives for the survival of the Fatherland.

This opportunity is like an attack on an enemy post in which we have reached the last fence and the enemy puts up a fierce resistance. We only need to make a swift assault to secure the target and gain total victory.

If we are hesitant and fearful of hardships and misery, we will suffer heavy losses, fail to accomplish the mission and feel guilty for failing our nation, our people, our families and our comrades who have already sacrificed themselves. It is time for us to take the initiative in penetrating into enemy bases in provinces, districts and villages, attacking him five or ten times more violently to score brilliant achievements.

Make all comrades realize that the purpose of the revolutionary activities conducted for many years is mainly to support this phase, in this decisive hour.

59. Porter, *Vietnam: The Definitive Documentation*, 2:477–78.

Even though we make sacrifices, we will gain glorious victory, not only for the people, but also for our Fatherland and families. . . .

38 President Johnson, address to the nation, 31 March 1968, limiting the war in Vietnam and withdrawing from the presidential race.[60]

[The North Vietnamese] attack—during the Tet holidays—failed to achieve its principal objectives.

It did not collapse the elected government of South Vietnam or shatter its army—as the Communists had hoped.

It did not produce a "general uprising" among the people of the cities as they had predicted.

The Communists were unable to maintain control of any of the more than 30 cities that they attacked. And they took very heavy casualties.

But they did compel the South Vietnamese and their allies to move certain forces from the countryside into the cities.

They caused widespread disruption and suffering. Their attacks, and the battles that followed, made refugees of half a million human beings.

. . .

We are prepared to move immediately toward peace through negotiations.

So, tonight, in the hope that this action will lead to early talks, I am taking the first step to deescalate the conflict. We are reducing—substantially reducing—the present level of hostilities.

And we are doing so unilaterally, and at once.

Tonight, I have ordered our aircraft and our naval vessels to make no attacks on North Vietnam, except in the area north of the demilitarized zone where the continuing enemy buildup directly threatens allied forward positions and where the movements of their troops and supplies are clearly related to that threat.

. . .

Tonight, we and the other allied nations are contributing 600,000 fighting men to assist 700,000 South Vietnamese troops in defending their little country.

Our presence there has always rested on this basic belief: The main burden of preserving their freedom must be carried out by them—by the South Vietnamese themselves.

. . .

60. *PPP: Lyndon B. Johnson, 1968* (Washington: GPO, 1970), 469–71, 473–74, 476.

. . . [W]e are prepared to withdraw our forces from South Vietnam as the other side withdraws its forces to the north, stops the infiltration, and the level of violence thus subsides.

. . .

. . . During the past 4 ½ years, it has been my fate and my responsibility to be Commander in Chief. I have lived—daily and nightly—with the cost of this war. I know the pain that it has inflicted. I know, perhaps better than anyone, the misgivings that it has aroused.

Throughout this entire, long period, I have been sustained by a single principle: that what we are doing now, in Vietnam, is vital not only to the security of Southeast Asia, but it is vital to the security of every American.

. . .

With America's sons in the fields far away, with America's future under challenge right here at home, with our hopes and the world's hopes for peace in the balance every day, I do not believe that I should devote an hour or a day of my time to any personal partisan causes or to any duties other than the awesome duties of this office—the Presidency of your country.

Accordingly, I shall not seek, and I will not accept, the nomination of my party for another term as your President.

39 Ho Chi Minh, testament of 10 May 1969, issued following his death on 3 September 1969.[61]

The war of resistance against US aggression may drag on. Our people may have to face new sacrifices of life and property. Whatever happens, we must keep firm our resolve to fight the US aggressors till total victory.

Our mountains will always be, our rivers will always be, our people will always be;

The American invaders defeated, we will rebuild our land ten times more beautiful.

. . . The US imperialists will certainly have to quit. Our Fatherland will certainly be reunified. Our fellow-countrymen in the South and in the North will certainly be re-united under the same roof. We, a small nation, will have earned the signal honour of defeating, through heroic struggle, two big imperialisms—the French and the American—and of making a worthy contribution to the world national liberation movement.

61. Ho, *Selected Writings*, 361.

7

Confronting
Revolution in Iran,
1953–1980

THE PERILS OF MODERNIZATION

In the late 1940s and early 1950s Iran emerged as an important point on the Cold War containment line. American policymakers came to regard internal political stability and economic development in that country as an indispensable check on Soviet-sponsored subversion. As a consequence, they plunged deeply into Iran's internal affairs, with Muhammad Reza Shah Pahlavi serving as the chief instrument for this U.S. policy. They restored him to power in 1953 and vigorously backed him as the agent of progress. He was to promote industrialization, Western education, and other initiatives that would bring his country into the modern world, and thus he would keep Iran stable and secure. Thanks to the shah's strong leadership, no communist scavengers would prey on this country as it made the difficult but promising transition to modern conditions.

The surrogate strategy worked for a quarter of a century—only to blow up in Washington's face. In the end "modernization" failed in Iran to produce the economic development and political stability that its advocates expected. Instead, it sharpened long-developing divergences among Iranians over their country's future and ultimately gave rise to a powerful revolutionary impulse. The Shi'ite clergy, articulating popular discontents, turned on the shah's regime and in 1979 overwhelmed it, pitching the administration of President Jimmy Carter into an unexpected crisis. Incredulous as "religious fanaticism" triumphed over "progressive modernization," U.S. policymakers sought without success to save the Shah or at least the Iran they had helped to create. Their palpable reluctance to come to terms with the new revolutionary order deepened the suspicion of an already hostile clergy. The taking of American diplomats as hostages in 1979 dramatically revealed the limits of American influence in Iran. A humiliated Carter would pay a heavy domestic political price for the collapse of a policy that he had inherited, not created, and for the end of a relationship with Iran that he had struggled to salvage.

*　*　*

The origins of the American political involvement in Iran (originally known as Persia), an arid, mountainous, and oil-rich country, date back to World War II. Americans arriving on the scene found Britain and the USSR already ensconced. Rivals for influence in the region since the nineteenth century, in 1941 those two powers had sent occupation forces into Iran to secure transport routes for military aid going to the Soviet Union. They also joined together to drive out the pro-German Reza Shah Pahlavi—an army officer who had helped to overthrow the Qajar dynasty in 1921 and then in 1925 established his own, the Pahlavi dynasty. They put in his place his more pliable, twenty-two-year-old son, Muhammad Reza. At the same time the two powers had sought to advance their own interests—the British in the south, the site of the valuable oil concession held by the Anglo-Iranian Oil Company (AIOC), and the Soviets in the north, near their border.

Once the United States entered the war, it too joined in the occupation, running the railroad carrying matériel into the Soviet Union and wielding political influence primarily as adviser to the Iranian government. By 1943 the Roosevelt administration was contemplating a long-term role in Iran. It wanted above all to head off Anglo-Russian rivalry, to promote Iran's independence, and to protect U.S. petroleum interests in the region (Document 1).

In the immediate postwar period the United States gradually established itself as the dominant power. In the spring of 1946 the Truman administration, already deeply distrustful of Moscow's ambitions, confronted the Soviets in the United Nations Security Council over their troops still in Iran and over their support of secessionist sentiment in Iran's Azerbaijan as well as among the Kurds (also in the northwest corner of the country). Joseph Stalin retreated. After concluding a deal with the Iranian government for an oil concession in the north comparable to what the British already enjoyed in the south, Stalin pulled his troops back. The government in Tehran soon crushed the separatists, and the Iranian parliament (the Majlis) refused to ratify the oil deal. Stalin was left with nothing to show for his efforts.

After 1946 the policy of the Truman administration reflected with growing emphasis the conviction that Iran was a strategic point on the containment line and was deserving of defense (Documents 2 and 3). While a Soviet inva-

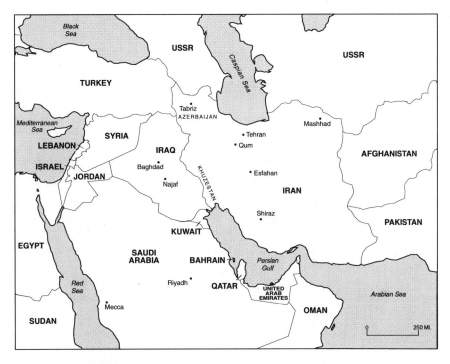

Black
Sea

USSR

USSR

TURKEY

Caspian Sea

Tabriz
AZERBAIJAN

Mashhad

Mediterranean
Sea

SYRIA

• Tehran
• Qum

LEBANON

IRAQ

AFGHANISTAN

ISRAEL

Baghdad

• Esfahan

JORDAN

Najaf

KHUZESTAN

IRAN

Shiraz
•

PAKISTAN

KUWAIT

EGYPT

SAUDI
ARABIA

BAHRAIN

Persian
Gulf

Riyadh

QATAR

Red
Sea

UNITED
ARAB
EMIRATES

Arabian Sea

Mecca

OMAN

SUDAN

0   250 Mi.

Iran and the Middle East

sion was a remote possibility, the more imminent danger seemed to come from within the country—from the well-organized, Soviet-connected Iranian communist party (known as the Tudeh or "Masses" Party). It had had success, the Central Intelligence Agency (CIA) reported in 1949, "in rousing certain important [urban] elements of the Iranian people from their political apathy" and now constituted "the logical nucleus for a quisling government should the USSR accelerate its efforts to interfere in Iran."[1]

But through the end of the decade Washington did little to translate its concerns into action. Policymakers doubted the ability of a politically fac-tionalized Iran to make good use of even minimal assistance at a time when U.S. resources lagged far behind multiplying global commitments. In any case, why not leave the task of defending Iran to the British, who had a larger stake in that country? And although the shah sought U.S. backing, Washington faced resistance from other Iranians more interested in ousting the British than in getting pulled deeply into the U.S. rivalry with the USSR. Finally, in 1950, the Truman administration put its hesitations aside and began to inte-

1. CIA report, "The Tudeh Party: Vehicle of Communism in Iran," 18 July 1949, in *The United States and Iran: A Documentary History,* ed. Yonah Alexander and Allen Nanes (Frederick, Md.: University Publications of America, 1980), 200.

grate Iran into its alliance system. It started a modest program of economic and military aid, expanded its diplomatic and its CIA presence, and organized a campaign of dirty tricks against the Tudeh Party.

The major threats to Iran's role as an anti-Soviet outpost would indeed come from within—but from unexpected quarters. The first indigenous threat came in the early 1950s from secular nationalists led by Muhammad Musaddiq. Born in 1882, he belonged to one of Iran's most prominent aristocratic families with major landholdings. He had been educated in France and Switzerland, acquired a doctorate in law, and already entered politics before the turn of the century. Between 1928 and 1941 he had suffered through internal exile and imprisonment for his opposition to Reza Shah. The latter's overthrow brought Musaddiq back into the public arena, and in the late 1940s this principled, high-strung politician had played a leading role in organizing the National Front, a diverse and (as it turned out) fragile urban coalition of foreign-educated technocrats, clergy, leftist intellectuals, and bazaar merchants.

In April 1951 the parliament elected Musaddiq prime minister. His main concerns were reflected in the program that brought him to power. He wanted to reclaim oil, the country's main economic resource, from the British. Like other Middle Eastern oil companies at the time, the AIOC decided on the rate of extraction, set the price, and thus in effect controlled the level of revenues from royalties that Iran would receive. Musaddiq also wanted to promote democracy, a commitment that set him at odds with Muhammad Reza Shah, just as it had with the shah's father. Along with his allies, he pressed for electoral, social, land, and military reforms.

Just as Musaddiq took office, a bill nationalizing oil and thus nullifying the AIOC concession went into effect. While a Britain weakened by two world wars was ready to abdicate its position of strategic dominance in favor of the United States, it was not ready to surrender this tremendous economic asset despite several decades of accumulating resentment among Iranians. The government in London, half-owner of the AIOC, at once set to work to regain its concession. An international oil embargo failed to bring the Iranian economy down. The machinations of pro-British Iranian politicians did not dislodge Musaddiq. Repeated coup attempts failed. Musaddiq finally broke diplomatic relations with London in October 1952. British diplomats and secret service agents departing Tehran passed the baton to the Americans.

The Truman administration had from the start of the petroleum dispute been leery of the British calls for help. Both President Harry Truman and Secretary of State Dean Acheson urged a negotiated settlement. They judged stability in the region more important than oil. When London in frustration began to contemplate an invasion of the southern oil fields, Washington quickly signaled its disapproval, thus killing the plans.

In early 1953 the new Eisenhower administration heard British petitions with a great deal more sympathy. Already in the Truman years some high-level officials in the CIA were ready not only to support the British but also to join them in a coup. They were not deterred by warnings from Iran specialists and the station chief in Tehran that such an effort would in effect be "putting U.S. support behind Anglo-French colonialism."[2] President Dwight Eisenhower and the Dulles brothers (John Foster, in charge in the State Department, and Allen, directing the CIA) quickly embraced coup plans, code-named AJAX (Document 5). They reasoned that the tightening noose of the oil boycott was creating strains within Iran that the Tudeh Party might exploit to seize power. They were also determined to control the country's oil, an essential resource in the prosecution of the Cold War. Musaddiq personally appealed to Eisenhower for sympathy and support (Document 4). But the American leader, who had already made his decision, publicly parried the overture.

By early 1953 Musaddiq was vulnerable. Deep fissures had formed within the National Front, and by the summer Tehran streets had become the battleground of pro- and anti-Musaddiq demonstrations, just as the CIA began its destabilization effort. The CIA brought to the project ample funding, the cooperation of British intelligence "assets" and conservative politicians within Iran, and a project officer, Kermit Roosevelt, with a gift for improvisation. When his elaborate plans for a coup miscarried, he put together a campaign of street demonstrations. Musaddiq, then over seventy years old, refused to resort to a brutal, bloody repression to save his government and fell from power on 19 August. Jailed for three years, he remained under confinement until his death in 1967. Unbending to the end, Musaddiq established himself as a hero to the anti-shah opposition and a legend in Iranian politics.

The main beneficiary of Musaddiq's overthrow was Muhammad Reza Shah. He had played a weak hand indecisively through the intricate plotting of 1951–1953. After having had Musaddiq thrust on him in 1951, the shah had made an ineffectual effort to oust this challenger to the court's prerogatives and power and thereafter watched passively as Musaddiq implemented his program of nationalization. In 1953 he reluctantly signed on to the Anglo-American coup plans but abruptly fled in mid-August when they seemed to fall apart. A few days later he returned in triumph. When he received Roosevelt (so the latter recalled), a grateful shah offered thanks: "I owe my throne to God, my people, my army—and to you!"[3] Eisenhower moved quickly to shore up the young monarch by granting the emergency economic assistance earlier denied

2. Quoted in Mark J. Gasiorowski, "The 1953 Coup d'Etat in Iran," *International Journal of Middle East Studies* 19 (August 1987): 270.

3. Kermit Roosevelt, *Countercoup: The Struggle for the Control of Iran* (New York: McGraw-Hill, 1979), 199.

Musaddiq. Washington had forged a new relationship while concealing at least for Americans the means by which it had been created.

The shah now pursued a two-track policy intended in the short term to consolidate his family's hold on the throne and ultimately to restore his country's imperial greatness. As a strong centralizer and authoritarian, the son followed lines laid down by his deposed father. To buttress his own political authority, the shah purged dissidents from the army, built up the police force, including the feared secret police (SAVAK), and brought the parliament under tight control. He built support for the revived monarchy among the wealthy landed elite and the middle class of bureaucrats and merchants. At the same time, to ensure external support, he cultivated a close relationship with the United States. The fruits of that effort were security against pressure from his Soviet neighbor and a large influx of American advisers and American economic and military aid (the largest outside western Europe). By 1960 Washington had funneled $1 billion into creating a reliable client and a solid base for containment in the Middle East.

The turning point of the shah's rule came in the early 1960s. The shah's grip on power finally seemed assured. In 1963 repressive measures stopped the last major outbreak of political discontent for more than a decade, and the shah pushed ahead on what became known as the White Revolution. Formally launched in January 1963, this so-called revolution was a top-down effort to develop industry, to give women political rights, to promote advanced education as well as basic literacy and health, to carry out land reform, and to establish civil law in place of Koranic law. The shah was responding to U.S. pressures as well as signs of internal discontent, but the program also advanced Iran's modernization, at least as the shah envisioned it.

The funding for this multifaceted program came from oil. The shah had negotiated a new deal in 1954. Iran's own oil company took control of oil reserves, leaving the AIOC (now joined by other foreign companies) in charge of operations. The bargain included an increase of royalties, and the shah pressed for greater production. As a result, oil revenues jumped from $10 million in 1954 to $285 million in 1960 as Iran emerged as the world's second-largest oil exporter. Thanks to higher international oil prices resulting from the 1973–1974 Arab oil embargo and to the full nationalization of the Iranian oil industry in 1973, the shah was enjoying an annual revenue of $20 billion by 1975–1976. It was this oil money that paid for industry, urban development, military power, and courtly pomp.

These internal developments gradually recast Iran's relationship with the United States. Washington in the late 1950s and early 1960s had pressed for a policy of modernization in Iran that was thought essential to achieving long-term stability along the containment line. Led by the State Department and the

CIA, the warmest supporters of the shah in the U.S. government, Washington urged Tehran to pay less attention to its military buildup and more attention to reforms needed to win popular support. Though Muhammad Reza Shah feared that reform might go too far and undermine his position, he nonetheless sought to accommodate the Americans not only to get the arms critical to becoming a regional power but also to leave no doubt at home about U.S. political backing of him personally. Whenever Washington refused him some of the weapons he wanted, he turned to Moscow, counting on American anxieties to get him his way. The muted tensions in the relationship were evident in the shah's 1962 meeting with President John F. Kennedy, one of many that Iran's leader had with a succession of U.S. presidents going back to Harry Truman (Document 6).

By the late 1960s rapid economic growth was giving the shah more leverage in his dealings with Washington. The oil shocks of the early 1970s forced Americans to look to Iran as a secure source of supply and a moderating voice in the oil cartel. The termination of the U.S. aid program during the administration of Lyndon Johnson was not only a recognition of the shah's success but also a milestone along Tehran's road to a more independent role. Under President Richard Nixon the relationship with Iran took another notable turn as Nixon embraced the shah as a partner rather than a client in the Middle East. Putting reform to the side, the president gave the shah carte blanche in May 1972 to buy whatever arms he wanted.

Despite Nixon's fall from political power, the shah's Iran remained a cornerstone of U.S. policy. Henry Kissinger, who had worked closely with Nixon and continued in office as Gerald Ford's secretary of state, privately instructed the new president in how to handle the shah (Document 11). Publicly Kissinger praised the maturing American partnership with Iran, a country that had become "a major factor in the stability of the Middle East."[4]

Muhammad Reza Shah proceeded to spend lavishly, to the benefit of the American arms industry and balance of trade. Between 1973 and 1977 the outlays on modern U.S. military equipment came to over $15 billion, and in 1977 Iran accounted for half of all U.S. arms sales abroad. With those weapons Nixon and Kissinger expected Iran to keep in check regional radicals with ties to the Soviet Union and to safeguard the oil supply on which Europe, Japan, and now even the United States was dependent. In the bargain American corporations profited handsomely, a point given some stress by Nixon and other advocates of a close collaboration.

In this golden age of intimacy between the two countries, thousands of

4. Toast at a state dinner in Tehran, 6 August 1976, in *Department of State Bulletin* 75 (6 September 1976): 306.

Americans (as high as fifty thousand by the late 1970s) flocked to Iran to do business, while some sixty thousand Iranians came to the United States to study. The CIA and SAVAK cooperated closely. The Iranian embassy cut a wide swath among Washington influentials, and an American embassy in Tehran kept a distance from dissidents that was meant to reassure the shah (while obscuring any cracks in the pillar of apparent stability). Already in the late 1960s a few specialists began warning of problems ahead, but Nixon and Kissinger ignored them, as Carter would also.

*   *   *

Within Iranian politics the collaboration between the Pahlavis and foreign powers had long been an explosive issue. Musaddiq and his National Front supporters had sought to break the pattern of dependency and find a middle way between the two superpowers. They especially resented the Pahlavis' pro-Western policy, which left Iran's oil resources under the control of foreigners, and the Pahlavis' autocratic ways, which were distinctly at odds with widely accepted constitutional principles. The shah was able to deprive the National Front of an active political role, but at the price of confirming its leaders' charges that he was beholden to a foreign power.

The shah's strategy left the Shi'ite clergy as the proponents of the only viable alternative vision of Iran's future. While the shah and Washington spoke approvingly of breaking the grip of "traditional" and "feudal" ideas and institutions, the clergy clung to their Shia faith, promoting the tenet that the only legitimate state was one that followed Shi'ite religious ideals as interpreted by religious authorities (the ayatollahs).[5]

As a disaffected elite, the clergy came to constitute a revolutionary party. They had their theological schools, mosques, study groups, Islamic associations, publications, and even audio tapes to develop and popularize their doctrine of resistance to unjust civil authority. Thus they created a revolutionary ideology—populist, Manichean, xenophobic—that could mobilize support. They also had a power base in local society, one that could make them a valuable ally of dynasts—or, as now, a dangerous threat. They collected and spent large sums, maintained landholdings to finance their operations, dispensed justice, managed basic education, and attended to social welfare.

Alone the clergy would have been a strong but not overwhelming opposition. However, they won followers as a result of the far-reaching social and

5. Shia, meaning literally "sectarian," refers to the minority branch of Islam. In contrast to the more numerous Sunni, the Shi'ites stress rigorous application of religious laws to everyday life and the strict observance of religious ritual. Shi'ites are the majority in Iran and constitute sizable communities in Iraq, Yemen, Pakistan, Lebanon, and Oman.

economic ramifications of the shah's modernization program. Land reform, begun in 1962, improved the lot of some peasants, but many still had no land or too little for subsistence, and land remained concentrated in a few hands and increasingly subject to mechanized cultivation that displaced peasants. Many projects associated with the shah's program were dramatic and visible but did little for economic development or popular welfare. Large dams, airports, grand avenues, modern military equipment, and new government buildings absorbed much of the government spending. At the same time, corruption and patronage were widespread, extending from the court down into the bureaucracy.

Although oil made Iran wealthy, the distribution of that wealth was marked by extreme disparities, among the worst in the world. Compounding growing inequalities was the rise of an alienated and unemployed urban underclass driven to the city by the consolidation of rural holdings. By 1979 half of the population was urban. The peasants who poured into the city suffered from inflation, poor housing, general government neglect, and the cultural shock of urban ways at odds with values brought from the countryside.

Adding to these social strains was an officially approved Western presence that stirred anger over cultural defilement, economic exploitation, and the loss of jobs to foreigners. This resentment was reenforced by memories of the 1953 coup (widely attributed to the Americans), and it helped keep alive the view that the shah was the tool of U.S. interests. He was also increasingly seen as a tool of Israel. Though he sought to conceal the contacts, he and his advisers did indeed meet frequently with Israeli officials. The military and especially SAVAK cooperated closely with their Israeli counterparts. And Iran guaranteed Israel a steady flow of oil.

By the 1970s political discontent had become widespread. Land reform had alienated the dispossessed landowners while failing to win for the shah the loyalty of the peasantry. The urban poor felt neglected in cities where the privileged were awash in newfound riches. Students and educated professionals, committed to greater political and social democracy and more balanced economic development, stirred under the influence of socialist and nationalist ideas. The bazaari—a long-established class of merchants engaged in small-scale production as well as banking and trade—grew restive as Western imports and investments and a new class of industrialists linked to the court threatened their position.

Ruhollah Khomeini was the inspirational figure that combined these varied discontents into a successful revolutionary movement. He articulated the Islamic values of the clergy and echoed the complaints of the other alienated groups. One of his admirers described the complex and charismatic cleric as a person of "spirituality and erudition, asceticism and self-discipline, sobriety and determination, political genius and leadership, compassion for the poor and deprived, and relentless hatred of oppression and imperialism."[6] He proved an adept revolutionary leader whose determination, vision, and appeal American leaders consistently underestimated.

Khomeini had been born in 1902 into a religious family. Both his father and grandfather had been religious scholars. Khomeini had not known his father, who had been killed by bandits. He had been raised by his mother and an aunt. Both were dead by the time he was fifteen, and thereafter the young Khomeini was guided in his education by an older brother. At nineteen he left home to study religion. Later, at the religious center of Qum, he gained distinction as a teacher of ethics and philosophy, with a strongly mystical cast and with an activist interest in politics. His first book appeared in 1941, an overtly political critique of Reza Shah.

Khomeini emerged in the early 1960s as a preeminent opponent of Reza Shah's son. His denunciations in 1963 of the secular, U.S.-backed White Revolution and the court's corruption, immorality, and materialism had nationwide impact (Document 7). This attack marked the beginning of a prolonged and bitter struggle. Muhammad Reza Shah immediately countered, assaulting religious centers, harassing clergy, and imprisoning Khomeini. When demonstrations broke out in major cities, the shah's forces suppressed them. Continued popular pressure, however, secured Khomeini's release in April 1964.

The cleric continued to speak out on political issues. In one of his most dramatic political interventions, Khomeini turned on the subservient parliament in October 1964 after it had voted full diplomatic immunity to all American military personnel and their families. Nationalist anger turned to outrage when almost immediately after the vote that body approved a $200 million American loan to buy U.S. military equipment. Khomeini was not alone in asking who was running the country (Document 8). The shah, exasperated, sent him into exile. Khomeini stayed briefly in Turkey and in 1965 moved to Najaf, a Shi'ite religious center in Iraq. In October 1978 as demonstrations began to beat down the shah's government, he moved to Paris. At each step of the way, Khomeini maintained contact with opposition groups inside Iran as well as abroad and with his own wide network of former students. He offered encouragement, guidance, and a fresh political vision of an Islamic state taking the place of a discredited monarchy (Documents 9, 14, and 16). He was beginning to project religious authority rare for Iranian Shi'ites.

In the early 1970s opposition within Iran began to turn violent as terrorists directed their attention to Americans and American facilities as well as the

6. Hamid Algar, ed. and trans., *Islam and Revolution: Writings and Declarations of Imam Khomeini* (Berkeley, Calif.: Mizan Press, 1981), 21.

shah's regime. Spreading disaffection left Muhammad Reza Shah with a shrinking base of political support, even within the urban middle class and the members of the court and its clients, who had been the primary beneficiaries of Iran's new wealth. But despite all the warning signs, the shah failed to make the adjustments necessary to save himself. He was surrounded with sycophants, whose corruption ate away at the integrity of the regime, and he was out of touch with worsening social conditions—as was all too evident when in 1971 he poured $200 million into an extravagant celebration of the twenty-five-hundredth anniversary of the Persian monarchy.

After 1973 three adverse developments converged to plunge the shah into ever deeper difficulty and ultimately to undermine what American policymakers were coming to regard as a model modernizing autocrat. First, a previously strong economy entered a rough patch. Oil revenues that had fueled growth soared at mid-decade, igniting inflation and inspiring grandiose development projects that outran the capacity of the government to manage. This combination of inflation and mismanagement inspired widespread discontent. Nevertheless, the shah resisted scaling back his general program, and he particularly insisted on making massive arms acquisitions.

Second, the highly centralized and autocratic nature of the regime was increasingly at odds with a more complex society produced by the earlier economic success. In thrall to the shah's own vision of a glorious, imperial future for the country and constrained by his dynastic ambitions, the regime was unresponsive to the diverse concerns and immediate needs of the population, even as more and more voices called for some kind of political opening. Here too the shah responded perversely, remaining adamant in his resistance to calls to open up the political system and leaving to SAVAK the brutal business of repressing dissent, exiling prominent critics, and crushing the newly formed guerilla organizations.

Third, the shah himself seemed out of touch as the economy stumbled and the political legitimacy of his regime came into question. Fixated on world affairs, he reacted indecisively to the mounting domestic problems. He seemed guided by wishful thinking: surely his people would patiently endure this time of difficulty and trust his leadership (Documents 10 and 12). Illness may to some extent account for this striking failure of judgment. Although French doctors diagnosed leukemia in 1974, the queen did not find out until 1976, and it was still later (possibly 1979, after he had gone into exile) before the shah fully realized the gravity of his condition. (Cancer was to take his life in 1980.) It is possible that the disease may already have begun to affect his personal outlook and judgment earlier in the decade, but even in his first years on the throne the shah had shown in times of crisis a lack of confidence and a striking indecision.

In January 1978 Iran entered a period of sustained conflict. The whole country was shaken by strikes, peaceful demonstrations, and rioting led by militant youths who served as anti-shah shock troops. Bloody repression, resulting in the death of between ten thousand and twenty thousand people, fed the feeling of outrage. Each period of mourning set the stage for more massive protests. By the fall Muhammad Reza Shah's confidence was shattered, leaving him politically irresolute, psychologically depressed, and looking for a CIA hand behind the opposition. In the end he could not bring himself to order a ruthless repression, even though his security forces gave him the means to save himself. By December he was looking for a graceful way out. On 16 January 1979 Muhammad Reza Shah left the country, ostensibly on a vacation, and on 1 February Khomeini, the central figure in the loose anti-shah coalition, returned to Tehran in triumph to establish an Islamic republic.

*　*　*

It fell to the unfortunate Jimmy Carter, a genial Southern Baptist, to confront this powerful, strongly anti-American Islamic revolution. He was burdened above all else by his own limited sense of the past, especially his complete inability to imagine the way memories of foreign interference might color the thinking of the new men in power in Tehran. He was also hampered by his increasing reliance on Zbigniew Brzezinski, whose sense of the past—one filled with Soviet goblins from his homeland of Poland—was as strong as Carter's was weak, but was no less irrelevant to understanding events in Iran.

When Carter entered the White House, Iran was peripheral to his foreign policy concerns. In a major address in May 1977 he warned against any longer letting "inordinate fear of communism" lead the United States to embrace dictators. Instead he called on his countrymen to follow a policy consistent "with our essential character as a nation" and confront "the new global questions of justice, equity, and human rights."[7] In that speech Carter passed over Iran in silence, and in the months ahead not only did he continue arms sales, but he also came to appreciate that country's stability and strength in a region of dangerous conflict. The CIA, which reported in August that it saw no major crisis on the horizon, supported the view of a shah bringing development to Iran and stability to the region.

Although a state visit in November 1977 was marred by anti-shah demonstrations held right outside the White House, Carter was impressed with the

7. Commencement address at Notre Dame, 22 May 1977, in *Public Papers of the Presidents of the United States* [hereafter *PPP*]: *Jimmy Carter, 1977* (2 vols.; Washington: Government Printing Office, 1977–78), 1:955–57.

Iranian leader. In a show of support he paid a return call the next month. Surrounded by the opulence of the court, Carter served up an effusive endorsement of the sort that had become commonplace in these last years of the regime, and made only brief, pro forma references to human rights (Document 13). Just days after his departure Iran entered the prolonged cycle of violence that would give the lie to its vaunted stability and that would a year later put the shah to flight.

As the revolution gathered momentum in 1978, the Carter administration was perplexed and uncomprehending. Indeed, it spent more time during the last stage of the protests, in the fall of that year, debating the shah's arms sales requests than appraising his opposition. In any case, Iran seemed small potatoes compared to the negotiations over nuclear arms control, the Middle East peace talks, and the process of normalizing relations with China. Once Washington began to recognize the depth of the crisis, U.S. leaders still found it difficult to fashion a response. It was hard to accept a political movement led by clerics seeking to restore Islamic values as anything but a passing inconvenience or a last gasp of resistance to a quarter century of modernization sponsored by the shah and the United States and generously funded by U.S. aid and oil revenues. It was also hard to abandon hope that the shah would weather this challenge, as he had earlier ones. One intelligence analysis in September gave the regime a fifty-fifty chance of survival and predicted that "the Shah will probably be able to maintain his position through the early 1980s."[8]

With Muhammad Reza Shah in undeniable trouble by the fall, the Carter administration struggled to find its way between the strident and hostile revolutionaries and the collapsing regime of the failed modernizer. Washington divided over how this might best be done, foreshadowing the increasingly sharp clash between Carter's secretary of state, Cyrus Vance, and his national security adviser, Zbigniew Brzezinski. Through late 1978 the State Department, including the Iran desk and Ambassador William Sullivan in Tehran, doubted that the shah could hold on and urged making contacts with the opposition. Brzezinski, by contrast, argued that the shah could save himself by the firm exercise of force and that the United States should push him in that direction. The transition to a new regime, Brzezinski warned, might open the door to Soviet intervention. Carter finally aligned with his White House adviser and

8. Defense Intelligence Agency, "Assessment of the Political Situation in Iran," c. 1 September 1978, in *Iran: The Making of U.S. Policy, 1977–1980*, ed. Eric J. Hooglund (Washington: National Security Archives; Alexandria, Va.: Chadwyck-Healey, 1990), microfiche no. 01497.

signaled his continued support for an old ally (Document 15). As late as 12 December he was publicly discounting "the predictions of doom and disaster" in Iran and voicing confidence that the shah would survive.[9]

Muhammad Reza Shah was soon on the way out, however. So the Carter administration turned to Shapour Bakhtiar, a centrist whom it hoped might hold the government together. Bakhtiar had served in the Musaddiq government and later joined the opposition to the shah. The shah made him prime minister late in December 1978 in a desperate bid to save a deteriorating situation. Carter quickly dispatched Robert Huyser, an American general with wide contacts in the Iranian military, to Tehran to rally that force behind Bakhtiar and to urge it otherwise to take power itself. Carter also reluctantly approved the first secret contacts with a Khomeini aide in Paris.

The frantic U.S. effort to maintain a stable, friendly government in Tehran proved unavailing. The shah soon fled, and Khomeini arrived in a tumult of celebration. The Bakhtiar government fell in the middle of February (only two weeks after Khomeini's return), with Bakhtiar going at once into exile. (He would be stabbed to death in Paris in 1991.) By then military resistance to the revolution had ended, scotching Brzezinski's lingering hope that a military coup would save the day. In the wake of these reverses in January and February Carter had to defend himself against charges by Kissinger and others that he had "lost" Iran, and he expressed guarded optimism that an acceptable government might yet emerge (Documents 17 and 19).

Once back home, Khomeini held adamantly to his vision of an Islamic Iran (Document 18). He soon began to translate that vision into institutions and programs. A revolutionary council, revolutionary courts, local revolutionary committees, and revolutionary guards were created to exercise power and enforce the will of the clergy. In the struggle to consolidate the revolution in a country now splintered politically, roughly ten thousand died and half a million (mostly the old political elite and middle-class professionals) fled between 1979 and 1981. Even the organization of the Khomeini loyalists, the Islamic Revolutionary Party, suffered heavy losses from bombings and assassinations. Insurrections along the border—among Kurds, Arabs, Turkomans—compounded the confusion. As the revolution turned more radical in the early 1980s, it began to devour its own. The Islamic Revolutionary Party turned on those loosely aligned with Khomeini earlier in the anti-shah struggle—militant leftists, liberals, merchants, and even conservative clerics. All had gone too far in accepting Western ideas of modernity and thus were an obstacle to creating an Islamic state and society.

9. Press conference comment, 12 December 1978, in *PPP: Jimmy Carter, 1978* (2 vols.; Washington: GPO, 1979), 2:2226.

By early 1983 the Islamic Revolutionary Party had destroyed all rival political organizations and monopolized control of the state. Parliament was restricted in its membership, and its laws were subject to review by a veto-wielding Council of Guardians, a majority of whom were appointed by Khomeini. The new government drove out the old bureaucrats and purged the army. It set out to make public behavior conform to religious ideals. Alcohol and coeducation were banned, and Western cultural influence was purged from the media, the schools, and the street. Women were enjoined to return to the veil in public and to abandon business and public affairs. The new government channeled some benefits to the urban poor, pursued briefly and with considerable controversy a limited land reform program, and took measures such as road and school building to integrate rural areas with the rest of the nation. It also took control of important sectors of the modern economy such as banks, industry, large agricultural enterprises, and foreign trade.

As the revolution turned ever more radical, Washington was caught in the trap of constantly doing too little too late to stabilize relations. Mistrust on one side and resentment on the other may in any case have made accommodation impossible. With high-level official contacts still in limbo through the summer of 1979, American officials contemplated possible overtures, including the unpleasant but necessary first step of a meeting with Khomeini (Document 20). But Carter could not bring himself to countenance any such approaches, especially in the face of the revolutionary madness that Khomeini and his followers seemed to stand for. Such a move would in any case have stirred up a hornet's nest of opposition in Congress and the public. On the other side, in the revolutionary camp, the ghost of Musaddiq whispered warnings that American agents were everywhere. As the embassy rebuilt its presence in Tehran in 1979, it sought out noncleric moderates in the new regime. This transparent American bias inspired fears that the CIA had some new plot afoot. Just talking to the Americans would prove for some within the government the kiss of death.

By the fall the United States and Iran were unable to turn the page in their relationship. Carter finally insured that it stayed stuck when he decided in October 1979 to admit the shah into the United States for cancer treatment. The seriously ill former monarch had wandered from Egypt to Morocco, the Bahamas, and Mexico seeking a permanent home. A circle of influential American supporters built up during the glory days of his reign, including the banker David Rockefeller and Henry Kissinger, applied pressure to let the exile into the United States. Brzezinski argued that the U.S. reputation for strength and loyalty to an ally hung in the balance. With the shah in critical condition Vance reversed himself and voiced support for admission for medical treatment. On 21 October Carter ordered the door open on humanitarian grounds.

The shah landed in New York on 22 October, and on 4 November predictions of attacks on Americans in Iran were realized. Some five hundred militants took the embassy in Tehran. Fifty-two Americans became hostages, and the documents found there cast U.S. contacts with the moderates within the revolutionary camp in a lurid light and confirmed suspicions that the embassy was indeed a "nest of spies." The provisional government headed by one of those moderates, Mehdi Bazargan, had turned back an attempted embassy occupation the previous February. He now resigned in protest against this successful seizure of the embassy, although in fact the days for his government were already numbered. Khomeini defended this bold stroke by the revolutionary youths while also warning them, supposedly, to safeguard the captives' lives on risk of losing their own. Throughout the hostage dispute he would shower denunciations on the United States and even begin to call for exporting the revolution (Documents 21, 24, and 25).

For fifteen months Carter was hostage to the crisis, almost as much as the American officials held in Tehran. As the American media began to count one by one the 444 days of humiliation, the hostages became a virtual obsession for the public and Carter himself. At first the president followed Vance along the path of negotiations and caution to preserve the lives of the hostages (Documents 22 and 23). His strongest measures of retaliation were to ban Iranian oil, freeze Iranian assets in U.S. banks, and crack down on Iranian students in the United States. Iran for its part demanded as a price for the hostage release the return of the shah for trial. As long as he remained abroad, so the new regime in Tehran reasoned, he would serve as a rallying point for supporters of the old regime and a potential front for the United States to use in a replay of the 1953 coup. Tehran also wanted the return of frozen Iranian assets and a U.S. apology for putting the shah in power and keeping him there.

By early April 1980 international efforts to work out with Foreign Minister Sadeq Ghotbzadeh and President Abol Hassan Bani Sadr some basis for freeing the hostages had made no headway. The American public in polls taken in March pronounced Carter's handling of the crisis a failure, by a five-to-four margin.[10] Carter decided to try the option that Brzezinski favored. The president had already built up the U.S. naval presence in the Persian Gulf. He broke diplomatic relations on 7 April and two weeks later launched a daring military rescue with the hope that it would save not only the hostages but also the U.S. reputation. The operation turned into a fiasco, exacerbating the public sense of impotence and humiliation and sending Carter's own political stock still lower. Vance, away on vacation when Carter had made the rescue decision, had sought a reversal and then after the mission's failure resigned in protest.

10. *Gallup Poll Index*, no. 177 (April–May 1980): 14.

Carter was now back to negotiations, putting the new secretary of state, Edmund Muskie, in charge. Unexpected events in the course of the summer of 1980 improved the prospects for success. In late July the death of the shah (then aged sixty) rendered moot demands for his return to his country for trial. Following medical treatment in the United States, he had moved on to Panama and then Egypt, where he died. In September clashes along the border with Iraq, a prelude to war, raised concerns in Tehran about its isolation. Even if Washington was behind the Iraqi attack, Tehran could not allow the lingering dispute with the United States to cost Iran much-needed international sympathy and support. That month Khomeini announced new terms for a settlement: a U.S. pledge of noninterference in Iran's internal affairs, the release of frozen assets, the cancellation of American claims against Iran, and the return of the shah's wealth. (Gone was the demand for an apology.)

Talks began to make progress, with Algeria serving as intermediary between Tehran and a U.S. team led by Warren Christopher—but too late to save Carter's presidency. He faced an electorate soured by the daily televised exposure to revolutionary militants denouncing the United States and holding American citizens captive with complete impunity. Not until 18 January 1981 did the two sides sort out the tangled financial issues and determine that the United States would have to pay almost $8 billion to Iran at the time of the hostage release. Finally, the hostages gained their freedom on 20 January 1981, just hours after Carter had vacated the White House to Ronald Reagan, the landslide winner of the November election. To the end Iran made life difficult for Carter.

Reagan swore as he welcomed the hostages home that it would be different with him. He warned terrorists of "swift and effective retribution" and "limits to our patience."[11] But even Reagan would become in his own way ensnared in the plight of hostages. Despite his strong language, Reagan would supply Tehran arms to secure the release of Americans held in Lebanon in a project begun in 1985 that went badly awry. Once again Iran would play the spoiler of presidential reputations.

* * *

A deep bitterness and incomprehension had come to infect relations between Iran and the United States, an outcome that the architects of the earlier era of intimacy could hardly have imagined. For fundamentalists in Iran the United States remained a satanic force committed to the support of Israel and conservative Arab regimes. Americans for their part continued to see Iran as a

---

11. Reagan remarks, 27 January 1981, in *PPP: Ronald Reagan, 1981* (Washington: GPO, 1982), 42.

land of fanatics who condoned the taking of hostages and fomented unrest throughout the Middle East.

The Iran-Iraq war accentuated the antagonism. Iran had provoked Baghdad by appealing to the Shia faithful in Iraq to overthrow the secular regime headed by Sunni Muslims. Baghdad responded in September 1980 by taking disputed oil-producing territory (Khuzestan) on the southern border. For the United States the conflict that followed was an irresistible opportunity for revenge. Washington would make the regime of Saddam Hussein the new stabilizing element in the region, and it would support his war with Iran with credits, technology, and intelligence. While obstructing international arms sales to Iran, Washington lifted restrictions on arms sales to Iraq. An internationally isolated Iran, driven by economic exhaustion and heavy loss of life, finally in 1988 made peace with the hated rulers in Baghdad. For Americans sweet revenge turned to gall when in 1990 the instrument of that revenge, Saddam Hussein, invaded Kuwait and thus became in the American imagination a fitting successor to Khomeini.

The decade ended with Iran wounded and in disarray. Economic development policy, redistribution of wealth, and respect for private property remained bones of contention within a political arena that was ideologically narrow but not clearly or rigidly defined. Revolutionary turmoil and the war with Iraq had left the economy in shambles—shaken by inflation, a slump in production and foreign trade, and low oil prices. In 1985 demonstrations began in Tehran in the very neighborhoods that had earlier been strongest for the revolution. Their spread nationwide suggested popular disappointment with the government and aversion to the war with Iraq. In addition, Iran was missing a generation that had been martyred or maimed in that conflict. Finally, the ruling elite had been divided over whether to extend their fundamentalism beyond Iran's borders (as Khomeini had wished) or to concentrate on domestic transformation (as his successor, Ali Akbar Hashemi-Rafsanjani, preferred).

A look back at the tangled U.S.-Iran relationship and the crisis that it gave rise to confronts us with a troubling set of questions. Was U.S. policy consciously and purposefully counterrevolutionary, or is it more fairly described as ethnocentric and uncomprehending? Was the United States responsible for creating the revolutionary powderkeg that exploded in 1979? Could Washington have done something to avert or at least dampen the explosion? Or were the developments all along beyond American control? On these questions hinge a verdict on American policy and an analysis of this case.

This crisis, with its denouement in the taking of hostages, helps us see how those of us looking back are also hostages—closed off by the veil of secrecy that our own and other governments wrap around their policy records. Without access to the documents that would provide an inside perspective on the thinking and decisions of policymakers, we are constrained to base our judgments in this case—to a far greater degree than any of the others examined in this book—on a critical reading of the public record. There are almost certain to be revelations, above all from the private records of Carter and Khomeini, that will in time force important revisions in the story told here and by extension a fundamental rethinking of this painful episode.

FOR FURTHER READING

The best overall accounts of this crisis are James A. Bill, *The Eagle and the Lion: The Tragedy of American-Iranian Relations* (1988), and Richard W. Cottam, *Iran and the United States: A Cold War Case Study* (1988).

On early U.S. involvement and the Iranian political context in which Americans operated, see Mark H. Lytle, *The Origins of the Iranian-American Alliance, 1941–1953* (1987); Mark J. Gasiorowski, *U.S. Foreign Policy and the Shah: Building a Client State in Iran* (1991); James A. Bill and Wm. Roger Louis, eds., *Musaddiq, Iranian Nationalism, and Oil* (1988); and Homa Katouzian, *Musaddiq and the Struggle for Power in Iran* (1990).

For an understanding of the revolutionary discontents that overthrew the shah and stunned the United States, the places to begin are Shaul Bakhash, *The Reign of the Ayatollahs: Iran and the Islamic Revolution* (1984), and Roy P. Mottahedeh, *The Mantle of the Prophet: Religion and Politics in Iran* (1985). Nikki R. Keddie has perhaps done more than any other scholar to promote serious examination of the course and nature of Iran's revolution in *Roots of Revolution: An Interpretive History of Modern Iran* (1981); in an influential and contested essay, "Iranian Revolutions in Comparative Perspective," *American Historical Review* 88 (June 1983): 579–98; and in a string of valuable edited volumes. Shaul Bakhash, "Iran," *American Historical Review* 96 (December 1991): 1479–96, helpfully reviews the literature on Iran's revolution.

Good insights on the Carter administration's response to this revolutionary upheaval can be found in David S. McLellan, *Cyrus Vance* (1985), and Gaddis Smith, *Morality, Reason, and Power: American Diplomacy in the Carter Years* (1986), both of which build on memoirs and interviews and supply a helpful policy context. Gary Sick, who served under Brzezinski, has provided the most detailed of the participant accounts, *All Fall Down: America's Tragic Encounter with Iran* (1985).

A representative sampling of documentary materials on American policy going back to the 1940s can be found in Yonah Alexander and Allen Nanes, eds., *The United States and Iran: A Documentary History* (1980). Eric J. Hooglund, ed., *Iran: The Making of U.S. Policy, 1977–1980* (1990), makes a fuller, microfiche collection available. Asadollah Alam, *The Shah and I: The Confidential Diary of Iran's Royal Court, 1969–77,* ed. Alinaghi Alikhani and trans. Alikhani and Nicholas Vincent (1992), and Hamid Algar, ed. and trans., *Islam and Revolution: Writings and Declarations of Imam Khomeini* (1981), offer valuable insights on the Iranian side.

DOCUMENTS

I **U.S. Department of State paper, "American Policy in Iran," conveyed by Secretary of State Cordell Hull to President Franklin D. Roosevelt, 16 August 1943, making the case for an active U.S. policy in defense of Iranian independence.**[12]

The historic ambitions of Great Britain and Russia in Iran have made that country a diplomatic battleground for more than a century. . . . [There is] strong reason to fear that their rivalry will break out again as soon as the military situation permits. This danger is greatly increased by the existing economic and political weakness of the Iranian Government and the presence on Iranian soil of British and Soviet armed forces.

. . .

The United States is the only nation in a position to render effective aid to Iran, specifically through providing American advisers and technicians and financial and other material support. We are also the only nation in a position to exercise a restraining influence upon the two great powers directly concerned.

. . . [I]t is to the advantage of the United States to exert itself to see that Iran's integrity and independence are maintained and that she becomes prosperous and stable. Likewise, from a more directly selfish point of view, it is to our interest that no great power be established on the Persian Gulf opposite the important American petroleum development in Saudi Arabia.

Therefore, the United States should adopt a policy of positive action in Iran. . . . We should take the lead, wherever possible, in remedying internal difficulties, working as much as possible through American administrators freely employed by the Iranian Government. We should further endeavor to lend timely diplomatic support to Iran, to prevent the development of a situation in which an open threat to Iranian integrity might be presented. . . .

The success of the proposed course of action is favored by the exceptionally high regard in which this country is held by the Iranian people. There is also reason to believe that the British Government would acquiesce, or even lend its active support. The attitude of the Soviet Government is doubtful. . . . It goes without saying that the safeguarding of legitimate British and Soviet economic interests in Iran should be a basic principle of American action.

12. U.S. Department of State, *Foreign Relations of the United States* [hereafter *FRUS*], *1943*, vol. 4 (Washington: GPO, 1964), 378–79. Roosevelt had earlier expressed informally his approval of similar points made in a memo of 23 January 1943 by John D. Jernegan, a junior member of the State Department's Division of Near Eastern Affairs. *FRUS, 1943,* 4:331–36.

2   Department of State memorandum, conveyed by Acting Secretary of State Robert A. Lovett to President Harry S. Truman, 24 November 1947, committing the United States to the defense of Iran as part of a broader, Anglo-American policy in the region.[13]

The security of the Eastern Mediterranean and of the Middle East is vital to the security of the United States. . . .

The security of the whole Eastern Mediterranean and Middle East would be jeopardized if the Soviet Union should succeed in its efforts to obtain control of any one of the following countries: Italy, Greece, Turkey, or Iran.

. . . [T]he United States should assist in maintaining the territorial integrity and political independence of Italy, Greece, Turkey, and Iran.

. . .

It would be unrealistic for the United States to undertake to carry out such a policy unless the British maintain their strong strategic, political and economic position in the Middle East and Eastern Mediterranean, and unless they and ourselves follow parallel policies in that area.

One of the greatest dangers to world peace may be the failure of the Soviet Union to understand the extent to which the United States is prepared to go in order to maintain the security of the Eastern Mediterranean and the Middle East. It should, therefore, be the policy of this Government to make evident in a firm but nonprovocative manner the extent of the determination of the United States to assist in preserving in the interest of world peace the security of the area.

3   National Security Council report 54, 21 July 1949, setting Iran formally and firmly within the framework of the Cold War containment policy.[14]

Because of its resources, strategic location, vulnerability to armed attack and exposure to political subversion, Iran must be regarded as a continuing

13. This memo was the product of detailed discussions between the U.S. and British governments. *FRUS, 1947*, vol. 5 (Washington: GPO, 1971), 575–76. Truman immediately gave his approval to the general policy outlined here. Ibid., 623n.

14. *FRUS, 1949*, vol. 6 (Washington: GPO, 1977), 545–48. Truman did not explicitly approve this report on "the Position of the United States with Respect to Iran," but it did lay the foundation for a series of similar NSC reports on Iran in 1951–1952 that Truman did approve. During that time mounting Anglo-Iranian tensions over oil caused Washington

objective in the Soviet program of expansion. If Iran should come under Soviet domination, the independence of all other countries of the Middle East would be directly threatened. Specifically the USSR would (1) acquire advance bases for subversive activities or actual attack against a vast contiguous area including Turkey, Iraq, the Arabian Peninsula, Afghanistan, and Pakistan; (2) obtain a base hundreds of miles nearer to potential US-UK [United Kingdom] lines of defense in the Middle East than any held at present; (3) control part and threaten all of the Middle Eastern oil reservoir upon which the western community draws to conserve limited western hemisphere resources; (4) control continental air routes crossing Iran, threaten those traversing adjacent areas, and menace shipping in the Persian Gulf, and (5) undermine the will of all Middle Eastern countries to resist Soviet aggression.

. . .

. . . [T]he primary objective of our policy toward Iran is to prevent the domination of that country by the USSR and to strengthen Iran's orientation toward the West. . . .

. . . In response to Iranian inquiries, we have authorized the Embassy in Teheran to say that in the event of war with the Soviet Union involving both Iran and the United States, Iran may count on all assistance compatible with U.S. resources in a global conflict.

Current U.S. efforts to assist Iran internally include two military missions now advising the Iranian Army and the *Gendarmerie,* the willingness of the United States to support Iran's efforts to secure financial aid through appropriate agencies (such as the World Bank) for well justified economic development projects, encouragement and advice in connection with the Iranian Government's consideration of political and economic reforms designed to strengthen popular loyalty to the central government, and the provision of surplus light military equipment on credit for internal security purposes. . . .

. . .

Although the USSR will continue to apply strong political and psychological pressures against Iran in an effort to force the government of that country into submission, it is considered unlikely that the Soviet Union would be willing to resort to direct armed intervention at this time. In the absence of such armed intervention, Iran is expected to maintain successful resistance to Soviet pressure and to strengthen its western alignment, provided it continues to have confidence in U.S. support. However, the Iranian Government must press its

---

growing concern that Iran's instability might lead to a communist takeover. See NSC 107 of 14 March 1951, NSC 107/2 of 27 June 1951, and NSC 136/1 of 20 November 1952, in *FRUS, 1952–1954,* vol. 10 (Washington: GPO, 1989), 21–24, 71–76, 528–34.

planned economic and social reforms or the internal stability of the country may be seriously threatened.

4 Prime Minister Muhammad Musaddiq to President-elect Dwight Eisenhower, letter, 9 January 1953, justifying Iran's nationalization of the British oil concession and appealing for support.[15]

It is my hope that the new administration which you will head will obtain at the outset a true understanding of the significance of the vital struggle in which the Iranian people have been engaging and assist in removing the obstacles which are preventing them from realizing their aspirations for the attainment of... life as a politically and economically independent nation. For almost two years the Iranian people have suffered acute distress and much misery merely because a company [Anglo-Iranian Oil] inspired by covetousness and a desire for profit supported by the British Government has been endeavoring to prevent them from obtaining their natural and elementary rights.

. . . Unfortunately the government of the United States while on occasions displaying friendship for Iran has pursued what appears to the Iranian people to be a policy of supporting the British Government and the former company. In this struggle it has taken the side of the British Government against that of Iran in international assemblies. It has given financial aid to the British Government while withholding it from Iran and it seems to us it has given at least some degree of support to the endeavors of the British to strangle Iran with a financial and economic blockade.

. . .

The Iranian people finally became convinced that so long as this company continued to operate within Iran its systematic interference in Iranian internal life would continue. The Iranian people therefore had no choice other than to exercise their sovereign rights by nationalizing their oil and terminating the activities of the former company in Iran. The Iranian Government made it clear at the time of nationalization that it was willing to pay fair compensation to the former company due consideration being given to such claims and counterclaims as Iran might have against the former company. The former company instead of entering into negotiations with Iran for the purpose of determining the amount of compensation due took steps with the support of the British Government to create an economic and financial blockade of Iran

15. *Department of State Bulletin* 24 (20 July 1953): 76–77.

with the purpose of forcing the Iranian people again to submit to the will of the former company and to abandon their right to exploit and utilize their own natural resources.

5 President Dwight D. Eisenhower, meeting with National Security Council advisers, 4 March 1953, discussing dangers of a communist takeover as the Anglo-Iranian oil dispute sharpens.[16]

[CIA director Allen W. Dulles foresaw] a dictatorship in Iran under Mossadegh [Musaddiq]. As long as the latter lives there was but little danger, but if he were to be assassinated or otherwise to disappear from power, a political vacuum would occur in Iran and the Communists might easily take over.... [I]f Iran succumbed to the Communists there was little doubt that in short order the other areas of the Middle East, with some 60% of the world's oil reserves, would fall into Communist control.

. . .

In reply, Secretary [of State John Foster] Dulles said that for a long time now he had been unable to perceive any serious obstacle to the loss of Iran to the free world if the Soviets were really determined to take it. We do not have sufficient troops to put into the area in order to prevent a Communist take-over, and the Soviets had played their game in Iran very cleverly and with a good sense of timing. Nevertheless, continued Secretary Dulles, he believed it was possible to gain time....

. . .

Secretary [of Defense Charles E.] Wilson inquired whether we were not in fact in partnership with the British in Iran, and whether the British were not the senior partner.

Secretary Dulles answered that this had been the case until fairly lately, but that the British had now been thrown out.

The President added that we do have to respect the enormous investment which the British had in Iran.... It was certainly possible, he added, for the United States to do what it thought necessary to do in Iran, but we certainly don't want a break with the British.

. . .

Mr. Cutler [Robert Cutler, administrative assistant to the president] . . . pleaded the wisdom of American policy in Iran independent of the British, and suggested that it might even be wise for the United States to buy out the British oil company.

16. Memo of discussion by S. Everett Gleason, in *FRUS, 1952–1954*, 10:693–96, 698–700.

The President replied that he had long believed that this should be done, but he could see no way of convincing Congress that it was the part of wisdom for the United States Government or any American oil company to buy the bankrupt Anglo-Iranian [Oil Company].

. . .

Reverting to the President's worries about the attitude of Congress, Mr. Cutler inquired how Congress would like it if the United States stood idly by and let Iran fall into the hands of the Soviet Union.

It was generally agreed that Congress would take a poor view of this eventuality.

. . .

The President said that if a real Soviet move against Iran actually comes, we shall have to face at this council table the question of going to full mobilization. If we did not move at [that] time and in that eventuality, he feared that the United States would descend to the status of a second-rate power. "If", said the President, "I had $500,000,000 of money to spend in secret, I would get $100,000,000 of it to Iran right now."

. . .

Secretary Wilson said that there seemed to him to be two great things in the world to which the United States did not have an answer. One was the obvious collapse of colonialism; the other was Communism's new tactics in exploiting nationalism and colonialism for its own purposes. In the old days, when dictatorships changed it was usually a matter of one faction of the right against another, and we had only to wait until the situation subsided. Nowadays, however, when a dictatorship of the right was replaced by a dictatorship of the left, a state would presently slide into Communism and was irrevocably lost to us.

. . .

Apropos of a statement by the President, that he also wished that for a change he could read about mobs in these Middle Eastern states rioting and waving American flags, Mr. Jackson [C. D. Jackson, special assistant to the president] said that if the President wanted the mobs he was sure he could produce them.

The President said in any case it was a matter of great distress to him that we seemed unable to get some of the people in these down-trodden countries to like us instead of hating us.

. . .

. . . Mr. Stassen [Director for Mutual Security Harold E. Stassen] inquired whether it was indeed the President's view that some funds should be expended at once in Iran if the Secretary of State agreed.

The President replied that of course this was a gamble, but if upon examination it seemed a good gamble, he was prepared to take it.

6   President John F. Kennedy and Muhammad Reza Shah Pahlavi, meeting in Washington, 13 April 1962, discussing a development program that would make Iran stable and strong.[17]

The President said that nothing contributed so much to the Shah's prestige as Iran's economic development program. . . .

The President noted that he, the President, could leave his present job and the United States would go on, but Iran would collapse if the Shah were to leave his post. The President assured the Shah that he had the support of the United States.

The Shah acknowledged the importance of this point, and noted that he had been working for twenty years at the task of building a strong anti-Communist society through social reform and economic development. But even if the USSR did not exist, he would still have a duty to work for the progress of the Iranian people. The Shah remarked that he felt responsible to the majority of his people and he cannot belong to the few. . . .

The President told how Franklin Roosevelt was still regarded almost as a god in places like West Virginia, because Roosevelt, though a rich man, had worked for the interests of the common people. . . . [H]e said it was necessary to identify ourselves with the small people, and he was aware that the Shah had done precisely this. This particular thunder must be taken away from the Communists. He wanted the Shah to realize the depth of his feelings on this subject. Life is a burden, but unless the Shah survives, Iran and then the whole Middle East would crumble.

The Shah stated that this concept was the goal of his life, and that he had devoted his life to this end. He gathers strength from seeing that Iran is moving forward. To succeed on the economic side Iran needs time and security. . . . The Iranian people expect strength from their government. Iran needs an honest, first-class army with a decent standard of living. With such an army Iran can resist Communist pressures and build the country into a showcase so that other peoples can see that it is possible to work with the West. . . .

. . .

The Shah . . . remarked that he is not by nature a dictator. But if Iran is to

17. Department of State, memo of conversation, 13 April 1962, in Hooglund, *Iran*, microfiche no. 00450.

succeed its government would have to act firmly for a time, and he knew that the United States would not insist that Iran do everything in an absolutely legal way.

. . .

The President said that as a politician he would like to emphasize that national leaders must identify themselves with the common people. The President said that he knew this was the Shah's course, and that politically it is the most successful course.

. . .

At this point Mrs. Kennedy and Caroline entered the office for a brief visit with the Shah. . . .

7   Ayatollah Ruhollah Khomeini, sermon delivered in Qum, 3 June 1963, laying down a religious challenge to the shah.[18]

Iranian nation! Those among you who are thirty or forty years of age or more will remember how three foreign countries attacked us during World War II. The Soviet Union, Britain, and America invaded Iran and occupied our country. The property of the people was exposed to danger and their honor was imperilled. But God knows, everyone was happy because the Pahlavi had gone!

Shah, I don't wish the same to happen to you; I don't want you to become like your father. Listen to my advice, listen to the *'ulama* [learned clergy] of Islam. They desire the welfare of the nation, the welfare of the country. Don't listen to Israel; Israel can't do anything for you. You miserable wretch, forty-five years of your life have passed; isn't it time for you to think and reflect a little, to ponder about where all this is leading you, to learn a lesson from the experience of your father? If what they say is true, that you are opposed to Islam and the religious scholars, your ideas are quite wrong. . . . Are the religious scholars really some form of impure animal? If they are impure animals, why do the people kiss their hands? Why do they regard the very water they drink as blessed? . . .

8   Ayatollah Khomeini, sermon delivered in Qum, 27 October 1964, attacking the privileged U.S. position in Iran.[19]

A law has been put before the Majlis [parliament] . . . that all American

18. Algar, *Islam and Revolution*, 178–79.
19. Algar, *Islam and Revolution*, 181–82, 184–86.

military advisers, together with their families, technical and administrative officials, and servants—in short, anyone in any way connected to them—are to enjoy legal immunity with respect to any crime they may commit in Iran.

If some American's servant, some American's cook, assassinates your *marja'*[20] in the middle of the bazaar, or runs over him, the Iranian police do not have the right to apprehend him! Iranian courts do not have the right to judge him! The dossier must be sent to America, so that our masters there can decide what is to be done!

. . . [The Majlis] passed it without any shame, and the government shamelessly defended this scandalous measure. They have reduced the Iranian people to a level lower than that of an American dog. If someone runs over a dog belonging to an American, he will be prosecuted. Even if the Shah himself were to run over a dog belonging to an American, he would be prosecuted. But if an American cook runs over the Shah, the head of state, no one will have the right to interfere with him.

Why? Because they wanted a loan and America demanded this in return. A few days after this measure was approved, they requested a $200 million loan from America and America agreed to the request. . . . Iran has sold itself to obtain these dollars. The government has sold our independence, reduced us to the level of a colony, and made the Muslim nation of Iran appear more backward than savages in the eyes of the world!

. . .

I don't know where this White Revolution is that they are making so much fuss about. God knows that I am aware of (and my awareness causes me pain) the remote villages and provincial towns, not to mention our own backward city of Qum. I am aware of the hunger of our people and the disordered state of our agrarian economy. Why not try to do something for this country, for this population, instead of piling up debts and enslaving yourselves? . . .

. . .

Let the American President [Lyndon Johnson] know that in the eyes of the Iranian people, he is the most repulsive member of the human race today because of the injustice he has imposed on our Muslim nation. Today the Qur'an [Koran] has become his enemy, the Iranian nation has become his enemy. Let the American government know that its name has been ruined and disgraced in Iran.

20. A *marja'* is a scholar of proven learning and piety whose rulings are authoritative in matters of religious practice.

9 Ayatollah Khomeini, lectures delivered to students of religion in Najaf, Iraq, January-February 1970, advocating the application of Islamic political principles in Iran.[21]

At a time when the West was a realm of darkness and obscurity—with its inhabitants living in a state of barbarism and America still peopled by half-savage redskins—and the two vast empires of Iran and Byzantium were under the rule of tyranny, class privilege, and discrimination, and the powerful dominated all without any trace of law or popular government, God, Exalted and Almighty, by means of the Most Noble Messenger [the prophet Muhammad] (peace and blessings be upon him), sent laws that astound us with their magnitude. He instituted laws and practices for all human affairs and laid down injunctions for man extending from even before the embryo is formed until after he is placed in the tomb. In just the same way that there are laws setting forth the duties of worship for man, so too there are laws, practices, and norms for the affairs of society and government. Islamic law is a progressive, evolving, and comprehensive system of law. All the voluminous books that have been compiled from the earliest times on different areas of law, such as judicial procedure, social transactions, penal law, retribution, international relations, regulations pertaining to peace and war, private and public law—taken together, these contain a mere sample of the laws and injunctions of Islam. There is not a single topic in human life for which Islam has not provided instruction and established a norm.

. . .

The imposition of foreign laws on our Islamic society has been the source of numerous problems and difficulties. Knowledgeable people working in our judicial system have many complaints concerning the existing laws and their mode of operation. If a person becomes caught up in the judicial system of Iran . . . , he may have to spend a whole lifetime trying to prove his case. . . .

. . .

. . . Huge amounts of capital are being swallowed up; our public funds are being embezzled; our oil is being plundered; and our country is being turned into a market for expensive, unnecessary goods by the representatives of foreign companies, which makes it possible for foreign capitalists and their local agents to pocket the people's money. A number of foreign states carry off our oil after drawing it out of the ground, and the negligible sum they pay to the regime they have installed returns to their pockets by other routes. As for the small amount that goes into the treasury, God only knows what it is spent on.

21. A student recorded these lectures, subsequently published as a book titled *Islamic Government*. Algar, *Islam and Revolution*, 29–30, 32, 115, 120, 126–27, 132.

All of this is a form of "consumption of what is forbidden" that takes place on an enormous scale, in fact on an international scale. It is not merely an evil, but a hideous and most dangerous evil. . . .

. . .

Our wretched people subsist in conditions of poverty and hunger, while the taxes that the ruling class extorts from them are squandered. They buy Phantom jets so that pilots from Israel and its agents can come and train in them in our country. So extensive is the influence of Israel in our country—Israel, which is in a state of war with the Muslims, so that those who support it are likewise in a state of war with the Muslims—and so great is the support the regime gives it, that Israeli soldiers come to our country for training! Our country has become a base for them! The markets of our country are also in their hands. . . .

. . .

It is our duty to work toward the establishment of an Islamic government. The first activity we must undertake in this respect is the propagation of our cause; that is how we must begin.

. . .

You must teach the people matters relating to worship, of course, but more important are the political, economic, and legal aspects of Islam. These are, or should be, the focus of our concern. It is our duty to begin exerting ourselves now in order to establish a truly Islamic government. We must propagate our cause to the people, instruct them in it, and convince them of its validity. We must generate a wave of intellectual awakening, to emerge as a current throughout society, and gradually, to take shape as an organized Islamic movement made up of the awakened, committed, and religious masses who will rise up and establish an Islamic government.

. . .

. . . So, courageous sons of Islam, stand up! Address the people bravely; tell the truth about our situation to the masses in simple language; arouse them to enthusiastic activity, and turn the people in the street and the bazaar, our simple-hearted workers and peasants, and our alert students into dedicated *mujahids* [those engaged in jihad or holy struggle]. The entire population will become *mujahids*. All segments of society are ready to struggle for the sake of freedom, independence, and the happiness of the nation, and their struggle needs religion. Give the people Islam, then, for Islam is the school of *jihad*, the religion of struggle; let them amend their characters and beliefs in accordance with Islam and transform themselves into a powerful force, so that they may overthrow the tyrannical regime imperialism has imposed on us and set up an Islamic government.

10 Muhammad Reza Shah and Minister of Court Asadollah Alam, discussing affairs of state between 1972 and 1974.[22]

—Consideration of popular alienation, audience of 19 April 1972:[23]

"Your Majesty is always saying that he wishes to be ahead of events," I said, "why not then implement change before change is forced upon us?" "But what more do you expect me to do?", he replied; "No one could have accomplished more than us." He then went on to say that he has discovered the root cause of discontent amongst the younger generation; the disparity between their wages and those of men already in established positions. I suggested that this is only one of several factors at work. If people could be persuaded that they are working to achieve some basic goal, a goal respected by the ruling class, they would be prepared to put up with any amount of deprivation, even real hunger. "But what principles do you suggest we put to the nation?", asked HIM [His Imperial Majesty]. I replied that the public must feel that they are more than mere spectators of the political game. We must prepare the ground for their greater integration into this game; only then will they be satisfied and learn to play by the rules. HIM totally lost track of what I was saying, since he objected: "But we lack the equipment; our department of physical education hasn't enough sports fields, trainers or even simple cash." I explained that this wasn't exactly what I had in mind; that I was talking about popular participation in the game of politics. For example, why does the government continue to meddle in local elections? Leave the public to fight their own political contests and to choose whatever local representatives they prefer. Parliamentary elections may still require a degree of management, but surely this is untrue of elections in the municipalities. Why not allow the people free discussion of their local cares and concerns? What harm could it possibly do? "What are you talking about; of course it would be harmful," he declared, "they'd begin moaning about inflation, or some such rot." "Sadly", I replied, "what they say about inflation is all too true. But even assuming it to be nonsense, why not open the safety valve and allow them to talk nonsense, freely, amongst themselves?" "Precisely the reason I've allowed the opposition party to continue in existence," he replied. "Yes," I said, "but an opposition deprived of free

22. Alam was a close and loyal adviser to the shah. Descended from an aristocratic family, he had supported the young shah in the 1940s and went on to serve him in a variety of capacities. As prime minister between 1962 and 1964 Alam carried out the repression needed to end protest. He later served as minister of court and the shah's confidant, from 1966 until 1977 (the year before his death).

23. Asadollah Alam, *The Shah and I: The Confidential Diary of Iran's Royal Court, 1969–1977*, ed. Alinaghi Alikhani and trans. Alikhani and Nicholas Vincent (New York: St. Martin's, 1992), 210–11.

discussion is surely no opposition at all?" At this point he asked [me] why the people pay so little attention to the progress we have made. "Because" I told him, "our propaganda is applied in quite the wrong directions. So much of our self-advertisement is patently untrue, and for the rest it's so mixed up with adulation of Your Majesty's own person that the public grows tired of it. . . ."

—Reaction to foreign criticism, audience of 7 October 1973:[24]

Referring to a recent broadcast on the BBC [British Broadcasting Corporation], he [the shah] declared, "The bastards have the audacity to state that the chances of a revolution in Iran have receded, since our army will be able to crush any rising, now that we've purchased so many new weapons. What the hell do they mean 'the chances of a revolution'? Our farmers and workers are far too happy ever to contemplate becoming revolutionaries." In the same way, he's outraged by an article in the [London] *Financial Times,* describing the problems we face with inflation ...

—Discussion of student unrest, audience of 9 December 1973:[25]

[The shah] is extremely anxious about student unrest which has now infected every campus save the Pahlavi University at Shiraz. "Mark my words, Moscow is behind it all," he said. I replied that this might be so, but that we should bear in mind that they would have to be sowing fertile ground if their success is to be explained. For my own part, I'm convinced that the university authorities have made the mistake of refusing any sort of dialogue with the students. The same goes for the country at large; our government behaves like the conqueror of a vanquished land. As I said to HIM, for all his achievements and his tireless endeavour, there's a growing sense of alienation between regime and people. "I'm afraid you're right," he replied. "I've sensed the same thing myself. Something must be done."

—Aspiration to make Iran a world power, informal conversation sometime between 22 March and 3 April 1974:[26]

I remarked to him [the shah] that every one of his dreams seems to have come true. It's almost unbelievable, but our oil income has rocketed from $2 billion to $16 billion; heavy rainfall suggests a bumper harvest, and HIM is now unrivalled amongst Middle Eastern statesmen. "But I have so many more aspirations," he replied. "To be first in the Middle East is not enough. We must

24. Alam, *The Shah and I,* 323. Suspension points in this text indicate an omission in the published version of the diary.

25. Alam, *The Shah and I,* 341.

26. Alam, *The Shah and I,* 360. Suspension points in this text indicate an omission in the published version of the diary.

raise ourselves to the level of a great world power. Such a goal is by no means unattainable.".....

I I Secretary of State Henry A. Kissinger to President Gerald R. Ford, memorandum of 13 May 1975, offering a "Strategy for Your Discussions with the Shah of Iran."[27]

The Shah made the first of his eleven visits to the United States in 1949. Beginning with President Truman, every U.S. President has reaffirmed the steadfastness of our relationship with Iran.

. . .

In recent years, the Shah has stepped up his arms purchases from the U.S. After President Nixon visited Tehran in May 1972, we adopted a policy which provides, in effect, that we will accede to any of the Shah's requests for arms purchases from us (other than some sophisticated advanced technology armaments, and with the very important exception, of course, of any nuclear weapons capability . . .).

. . .

. . . [T]he Shah comes to the U.S. apparently in firm control at home, although student/intellectual dissent and a persistent terrorist movement are causes for concern. The Iranian economy is booming, having enjoyed GNP increases at the average rate of some 15 per cent annually for a number of years. The domestic development program continues apace. . . . He personally makes all important decisions, and this reliance on one man—albeit one of extraordinary ability and knowledge—is at once Iran's strength and Achilles' heel.

. . .

The Shah's main concern in visiting Washington is to test the firmness and reliability of his ties with the U.S., on which he has so heavily staked his position over the past three decades. He is worried about our ability to continue to play a strong world role, to retain a dominant position over the USSR in the Middle East and Indian Ocean, and to maintain close cooperation with Iran in the political, military, and economic fields. . . .

Closer to home, the Shah is upset by Congressional and American public criticism of Iran's oil pricing policies; widespread criticism in the U.S. of our military supply to Iran, now our largest foreign buyer of weapons; and problems in completing some major proposed deals with private American corporations. . . .

27. Memo of 13 May 1975, drafted by Sidney Sober in anticipation of the shah's arrival in Washington on 15 May, in Hooglund, *Iran*, microfiche no. 00955.

I see the Shah as playing an increasingly important role in the Persian Gulf, the Middle East, South Asia, and further afield. He may have some excessive ideas of his importance and some people consider him arrogant, but there is no gainsaying the sharply rising economic and military strength of which he disposes. . . . [H]e is a man with a clear vision of where he wants to go and an ability to project that vision in political terms in his relationships with other countries.

. . .

Your objective will be to leave the Shah confident of our determination to work ever more closely with Iran over an expanding field of relationships both at the Government and private levels. He will be anxious to have your affirmation that continued American advances in new technology and our vast economic know-how, as well as our collaboration in providing the defense materiel he believes it necessary to have, will continue to be available to Iran. . . . We currently estimate that over the next five years our non-oil, non-military trade will total $26 billion with the balance heavily in our favor.

The one big bilateral problem we have with Iran is over oil prices. I see little point in your trying to argue with the Shah that prices were raised too fast and too much, inasmuch as he is utterly convinced of the correctness of what was done and easily takes umbrage at suggestions to the contrary. . . . In any event, you will want to leave the Shah in no doubt about our interest in a positive, mutually beneficial relationship on oil matters.

12 Muhammad Reza Shah and Minister of Court Alam, diary entries from May 1977, discussing the religious opposition and U.S. support for Iran.

—Audience of 21 May:[28]

Much to HIM's disgust the new US ambassador, William Sullivan, has issued a statement to Congress, referring to the existence of religious opposition groups here in Iran... "Doesn't he realize these people are Islamic Marxists, mere Soviet puppets," HIM said. I replied that, whilst various of them may well be manipulated by the Soviets, or for that matter by Washington, there are others who act solely out of ignorant fanaticism... HIM remarked that he had no objection to girls wearing scarves at school or university; "But veils are out of the question... Tell my private secretariat to inform the government accordingly."...

28. Alam, *The Shah and I*, 544. Suspension points in this text indicate an omission in the published version of the diary.

Referring to [President Jimmy] Carter's speech of last night, HIM said, "He's announced he's willing to supply weapons to NATO, Israel, the Philippines, South Korea, Australia and New Zealand without any conditions attached; he didn't so much as mention Iran. Does he suppose that, strategically speaking, Iran is less significant than a country like New Zealand? Perhaps the Americans and the Soviets have devised some scheme to divide the world between themselves." I replied that this was quite out of the question. The Americans will never abandon us. As for Carter's pronouncements, they're intended merely to impress American public opinion. Like it or not, these idiot Americans are convinced we're violating human rights...

13 President Jimmy Carter, toast at a state dinner in Tehran, 31 December 1977, praising the achievements of the shah.[30]

Iran, because of the great leadership of the Shah, is an island of stability in one of the more troubled areas of the world.

This is a great tribute to you, Your Majesty, and to your leadership and to the respect and the admiration and love which your people give to you.

. . .

The cause of human rights is one that . . . is shared deeply by our people and by the leaders of our two nations.

. . .

We have no other nation on Earth who is closer to us in planning for our mutual military security. We have no other nation with whom we have closer consultation on regional problems that concern us both. And there is no leader with whom I have a deeper sense of personal gratitude and personal friendship.

14 Ayatollah Khomeini, statement delivered from exile in Najaf, Iraq, 19 February 1978, supporting anti-shah demonstrations and attacking American policy.[31]

[A]ccording to the information reaching us, all the major cities of Iran are closed down: Tehran, Tabriz, Mashhad, Qum. . . .

29. Alam, *The Shah and I*, 545. Suspension points in this text indicate an omission in the published version of the diary.

30. *PPP: Jimmy Carter, 1977*, 2:2221–22.

31. Algar, *Islam and Revolution*, 212–14, 221–22, 224.

These closings represent a form of active protest against the person of the Shah. The people have identified the true criminal. It was obvious before, it is true, but some people didn't recognize him as such or didn't dare speak out. Thanks be to God, this barrier of fear has collapsed and the people have discovered the true criminal and come to understand who is responsible for the misery of our nation.

. . .

All the miseries that we have suffered, still suffer, and are about to suffer soon are caused by the heads of those countries that have signed the Declaration of Human Rights,[32] but that at all times have denied man his freedom. . . .

The U.S. is one of the signatories to this document. It has agreed that the rights of man must be protected and that man must be free. But see what crimes America has committed against man. As long as I can remember—and I can remember back further than many of you, for you are younger than I— America has created disasters for mankind. It has appointed its agents in both Muslim and non-Muslim countries to deprive everyone who lives under their domination of his freedom. The imperialists proclaim that man is free only in order to deceive the masses. But people can no longer be deceived. . . .

. . .

. . . Before, it was the British that brought us misfortune; now it is the Soviets on the one hand, and the Americans on the other. All our miseries are caused by those imperialists; if they would stop protecting the Iranian government, the people would skin them alive. The Iranian government granted absolute immunity to the American advisers and got a few dollars in exchange. How many American officers there are in Iran now, and what huge salaries they receive! That is our problem—everything in our treasury has to be emptied into the pockets of America, and if there is any slight remainder, it has to go to the Shah and his gang. They buy themselves villas abroad and stuff their bank accounts with the people's money, while the nation subsists in poverty. . . .

. . .

This Carter fooled people for a time, and they said he would do all kinds of things if he came to power. . . . First he says human rights are inalienable, and then he says, "I don't want to hear about human rights." Of course, he's right from his own point of view; he uses the logic of bandits. The head of a government that has signed the Declaration of Human Rights says, "We have military bases in Iran; we can't talk about human rights there. Respect for human rights is feasible only in countries where we have no military bases." What miseries America, for all its boasting about human rights, has inflicted on the peoples of Latin America, in its own hemisphere!

32. The international accords signed in Helsinki, Finland, in 1975 protecting human rights but providing no enforcement mechanism.

15 President Carter, press conference comments, 10 October 1978, voicing continued support for the shah in the face of antigovernment demonstrations.[33]

[REPORTER:] How important is it to U.S. interests that the Shah remain in power? And what, if anything, can the United States Government do to keep him in power?

[CARTER:] The strategic importance to our country, I think to the entire Western World, of a good relationship with a strong and independent Iran is crucial. We have historic friendships with Iran. I think they are a great stabilizing force in their part of the world. They are a very important trade partner. They've acted very responsibly.

My own belief is that the Shah has moved aggressively to establish democratic principles in Iran and to have a progressive attitude toward social questions, social problems. This has been the source of much of the opposition to him in Iran.

We have no inclination to try to decide the internal affairs of Iran. My own hopes have been that there could be peace there, an end to bloodshed, and an orderly transformation into more progressive social arrangements and, also, increased democratization of the government itself, which I believe the Shah also espouses. He may not be moving fast enough for some; he may be moving too fast for others. I don't want to get involved in [the] specifics.

16 Ayatollah Khomeini, declaration issued from exile in Paris, 11 October 1978, praising the waves of anti-shah demonstrations in Iran.[34]

According to the way Carter thinks, all the crimes, savagery, and repression the Shah practices represent efforts to establish democracy and find progressive solutions for social problems. He accuses the Iranian people of being opposed to the freedom the Shah wishes to give them—as if all the strikes and protest movements taking place all over Iran were an attempt to evade freedom! But he should realize that this kind of nonsense no longer has any effect and people have come to recognize the Shah for what he is.

Great people of Iran! The history of Iran, even world history, has never

33. *PPP: Jimmy Carter, 1978,* 2:1750.
34. Algar, *Islam and Revolution,* 239–40.

witnessed a movement like yours; it has never experienced a universal uprising like yours, noble people!

Today primary school children of seven or eight stand ready to sacrifice themselves and shed their blood for the sake of Islam and the nation; when has anything like that been seen? Our lion-hearted women snatch up their infants and go to confront the machine guns and tanks of the regime; where in history has such valiant and heroic behavior by women been recorded? Today the thunderous cry of "Death to the Shah!" arises from the heart of the primary school child and the infirm old man alike, and it has blackened the days of this vile Pahlavi regime and so shattered the nerves of the Shah that he seeks to calm himself with the blood of our children and young people.

Beloved sisters and brothers! Be steadfast; do not weaken or slacken your efforts. Your path is the path of God and His elect. Your blood is being shed for the same cause as the blood of the prophets and the Imams [recognized religious leaders] and the righteous. You will join them, and you have no cause to grieve, therefore, but every reason for joy.

17 President Carter, press conference comments, 17 January 1979, reacting to the shah's fall from power.[35]

[REPORTER:] [W]hat will the posture of our Government be now toward the various contending factions in Iran . . . ?

[CARTER:] We have very important relationships with Iran. . . . They have been good allies of ours, and I expect this to continue in the future.

. . .

We have encouraged to the limited extent of our own ability the public support for the [Shapour] Bahktiar [Bakhtiar] government, for the restoration of stability, for an end of bloodshed, and for the return of normal life in Iran.

As you know, the Shah has left Iran [on 16 January 1979]; he says for a vacation. How long he will be out of Iran, we have no way to determine. . . .

[REPORTER:] [A] month ago, at a news conference, you said the Shah would maintain power. How could you be so wrong, and is it typical of our intelligence elsewhere in the world? And are you in touch with Khomeini in case he winds up at the top of the heap?

[CARTER:] Well, it's impossible for anyone to anticipate all future political events. And I think that the rapid change of affairs in Iran has not been predicted by anyone so far as I know.

35. *PPP: Jimmy Carter, 1979* (2 vols.; Washington: GPO, 1980), 1:50–52.

. . .

I have confidence in the Iranian people to restore a stable government and to restore their economic circumstances for the future.

No, we have not communicated directly with Mr. Khomeini. Our views have been expressed publicly that he support stability and an end to bloodshed in Iran and, no matter what his deep religious convictions might be—and I don't doubt their sincerity—that he permit the government that has now been established by the legal authorities in Iran, and under the Constitution, to have a chance to succeed. We do know that the Iranian military and many of the religious and political opponents to the Shah have given their pledge of support to the Bahktiar government. And that's our hope.

And I would like to add one other thing. We have no intention, neither ability nor desire, to interfere in the internal affairs of Iran, and we certainly have no intention of permitting other nations to interfere in the internal affairs of Iran.

[REPORTER:] If we had had better intelligence in Iran, is there anything that we could have done to save the Shah? . . . Would you authorize new weapons shipments to the Bahktiar regime?

[CARTER:] Even if we had been able to anticipate events that were going to take place in Iran or other countries, obviously, our ability to determine those events is very limited. The Shah, his advisers, great military capabilities, police, and others couldn't completely prevent rioting and disturbances in Iran. Certainly we have no desire nor ability to intrude massive forces into Iran or any other country to determine the outcome of domestic political issues. This is something that we have no intention of ever doing in another country. We've tried this once in Vietnam. It didn't work well, as you well know.

We have some existing contracts for delivery of weapons to Iran, since sometimes the deliveries take as long as 5 years after the orders are placed. Our foreign military sales policy is now being continued. We have no way to know what the attitude of the Bahktiar government is. We've not discussed this with them.

After the Iranian Government is stable, after it assuages the present disturbances in Iran, then I'm sure they'll let us know how they want to carry out future military needs of their own country. It is important to Iran, for their own security and for the independence of the people of Iran, that a strong and stable military be maintained. And I believe that all the leaders of Iran, whom I have heard discuss this matter, agree with the statement that I've just made.

[REPORTER:] [T]here is a suggestion that if Iranian oil supplies do not begin flowing again, perhaps within 2 months, there may be a shortage and perhaps a price increase for us. Does our intelligence indicate that might happen, or is there such a prospect as you see it?

[CARTER:] We derive about 5 percent of our oil supplies from Iran in recent months—much less than many other countries. . . . I think an extended interruption of Iranian oil shipments would certainly create increasingly severe shortages on the international market.

So far, other oil-producing nations have moved to replace the lost Iranian oil supplies. . . .

18 Ayatollah Khomeini, speech delivered at the cemetery outside Tehran, 2 February 1979, indicting the shah's legacy and calling for the overthrow of the Bakhtiar government.[36]

I offer my condolences to the mothers who have lost their children, and I share in their grief. I offer my condolences to the fathers who have lost their young offspring. And I offer my condolences to all the children who have lost their fathers.

. . .

Muhammad Riza Pahlavi, the vile traitor, has departed; after destroying everything, he has fled. In his time, only the cemeteries prospered; the country itself, he destroyed. The economy has been disrupted and ruined, and years of continuous effort by the whole population will be needed to restore it; the efforts of the government alone, or a single segment of the population, will not be enough. Unless the whole nation joins hands, our shattered economy cannot be restored.

You will remember that the Shah's regime carried out land reforms on the pretext of turning the peasants into independent cultivators, and that those reforms ultimately resulted in the complete destruction of all forms of cultivation. Our agrarian economy was ruined, and we were reduced to depending on the outside world for all our essential needs. In other words, Muhammad Riza enacted his so-called reforms in order to create markets for America and to increase our dependence upon America. We were forced to import wheat, rice, and chickens either from America or from Israel, which acts as an agent of America. In short, the so-called reforms constituted a blow that it will take us maybe as long as twenty years to recover from, unless all our people work hard, hand in hand.

Our educational system has been kept in a retarded condition, so that our youth cannot receive a complete education in Iran; after being half-educated at

36. Algar, *Islam and Revolution*, 254, 257–60.

home, at the cost of great suffering, they are obliged to go abroad to complete their studies. . . .

That man destroyed all our human resources. In accordance with the mission he was given as the servant of foreign powers, he established centers of vice and made radio and television subservient to immoral purposes. Centers of vice operated with complete freedom under his rule. As a result, there are now more liquor stores in Tehran than there are bookstores. Every conceivable form of vice was encouraged.

. . .

As for our oil, it was given away to America and the others. It is true that America paid for the supplies it received, but that money was spent buying arms and establishing military bases for America. In other words, first we gave them our oil, and then we established military bases for them. America, as a result of its cunning policies (to which that man was also a party), thus benefited doubly from us. It exported weapons to Iran that our army was unable to use so that American advisers and experts had to come in order to make use of them.

This man, Bakhtiar, is accepted by no one. The people do not accept him, the army does not accept him, his friends do not accept him, he does not even accept himself. It is only America, which has sent an envoy to instruct the army to support him, and Britain that recognize him. No segment of the population recognizes him, except the few ruffians he sends into the streets to make a noise on his behalf.

. . .

This Bakhtiar must be put in his place. As long as I live, I will not let him and his associates gain a firm hold on power. I will never permit the former situation to be restored, with all its accompanying cruelty and oppression. I will never allow Muhammad Riza to return to power, for that is what they are planning to do. Yes, people, be alert. . . . They want to return us to the period when all we knew was repression and America swallowed up all of our wealth. We will never allow that to happen. . . .

. . .

Army commanders, do you not want to be independent? Do you want to be the servants of others? My advice to you is to enter the ranks of the people and to add your voices to their demand for independence. The people want their army to be independent, not under the orders of American and other foreign advisers. They are making this demand on your behalf, so you too should come forward and say, "We want to be independent and to be rid of those advisers." But instead, you reward us by slaughtering the young soldiers on the streets who have joined the ranks of the people and thus saved the nation's honor as well as their own.

19 President Carter, press conference comments, 27 February 1979, discussing prospects for working with the new government in Iran.[37]

[REPORTER:] [G]enerally, how would you describe the relationship between our Government and the Khomeini government?

[CARTER:] The Khomeini government has made it clear ever since it came into power ... that they desire a close-working and friendly relationship with the United States.

They have also announced that oil production in Iran will be increased, and that, very shortly, exports will be recommenced. And my own assessment is that they have strong intentions to carry out both these goals and that they are capable of doing so.

[REPORTER:] ... [T]here appears to be starting a public debate on the question, "Who lost Iran?" I noticed that former Secretary [Henry] Kissinger was suggesting that your administration should bear some responsibility; former Under Secretary of State George Ball suggested that the Nixon-Kissinger administration did much to destabilize Iran with their billions in sophisticated military hardware. My question was, I suppose, do you agree with Ball? Who lost Iran, or was Iran ours to lose in the first place?

[CARTER:] Well, it's obvious that Iran was not ours to lose in the first place. We don't own Iran, and we have never had any intention nor ability to control the internal affairs of Iran. For more than 2,000 years, the people in the Iran area, the Persians and others, have established their own government. They've had ups and downs, as have we. I think it's obvious that the present government in Iran ... would like to have good relationships with us. I don't know of anything we could have done to prevent the very complicated social and religious and political interrelationships from occurring in Iran in the change of government. And we'll just have to make the best of the change.

But, as I say, we cannot freeze the status quo in a country when it's very friendly to us. When the change is made by the people who live there, we do the best we can to protect American interests by forming new alliances, new friendships, new interrelationships, new trade relationships, new security relationships, perhaps, in the future, with the new government, and that's the best we can do.

But to try to lay blame on someone in the United States for a new government having been established in Iran, I think, is just a waste of time and avoids a basic issue that this was a decision to be made and which was made by the Iranian people themselves.

37. *PPP: Jimmy Carter, 1979,* 1:351–52.

20   Assistant Secretary of State Harold Saunders to Secretary of State Cyrus Vance, briefing memorandum of 5 September 1979, assessing the pros and cons of contacts with Khomeini.[38]

—We have had no direct contact with the man who remains the strongest political leader in Iran. His hostility towards us is unlikely to abate significantly, although there have been fewer venomous statements against us recently. Clearly, a first meeting could be a bruising affair.

—A meeting with Khomeini will signal our definite acceptance of the revolution and could ease somewhat his suspicions of us. . . .

—On the other hand, we would risk appearing to cave in to a man who hates us and who is strongly deprecated here and by Westernized Iranians. Thus, we would want to be careful not to appear to embrace Khomeini and the clerics at the expense of our secular friends. . . .

—The symbolism of a call on Khomeini would not attach to visits to the other religious leaders, but they will not see us until we have seen him. We badly need contacts with . . . moderate clerics. We want to reassure them of our acceptance of the revolution as their influence may rise in the months ahead.

21   Ayatollah Khomeini, address delivered to Monsignor Bugnini, special papal emissary to Iran, 12 November 1979, taking a defiant stance after the seizure of American hostages.[39]

[T]he young people of our nation, after long years of oppression and misery, have decided to hold in that nest of spies a few individuals who were spying on our nation and conspiring against it, or rather, against the whole region.

. . .

What our nation wants is for that man who is now in the U.S., under whom it suffered for about thirty-seven years, who betrayed it continuously for thirty-seven years, who deprived our young people of freedom for thirty-seven years, who stifled our country and people with his all-embracing repression for thirty-seven years . . . [which] resulted in the killing of more than one hundred thousand people and the wounding and maiming of hundreds of

38. Saunders, a Mideast specialist, had earlier been a strong supporter of the shah's regime. His long experience in the government included the CIA, the National Security Council, and the State Department's Bureau of Intelligence and Research. Henry Precht, the Iran desk officer, drafted this memorandum. It was seized in the U.S. embassy in 1979 and then made public. Hooglund, *Iran*, microfiche no. 02996.

39. Algar, *Islam and Revolution*, 278–81, 285.

thousands of others—what our nation wants is for that criminal under whom it has thus suffered to be returned to face a just trial.

If he is found guilty, the money he has stolen from us should be returned. Huge amounts of money have been taken out of the country by him and persons associated with him and now fill the banks in America and other Western countries. . . .

. . .

. . . [W]e would have welcomed a soothing expression of concern on the part of His Eminence, the Pope, or an attempt by him to discover why our nation has acted as it has. Let him ask Carter why he enabled a man like the Shah to keep ruling us; let him inquire of Carter why he has brought to America, under his protection, the man who blatantly committed so many crimes and acts of treachery for more than thirty years, and why he now wishes to hatch conspiracies with that man.

. . .

. . . [W]e fear neither military action nor economic boycott, for we are the followers of Imams who welcomed martyrdom. . . . We are warriors and strugglers; our young men have fought barehanded against tanks, cannons, and machine guns, so Mr. Carter should not try to intimidate us. . . .

As for economic pressure, we are a people accustomed to hunger. We have suffered hardship for about thirty-five or fifty years. Assuming that the Americans can impose an economic embargo on us by persuading all nations to sacrifice their own interests—which is nothing more than an idle dream, something that will never happen—we can always fast, or content ourselves with the barley and corn that we sow on our own land. That will be enough for us. . . .

22 Carter, press conference comments, 28 November 1979, condemning hostage-taking.[40]

[CARTER STATEMENT:] For the last 24 days our Nation's concern has been focused on our fellow Americans being held hostage in Iran. We have welcomed some of them home to their families and their friends. But we will not rest nor deviate from our efforts until all have been freed from their imprisonment and their abuse. We hold the Government of Iran fully responsible for the well-being and the safe return of every single person.

. . .

The actions of Iran have shocked the civilized world. For a government to applaud mob violence and terrorism, for a government actually to sup-

40. *PPP: Jimmy Carter, 1979*, 2:2167–68, 2172–74.

port and, in effect, participate in the taking and the holding of hostages is unprecedented in human history. This violates not only the most fundamental precepts of international law but the common ethical and religious heritage of humanity. There is no recognized religious faith on Earth which condones kidnaping. There is no recognized religious faith on Earth which condones blackmail. There is certainly no religious faith on Earth which condones the sustained abuse of innocent people.

We are deeply concerned about the inhuman and degrading conditions imposed on the hostages. From every corner of the world, nations and people have voiced their strong revulsion and condemnation of Iran and have joined us in calling for the release of the hostages.

. . .

We hope that [the] exercise of diplomacy and international law will bring a peaceful solution, because a peaceful solution is preferable to the other remedies available to the United States. At the same time, we pursue such a solution with grim determination. The Government of Iran must recognize the gravity of the situation, which it has itself created, and the grave consequences which will result if harm comes to any of the hostages.

I want the American people to know and I want the world to know that we will persist in our efforts, through every means available, until every single American has been freed. We must also recognize now, as we never have before, that it is our entire Nation which is vulnerable, because of our overwhelming and excessive dependence on oil from foreign countries. We have got to accept the fact that this dependence is a direct physical threat to our national security, and we must join together to fight for our Nation's energy freedom.

. . .

[REPORTER:] . . . [T]here's a feeling of hostility throughout the country toward Iran, because of the hostages. . . . I ask you, as our Commander in Chief, is war possible, is war thinkable?

[CARTER:] It would be a mistake for the people of our country to have aroused within them hatred toward anyone; not against the people of Iran, and certainly not against Iranians who may be in our country as our guests. We certainly do not want to be guilty of the same violation of human decency and basic human principles that have proven so embarrassing to many of the Iranian citizens themselves.

We obviously prefer to see our hostages protected and released completely through peaceful means. And that's my deepest commitment, and that will be my goal. The United States has other options available to it, which will be considered, depending upon the circumstances. But I think it would not be well-advised for me to speak of those specifically tonight.

. . .

[REPORTER:] . . . [M]any Americans view the Iranian situation as one in a succession of events that proves that this country's power is declining. . . .

[CARTER:] The United States has neither the ability nor the will to dominate the world, to interfere in the internal affairs of other nations, to impose our will on other people whom we desire to be free, to make their own decisions. This is not part of the commitment of the United States.

. . .

. . . We are strong, and we are getting stronger, not weaker. But if anybody thinks that we can dominate other people with our strength, military or political strength or economic strength, they are wrong. That's not the purpose of our country.

23 President Carter, comments at a White House meeting with members of Congress, 8 January 1980, reacting to the hostage standoff.[41]

The most difficult part of the Iranian question is that there's no government entity with whom we can communicate or negotiate or register a complaint or a request. When the Secretary-General [of the United Nations] went over to Iran, he came back and reported the same thing that we had already known, and that is that the most powerful single political entity in Iran consists of the international terrorists or the kidnapers who are holding our hostages. Whenever there has been a showdown concerning the hostages between Khomeini or the Revolutionary Council versus the terrorists, the terrorists have always prevailed.

We don't know what will happen in the future, but I think you possibly recognize that this small group of people . . . have achieved, with the holding of American hostages, a great and significant political influence in Iran. They don't necessarily have as one of their prime interests the integrity of Iran as a nation or the well-being of the Iranian people or even the security of the country within which they live. And so there is no legitimate political bargaining leverage that can be exerted on them, and there is no entity there with whom one can negotiate.

They know that the consequences to Iran will be quite severe if our hostages are injured or killed, and I think only the presence of a very strong military force in the Arabian Sea has deterred them so far from taking action that would have been even more abhorrent to the rest of the world. That problem

41. *PPP: Jimmy Carter, 1980–81* (3 vols.; Washington: GPO, 1981–82), 1:39.

persists. It's an ever-present consideration of mine and yours. And I'm determined that this country will not forget for a moment those hostages. And the last hostage there is just as important to me as the first one.

24 Ayatollah Khomeini, message on the occasion of the Iranian New Year, Tehran, 21 March 1980, advocating support for the fundamentalist cause outside Iran.[42]

We must strive to export our Revolution throughout the world, and must abandon all idea of not doing so, for not only does Islam refuse to recognize any difference between Muslim countries, it is the champion of all oppressed people. Moreover, all the powers are intent on destroying us, and if we remain surrounded in a closed circle, we shall certainly be defeated. We must make plain our stance toward the powers and the superpowers and demonstrate to them that despite the arduous problems that burden us, our attitude to the world is dictated by our beliefs.

. . .

Once again, I declare my support for all movements and groups that are fighting to gain liberation from the superpowers of the left and the right. I declare my support for the people of Occupied Palestine and Lebanon. I vehemently condemn once more the savage occupation of Afghanistan by the aggressive plunderers of the East, and I hope that the noble Muslim people of Afghanistan will achieve victory and true independence as soon as possible, and be delivered from the clutches of the so-called champions of the working class.

25 Ayatollah Khomeini, message to pilgrims, issued in Tehran, 12 September 1980, discussing the successes of the Iranian revolution and setting terms for resolving the hostage crisis.[43]

Part of the extensive propaganda campaign being waged apparently against Iran, but in reality against Islam, is intended to show that the Revolution of Iran cannot administer our country or that the Iranian government is about to fall. . . . But by the blessing of Islam and our Muslim people, in the space of less than two years, we have voted on, approved, and put into practice all the measures necessary for the administration of the country. Despite all the

42. Algar, *Islam and Revolution*, 286–87.
43. Algar, *Islam and Revolution*, 303, 305–6.

difficulties that America and its satellites have created for us—economic boycott, military attack, and the planning of extensive coups d'etat—our valiant people have attained self-sufficiency in foodstuffs. Soon we will transform the imperialist-inspired education system that existed under the previous regime into an independent and Islamic education system. The armed forces, the Revolutionary Guards, the gendarmerie, and the police stand ready to defend the country and uphold order, and they are prepared to offer their lives in *jihad* for the sake of Islam. In addition, a general mobilization of the entire nation is under way, with the nation equipping itself to fight for the sake of Islam and the country. Let our enemies know that no revolution in the world was followed by less bloodshed or brought greater achievements than our Islamic Revolution, and that this is due entirely to the blessing of Islam. . . .

. . .

America is the number-one enemy of the deprived and oppressed people of the world. There is no crime America will not commit in order to maintain its political, economic, cultural, and military domination of those parts of the world where it predominates. . . .

Iran has tried to sever all its relations with this Great Satan and it is for this reason that it now finds wars imposed upon it. America has urged Iraq to spill the blood of our young men [in border clashes that were a prelude to the long Iran-Iraq war], and it has compelled the countries that are subject to its influence to boycott us economically in the hope of defeating us. . . . This is a result of the Islamic content of our Revolution, which has been established on the basis of true independence. Were we to compromise with America and the other superpowers, we would not suffer these misfortunes. But our nation is no longer ready to submit to humiliation and abjection; it prefers a bloody death to a life of shame. . . .

. . .

I have said repeatedly that the taking of hostages by our militant, committed Muslim students was a natural reaction to the blows our nation suffered at the hands of America. They can be set free if the property of the dead Shah is returned, all claims of America against Iran are annulled, a guarantee of political and military non-interference in Iran is given by America, and all our capital is released. Of course, I have turned the affair over to the Islamic Assembly for it to settle in whatever way it deems best. . . .

I ask God Almighty that He grant all captive people freedom, independence, and an Islamic republic.

And peace be upon the righteous servants of God.

8 Afterthoughts

Readers who have moved methodically through this book to reach this point find themselves—perhaps without realizing it—in an extraordinarily privileged position. They have survived more crises than any policymaker can hope or would want to see in a lifetime. Readers have witnessed those crises, moreover, from a better vantage point than that afforded any of the individual participants. Blinded by passion, engulfed in confusion, and plagued by accidents, the individuals controlling the levers of state power frequently embroiled themselves in diplomatic quarrels and sometimes armed encounters, even major wars. Readers are in a position to see how easily crises arise and how difficult they are to control. International history offers a perspective on ambition, human folly, and misfortune that can be both exhilarating and sobering.

* * *

Not surprisingly, crises have attracted a large and avid body of students. These dramatic events mean life or death for sizable populations that are pitted against each other in international rivalries. While a crisis in any age can carry a high price and set off profound, long-term social and economic effects, a misstep during the latter stages of the Cold War could have launched thousands upon thousands of nuclear-tipped missiles, each capable of creating its own terrible inferno and collectively inflicting unimaginable destruction.

One notable group drawn to crises has been social scientists bent on discovering regular patterns of behavior in international relations, above all in the confrontations of the Cold War. They have variously depicted crises as an organism, an exercise in rational choice, a collision of interests within the international system, or a frightening feature of the nuclear age. By applying

The observations in this chapter are drawn in part from my "Internationalizing U.S. Diplomatic History: A Practical Agenda," *Diplomatic History* 15 (Winter 1991): 1–11. I am grateful to the Society for Historians of American Foreign Relations for its permission.

tools such as social and cognitive psychology, statistical analysis, organization theory, bureaucratic politics, and the concepts of deterrence and compellence, social scientists have attempted to pry loose hidden laws, regularities, and rules.[1]

This social science enterprise has struggled, however, for reasons that those who have looked at the seven cases treated here can easily understand. For those seeking broad and rigorous generalizations, the high degree of complexity and contingency that mark each case and the substantial variations from case to case pose almost intractable problems. Taken collectively, crises assume a decidedly quicksilver quality.[2]

Social science generalizations have encountered added difficulty because they have drawn heavily on poorly documented Cold War cases. Most of the theory building proceeded without significant quantities of declassified material on U.S. policy to complicate the search for patterns. Today that record is open only to the early 1960s, and even there large gaps in the intelligence and covert-operations part of the record remain. Evidence has been in notably shorter supply on the foreign side, leading some scholars to treat the international dimension of crisis as if it were only incidental rather than essential to understanding and evaluating policymakers in crisis.[3] This misapprehension,

1. Prime examples from a sustained effort by political scientists and some historians at extracting theoretical insights from past crises include Graham T. Allison, *Essence of Decision: Explaining the Cuban Missile Crisis* (Boston: Little, Brown, 1971); Alexander L. George and Richard Smoke, *Deterrence in American Foreign Policy: Theory and Practice* (New York: Columbia University Press, 1974); Paul Gordon Lauren, "Crisis Management: History and Theory in International Conflict," *International History Review* 1 (October 1979): 542–56; Irving L. Janis, *Groupthink: Psychological Studies of Policy Decisions and Fiascoes* (first published 1972; rev. ed.; Boston: Houghton Mifflin, 1982); Gordan A. Craig and Alexander L. George, *Force and Statecraft: Diplomatic Problems of Our Time* (rev. ed.; New York: Oxford University Press, 1990); and Russell J. Leng, *Interstate Crisis Behaviour, 1816–1980: Realism versus Reciprocity* (Cambridge, Eng.: Cambridge University Press, 1993).

2. The classic critique of social science-based study of international relations is Stanley Hoffman, "An American Social Science: International Relations," *Daedalus* 106 (Summer 1977): 41–60. For more recent critiques, see Robert W. Cox, "Social Forces, States and World Orders: Beyond International Relations Theory," in *Neorealism and Its Critics*, ed. Robert O. Keohane (New York: Columbia University Press, 1986), 204–54, and Joseph S. Nye, Jr., and Sean M. Lynn-Jones, "International Security Studies: A Report of a Conference on the State of the Field," *International Security* 12 (Spring 1988): 5–27. A special issue of *Journal of Interdisciplinary History* 18 (Spring 1988), "The Origins and Prevention of Major Wars," edited by Joseph Nye; and Robert Jervis, Richard Ned Lebow, and Janice Stein, *Psychology and Deterrence* (Baltimore: Johns Hopkins University Press, 1985), reveal the caution with which some crisis theorists have come to approach historical phenomenon and data.

3. Striking instances of this tendency are Gregory M. Herek et al., "Decision Making during International Crises: Is Quality of Process Related to Outcome?" *Journal of Conflict*

perhaps the most serious that students of crises can make, is only gradually being corrected as the winding down of the Cold War in the 1980s has brought forth documentation and recollections by former foes. That this evidentiary opening has already transformed our understanding is clear in the Korean and Cuban crises. Those who want to construct a science of international relations and even perhaps to guide policymakers will have to wrestle with the increasingly rich evidence for older crises[4] or look to more recent ones, where the paucity of evidence permits bold, if highly provisional, generalizations.

A second major set of crisis devotees consists of former policymakers looking back on their own experience and offering insights that might serve as a compass for future leaders crossing stormy international seas. Even this more modest, down-to-earth attempt at understanding, evaluating, and generalizing has faced obstacles. To some extent these are the same ones that frustrated the theoretically inclined—the lack of a broad range of evidence, especially on Washington's antagonists. Those writing in retirement create further obstacles of their own as they all too often succumb to special pleading. Preoccupied with the "verdict of history," they write to burnish their own reputations or that of the administration they served, or to even old scores with bureaucratic foes or public critics.

These former policymakers, with the greatest personal and political stake in the evaluation of particular crises, also are among the first to offer an authoritative verdict. The first order of business after retirement is passing judgment on their own careers and along the way making sure that "their" crises are "properly" understood. This disproportionate insider influence is made possible, at least in the United States, by a system of declassification that blocks public access to government records for thirty years or more. With their memories, desk notes, and contacts in high places, the insider is in a uniquely privileged position to describe and judge without fear of convincing rebuttal except by other insiders. The insider accounts in turn become the stuff on which scholars most heavily rely, thus making them unwitting proponents of partisan accounts. The tendentious tales of former policymakers, reenforced by scholarly repetition, harden into common wisdom that will survive at least until the opening of a fuller record permits a critical assessment.

Resolution 31 (June 1987): 203–26; John P. Burke and Fred I. Greenstein, *How Presidents Test Reality: Decisions on Vietnam, 1954 and 1965* (New York: Russell Sage, 1989); and Robert B. McCalla, *Uncertain Perceptions: U.S. Cold War Crisis Decision Making* (Ann Arbor: University of Michigan Press, 1992).

4. For an example of this wrestling see the exchange between Jack Snyder and Scott D. Sagan over "The Origins of Offense and the Consequences of Counterforce," *International Security* 11 (Winter 1986–87): 187–98, and Richard Ned Lebow and Janice Gross Stein, "Deterrence: The Elusive Variable," *World Politics* 42 (April 1990): 336–69.

This interpretive dominance of insiders stands in the way of a more complex understanding of crisis as long as "national security" restrictions deprive Congress and the public of the record on which an informed, intelligent discussion of foreign policy depends. As one might expect, a debate in which only the insiders and their allies have full access to the pertinent information is not likely to offer a true or illuminating test of ideas. Democracy is poorly served, indeed seriously compromised, when the foreign policy part of the public agenda is thus put effectively out of bounds. However, bureaucratic resistance, vague anxieties over security breaches, and the cost and complexity of declassification have frustrated spasmodic attempts to put in place a system that would vindicate the public's and Congress's right to know what the executive branch has done in the name of the nation in foreign affairs.

The Cuban missile crisis offers a fine example of the insiders' impact. In 1969, just seven years after the event, President John F. Kennedy's brother Robert offered in *Thirteen Days* the most influential account—one that held up for nearly twenty years and contributed to the Camelot myth that still captivates the popular imagination. The account depicted the president and his team confronting a clear-cut Soviet challenge and then responding with resolution, nerve, and intelligence. Robert Kennedy concluded by holding up this first instance of nuclear crisis as a model that others intent on averting disaster could study with profit. The impact of this influential insider was reenforced by the accounts of others following a similar interpretive line. For example, much like Robert Kennedy, Arthur M. Schlesinger, Jr, praised John Kennedy for bringing the Cuban crisis to a successful close through a "combination of toughness and restraint, of will, nerve and wisdom, so brilliantly controlled, so matchlessly calibrated."[5]

The insider accounts, with their selected peeks into the policy process in October 1962, have not stood up well to the test of new evidence. In the mid-1980s the release of American documents began to prompt second thoughts, and the subsequent addition of the Soviet and (to a limited extent) Cuban perspectives has given a powerful new impetus to revision of the Cam-

5. Robert F. Kennedy, *Thirteen Days: A Memoir of the Cuban Missile Crisis* (New York: Norton, 1969); Arthur M. Schlesinger, Jr., *A Thousand Days: John F. Kennedy in the White House* (Boston: Houghton Mifflin, 1965), 841. See also Theodore C. Sorenson, *Kennedy* (New York: Harper and Row, 1965), and Roger Hilsman, *To Move a Nation: The Politics of Foreign Policy in the Administration of John F. Kennedy* (Garden City, N.Y.: Doubleday, 1967). Graham Allison quickly built on these insider revelations in his 1971 study, *Essence of Decision*. Critics of Camelot tried to construct a countermythology in which the missile crisis played a prominent role. But Richard J. Walton, *Cold War and Counterrevolution: The Foreign Policy of John F. Kennedy* (New York: Viking, 1972), and other works in this vein lacked the documentation to develop a nuanced alternative.

elot story. Nowhere in Robert Kennedy's neat and reassuring model was there room for the American contributions to the crisis in the first place or for the misperception, miscommunication, and error during the crisis itself. The white knights sitting around the Executive Committee roundtable seem now more complicated and human figures than they once appeared, capable of duplicity, indecision, inconsistency, and even—especially in the president's case—incoherence. The confidence-inspiring certitudes of *Thirteen Days* have begun to dissolve into interpretive complexities and doubts.

Other cases dealt with here reveal the same pattern of insiders' trading on their knowledge and contacts for political and historical profit. Soon after the end of the Pacific War two "court historians," both former officials, gained special access to the prewar record. Former colleagues expected that this prompt review would promote a "proper" understanding of U.S. policy before Pearl Harbor. Just as much as the conventional memoirs, their scholarly treatments were also aimed at preempting critics, in this case "isolationists" charging Franklin D. Roosevelt with drawing Japan into war.[6] Once in retirement Harry Truman took up his pen to use as a cudgel to beat Joseph Stalin for starting the Cold War and Douglas MacArthur and others for opposing limited war in Korea.[7] For the origins of the Cold War and, even more dramatically, for the first year of the Korean War, the appearance of fuller documentation, Soviet and Chinese as well as American, has exploded Truman's simple moral dramas and introduced complexities not even imagined at the time. The Iranian failure—to take a final instance—propelled senior Carter administration officials into print with extenuating claims and shifts of blame.[8] Assessing

6. See *The World Crisis and American Foreign Policy* (2 vols.; New York: Harper, 1952–53), by William L. Langer and S. Everett Gleason, who had served in the Office of Strategic Services, as well as *The Road to Pearl Harbor: The Coming of the War between the United States and Japan* (Princeton: Princeton University Press, 1950), by Herbert Feis, a former State Department official. The "isolationist" voice that these "establishment" histories sought to head off can be heard in Charles A. Beard's *President Roosevelt and the Coming of the War, 1941: A Study in Appearances and Realities* (New Haven: Yale University Press, 1948) and Charles C. Tansill's *Back Door to War: The Roosevelt Foreign Policy, 1933–1941* (Chicago: H. Regnery, 1952).

7. Harry S. Truman, *Memoirs* (2 vols.; Garden City, N.Y.: Doubleday, 1955–56). Robert L. Messer, *The End of an Alliance: James F. Byrnes, Roosevelt, Truman, and the Origins of the Cold War* (Chapel Hill: University of North Carolina Press, 1982), chap. 12, shows Byrnes and Truman competing in their recollections between 1947 and 1958 to indict the Soviets and establish anticommunist credentials, thus in effect obscuring from the public the origins of the Cold War.

8. Jimmy Carter, *Keeping Faith: Memoirs of a President* (New York: Bantam, 1982); Zbigniew K. Brzezinski, *Power and Principle: Memoirs of the National Security Adviser, 1977–1981* (New York: Farrar, Straus, Giroux, 1983); and Cyrus R. Vance, *Hard Choices: Critical*

those accounts will have to wait another decade or more—until a full set of sources finally come available.

However influential, insiders eventually lose their monopoly on information. For our understanding of entry into the two world wars, that monopoly is long gone. For the early Cold War and Korea, the opening of archives in the late 1960s and the 1970s began to break the stranglehold of the insiders. For Cuba and Vietnam, the process of opening (dare we say *glasnost*) is now well underway, though hardly complete. Iran is the case most instructive on how heavily mortgaged we are to the story former policymakers tell and how deeply we remain interpretively in debt to them until sources become public.

Restrictions on evidence, particularly for recent crises that are most likely to be the subject of debate and the source of lessons, would seem to hobble the very policymakers who perpetuate the current far-reaching classification system. Lessons drawn early from limited evidence are bound to be partial and in some respects fundamentally flawed. For example, the Kennedy administration's triumphal accounts of its victory over Nikita Khrushchev offered critical support to the generalization that the Soviets would back down in the face of a resolute, hard-line U.S. stand. Only now, more than thirty years later, has enough documentation come to public light to reveal the complexity of the bargaining and the degree of accommodation needed to bring the crisis to an early and satisfactory end.[9]

But policymakers have been reluctant to embrace openness. They fear that a fuller knowledge of the recent past would stir debate, tarnish the reputation of some revered predecessor, or even reveal skeletons lurking in their own closets. Bureaucrats within the foreign policy establishment reinforce this caution. They stand ready to frustrate any president foolhardy enough to upset the applecart of "national security" restrictions, and their capacity for delay, obfuscation, and obstruction can easily frustrate public and academic demands for greater accountability and openness.

Of the many policymakers who have reported and reflected on their experience with crisis, Robert McNamara has shown himself to be an interesting and instructive exception. As a powerful secretary of defense for both John Kennedy and Lyndon Johnson, he has an important story to tell. He figured prominently in the Cuban missile crisis and in the decision to commit American forces to war in Vietnam. His forcefulness and persistence on the Vietnam

Years in America's Foreign Policy (New York: Simon and Schuster, 1983). Lesser policy players such as Gary Sick in the National Security Council, Ambassador in Tehran William Sullivan, and John D. Stempel in the State Department moved quickly to get their views in print.

9. Barton J. Bernstein, "Reconsidering the Missile Crisis: Dealing with the Problems of the American Jupiters in Turkey," in *The Cuban Missile Crisis Revisited*, ed. James A. Nathan (New York: St. Martin's, 1992), 106.

question makes him in some ways the father (or at least godfather) of intervention. In 1968 he left the government, burdened by his sense of responsibility for what had turned into a multifaceted disaster, though not before setting in motion an in-house post-mortem (the "Pentagon Papers," later leaked by Daniel Ellsberg). Better than any self-serving memoir, that study, with its ample documentation, created an open and level field for public discussion of the Vietnam War.

Having made that one major contribution to public understanding, McNamara set off on a long personal journey of reflection and discovery that has assumed a decidedly and unusually somber tone. In his ruminations he moved beyond the easy critique of Vietnam policy to gathering doubts about the ostensibly successful Cuban case. Attendance at a series of conferences that brought together missile crisis participants, Russians and Cubans as well as Americans, afforded him an international perspective on the crisis not available at the time and seldom available to other former policymakers scrutinizing their own handiwork.

The resulting revelations proved unsettling, prompting McNamara to wonder at how easily the crisis that finally went right could have gone badly wrong. Only in retrospect and with the help of his former antagonists could he see how Operation Mongoose alarmed both Cuba and its Soviet patron, a point lost on Washington in October 1963 and certainly not anticipated in the planning to topple Fidel Castro. Hindsight, McNamara conceded, convinced him that "if I had been a Cuban leader, I think I might have expected a U.S. invasion." He also glimpsed significant flaws in U.S. intelligence, notably a gross underestimate of Soviet troop strength in Cuba and a failure to identify tactical nuclear weapons available for the Soviet commander on the island to use at his discretion. An invasion not only would have cost more lives than anticipated but might well have resulted in the local use of nuclear weapons that could have escalated toward civilizational disaster.

McNamara publicly revealed how much prolonged reflection and fresh revelations had eroded the confidence that was so notable a feature of his policy years.[10] He now thought of the Cuban missile crisis as a close brush with death. "Events were really out of the control of either party, though both the Russians and we were trying to maintain control." He recalled a particular

10. The quotations that follow draw from Carl Bernstein's interview with McNamara, "On the Mistakes of War," *Time* 137 (11 February 1991): 70–71, and from McNamara's conference remarks, recorded in James G. Blight and David A. Welch, *On the Brink: Americans and Soviets Reexamine the Cuban Missile Crisis* (2nd ed.; New York: Noonday Press, 1990), 280–81, and in Bruce J. Allyn et al., *Back to the Brink: Proceedings of the Moscow Conference on the Cuban Missile Crisis, January 27–28, 1989* (Lanham, Md.: University Press of America, 1992), 7, 168.

moment, Saturday, 27 October 1962, "when, as I left the President's office to go back to the Pentagon—a perfectly beautiful fall evening—I thought I might never live to see another Saturday night." He could deal with Vietnam only as one would with an old and still painful wound. Tellingly, in the interview he could address it only by avoiding the first person. "Psychologically, you're dealing with a problem for which there was no satisfactory answer, an answer that in part you're responsible for. And that is a terrible situation to be in."

From these two cases McNamara drew larger generalizations revealing his second thoughts on the Cold War. "I suspect we exaggerated, greatly exaggerated, the strength that lay behind those [Communist] threats, and therefore I think we probably misused our resources and directed excessive resources toward responding to those threats at considerable cost to our domestic societies." On the nuclear arms buildup, which he helped push ahead in the early 1960s, McNamara belatedly conceded, "We could have maintained deterrence with a fraction of the number of warheads we built. The cost is tremendous—not just of warheads. It's research, and it's building all the goddam bombers and missiles. Over the past 20 years the unnecessary costs are in the tens of billions. Insane. And moreover, our actions stimulated the Russians ultimately."

The McNamara of 1991 had come to accept what the McNamara of the 1960s could not—that policymaking was in effect about limits of understanding and control and hence about the unavoidability of mistakes. Policymakers are "subject to misinformation, miscalculation, and misjudgments," and thus "crisis management is a very uncertain and very difficult thing to do." McNamara's prudential maxim boiled down to "You've just got to avoid the crises in the first place." And he could have added: Once in, be careful!

Whatever its wisdom, McNamara's law is pretty thin gruel for the consumption of future policymakers hungry for heartier fare from the wise men of the past. In questioning the perceptiveness of policymakers, their control over events, and the gap between their desired or intended goals and the actual results, McNamara's observations corrode the faith in instrumental rationality. In his hands crises serve us less as a source of practical lessons for activist policymakers than as a repository of cautionary tales. Prudence, depicted during the Renaissance as triply armed against error, emerges as the new patron saint of crisis managers. The prudent policymaker looks to the past as a source of instruction, gazes into a mirror seeking self-knowledge, and seeks to strain the true from the false.

Historians have made up a third group fascinated by crises. They have tended to hang back from recent ones, leaving political scientists to make the early pronouncements and former policymakers to offer the exciting revelations. This tendency has much to do with the training of historians. They have learned to immerse themselves in the evidence and proceed with caution where it is in short supply. But as the century draws to a close, historians will increasingly be looking back at its crises as the prospects for a more comprehensive and more detached understanding improve. And as they do, McNamara's reflections (however discouraging) are likely to find a strong resonance.

Impatiently historians have watched American archives open slowly. Whereas evidence on the pre–World War II period is fairly full, documentation on the postwar period is still very far from complete. Historians now have access to almost two decades of U.S. Cold War records, but even they contain major gaps; and the final twenty-five years of the Soviet-American rivalry is poorly documented for the U.S. side and hence are treacherous to interpret. Foreign archives, the British excepted, lag far behind the American. Those trained in the language, history, and culture of former U.S. rivals have begun to trek abroad to Moscow, Beijing, Havana, Hanoi, and other previously off-limits capitals in order to fit foreign documents with the American record and thereby produce a genuinely international history of crisis. But a full international history of the Cold War is still decades away.

Those who have read through the seven case studies that make up this volume will better understand historians' preoccupation with evidence, insistence on taking as international a view as the documentation allows, and caution in drawing conclusions. Readers will recall the sharp contrast between the full record of the early crises treated here and the gaps in the later ones. What passed through Stalin's mind in the immediate aftermath of World War II? How did Khrushchev arrive at his decision to send missiles to Cuba? What private calculations guided Hanoi as Washington moved toward escalation in South Vietnam? How did President Jimmy Carter and Ayatollah Ruhollah Khomeini see each other? Only a fuller accounting on the part of all the participants will make possible not just answers to questions of this sort but a more secure understanding and evaluation of crises in general.

Beyond the issue of evidence and its interpretation is the somewhat more abstruse but no less important question of how to delineate an international crisis comprehensibly. A crisis unfolds in many layers, drawing leaders and their agents in different countries into shifting relationships. An international history that asks us to interpret a crisis in terms of its multiple participants compounds the problem of extracting a stable meaning out of a highly dynamic and interactive process. Only when all the parties involved are combined to achieve a rounded picture are these difficulties most fully apparent. It is then that we are forcefully reminded of how uneven and discrepant the evidence is from which we work, how thick the fog of uncertainty was as each side tried to impose an artificial clarity on the outlook of the other, and how deep the confusion and misperception could become as the information on which estimates were made lagged behind the evolving thinking and changing stances of the other side.

Some may wish to deal with this confusion by focusing on the morphology (the form and structure) of crisis. Crises are segmented. They unfold in rough stages discernible to the historian, if not to the eyewitnesses. A crisis has its prehistory, the confluence and accumulation of tensions and misapprehensions. It ignites when contention becomes so sharp that it galvanizes policymakers and commands their close attention. It then moves toward climax and resolution—either back from the brink or toward a test of arms. Regardless, there is an aftermath to describe and evaluate. Who won, who lost, why, and with what long-term consequences?

This complexity, inherent in the historical reconstruction of crises, creates a challenge—how to create narrative order. The task is imposing enough when dealing with just one set of policymakers, and it becomes more daunting when dealing with two or more sets interacting with each other under intense pressure and with great rapidity. Yet students of foreign policy crises have put a premium on imposing narrative order. For social scientists, this proclivity may be the result of the interpretive paradigm that they have operated within, one committed to engaging theory, evaluating the "rationality" of policy, and offering lessons to policymakers. The poverty of documentation on most of the crises they study and the tendency to focus on one side of a crisis (usually the better-understood American role) rather than the international interplay has facilitated and reenforced this impulse to reduce crises to an easily encapsulated and evaluated form.

But is it possible that crisis studies go too far in imposing order and as a result fundamentally distort our understanding? Should our accounts pay more attention to the role of chaos in decision-making, as one set of leaders formulates policy, and to the element of contingency in the unfolding of crises, as one set interacts with another? The cases treated in this book would suggest that the answer to both questions is yes. Misperception, miscalculation, and confusion were prominent, perhaps dominant features of the policy process in all cases and on all sides. Leaders in all capitals came to crises with attitudes that were ambivalent, even contradictory, and as each explored options ranging from inaction to all-out assault their views did not so much clarify as shift messily about.

These observations are not meant to deny rationality on the part of any set of policymakers but to highlight the difficulty of using rationality as an interpretive or evaluative device by those seeking to understand crises, especially in an international setting. It could be argued that policies within one capital—however diverse their sources, however jumbled their elements, however tentative their acceptance, however divergent their possible meanings—are none-theless thought through by policymakers and thus can be subjected to the test of rationality within that country's prevailing political, cultural, and institutional framework.

But when a crisis is viewed internationally and an analyst must deal with two or more historical actors, each operating within strikingly different frameworks, then rationality as an interpretive theme or as an overarching standard of evaluation is much harder to apply. In this altered context we are more likely to be struck by the degree to which each party in a crisis is radically and necessarily hobbled by badly flawed or seriously incomplete information about the other. Even if the crisis environment were transparent, information would not necessarily assemble into a coherent and correct picture. And even if the available information were assembled into such a picture, a rapidly changing situation would soon leave it outdated.

Crisis studies need to temper their preoccupation with rationality by developing a greater sensitivity to policymakers' inevitable lack of clairvoyance, their unavoidable cultural blinders, and their extreme vulnerability to contingency. These studies need to recognize in turn the degree to which this debilitating trio introduces a dynamic element into crisis as each side rushes to keep its estimate of the situation, the adequacy of its will and resources, and the nature of its overall goals current with the gyrations of equally agitated policymakers on the other side. Under stress the multiple, perhaps divergent goals of each policymaker become exposed and the ambiguities of calculations are revealed. Viewed in international terms, "crisis management" ceases to be a simple exercise in cool ends-means analysis (or a failure to match up to that standard) and becomes instead a kind of psychological Saint Vitus' dance that two rivals induce in each other and that ends only after exhaustion sets in.

If this characterization of crises as events thickly enveloped in confusion and misinformation is correct, then historians and other students of crises are left to confront the paradox that they must speak clearly about something that is inherently disorderly and governed to a large degree by chance. While it might be more convenient to think of a crisis in terms of a straightforward game of chess, other analogies might be more appropriate, particularly analogies that allow for less transparency and rule-bound behavior.

For example, participants in a crisis might be thought of as creators of narratives. Each is by necessity compelled to impose sense on looming problems—to construct a reality in the mind—in order to determine ways to deal with them. In the context of crisis each party thus creates narratives meant to account for the behavior of the other side, and these distinct narratives carry "truths" that provide the basis for action—however distant those truths may be from the confusion, mixed motives, and changing calculations that in reality characterize the behavior of the other side as it writes, revises, and acts on its own narrative.

Viewed internationally, a crisis is made up of narratives that seldom overlap, or for that matter even converge, in a way that puts all parties in the same narrative framework. Rather, the distinct narratives intertwine, and as they do, each narrator appropriates narrative fragments from the others, prompting in turn the revision or extension of that party's narrative. Thinking of policymakers as creators of narratives may help us see more clearly the many unpredictable twists a crisis (like a piece of fiction) may take. And thinking of a crisis as the interweaving of narratives spun out by each of the major participants in the crisis underlines not just the complexity but also the subjectivity of the phenomenon that we struggle to pin down. Students of crisis are thus cast in the difficult role of having to reconstruct a collection of outlooks, each inherently limited and highly subjective and thus inevitably prey to misjudgments and miscalculations in its appraisal of others.

This kind of history leaves little room for those bent on apportioning blame or vindicating particular moral or nationalist claims. There is not one but several good stories to tell in each dangerous international confrontation, and depending on whose perspective the story reflects, the identity of the aggressor and the victim will change. Those who write and read these stories remain free to draw their own ultimate judgments, but they must do so from a complex body of evidence, in the face of openly competing claims, and with the specter of moral relativism fluttering quietly overhead.

*   *   *

However insistent the counsel of caution, readers will still indulge the human instinct to want to reduce crises to comprehensible form—to tell stories, to trace patterns, to find themes, to draw conclusions, to consider might-have-beens. Some of the specific reactions are fairly predictable, to judge from the comments of readers of these cases in draft. Laying out the more common of those reactions may help current readers to refine their own similar views or provoke them to formulate alternatives positions.

Some readers may be surprised to find, first of all, that policymakers are people. Political leaders who create and handle crises are not supermen, computers, or the sum of the admirable traits promoted by their own public relations. As people, they reveal personal limitations, diverse outlooks, and situational constraints that are all too familiar from our own everyday observation of the human condition.

To take a prime example, leaders bring to moments of crisis varying degrees of experience, assurance, and well-being. A striking number of presidents treated here, including Woodrow Wilson, Harry Truman (during the postwar settlement), John Kennedy, and Jimmy Carter, entered the White House with little or no practical experience with the making of foreign policy. They thus had to engage in hurried and extensive on-the-job training. Policymakers embarked on that education with varying levels of confidence and health. Truman, in his handling of both the USSR and the Korea conflict, shows how a fragile sense of self-worth can play an important role, while physical problems may help us understand the Kennedy performance and perhaps the difficulties experienced by the shah of Iran in the 1970s.[11]

Leaders in crisis also display wide variations in fundamental values and in their capacity for empathy. They need a moral compass to ground and guide policy, but they also need to be able to get in the others' shoes—to grasp their concerns and limits. A moral vacuum, no less than a lack of empathy, makes for poor policy. Yet the two do not mix easily. Wilson's moral impulses and Truman's brittle self-confidence led to demonizing the enemy. Roosevelt's moral condemnation of and myopia on Japan fit easily together and reenforced each other. Kennedy's effort to understand Khrushchev's motives may have been the natural concomitant of his "cool" style that tempered any strong moral impulse.

Far from being predictable, individuals can show surprising variations in their policy stance when put in different circumstances. Just within the cases treated here we can see how dramatically positions can shift. Roosevelt administered the final blow to the idea of a Pacific condominium with Japan and then set to work on a global condominium with Joseph Stalin and Winston Churchill. Henry L. Stimson stood as a hard-liner pushing toward confrontation with Japan, and then turned around after World War II and argued against confrontation with the Soviet Union. Clark Clifford, an exponent alongside Truman in 1946 of a manichean Cold War view, became the voice of caution to Lyndon Johnson in 1965. George Ball was a hawk during the Cuba crisis but a dove on Vietnam three years later. McNamara, who sounded caution to Kennedy on Cuba, would quickly turn around and urge Johnson to action in Vietnam.

Personality differences also expressed themselves in policymakers' differing approaches to decision-making. Wilson held decisions tightly in his own hands and kept his advisers at a distance. Roosevelt admitted a far wider range of advisers in a pattern of informal consultation that angered bureaucrats,

11. Jerrold M. Post and Robert S. Robins, *When Illness Strikes the Leader: The Dilemma of the Captive King* (New Haven: Yale University Press, 1993), and Robert E. Gilbert, *The Mortal Presidency: Illness and Anguish in the White House* (New York: Basic Books, 1992), draw attention to physical frailty that often afflicts political leaders, but these works also underline the difficulty of identifying their illnesses (often for want of adequate medical records) and relating them to performance with any precision.

tangled lines of authority, and reserved for the president the last word. With little experience Truman relied heavily on advisers in 1945–1947—but only those whose values fundamentally tracked with his own. Kennedy and Johnson allowed considerable scope for consultation and encouraged debate, although some formal exchange may have served as mere window dressing for decisions already made.

The case of the China-U.S. collision over Korea offers a revealing illustration of the critical importance of these various facets of personality. The war plunged the Truman presidency into difficulties on several fronts. It was at once internally divided, under the growing scrutiny of its worried allies, besieged by domestic critics, and confused by the failure of the Soviets to behave belligerently and the Chinese to take American professions of goodwill at face value. At the root of these troubles was a president whose involvement in making policy might be described as spasmodic rather than either weak or strong. He hesitated at critical moments to play a decisive role even though the interminable and inconclusive debates among his aides cried out for presidential direction.

During the summer and into the fall of 1950 Truman was an almost invisible man, resistant to sitting down with his key advisers and engaging in formal discussion of the chief issue that divided them—whether to cross the thirty-eighth parallel and, if so, how to do it. As MacArthur's public outbursts became increasingly serious, Truman once again proved reluctant to act until he had the backing of another general, George C. Marshall, then serving as secretary of defense. Only then did Truman overcome his lack of self-confidence and abruptly sack MacArthur. This decision brought to a close the contest over presidential prerogative and personal prestige, but the debate over limited war that had begun in earnest in December 1950 continued unabated to the end of the Truman presidency. Once again, Truman sat quietly at the center of the storm while the argument within his administration over the use of nuclear weapons, the bombing of China, a naval blockade of the China coast, and the unleashing of the Nationalist army on Taiwan swirled about him.

Viewing the Korean crisis internationally reminds us that personality is as important in foreign capitals as it is in Washington. Mao's assertive style, his hands-on approach, and the general deference accorded him contrasts with Truman's notable lack of assurance, his episodic involvement in policymaking, and the leadership vacuum that MacArthur and others sought to fill more or less constructively. For Mao the close link between politics and warfare was a given, a point that Truman was slow to grasp or at least to act on. Even when Mao withdrew from daily direction of military affairs from January to May 1951, he still provided a guiding hand.

Other cases treated here reveal equally striking contrasts between the decision-making style of international antagonists. Wilson dominated neutrality issues and shied away from formal meetings of his advisers. German decision-making, on the other hand, was marked by a wider range of participants and required regular formal conferences to reconcile differences and arrive at a policy. The same picture emerges from the Pearl Harbor case of a democratic United States endowed with a strong presidential system with relatively few checks and infrequent occasions for formal debate beyond what the president was prepared to allow. As with the Germans during World War I, the Japanese decision-making before Pearl Harbor pitted a range of influentials in debate and moved them toward consensus ultimately registered in major conferences attended by the emperor. The paradox that emerges is that policymakers in the more open, democratic U.S. system took refuge in a relatively closed policy process, while policymakers in societies less tolerant of public debate could afford to embrace a more formal system with built-in opportunities for give and take. Whether one worked better than another is for readers to decide.

However diverse policymakers may be, they all encounter a predictable range of constraints. To begin with, they operate under inherited policy doctrines and policy precedents internalized by the bureaucracy, entrenched in the minds of advisers, and engraved in the public discourse. For example, Johnson approached a fateful decision on Vietnam hemmed in by widely accepted notions of the dangers of appeasement and the domino-like toppling of Asian nations, by the need to make good on containment, and by the decisions of his predecessors (not least John Kennedy's overthrow of Ngo Dinh Diem). The image Khrushchev invoked in October 1962 is just right. A crisis is like a knot tied and pulled tight by many hands, perhaps over many years, and not easily or quickly undone. Just as a policymaker usually does not create the grievances and resentments that nurture and sustain a crisis, a policymaker cannot remove them with a simple snap of the finger.

Policymakers are also bound by the obligations of multiple roles. The U.S. president, for instance, is head of a political party, and his performance in a crisis may win or lose elections, please or alienate vital constituencies, and boost or depress public approval. Presidents are also spokesmen and symbolic embodiments of the nation. Scoring victories against foreign foes serves to affirm national values and enhance the national morale. On the other hand, crises gone awry humiliate not just the president but the country that he stands for. These political and symbolic concerns are not hard to glimpse in the Kennedy White House during the Cuban crisis or in the Carter White House during the Iran crisis.

The second broad point likely to impress readers is the critical role of communications to policymakers in crisis. Leaders in different capitals need to speak clearly, directly, and coherently to each other if they wish to avoid crisis in the first place and then, once engulfed by one, to get themselves out. Yet as the cases in this book reveal, communication is plagued by a worrisome array of obstacles, filters, and pitfalls that can waylay or distort messages from one side to the other. It is as if crisis communication were in practice conducted through a telephone system riddled with broken cables and crossed wires, cursed with faulty receivers, and staffed by harried, monolingual operators.

While open, direct diplomatic lines would seem the bare minimum for crisis management, such direct formal contacts were in fact completely lacking in three of the seven cases dealt with here: Korea, Cuba, and Vietnam. This high incidence of isolation of American policymakers from their opposite numbers is in large measure the heritage of the Wilsonian contention that diplomatic contact is not a practical necessity but a sign of moral approbation. The paradoxical result is that Washington had no way to talk with those whom Washington was most likely to condemn and thus confront. Without direct contact, a host of problems can arise. Public statements assume greater prominence, with the risk that a statement intended for one audience (perhaps domestic) may be misinterpreted by policymakers abroad for whom it was not intended. Mao mistakenly thought that the China White Paper was aimed at China, and Washington in turn saw its name on Mao's response, which was in fact written to educate intellectuals he thought susceptible to American appeals.

But even where diplomatic lines are open, messages passing through several hands can easily get garbled. Drawing on an old parlor game, I once entrusted the following note to a student in the first row of one of my classes: "Please pass the following message to President Clinton: remove all American forces from the Korean peninsula or I will go ballistic.—Kim Il Sung." Halfway through the second row, after whispered relay from student to student, the message had become, "President Clinton has told the President of Korea that if he doesn't get his forces out the United States will invade." Crisis garbling is usually not so extreme, but the more intermediaries there are, the greater the danger of miscommunication. John Kennedy's resort to his brother to contact the Russian ambassador, who in turn passed messages into the Soviet system (through how many additional hands?) and ultimately to Khrushchev, will provide a fascinating test of this generalization once adequate materials on both sides can be assembled.

Perhaps the most profound gulf that policymakers communicating in crisis must bridge is cultural. The frequent inability to understand the language of the other, literally or symbolically, closes the window onto the mental world of the other side and thus renders virtually incomprehensible its guiding concerns. A cadre of specialists do not always exist for policymakers to turn to, and where they do exist they are often kept on the margins of policy. The most conspicuous failures not just to speak the language but to understand the key words and phrases, with their historical resonance and societal ramifications, appear in Cold War cases where Marxism as a simple, forbidding doctrine combined with the radical rhetoric of third-world liberation. Problems of communication, which were substantial in dealing with Soviet Marxists or Iranian fundamentalists, became well-nigh impossible when Marxism and liberation combined, as they did in the cases of Korea, Vietnam, and Cuba. It was there that U.S. policy was most likely to get into a muddle, to set off on misguided programs of cultural transformation, to fall victim to the recurrent patterns of cultural misperception, and to suffer the worst setbacks.

The third general point to strike readers may be that compelling lessons about crises are few and that even the most plausible evoke objections. It would be comforting to believe that immediately on recognizing a crisis in progress, policymakers can draw off the shelf a manual summarizing the accumulated wisdom of their predecessors and sit down for a hasty reading that will initiate them into the secret maxims of good crisis conduct. But alas, policymakers in crisis have no ready checklist of procedures to follow or mantras to recite—at least none that will enhance their chances of success or even simple survival. A look at some of the injunctions to policymakers much heard of late should help make this pessimistic point.[12]

"The United States should risk crises only where clear national interests are at stake and, conversely, avoid military conflict except where U.S. interests are so clear as to justify the use of all necessary force to win it." Sensible on the surface, this point forgets what the cases here show repeatedly—that definitions of interest are frequently contested and seldom stable. Wilson and Carter, for example, steadily adjusted their sense of national interest to the march of events at home and abroad. To translate this injunction into practice, a policymaker not only would have to be a paragon of certitude but would also need the clairvoyance to know how far particular international opponents intended to proceed along their own line of policy and at what point the domestic reaction might force the president's hand. Wilson could not know how far Germany would press its submarine warfare, not least because the Germans themselves had no script to follow. Similarly, Carter could not be sure of the course that Iran would take because that revolution, like others, followed no predetermined course. Indeed, the internal conflict within Iran from 1978 to 1980 kicked up dust that was impenetrable to outsiders keen to know the future.

12. The following lessons were drawn by undergraduates at the University of North Carolina at Chapel Hill after having read this set of crises in the fall semester of 1993.

It is commonsensical to believe that policymakers, with their heavy responsibilities and circle of experienced advisers, must operate in a clearheaded fashion, their minds purged of ambiguities and tensions, even in time of crisis. But this belief is questionable. Indeed, a contrary case could be made. Far from being clear, the thinking of policymakers, particularly under the cross-cutting pressures that attend crises, is marked by pronounced ambiguities and shifts that are bound to frustrate the efforts of historians and theorists bent on extracting sharply defined intentions from the record.[13]

Scholars may differ over what the principals in a past crisis wanted precisely because the principals themselves were not certain either as individuals or as a group about the dangers they faced or the outcomes they desired. Far from having a simple or settled point of view, policymakers caught in a complex and tension-filled situation, in which the outcome may carry great personal and national consequences, themselves often display a fuzzy, inchoate, or even shifting definition of their interests and goals. To say that leaders want more than one thing at a time and that they change over time may only underline the point already made: they are human and think like ordinary people.

"Never get involved in a crisis that does not justify the heavy use of economic and military resources that victory may require." This second injunction, like the first, offers entirely sensible guidance that also requires clairvoyance—particularly an ability to count costs before the other side has even decided what resources it is prepared to invest in a confrontation. Virtually impossible in advance of crises, calculations of cost get no easier once the crisis has begun. Action and response are tightly but unpredictably linked together in a dynamic that leaves unclear the risks or sacrifices either side is prepared to make. Particularly problematic, at least in the United States, is the role of the public, which is permissive at first but grows restive as intervention drags on and becomes costly. The cases of Korea and Vietnam are prime instances of this tendency.

An emphasis on matching ends and means is thus not just a bromide; it is something more dangerous, based as it is on a fundamental misapprehension of the nature of crisis. Policymakers under pressure and in the midst of rapidly unfolding events usually do not have a single fixed notion of interest in mind. And even if policymakers did have such a notion, they would need to find a foe with an equally fixed notion of interest whose views and level of determination were transparent, so that the level of resistance and hence the level of cost

13. Works illustrating the difficulty that policymakers have in defining interests and goals include Leon V. Sigal, *Fighting to a Finish: The Politics of War Termination in the United States and Japan, 1945* (Ithaca: Cornell University Press, 1988), and Richard K. Betts, "Analysis, War, and Decision: Why Intelligence Failures Are Inevitable," *World Politics* 31 (October 1978): 61–72.

could be established in advance of any initiative. Such clarity, stability, and transparency are seldom seen in everyday life, and those qualities seem even rarer in the world of policy. Ends-means analysis may more appropriately come from Polonius than from prudence.

"Listen to the experts in avoiding and managing crises." This injunction echoes the pet prescriptions offered by experts themselves in their unending campaign to bring their valuable insights to the attention of high officials. But it ignores the fact that experts differ, sometimes threaten chaos by questioning the fundamentals of established policy, and may have insights not easily assimilated by distracted, aging leaders. Experts may even obscure rather than illuminate the thinking on the other side. George Kennan, a leading government authority on the USSR, missed the significance of Stalin's speech in early 1946 at a critical moment of the Cold War by serving up his long-held indictment of the Soviet system. China specialists sent mixed signals on China's position on Korea. The community of Iran specialists differed on the nature and depth of the opposition to the shah in the 1970s.

The largest problem facing the advocates of expertise is that by the time a crisis breaks out, specialists may be too late and are almost certain not to find a seat at the table where a small, closed circle of tense, harried crisis managers gather. As one retired foreign service officer observed, "The more serious the international crisis, the less expertise is brought to bear on it. This is because these crises are handled at the very highest level."[14] One Vietnam specialist, Jeffrey Race, makes the same point in relating his frustrated and frustrating effort in 1971 to convey his insights on the war in the Vietnamese countryside. Invited to brief Pentagon officials, he found them literally refusing to listen to a line of argument that undercut the culture-bound premises of the policy they were then pursuing.[15] Race's account of this extraordinary encounter bears reading and remembering: specialists may speak truth to power, but power may not want to hear. Only a Pollyanna or a Pangloss can be confident that policymakers or for that matter the public will listen to, not to mention take to heart, the advice of such specialists even when they are right.

"Try to understand the other side." This call for empathy is important because the outlook and goals of other countries should not be confused with our own preferences or taken as blank or plastic. Policymakers do need to transcend the assumptions and convictions that cut them off from an understanding of the other's perspective. And they can do so only by strenuous acts

14. Quotation from an unidentified source, in James A. Bill, *The Eagle and the Lion: The Tragedy of American-Iranian Relations* (New Haven: Yale University Press, 1988), 11.

15. Jeffrey Race, "The Unlearned Lessons of Vietnam," *Yale Review* 66 (December 1976): 163–66.

of empathy that put them imaginatively at least in the psychological and intellectual framework of foreign leaders. By extension, policymakers need to assume the universality of the "Rashomon effect," named after a Japanese film, wherein one act of violence and brutality appears quite differently to different witnesses to the event.

Once more we are asking a great deal of policymakers. Holding two or even more versions of a single situation in mind at the same time requires a psychological and even political balancing act that should tax the skills of even the most confident and adept. But even more fundamental is the perceptual problem plaguing policymakers. Perceptions, which serve as the basis for policy, are profoundly conditioned by cultural values. In the case of relations between markedly different countries and peoples, those perceptions will do more to obscure than to illuminate the beliefs and behavior of the other. Hard-won understanding of other cultures has repeatedly revealed the gap between what policymakers thought they saw and the reality, at least as scholars today can reconstruct it. Policymakers, themselves culturally conditioned and carriers of unexamined ideological biases, struggle against long odds to understand a diverse, indeed bewilderingly complex world. That realization gives added weight to the voices of caution in policy discussions.

Even policymakers with a deep knowledge of the broad cultural and political context in which their opposites operate face an additional hurdle. They are not likely to have access to the specific concerns and calculations driving the other side. Policymakers, whatever the country, are generally secretive, and in the cases of China and the USSR they go a step or two farther. It is thus nearly impossible to gauge the cross-currents in the minds of antagonists, as Washington's surprise at the attack on Pearl Harbor and the intervention across the Yalu River suggests. It is particularly easy for policymakers to overlook the role of clients as hidden triggers or unnoticed symbols for their patrons. The obvious examples are Washington's failure to grasp the nature of the Soviet links to China and Cuba, Japan's inability to understand the depth of the American support for China on the eve of Pearl Harbor, and Kim Il Sung's and Stalin's misconception of American policy toward South Korea before the 1950 attack.

The final and perhaps most important general point is the degree to which an international history of crisis collides with the nationalist biases that normally inform our reading of foreign policy. Those biases remain latent, even unrecognized, as long as the story of crisis is told from an exclusively American perspective. Shifting to a more international perspective helps lay them bare— and in doing so prompts on the part of some readers a sense of betrayal.

Schooled in nationalist notions of the United States as a force for good in world affairs and as an exceptionally enlightened country, students often react with chagrin and disillusionment to discover that the record is muddy and that sometimes American policymakers fell short of their own publicly enunciated standards. At the same time foreigners often caricatured by American leaders and media emerge for the first time as real people with their own credible point of view, including contempt for what they took as hypocritical American support for such principles as self-determination and human rights. Shaken by these discoveries, one student bemoaned the fact that "the United States has not always done the most unselfish, morally correct, just things. . . . We are not always the 'good guys' that we have been made out to be." Another student was blunter. "The government of the United States is more sneaky and under-handed than I ever suspected."

These disillusioned reactions reflect in part the nationalistic bias conveyed in high-school texts. One wide-ranging and thoughtful survey described them as spotty in their treatment of foreign affairs, sometimes critical but since the 1950s generally self-righteous, self-congratulatory, or naively moralizing.[16] At the college level the situation is better. But even there American history texts, in which most students have their sole encounter with foreign policy, inadvertently perpetuate the nationalist perspective by slighting the reciprocal impact of the United States on the states and political movements arrayed against it and by picturing foreign leaders as shadowy figures particularly prone to nasty deeds.

This insularity may be inadvertent—the result of an understandable focus on American actions and debates, and on the underlying concerns of policy-makers and the public. But the effect is still to give short shrift to opponents of the United States. While foreign misbehavior is duly noted, the concerns be-hind that behavior are invariably omitted or summed up in a phrase or sen-tence that is neither likely to stick in students' heads nor to begin to suggest the foreign outlook and motives. Little wonder that students react with surprise and unease when they finally have the chance to transcend their national horizons and to see foreigners as something other than stock characters— usually victim or victimizer—in an American morality play.

An international history of crisis, one that sets U.S. policymakers and policy alongside those of other countries, has much to recommend it. It offers an antidote to American exceptionalism. The United States is no more a special case than any other country. It militates against establishing impossible goals and costly standards for our policy and people, and it quiets the spasms of blame and guilt when we fail to measure up to those standards. There is as little ground for picturing American dealings with the world as unusually blunder-

16. Frances FitzGerald, *America Revised: History Schoolbooks in the Twentieth Century* (Boston: Little, Brown, 1979).

ing or shamefully depraved as there is for retailing heroic tales of good intentions and sometimes magnificent achievements. A comparative perspective should make it clearer that the burdens, dilemmas, and constraints under which the United States has labored are weights that other countries have also felt, and thus such a perspective may help us argue for a less chauvinistic and more sophisticated appraisal of our nation's conduct.

Above all, a history that has room for international complexities may contribute to increased sensitivity to the role of cultural differences and remind us of how policymaking differs fundamentally from country to country. It reminds us that while we may think we live in a global village, its inhabitants still hold sharply divergent and surprisingly tenacious worldviews. An unlikely proponent of this point, Fidel Castro, coupled the release of new documents in 1992 with what he called with a chuckle "deideologizing international relations."[17] A more international history that promotes that goal may serve all people well—by raising the level of political understanding and discourse in our democracy and, in the final analysis, by making less crisis-prone our relationship with the outside world.

17. James G. Blight et al., *Cuba on the Brink: Fidel Castro, the Missile Crisis, and the Collapse of Communism* (New York: Pantheon, 1993), 225.

ACKNOWLEDGMENTS

Arthur S. Link, ed., *The Papers of Woodrow Wilson*. Copyright © 1966–94 by Princeton University Press. Reprinted by permission of Princeton University Press. Vol. 30: 393–94; vol. 31: 458–59; vol. 36: 66–67, 73; vol. 40: 534–39; vol. 41: 87, 437–44, 519–21, 523–27.

The Carnegie Endowment for International Peace, Division of International Law, comp. and trans. *Official German Documents Relating to the World War.* 2 vols.; New York: Oxford University Press, 1923. Vol. 2: 972–73, 977–78, 1122, 1125–26, 1134–36, 1138–40, 1142, 1155–59, 1161–62, 1183–86, 1201–1202, 1214–16, 1218–19, 1320–21, 1337. Reprinted by permission of the Carnegie Endowment.

The Letters of Theodore Roosevelt, vol. 7: 189–90, edited by Elting E. Morison. Cambridge, Mass.: Harvard University Press. Reprinted by permission of the publishers. Copyright © 1954 by the President and Fellows of Harvard College; © 1982 by Elting E. Morison.

Sources of Japanese Tradition, Ryusaku Tsunoda et al., eds. and trans., 2: 207–8, 256–58. Copyright 1964, © Columbia University Press, New York. Reprinted with permission of the publisher.

K. K. Kawakami, "A Japanese Liberal's View," *The Nation* 113 (9 November 1921): 530–31. Reprinted by permission.

Henry L. Stimson diary entries October 1931 through January 1932 and July 1945, Stimson Papers, Manuscripts and Archives, Yale University Library. Vol. 18: 111–12; vol. 19: 18–19, 103; vol. 20: 100–103; vol. 52: 31. Reprinted by permission.

Japan's Decision for War: Records of the 1941 Policy Conferences, edited and translated by Nobutaka Ike, reprinted with the permission of the publishers, Stanford University Press © 1967 by the Board of Trustees of the Leland Stanford Junior University. Pp. 9–10, 12, 94, 96–97, 99–102, 139–40, 147–48, 151, 201–4, 211–13, 220, 229–30, 236–38, 270–73, 281–83.

Joseph Stalin, *The Great Patriotic War of the Soviet Union.* New York: International Publishers, 1945, pp. 139–42 (Stalin speech, 6 November 1943). Joseph Stalin, *For Peaceful Coexistence: Postwar Interviews,* ed. Alexander Trachtenberg. New York: International Publishers, 1951, pp. 32, 34–35 (Stassen interview of April 1947). Joseph Stalin, *Economic Problems of Socialism in the U.S.S.R.* New York: International Publishers, 1952, pp. 26–30 ("Remarks on Economic Questions Connected with the November Discussion"). Reprinted by permission.

Excerpt from *The Price of Vision: The Diary of Henry A. Wallace 1942–1946,* edited by John Morton Blum, pp. 664–68. Copyright © 1973 by the Estate of Henry A. Wallace and John Morton Blum. Reprinted by permission of Houghton Mifflin Co. All rights reserved.

George Kennan (writing under the pseudonym "X"), "The Sources of Soviet Conduct," *Foreign Affairs* 25 (July 1947): 576, 581–82. Reprinted by permission of *Foreign Affairs,* July 1947. Copyright 1947 by the Council on Foreign Relations, Inc.

Fidel Castro, "The Second Declaration of Havana," in Martin Kenner and James Petras, eds., *Fidel Castro Speaks*. New York: Grove Press, 1969, pp. 105, 115–16, 122–23. Reprinted by permission.

Tran Hung Dao, proclamation of 1285, in *Patterns of Vietnamese Response to Foreign Intervention, 1858–1900*, ed. and trans. Truong Buu Lam. New Haven, Conn.: Yale Southeast Asia Studies, 1967, pp. 50, 53, 68–70. Reprinted by permission.

Gareth Porter, ed., *Vietnam: A History in Documents*. New York: New American Library, 1981, p. 217 (Porter translation). Gareth Porter, ed., *Vietnam: The Definitive Documentation of Human Decisions*. 2 vols. Stanfordville, N.Y.: Earl M. Coleman Enterprises, 1979, 2:383–85 (Porter translation). Reprinted by permission of Gareth Porter.

Peasant accounts (pp. 71–75, 93–95, 141–43) from *The Peasants of North Vietnam by Gérard Chaliand*, translated by Peter Wiles. Penguin Books, 1969, first published in France, 1968, copyright © Librairie François Maspero, 1968 translation copyright © Penguin Books Ltd, 1969. Reproduced by permission of Penguin Books Ltd.

Le Van Chan interview from Jeffrey Race, *War Comes to Long An: Revolutionary Conflict in a Vietnamese Province*. Berkeley: University of California Press, 1972, pp. 97–99, 110–11, 129–30. Reprinted by permission of Frances Collin, Literary Agent. Copyright © 1972 by Jeffrey Race.

Asadollah Alam, *The Shah and I: The Confidential Diary of Iran's Royal Court, 1969–1977*, ed. Alinaghi Alikhani and trans. Alikhani and Nicholas Vincent. New York: St. Martin's Press, 1992, pp. 210–11, 323, 341, 360, 544–45. Copyright © 1992 Asadollah Alam. Reprinted with permission of St. Martin's Press, Incorporated. Permission also granted by I. B. Tauris and Co. Ltd., London.

Hamid Algar, ed. and trans., *Islam and Revolution: Writings and Declarations of Imam Khomeini*. Berkeley: Mizan Press, 1981, pp. 29–30, 32, 115, 120, 126–27, 132, 178–79, 181–82, 184–86, 212–14, 221–22, 224, 239–40, 254, 257–60, 278–81, 285–87, 303, 305–306. Reprinted by permission.

I owe thanks to undergraduates at the University of North Carolina at Chapel Hill, who have over the last decade served as guinea pigs and critics. Several graduate students made special contributions to particular chapters: John Hepp (1, 2, and 8), Li Li (4 and 8), Xiaodong Wang (4), and Antonio Fins (5, 7, and 8). Colleagues who took time to provide a detailed critique of chapters overlapping with their special expertise include John Coogan (1), Miles Fletcher (2), Albert Resis (3), Odd Arne Westad (3 and 4), Rosemary Foot (4), Piero Gleijeses (5), Marilyn Young (6), and David Painter (7). Emily Rosenberg and Warren Cohen gave me the benefit of their readings of the entire manuscript. H. R. MacMaster, Thomas G. Paterson, and Vladislav M. Zubok provided welcome suggestions and materials. Mattie Hackney supplied much-appreciated help in getting many of the documents on disk, while Heather Hunt, Karen Thomas, Parker Doig, and Rosalie Radcliffe provided assistance with last-minute details. Paula Hunt has done much to help shape this collection by her practical assistance, thoughtful criticism, and sound advice. I have also to thank Charles Grench, Otto Bohlmann, and Richard Miller, at Yale University Press, who gave me strong and thoughtful editorial support critical to bringing this project to fruition, and Rachel M. Bowman at The

University of North Carolina's Center for Teaching and Learning, who prepared the maps that appear in this book. I alone am responsible for sins of omission and commission that inevitably creep into a globe-girdling enterprise such as this one. I would, however, be grateful to readers who wish to contribute to my salvation in some later edition by suggesting documents that would fill gaps and by pointing out errors.

INDEX

Page numbers in **boldface** indicate documents.

studies on Korea, **188–90, 229–30;** study on China policy, **196–97;** report on Vietnam, **323–24;** report on Iran, **386–88.** *See also* ExComm in Cuban crisis

Nehru, Jawahrlal, **204**

Ngo Dinh Diem, 302, 304, 305; Eisenhower letter to, **326–27;** Kennedy letter to, **335;** overthrow of, **338–40**

Ngo Dinh Nhu, 304, 305

Nguyen Chi Thanh, **336–37**

Nguyen Dinh Chieu, **315–16**

Nguyen Van Thieu, 310–11

Nie Rongzhen, 179

Nitze, Paul, **355**

Nixon, Richard, 232; Vietnam and, 310–11, 312; Iran and, 371, 372

Nomura Kichisaburo, 70, 71, **90–91;** Hull and, **98, 106, 107, 109–10**

Norris, George W., 20, 24; speech, **54–55;** letter from FDR, **132**

North Atlantic Treaty Organization (NATO), 125–26, 127

North Korea, 170. *See also* Kim Il Sung; Korean War

North Vietnam, 299, 301, 302, 305–6. *See also* Vietnam War

Novikov, Nikolai, **151–55**

Nuclear weapons, 120, 125, 182; arms race, 120, **142–43,** 248; danger of war, 128, 244, 246

Oikawa Koshiro, **94**

Organization of American States, 234

Ottoman Empire, 7

Outer Mongolia, 175

Pacific War. *See* United States–Japan conflict

Page, Walter Hines, **30–31**

Pahlavi, Muhammad Reza Shah, 365; Musaddiq and, 368, 369; supports modernization, 370–71; clashes with clergy, 372, 373–74; shrinking support for, 375–76, 377, 378; meets with JFK, **391–92;** discussions with Alam, **396–97, 399–400**

Pahlavi, Reza Shah (father of Muhammad Reza Shah), 366

Panay (gunboat), 65

Paris peace conference, 59

Pearl Harbor, 56, 71–72; FDR condemns attack on, **110–11.** *See also* United States–Japan conflict

Peng Dehuai, 179, 180, 183, 184; communications with Mao, **212–13, 216, 223, 226–27, 231**

"Pentagon Papers," 420

People's Republic of China (PRC). *See* China

Pham Van Dong, 306, **346–47**

Philippines, 15, 57, 60, 70

Pliyev, Issa A., 236

Poland: post-WWII issue of, 116, 117, 118, 119, 122, **133, 134–35**

Potsdam conference, 119, **140–42**

Raborn, William F., **352**

Race, Jeffrey, 432

Rafsanjani, Ali Akbar Hashemi. *See* Hashemi-Rafsanjani, Ali Akbar

Reagan, Ronald, 381

Resor, Stanley, **358**

Rhee, Syngman, 171, 175

Ridgway, Matthew, 181–82, 183

Rockefeller, David, 379

Romania, 116, 119

Roosevelt, Franklin D.: Japan policy, 65–68, 71–72, **89–90, 95, 106–7,** 129; speeches and radio messages, **81–82, 84, 88–89, 110–11;** post-WWII plans, 114–15, **132;** Stalin and, 116–17, **133–34;** death of, 117–18; atomic bomb and, 120; views on Indochina, 296–97, **318;** Iran and, 366, **385**

Roosevelt, Kermit, 369

Roosevelt, Theodore, 57, **74**

Rostow, Walt, 303–5, **331–33**

Rowan, Carl, **352**

Rusk, Dean, 239; role in Cuban crisis, 240, 241, **256, 257–58;** role in Vietnam, 303, 304, 310, **333–35, 352, 354**

Russia, 17, 21, 57. *See also* Soviet Union

Saionji Kimmochi, 62

Saito Hiroshi, **80**

Saito Yoshie, **92**

Sakhalin Island, 114

Japan's response to U.S. hostility, 68–71; interpretive questions about, 71–72; books about, 72–73